Planning for Development in Sub-Saharan Africa

Ann Seidman

The Praeger Special Studies program—
utilizing the most modern and efficient book
production techniques and a selective
worldwide distribution network—makes
available to the academic, government, and
business communities significant, timely
research in U.S. and international economic, social, and political development.

Planning for Development in Sub-Saharan Africa

PRAEGER SPECIAL STUDIES IN INTERNATIONAL ECONOMICS AND DEVELOPMENT

Praeger Publishers   New York   Washington   London

Library of Congress Cataloging in Publication Data

Seidman, Ann Willcox, 1926-
 Planning for development in sub-Saharan Africa.

 (Praeger special studies in international economics
and development)
 Includes bibliographical references.
 1. Africa, Sub-Saharan—Economic conditions.
2. Africa, Sub-Saharan—Economic policy. I. Title.
HC502.S45   338.967   73-19450

PRAEGER PUBLISHERS
111 Fourth Avenue, New York, N.Y. 10003, U.S.A.
5, Cromwell Place, London SW7 2JL, England

Published in the United States of America in 1974
by Praeger Publishers, Inc.

Printed in the United States of America

To my extended family, especially
my five children who have, over the
years, been very understanding about
the hours I have spent in writing.

Over forty African nations have won political independence in the last quarter of a century, most of them in the course of the few short years designated by the United Nations as the first Development Decade. All have initiated planning exercises of one kind or another. Yet, as the first Development Decade drew to a close, few had succeeded in achieving much improvement in the daily lives of the vast majority of their inhabitants. Long hours at backbreaking labor with a hoe to sow and harvest crops barely adequate to support life; rural under-employment and mounting unemployment in squalid urban slums; undernourishment and disease; a life expectancy of 35 years—these still shape the life perspectives of most babies born today in that vast continent, despite its rich stores of mineral and agricultural wealth.

This book seeks to explore the fundamental constraints inherent in the inherited institutional and resource allocation patterns which thwarted efforts to attain declared development goals in the 1960s. It is impossible, in a single volume, to survey in depth the constraints affecting the more than forty diverse, balkanized political-economic units which in the last few years, have broken the bonds of outright colonial rule. The aim here is to illustrate the problems they have confronted by examining in some detail the post-independence experience of the larger of the former British colonies in sub-Saharan Africa. It is hoped that such an analysis may contribute to the formulation of more realistic policies to implement plans for the improved allocation of resources required to enable African populations to enjoy, in the coming decades, levels of life commensurate with the technological possibilities of the Twentieth Century.

I would like to express thanks to many people whose comments and criticisms have contributed to the formulation of the hypotheses which have guided the development of the materials in this book. It would be impossible to list them all by name. The ideas have been debated and criticised back and forth by many students and faculty members during my seven years of teaching and research in universities in Ghana, Tanzania and Zambia. They were further crystallized in discussions at the Land Tenure Center in the University of Wisconsin with graduate students and colleagues who came from or had worked in many Third World countries, not only in Africa, but also in Latin America and Asia. I would like, in particular, to thank my husband Bob, with whom I have enjoyed debating many of these issues over the breakfast table as well as in the Law and Development seminars we have worked in together in several countries. I can only hope my appreciation is adequately expressed by this attempt to bring these ideas together here for further criticism and testing by those who may take the trouble to read this book.

CONTENTS

LIST OF TABLES AND FIGURES

PART

I

**THE CAUSES OF
UNDERDEVELOPMENT
IN AFRICA:
THE NEED TO RESTRUCTURE
AFRICAN POLITICAL-ECONOMIES**

GAMEIA

SIERRA
LEONE

GHANA

NIGERIA

SUDAN

UGANDA

KENYA

TANZANIA

ZAMBIA

MALAWI

BOTSWANA

SWAZILAND

LESOTHO

1

**A PROPOSED MODEL
OF UNDERDEVELOPMENT
IN AFRICA**

THE NEED FOR A NEW THEORETICAL
APPROACH

Since attaining independence nearly every African government
has initiated a national planning exercise. It is recognized that modern
specialization and exchange, essential for significantly increased
productivity, require large markets, large capital investments, a
broad range of natural resources, and the training of skilled manpower
—all of which require mobilization of resources at least on a national
level. Plans limited to allocating resources merely on a village or
even on a regional level are incapable of contributing to significant
increases of productivity because such small units cannot meet these
technological requirements. The record of national planning in Africa
has not, however, been very successful in contributing to significant
development.[1]

The Goals of Development

It is essential[2] to formulate an explicit statement of the generalized ends of development to establish even a tentative set of criteria
for a meaningful evaluation of national plans.

The current emphasis on economics as a "positive science,"
dealing primarily with investment and price-output relations in the
context of pre-existing institutions, has led to an emphasis on increased
production without regard to distribution.[3] It is becoming widely
accepted today that this approach to economic development must be
broadened to encompass the spread of productivity into all sectors
of more integrated, nationally balanced economies capable of providing

3

continually improved levels of living for the broad masses of the population.[4]

Adopted throughout this book is the view that development must encompass increased productivity in all sectors of the national economy directed to raising the levels of living of the broad masses of the inhabitants. This is essential to insure that demand and supply will expand simultaneously so as to contribute to attainment of a balanced, nationally integrated economy.[5]

The inadequacy of national plans in Africa becomes particularly evident when evaluated in terms of this development perspective. Several countries have achieved significant increases in per capita income; but these benefits have, more often than not, been concentrated in a few urban centers where modern office buildings just over the skyline, sleek automobiles crowd the streets, and the wealthy few live in luxurious villas furnished with refrigerators, air conditioners, television sets, and innumerable servants. The vast majority of the populations continue to live in the rural areas in thatched-roofed homes with dirt floors, scratching a bare living from lateritic soils with little more than hoes, their average life expectancy about 30 to 35 years. Hundreds of thousands of eager younger men and women flee the countryside annually, hoping to share some of the conspicuous advantages of twentieth-century life in the cities—but many of them are condemned to live in squalid urban slums, taking any job for wages as low as $15 or $20 a month, or joining the growing ranks of unemployed, who sometimes number as much as 20 to 30 percent of the urban labor force. In Liberia, the classic example, where gross domestic product multiplied four times over from 1950 to 1960, this pattern has justifiably been dubbed "growth without development."[6]

The Inadequacies of Traditional Planning Tools

Not only the stated goals of economic development, but the methodologies designed to attain them need to be fundamentally revised. The entire tool-kit of concepts and methods currently taught in Western universities remains permeated with the notion that price-output relations are the stuff of economic development. The dismal record of national plans underscores the fact that development cannot be attained merely by transplanting to Africa the refined planning techniques devised to allocate resources in developed countries such as input-output tables, linear programming, or macro-economic models based on assumed capital-output ratios. Yet foreign "instant experts," hired as short-term advisors to African planning ministries, continue to formulate mathematical macro-economic models based on projections of past trends. Monetary and taxation policies are typically proposed on the assumption that the existing sets of institutions may be expected to respond in the desired manner, as they are held to do in the United States or Europe.* The failure of these plans and policies may in part be attributed to the lack of data that requires that many of the essential coefficients must simply be "invented"; over time this is likely to lead to results significantly deviating from projected goals.[7] More critical, however, the imported techniques must, of necessity, make assumptions about the underlying sets of production relations and institutions in less developed countries that are simply not justified by the facts.

Georgescu-Roegen has emphasized that the content of the fundamental principles of standard economics, as taught in the United States and Western Europe, has been determined by the institutional setting existing there. He adds:

> Without this institutional content, the principles are nothing but "empty boxes" from which we can obtain only
> empty generalities. This is not to say that standard theory
> operates with "empty boxes." On the contrary . . . these
> boxes are filled with an institutional content distilled
> from cultural patterns of a capitalist society . . . it is
> precisely because the boxes of standard theory are
> already filled with a specific institutional content that
> this theory was unceremoniously rejected by the students
> of the economic process in non-capitalist settings.[8]

Examination of the rather dismal record of national planning[9] and economic policies of the type proposed by Western economic advisors and taught in educational institutions in Western developed countries provides insights into the reasons why Georgescu-Roegen and others are increasingly adopting the view that development cannot be attained merely by transporting to developing countries the refined econometric techniques being devised to allocate resources in developed countries.

Why a New Economic Model

Until recently, most standard theorists have argued that the shortage of capital constituted the greatest hindrance to development.

---

*Even in the United States, the persistence of "stagflation" in recent years—inflation combined with growing unemployment—suggests that these assumptions may not be warranted there either.

This notion was fostered by Harrod-Domar-type models, which link capital investment directly to expanded national income. Developing countries have been encouraged to create "hospitable investment climates" for foreign investors. Metropolitan countries have been urged to expand their loans and grants.

Initially, too, this argument was frequently coupled with the belief that expansion of the export sector, devoted to production of mineral or agricultural produce for sale overseas, provided a viable "engine for development"; the multiplier effects resulting from expansion of export production were expected to spread throughout the entire national economy, leading to growth in all sectors.[10]

As the anticipated spread effect has failed to materialize—not only in Africa, but throughout the Third World—various one-sided explanations have been devised. Several sociologically oriented theorists place the onus for the failure on alleged socio-psychological characteristics of the hinterland. The peasants are said to lack the necessary motivation to adapt their methods of production to participation in the spread of specialization and exchange and hence to benefit from the potentials of modern technology. This has been attributed to the lack of various behavioral characteristics that are said to have fostered development in countries like the U.S.; these include the peasants' alleged failure to act like "economic men,"[11] or, in a more refined analysis, their lack of N-achievement.[12] Sometimes it is said that traditional societies are characterized by insufficiently creative personalities.[13] Some social scientists have maintained that traditional institutions hinder growth: for example, it is sometimes held that extended families and status-oriented values obstruct development of attitudes necessary for effective participation in development;[14] or traditional political institutions hamper the emergence of the type of political competitiveness required to foster economic growth.[15]

Some economists, most notably Prebisch,[16] urge government planners to formulate policies to foster the investment of capital in import-substitution industries, rather than export trade, to reduce dependence on raw material exports. Over the years, however, evidence has accumulated that suggests that, given the narrow markets of most developing countries, such industries do not contribute much to the creation of nationally integrated economies capable of attaining increased productivity and higher levels of living for the majority of the populations. Rather, in Africa, as in Latin America and Asia,[17] import-substitution industries are typically concentrated in existing urban centers and are capital intensive, contributing little to employment. They produce a range of goods including luxury and semi-luxury items rather than needed farm inputs and consumer necessities that could augment productivity and levels of life in rural areas. They are predominantly dependent on imported parts and equipment, aggravating rather than reducing the pervasive dualism and external dependency characteristic of most, if not all, developing countries.

In the late 1950s, as African countries were winning political independence, many theorists concluded that greater investment in "human capital" was essential to facilitate the spread of modern technology to more backward areas.[18] But rapid multiplication of the numbers of educated men and women, unaccompanied by expansion of modern productive activities, has created large pools of unemployed school leavers, unwilling to return to the backbreaking drudgery of traditional rural life. This has for years been a serious problem in Asia. In Africa, particularly in regions like southern Nigeria and Ghana, educational facilities have been established for the majority of primary school age children, and secondary schools and universities have literally mushroomed in the years since independence. But the result has not been the spread of specialization and exchange to encompass the traditional areas in increasingly productive activities; rather it appears in recent years to have accelerated the flight of rural populations to the squalid slums of urban centers. Even university graduates find themselves without employment, competing bitterly for the limited numbers of posts available in the ministries, universities, and politics. Increasing numbers are leaving their countries in search of employment abroad. It has been suggested[19] that the "brain drain" may be a blessing in disguise, siphoning off "overeducated" high-level personnel who might, if they remained at home, constitute a serious source of discontent and political instability.

These experiences suggest that education by itself cannot solve the problems of underdevelopment; Myint pointed out that in Asia in the 1950s, "Too great an emphasis on 'under-investment in human capital' . . . tends to confuse the issues and distract attention from the more potent disequalizing factors."[20]

Still more recently, many U.S. development theorists have concluded that, since the anticipated expansion of GDP has not led to adequate growth in per capita incomes, it is necessary to cut down on population growth rates. This proposition finds sympathetic response in the U.S., where planned parenthood has come to be perceived as an important element in the liberation of women, as well as a vital necessity for the maintenance of ecological balance. The result has been a major emphasis by U.S. and international agencies on implementing programs designed to reduce population growth rates in less developed countries—programs that sometimes would go further than those now implemented in the United States itself. In Africa,[21] where population pressures are of entirely different dimensions than in India or China or even the U.S., this emphasis has, at best, been accepted by only a small percent of the population, frequently only the more wealthy urban dwellers; at worst, it has led to misunderstanding and even resentment. Traditional attitudes toward children

7

in Africa have been shaped by the age-old necessity for rural parents to rely on large families to hedge against high mortality rates, insuring provision of a future labor force and a form of old-age security. Not a few Africans find it hard to accept U.S. proposals for population control. Some maintain these proposals divert attention from other pressing development needs. Some even argue that such policies are nefariously designed to hold back population growth in Africa for selfish reasons related to a desire to maintain world hegemony.[22]

This book seeks to show that neither traditional institutions and attitudes, the lack of education, nor rapid population growth rates, alone, are responsible for the persistence of underdevelopment in Africa since independence. It is argued here, in contrast, that the characteristics of the political, economic, and social institutions created during the colonial era that shaped the export sector itself are the primary factors inhibiting the anticipated spread of modern technology. This is not to intimate that the institutional structures and norms in the traditional sector do not sometimes hinder the spread of development throughout the national economy. Nor is it to argue that industrialization is not necessary; that the planned spread of the appropriate kinds of education is not essential to the attainment of development; or that rapid population growth rates may not pose serious complications for national planners.

The underlying thesis here asserted is that all of these must be dealt with, not as one-sided, isolated phenomena, but as interrelated facets of an all-encompassing process of planning for development that can be implemented only after the attainment of certain essential preconditions in the form of fundamental changes of critical institutions. In other words, this thesis holds that national planning, in the context of the inherited sets of political-economic-social institutions and working rules that direct and control the dominant modern export sectors of all African countries, cannot meet the needs of the broad masses of the population. The primary function of those institutions, despite the attainment of political independence, continues to be the fulfillment of the requirements of large foreign trading and mining firms linked to metropolitan centers overseas. These institutions have established ties and relationships with elements in the traditional societies in a manner that has contributed to the emergence of the typical lopsided resource allocation pattern. As long as this institutional structure remains unchanged, despite the attainment of political independence, as long as these sets of institutions shape the fundamental decisions relating to resource allocation in the independent African countries, it appears unlikely that national planning will succeed in attaining broader development goals. It follows that any attempt to constrain analysis of development problems in the framework of traditional economic theory, with its concentration on price-output relations to the exclusion of these kinds of institutional factors, is bound to fail to provide an adequate guide for more effective development planning.

The approach here adopted, then, is in distinct disagreement with that of development theorists like Myint, who, while admitting the validity of some of the criticisms of traditional theory, rejects Myrdal's advice to "young economists" in developing countries to "throw away large structures of the meaningless, irrelevant and sometimes blatantly inadequate doctrine and theoretical approaches."[23] Myint insists that "underdeveloped countries are too poor to put up with the burden of preventable waste that arises even within the static framework of given wants, techniques and resources."[24] They should not "discard the existing static optimum theory before we have time or are clever enough to build up a satisfactory 'dynamic' approach to the underdeveloped countries."

Myint himself not only falls back on traditional models, but also re-endorses traditional timeworn remedies for attainment of development: expansion of exports and free trade policies. His proposals tend to overlook the very features of underdevelopment that his own earlier empirical investigations so sharply exposed:[25] the "fossilization" in so-called "backward" countries of a cheap labor force and a low-income cash crop peasantry into a system of producing raw materials for export through the mediation of oligopolistic foreign firms that remit a major share of the resulting investible surpluses to their home countries. These are the very features that have, in the African case, been major contributing causes of the repeated failures of the kinds of traditional remedies recommended by Myint. That Myint has come, over time, to simply ignore these crucial aspects of reality that he himself emphasized two decades ago illustrates the way reliance on an invalid model may direct one's attention away from critical explanatory features in a troubled situation. This is perhaps the best possible proof of the hypothesis that for economists working in developing countries it is more dangerous to cling to outmoded static models than to attempt to formulate new ones.

Perhaps this was the danger Georgescu-Roegen had in mind when he warned:

> The tenacity with which we cling to the tenet that standard theory is valid in all institutional settings . . . has far-reaching consequences for the world's efforts to develop the economy of nations which differ in their institutions from the capitalist countries. These consequences may go down in history as the greatest monument to the arrogant self-assurance of some of sciences' servants.[26]

If this is true, then the issue appears to be not whether but how to build a dynamic model capable of incorporating the critical inter-relationships of the key institutions and resource allocation patterns to explain the persistent problem of underdevelopment in Africa. Once such a model is created, it may focus on the crucial areas about which more fruitful hypotheses may be formulated for fostering more successful developing planning.

The basic premise adopted here is that a problem-solving approach provides a means of building a more dynamic model that incorporates, rather than excludes, the way in which the interaction of the critical institutional features with resource allocation patterns has, over time, shaped the persistent problem of underdevelopment confronting independent governments in Africa today.

The Problem-Solving Approach to Model-Building

The problem-solving approach provides a method for analyzing specific problems that is diametrically opposed to any approach that would attempt to insist dogmatically on the imposition of static models or methods drawn from one country to solve problems in another.[27]

Unfortunately, problem-solving has tended to become identified in the minds of some with an atheoretical practice of dealing with isolated, fragmented features of the existential world without attempting to develop a broader theoretical framework. It is argued here that the problem-solving method requires the development of general theory and is, at the same time, essential to it. In the case of social phenomena, theory provides a source of hypotheses for identifying and dealing with critical problems that emerge in the larger social context. The process of testing those hypotheses against existential reality is the only way of warranting them for reincorporation into, elaboration of, and/or reshaping the general theory to insure that it will provide a more useful guide for the formulation of hypotheses more capable of explaining and perhaps solving additional problems.

In this broader sense, the problem-solving approach is best conceived as involving a four-step process for dealing with problems of underdevelopment: first, a theory may suggest hypotheses to explain the particular "troubled situation" or problem identified in a less developed area. No matter how "positivist" a problem-solver may believe he is, he will in fact be drawing his explanation from some sort of theory—although it may be unstated and not thought out, little more than a value set.

The proposed explanation may be formulated in the form of a series of middle-level propositions that constitute a model[28] showing how the relevant sets of complex phenomena interact to cause the troubled situation. It would be preferable if all possible alternative hypotheses suggested by different theories, that is, the generalized experiences drawn from many countries—including socialist as well as capitalist, developing as well as developed—were conscientiously canvassed in an effort to obtain the best possible explanation at the outset. Whether or not this is done, it is essential that the assumptions or theoretical framework underlying the model initially utilized be stated as explicitly as possible, to enable a careful evaluation of their validity in light of the objective circumstances prevailing in the troubled situation being explained.

Second, the proposed model must be rigorously tested against all the available evidence relating to the specific troubled situation. No evidence may be excluded because it is not "covered" by the particular discipline of the investigator or because it does not seem to "fit" the model.[29] Even after the hypothesis appears to have been "warranted" by this test it should always be considered tentative, subject to revision in light of new evidence that may be revealed by subsequent investigations.

Third, on the basis of the explanation given of the problem, hypotheses should be formulated as to appropriate solutions. The explanation of the problem made explicit by the model will itself suggest solutions, or at least the areas in which solutions may be required. Again, it would be preferable if the investigator conscientiously examined a range of theories drawn from the experiences of other countries for possible hypotheses for solutions. He should again explicate the assumptions on which each hypothesis finally selected is based so that these, too, may be evaluated in light of prevailing circumstances of the particular problem situation explicated by the model.

Fourth, the proposed solution should be tested in light of the actual circumstances prevailing in the given situation. Here again, all the consequences, both anticipated and unexpected, must be considered. It should be noted that the implementation of the proposed solution will itself undoubtedly introduce a new set of problems that must also be solved; so that the procedure will have to be repeated. The problem-solving approach implies, in this sense, an on-going process of evaluation of the causes and consequences of problems and methods utilized in an effort to solve them in the context of particular circumstances.[30] In this process, the general theory will inevitably be changed and developed to provide a more useful heuristic guide, a source of more helpful hypotheses for explaining and solving problems.

The utilization of the problem-solving approach to formulate an appropriate model, rather than the automatic transference of a preconceived set of models, concepts, and methods derived from the experience of Western developed countries, would appear to provide a more appropriate foundation for realistic planning for development in Africa. An effort has been made to utilize this approach to formulate the model presented below. The proposed model seeks to select and incorporate into a set of interlinked middle-level propositions hypotheses as to the key variables that explain how complex institutional and resource phenomena interact to perpetuate underdevelopment in Africa, despite relatively favorable resource and population patterns. Such a model must, of course, be seen as tentative, continually subject to testing in light of the accumulation of both quantitative and qualitative evidence as to the validity of the individual middle-level propositions and their relationships to each other. The most crucial test is of course the implementation of policies based on hypotheses drawn from the explanatory model. The references cited in connection with the model indicate the extent of available supporting evidence upon which this tentative model has been built.

THE PROPOSED EXPLANATORY MODEL

The typical African economy is characterized by an all-pervasive dualism. Some theorists maintain development merely requires the spread of the advanced technologies and attitudes allegedly characteristic of the relatively "modern" sector to the traditional sector; others insist that the very notion of dualism obscures the basically exploitative relationships and underlying external dependence of underdeveloped countries.[31] The model here proposed (see Figure 1) accepts that the newly independent countries of Africa are characterized by dualism. It seeks to explain how the relatively modern, externally dependent export enclave is linked to and, in a sense, exploits the less developed traditional sector.

The Critical Variables in the Typical African
Dual Economy

The export enclave itself is characterized by the (sometimes relatively modern) production and export of a few raw materials to be processed in the factories of developed industrial countries, primarily those of the former colonial power.* Most of the more

_____

*In many African countries, agricultural exports that have been grown for decades by African farmers are sold to foreign trading firms that import manufactured consumer goods (e.g., Ghana, Nigeria, Gambia, Senegal, Uganda, Sierra Leone). In others, foreign or white-

12

FIGURE 1

A Model of the Inherited Dual Economy and Associated
Skewed Income Distribution Typical of the
Newly Independent African Countries

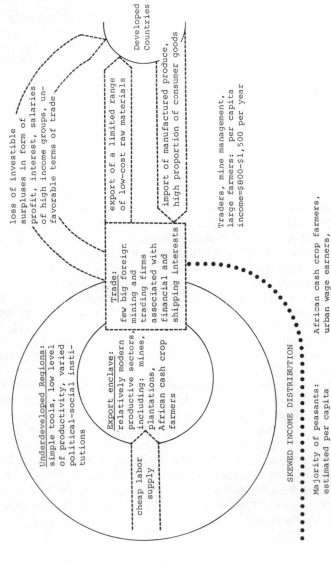

productive resources of the economy—particularly human and physical capital—are engaged in mines, plantations, or small peasant farms, extracting the main known natural resources of the nation for shipment abroad in crude form.[32] The nations utilize a large share of the foreign exchange thus earned to import the bulk of the manufactured goods consumed, again mainly from the factories of the former colonial power; together, the African imports provide a not unimportant outlet for the industrial exports of the latter. Domestic African industrial growth has been sharply curtailed, producing less than 10 percent of total Gross Domestic Product in all but a few cases, less than 5 percent in the majority.[33] Urban development, associated with export-import trade and the limited national industrial growth, has been concentrated in one or a few centers in the export enclave.[34]

The majority of the population in independent Africa lives and works in the agrarian economy in the remaining underdeveloped regions, using simple age-old productive techniques geared to survival in the face of the uncertainties of a harsh nature. There has, historically, been some trade in local produce, which even today extends across national borders; but it constitutes less than 10 percent of African trade for the continent as a whole, and in some areas tends to be declining rather than increasing. Most of the peasants in these regions continue to produce the bulk of their own needs: their food, their houses, sometimes even their clothes. Major mineral deposits may exist there, but they are often unknown, undeveloped, and, until recently, almost unsought.[35]

The underdeveloped regions contribute one important factor to the export enclave: cheap, unskilled migrant labor, workers willing to work in mines, on plantations, or as sharecroppers for more wealthy African cash crop farmers for incomes that barely cover subsistence.[36] The constant flow of labor to the export enclave may reflect the desire for a few of the modern conveniences of life. In a growing number of cases, however, it seems to reflect the inability of age-old productive techniques undermined by the loss of manpower to support even traditional levels of living in the face of mounting population pressure.[37]

---

settler plantations hire low-cost African labor to produce export crops (e.g., Congo-Kinshasa, Rhodesia, and, formerly, Kenya, Algeria, and Tunisia). In many, foreign firms employ African workers for subsistence wages to mine ores for export, frequently to factories owned by the same parent companies (e.g., Congo-Kinshasa, Zambia, Gabon, Mauritania, Sierra Leone, Liberia, Guinea). Regardless of the particular features of production, however, the export enclave usually exhibits the typical characteristics outlined here.

The inherited institutional structure has been developed on the foundation of and reinforces this distorted pattern of resource allocation. The dominant feature of the export enclave is the group of oligopolistic foreign private trading, and in some cases mining and plantation firms and associated banking, insurance, and shipping interests.[38] In the days of outright colonial rule, the entire political-economic institutional structure of government—from the administrative departments to the money and banking system—was shaped primarily to facilitate the operation of these firms and associated interests.[39] Since independence, with few exceptions,[40] these interests have continued to dominate the export enclave. They seek to maximize their profits[41] primarily by producing raw materials for their home industries in accord with the pattern shaped in the past. In the case of mines and large plantations, the firms still own the productive facilities outright. Increasingly, however, especially since independence, they have been purchasing agricultural raw materials from African farmers who—with lower overheads and, for the most part, providing their own foodstuffs—have sometimes been able to sell cash crops at lower prices than could large plantations. The foreign trading firms handle almost all of the profitable imports of relatively high-priced manufactured goods.[42]

All the foreign firms and associated interests transfer a major share of their profits home to their shareholders[43]—a significant loss of investible surpluses so badly needed by the developing countries. They formulate their investment and trade policies primarily in terms of their own interests as determined by the state of the world market and their own profits, rather than by the interests of the new nations; and the two sets of interests have not always coincided.[44]

Typically, too, a well-to-do farmer-trade group has emerged alongside the giant foreign firms as a result of and within the export enclave created by the expansion of a cash crop and/or mining sector. In parts of North, East, and South Africa, this group has historically been predominantly non-African. In West Africa and in areas in Central, East, and North Africa, especially where Africans have been permitted to engage in cash crop production, it also includes a limited group of African farmers. This group has tended to take advantage of its position in the expanding cash economy to accumulate a significant share of the investible surpluses remaining in the country.[45] Because the Africans in this group were the primary beneficiaries of the limited introduction of education in the colonial era, they constituted the main source of the African government politicians and civil servants who replaced the departing Europeans after independence. The vast majority of the Africans in the export enclave, on the other hand, remain as either low-paid wage earners in the mining plantation sector; poor peasants who, together with their families, till a few acres of land and sell a few bags of the export crop for a little cash; or sharecroppers working for the handful of larger African farmer-cum traders who have accumulated larger amounts of land and capital.

The political, social, and economic institutions that had developed over the centuries in the less developed regions tended to become linked to those dominating the export enclave, perpetuating and con-tributing to their underdevelopment.[46] The chief's control of land in the interest of the community was initially appropriate to shifting agriculture in that, with community sanction, he could allocate new land to families and individuals in terms of their needs. In some regions, chiefs and their followers had in pre-colonial times achieved enough power to arrogate a significant share of the surpluses produced by the community for themselves, to a greater or lesser degree con-forming with a pattern described by some sociologists as characteris-tic of more advanced stages of development.[47] The colonialists' efforts to win support in the traditional societies sometimes led them to rule indirectly through existing or newly appointed chiefs, often increasing the power and privilege of the latter vis-à-vis the com-munity as a whole. Chiefs and associated religious leaders have at times resisted changes in methods and institutions proposed by new national governments when they have perceived them as threatening their status and prestige. Opponents of change may also gain support in their community due to a not unreasonable fear that changes in-troduced at the prevailing marginal level of subsistence may, if they encompass error, be disastrous to community welfare. These factors may combine to perpetuate working rules and institutions that rein-force the institutional linkages with the export enclave which per-petuate and aggravate the characteristics of underdevelopment, despite the pressing requirements of population growth and mounting desires among growing numbers of peasants for some of the potential bene-fits of twentieth-century life. In this sense, the regions outside the export enclave have sometimes appeared "stagnant."[48] The only escape available to individual peasants has appeared to be migration in search of jobs in the cash economy of the export enclave: the mines, the plantations, the farms of well-to-do cash crop farmers, or the squalid urban slums festering on the outskirts of cities.

How the Interaction of the Key Variables Thwarts Development

Any development plan that relies on this set of inherited insti-tutions for implementation is unlikely to attain development defined as increasing the productivity and raising the level of living of the broad masses of the population. The inherent characteristics of the institutions are such that they will tend to perpetuate and extend the dual character of the economies, leaving them dependent on narrow, uncertain world markets for a limited range of raw material exports. Even if some of the institutions in the export enclave are reorganized to capture a greater share of the investible surpluses and invest them in economic and social infrastructure with a view to enhancing the national attractiveness to private enterprise, it appears unlikely that a significant degree of development as here defined will be attained.

The dominant private firms, seeking to maximize relatively short-term profits, will predictably invest in a manner that will merely extend the export enclave, rather than contribute to a fundamental restructuring of the economy. The oligopolistic foreign trading and mining firms shaped in the colonial era are likely to invest primarily in their known, going businesses,[49] producing for known existing markets. If national government policies require it, trading firms may invest in last-stage assembly and/or packaging import-substitute industries, primarily to maintain or extend their hold over existing markets among the higher income groups in the export enclave. They are apparently reluctant to invest in integrated plants in the African countries' truncated markets[50]—particularly because these would tend to compete with manufacturing facilities with which they are directly or indirectly affiliated in developed areas. They have been quite unwilling to invest in the hinterland, away from export enclaves where at least to some extent external economies have emerged as a result of decades of colonial export-oriented development. The exception may be the foreign firm seeking to carve out an additional enclave for the export of minerals[51] or, in decreasingly typical cases, agricultural produce,[52] or the use of cheap hydroelectric power resources for partial processing.[53]

Those few domestic African entrepreneurs who have accumulated a little capital in their export enclave activities are no more likely to contribute to restructuring the economy than are the foreign firms. They tend to invest in the business they know best: the production of cash crops for export, associated trade, and/or speculative real estate*—all within and inevitably expanding the export enclave.[54] Efforts to design government policies to redirect investment of surpluses to alter production patterns outside the export enclave—for example, in order to increase essential supplies of foodstuffs or raw materials for use in industrial and rural projects more closely related to internal development—are likely to encounter resistance by domestic

---

*In some cases they have loaned money to poorer peasants at high interest rates, but this appears to be less typical in Africa than in some other developing areas.

groups benefitting from the status quo.[55] The well-to-do elite, which historically benefitted most from the limited African participation in cash crop production and educational facilities available under colonialism, has tended to provide the main pool from which have come new office holders for national and local governmental posts. The temptation is considerable to use their positions in control of state machinery to advance their own status at the expense of efforts to restructure the economy.

Corruption,[56] too, has become a ready tool by which those in power may be influenced. Foreign firms and domestic entrepreneurs have tried to influence critical decisions by government officials to win favor for their projects, regardless of the impact on national economic developments. The evidence indicates that not a few office holders have succumbed to these temptations.

To the extent that fundamental restructuring of the national political-economic institutions does not take place, and the export enclave is merely extended, underdevelopment has tended to persist. World market prices for agricultural raw materials have tended to fall as all the Third World nations, seeking more foreign exchange to implement their development programs, compete in multiplying their exports in the face of the slowly growing demand in developed countries.[57] The companies purchasing the major mineral exports have occasionally restricted output, employment, and government revenues in developing countries in order to maintain stable high prices and their own profit levels on world markets. To the extent that larger numbers of the population have been engaged in production of raw materials for export, they have tended to spend their cash earnings on increased imports of manufactured goods and even foodstuffs competing for limited foreign exchange earnings with imported capital goods and equipment needed for development programs.[58] The prices of imported manufactured goods, governed by profit-oriented decisions of the oligopolistic foreign trading firms, have tended to remain constant or to rise.[59] Sooner or later, less developed countries pursuing such a strategy primarily dependent on export expansion have almost inevitably confronted a mounting deficit in their balance of payments.[60]

The extensive use of land for production of agricultural exports, coupled with the continued stagnation of traditional farming in the hinterland, has tended to contribute to growing shortages of foodstuffs as urban populations have expanded in the export enclave.[61] This has necessitated further imports of foodstuffs,[62] reducing available foreign exchange for buying needed capital equipment and machinery. At the same time, it has tended to foster rising local foodstuff prices, which have undermined the real incomes of wage earners. On the one hand, domestic traders, whose profits have tended to mount when prices

18

rose, have frequently pursued tactics that have hindered expansion of
farmer output for domestic consumption. On the other hand, wage
earners have become increasingly resentful of the governmental ex-
hortations to hold the line on wages in the interest of accumulating
capital for investment. This resentment has become doubly compiled
when the workers have seen new government officials driving Mercedes-
Benz and purchasing large houses, not only for their own use, but for
speculation.

Inflation has been fostered if the government has expanded
borrowing internally and/or externally to continue development expenditures when export-based revenues have failed to expand adequately.[63] This has been the case particularly when the loans obtained
have been used predominantly to build nonproductive or at best long-
term-payoff social and economic infrastructure in hopes of attracting
private enterprise, or prestige projects such as hotels and fancy airports. Indirect monetary controls typically available to the newly
established central banks have not been designed to alter the underlying
structural factors leading to rising prices. The introduction of high
interest rates to reduce inflation has, instead, reduced or even halted
existing limited domestic private investment.[64]

Past experience shows that what little private investment in
manufacturing has been attracted by heavy infrastructural expenditures
has been:

1. Directed to producing luxury goods—cigarettes, beverages,
or, in more advanced cases, assembly of radios and automobiles—
for the cash market that has emerged in the export enclave, particularly for the higher income elite;[65]

2. Heavily dependent on imported parts and materials, contributing to further dependency on overseas sources of supply and increased exports as well as balance of payments deficits;[66]

3. Capital intensive, since foreign firms usually simply transfer
to Africa the techniques devised for their home countries (often encouraged to do so by tax incentives); when urban wages have been
increased to cover inflated living costs, this trend may be accelerated.
As a result, little additional employment is provided;[67]

4. Concentrated, for the most part, in existing urban areas
to take advantage of existing markets and external economies,[68] thus
further aggravating the lopsided resource allocation pattern of the
dual economy.

To the extent that governments have made their own investment
in import-substitution manufacturing plants, they have tended to contribute still further to the growing internal and external imbalance
characteristic of the dual economy.[69]

19

The tragic culmination of this pattern of development has tended to be economic crisis. The more vigorously it has been pursued, the sooner the crisis has tended to be realized. Ensuing governmental efforts to overcome the crises by orthodox methods—reduction of government expenditures, layoff of government employees, devaluation, which reduces the per unit earnings of exports and causes still further increases in costs of living—have tended, directly, to reduce the real incomes of the wage earners and cash crop peasants in the export enclave and, indirectly, to add pressures to the marginal levels of living in the hinterland as the unemployed trickle back to traditional sectors. Continued emphasis on export production and the failure to restructure political-economic institutions in order to implement plans to reallocate resources for an increasingly integrated, balanced national economy has, in other words—far from contributing to development as here defined—typically led to the eventual deterioration of the levels of living of the broadest masses and general stagnation.

SUMMARY AND OUTLINE OF THE REMAINDER
OF THIS BOOK

The record of national planning has not, either in Africa or elsewhere throughout most of the Third World, been notably successful. For the most part, it has been based on traditional theories drawn from Western economic teachings that emphasize expansion of output without regard to the role of institutions in distorting the distribution of benefits. When "modern" growth has failed to spread (or even to "trickle down") as projected, a variety of one-sided, fragmented, static explanations have been offered: Africans do not respond like "modern" economic men; their traditional institutions are inadequate; their educational systems should be expanded; their population growth rates are too high; their governments should—depending on whose advice is followed—expand exports and/or limit imports to foster import-substitution industries.

More careful analysis of the problem permits identification of critical variables that may be incorporated into a comprehensive model to explain how the interactions of crucial institutional features have perpetuated the lopsided resource allocation patterns characteristic of underdevelopment in Africa. The model in turn suggests hypotheses as to critical areas in which changes must be made if increased productivity is to spread into all sectors of more integrated, balanced economies, contributing to raising the levels of living of the broad masses of the population.

The remainder of Part 1 is devoted to an exploration in greater depth of specific aspects of the explanation of underdevelopment provided by the model and to outlining some of the hypotheses it suggests as to more effective approaches to planning. Chapter 2 presents evidence relating to the five major exports of sub-Saharan Africa that tends to substantiate the model's explanation as to the limits imposed by external factors on the export sector as a potential engine for development. Chapter 3 analyzes the emergent conflicts among the historically shaped interest groups, or classes, which may be expected to influence efforts to formulate and implement national plans and policies. Chapter 4 outlines some of the implications of the model and the particular constraints identified in chapters 2 and 3 for efforts to implement more fruitful approaches to planning.

In sum, Part I attempts to explicate the problem of underdevelopment. The following parts of the book consider in more detail the evidence drawn from the experiences of the larger of the former British colonies in sub-Saharan Africa in an effort to assess the probable consequences of alternative strategies that have been or might be adopted in the critical areas suggested by the model. These areas include the productive sectors, industry and agriculture, which are analyzed in Part II; external and internal trade, Part III; and finance, Part IV.

NOTES

1. A. Waterston, Development Planning—Lessons of Experience (Baltimore: printed for the Economic Development Institute, International Bank for Reconstruction and Development, by the Johns Hopkins Press, 1965), passim.

2. Cf. W. J. Barber, The Economy of British Central Africa, A Case Study of Economic Development in a Dualistic Society (Stanford: Stanford University Press, 1961), p. 6. See R. B. Seidman, "The Jural Postulates of African Law" (paper presented to African Studies Association Conference, Boston, October 1970), for problems of determining goals of development in Africa, and P. Dorner, "Research Issues in Agricultural Developmental Policy," Land Tenure Center (submitted for journal publication).

3. E.g., R. E. Hunter, in "Throwing out the Baby: In Defense of Foreign Aid," The New Republic, Nov. 20, 1971, p. 18, emphasizes the "positive successes" of foreign assistance as indicated by the "spectacular achievement" of a 5 percent per year growth rate in the 1960s.

4. Cf. Currie, "The Relevancy of Development Economics to Development," D. Seers, "The Meaning of Development," Institute of Development Research, Dec. 1969, pp. 1-2; B. Nossiter, "Does Foreign Aid Really Aid?" Atlantic, Feb. 1970; and Mahbub ul Haq, "Employment

and Income Distribution in the 1970s: A New Perspective," Development Digest, Nov. 10, 1971, p. 6.

5. The necessity of a balanced economy was underscored by the Food Agricultural Symposium on Agricultural Institutions for Integrated Rural Development, FAO, Rome, 21-28 June 1971 (ESR: FAO/SIDA/IRD/71A, 16 April 1971). See also, R. McNamara, Address to Board of Governors, International Bank for Reconstruction and Development, Washington, 1971.

6. R. W. Clower, G. Dalton, M. Harwitz, A. A. Walters, Growth Without Development, An Economic Survey of Liberia, (Evanston: Northwestern University, 1966).

7. W. A. Lewis, Development Planning, The Essentials of Economic Policy (New York: Harper & Row, 1966), esp. pp. 15, 20-21.

8. Georgescu-Roegen, Analytical Economics, Issue and Problems (Cambridge: Harvard University Press, 1966), pp. 109-110.

9. Cf. Waterston, Development Planning—Lessons of Experience.

10. E.g., H. Myint, Economic Theory and the Underdeveloped Countries (London: Oxford University press, 1971), esp. Ch. 7; and P. T. Bauer, in Foreword to R. Szereszewski, Structural Changes in the Economy of Ghana, 1891-1911 (London: Weidenfeld and Nicolson, 1965).

11. For criticism of this concept see W. O. Jones, "Economic Man in Africa," Food Research Institute Studies, May 1960.

12. D. McClelland, Achieving Society (Princeton: Van Nostrand, 1961), esp. Chs. 2, 3.

13. E. E. Hagen, On The Theory of Social Change: How Economic Growth Began (Homewood, Illinois: Dorsey Press, 1962).

14. B. F. Hoselitz, "Unity and Diversity in Economic Structure," in Economics and the Idea of Mankind, Hoselitz (ed.), (New York: Colombia University Press, 1965), esp. pp. 88-89.

15. For a statement as to the conditions "required" for the functioning of democracy—including "a value system allowing the peaceful 'play' of power"—see S. M. Lipset, Political Man—The Social Bases of Politics (New York: Doubleday & Co., Inc., 1960), esp. Ch. 11 Lipset introduces this chapter with the declaration that, "Since most countries which lack an enduring tradition of political democracy lie in the underdeveloped sections of the world, Weber may have been right when he suggested that modern democracy in its clearest form can only occur under capitalist industrialization."

16. R. Prebisch, "Nuera politica commercial para el deserolla," inaugural address, UNCTAD, Geneva, Switzerland, 1964.

17. Myint, Economic Theory and the Underdeveloped Countries, esp. Ch. 6; and R. F. Johnston and P. Kilby, Agricultural Strategies, Rural-Urban Interactions, and the Expansion of Income Opportunities (Stanford: Mimeo Draft, 1971).

18. E.g., T. Schulz, "Investment in Human Capital," American Economic Review, March, 1961.

19. Cf. Myint, Economic Theory and Underdeveloped Countries, esp. Ch. 10.

20. Ibid., p. 88.

21. W. A. Hance, Population, Migration and Urbanization in Africa (New York: Columbia University Press, 1971), presents a detailed picture of the dimensions of this problem.

22. Cf. J. R. Hooker, Population Problems in Zambia, Central and Southern Africa Series (Hanover, N. H.: American Universities Field Staff, 1972), XV, no. 7, 5.

23. G. Myrdal, Economic Theories and Underdeveloped Regions (London: 1957), p. 101.

24. Myint, Economic Theory and Underdeveloped Countries, p. 16.

25. Ibid., Chs. 4, 5.

26. N. Georgescu-Roegen, Analytical Economics, Issues and Problems (Cambridge: Harvard University Press, 1966), p. 114.

27. Cf. J. Dewey, Logic, The Theory of Inquiry, (New York: Holt, Reinhart and Winston, 1938). Dewey argues that the problem-solving method of inquiry is as valid for the social as for the physical sciences, even providing a means of dealing with the perplexing question of the role of values in social science research. There are interesting parallels between the problem-solving approach to warranting hypotheses and the methodology implicit in historical materialism, for both require analysis of the complex contradictory interrelationships of changing material and ideological phenomena as the foundation of realistic policies directed to social change.

28. There is a growing literature on model-building for the social sciences. The following have been found useful in formulating the model presented here: G. C. Homans, "Contemporary Theory in Sociology," in Handbook of Modern Sociology, Faris, ed. (Chicago: Rand McNally & Co., 1964), pp. 951-977; M. Black, Models and Metaphors, Studies in Language and Philosophy (Ithaca: Cornell University Press, 1962); I. D. F. Black, Design for Decision (New York: The Free Press, 1953); R. A. Dahl and C. E. Lindblom, Politics, Economics and Welfare (New York: Harper and Bros., 1963); L. H. Mayo and E. M. Jones, "Legal Policy Decision Process: Alternative Thinking and the Predictive Functions," George Washington Law Review 33: 318-458; M. W. Riley, Sociological Research, I: A Case Approach (New York: Harcourt, Brace & World, Inc., 1963).

29. C. G. Homans, "Contemporary Theory in Sociology," Handbook of Modern Sociology, pp. 97-8.

30. For a useful tool for evaluating policies proposed for solving development problems, see paradigm as formulated by R. B.

Seidman, "Law and Development: A General Model," Law and Society Review, 1972; and the discussions among some 30 law students from 17 countries who participated in the Law and Development Institute, University of Wisconsin, summer 1971.

31. T. Szentes, Theories of Underdevelopment (Budapest: Akademiai Kiado, 1971), summarizes and evaluates this range of theories about "dualism" in the underdeveloped countries.

32. Cf. U. N. Economic Survey of Africa Since 1950, passim; also G. Hunter, The New Societies of Tropical Africa, A Selective Study (New York: Oxford University Press, 1963), passim; and Green and Seidman, Unity or Poverty? (African Penguin Library), Part I.

33. Cf. Economic Commission for Africa, Industrial Growth in Africa: A Survey and Outlook (E/CN.14/INR/I), Dec. 1962.

34. Cf. R. J. H. Church, "Some Problems of Regional Economic Development in West Africa," Economic Geography 45 (Jan. 1969): 53-62.

35. Only 10 percent of the African continent had been geologically surveyed by 1957, see Economic Commission for Africa, Industrial Growth in Africa, A Survey and Outlook, App. III.

36. For discussions of reasons for labor migration from traditional to urban areas in East Africa, see N. W. Forrester, Kenya Today (Hague, 1962), pp. 127-131; W. Elkan, Migrants and Proletarian Urban Labour in the Economic Development of Uganda (London: Oxford University Press, 1960); see also E. P. Skinner, "Labour Migration Among the Mossi of the Upper Volta," in H. Kuper (ed.), Urbanization and Migration in West Africa (Berkeley: University of California Press, 1965), p. 65. See also E. Berg, "French West Africa" in Galenson (ed.), Labour and Economic Development (New York: 1959), pp. 186-259; M. Harris, Portugal's African "Wards" (American Committee on Africa, 1960), pp. 17-30.

37. Labor migration was accelerated in North, East, and South Africa by colonial and white-settler land reserve policies that restricted the most fertile land areas to the white minority; see, e.g., Forrester, Kenya Today, op. cit.

38. Cf. P. T. Bauer, West African Trade, A Study of Competition, Oligopoly and Monopoly in a Changing Economy, revised (London: Rutledge and Kegan, Ltd. 1963), pp. 68-75; W. Thompson and R. Adloff, French West Africa (London: George Allen & Unwin, Ltd., 1958), pp. 432-435, and the Emerging States of French Equatorial Africa (Stanford: Stanford University Press, 1960), passim; Barber, The Economy of British Central Africa, especially chs. 5-7; R. Hall, Zambia (London: Pall Mall Press, 1965), especially Ch. 8.

39. E.g., D. E. Carney, Government and Economy in British West Africa, A Study of the Role of Public Agencies in the Economic Development of British West Africa in the Period 1947-1955 (New York: Bookman Associates, 1961), passim.

40. For efforts of Tanzania to escape this domination, see A. Seidman, Comparative Development Strategies in East Africa, and Ghana's Development Experience, 1951-1965 (Nairobi: East Africa Publishing House, 1972).

41. For discussion of the profit-maximizing aims of firms investing in the Third World, see M. Tanzer, The Political Economy of International Oil and the Underdeveloped Countries (Boston: Beacon Press, 1969), pp. 32-34; for a direct assertion, see A. Hacker, "The Making of a (Corporation) President," New York Times Magazine, April, 1967.

42. See International Monetary Fund, Annual Report, 1963, p. 58, for terms of trade trends, 1950-1962; also U. N. Statistical Yearbooks for terms of trade in the postwar period.

43. E.g., the Jeanneney Report of the French government pointed out that the outflow of funds from the African franc zone countries since the war on these accounts exceeded all official French government contributions to those countries, including those for military expenditures (the period included the Algerian War for Independence) (official text [Paris, 1963]). See also Barber, The Economy of British Central Africa; D. E. Carney, Government and Economy in British West Africa; and Newlyn and Rowan, Money and Banking in British Colonial Africa, passim.

44. See Green and Seidman, Unity or Poverty? especially Part II regarding policies of these firms and their governments vis-à-vis African states.

45. Cf. U. N. Economic Survey of Africa since 1950, Table I-LIV, "Annual Personal Income, African and Non-African, in Selected Countries," p. 94; D. Ghai, "Some Aspects of Income Distribution in East Africa" (mimeo), Nov. 24, 1964; G. Hunter, The New Societies of Tropical Africa, p. 135; R. Gullet, K. Caldwan, and L. Dina, Nigerian Cocoa Farmers (London: Oxford University Press, 1956), passim; C. C. Vrigley, "African Farming in Buganda" (East African Institute of Social Research Conference, 1953).

46. Cf. P. T. Ellsworth, "Factors in the Economic Development of Ceylon," In Betz, Choudhry, and Morgan (eds.), Readings in Economic Development, pp. 14-22.

47. G. Lenski, Power and Privilege, a Theory of Social Stratification (New York: McGraw Hill, 1966), pp. 209-210.

48. Cf. G. Ranis, "International Trade and Its Relation to National Development Planning" (mimeo), University of Wisconsin Library. Library.

49. Cf. Marcus, Investment and Development Possibilities in Tropical Africa, passim; Green and Seidman, Unity or Poverty? esp. pp. 21-126; and A. Seidman, "Foreign Firms in Africa: Old Goals, New Methods," African Perspectives Papers in the History,

Politics and Economics of Africa, presented to Thomas Hodgrin, (Cambridge University Press, 1970).

50. Cf. A. N. Hakam, "The Motivation to Invest and the Locational Pattern of Foreign Private Industrial Investments in Nigeria," The Nigerian Journal of Economic and Social Studies 8, no. 1 (March, 1966).

51. E.g., MIFERMA's postwar development of Mauritania's Iron ore deposits; LAMCO's Investment in Liberia's iron ore deposits; Shell-DP and Gulf's (among others) investments in Nigeria's and Libya's oil wells. For other examples, see Green and Seidman, Unity or Poverty? especially Part II.

52. Today the new pattern appears to be that in cases where there are economies of scale, especially in local processing of crops, foreign firms will establish nuclear estates and/or processing facilities and encourage peasant farmers to produce for them; e.g., Brook Bond-Leibig and American Tobacco Company in East Africa and the rubber estates purchases by Firestone Rubber in Ghana following the coup of 1966.

53. Cf. the Kaiser-Reynolds VALCO smelter in Ghana, using power from the Volta Dam; see Seidman, Ghana's Development Experience, 1951-1965 (Nairobi: East African Publishing House, 1972), Ch. VIII.

54. Cf. O. Aboyade, "A Note on External Trade, Capital Distortion and Planned Development," African Primary Products and International Trade, papers delivered at an international seminar at the University of Edinburgh, I. G. Stewart and H. Ord (eds.) (Edinburgh University Press, 1965).

55. See E. H. Hagen, On the Theory of Social Change, pp. 55-85, for operation of internal market forces; I. S. Livingstone, "Marketing Crops in Uganda and Tanganyika," African Primary Products; Bohannan and Dalton (eds.), Markets in Africa (Evanston, Illinois, 1962), A. Martin, Marketing of Minor Crops in Uganda (London: Her Majesty's Stationery Office, 1963); and W. A. Lewis, Development Planning, pp. 42-43.

56. For varying viewpoints concerning corruption in developing countries, see N. H. Leff, "Economic Development Through Bureaucratic Corruption," American Behavioral Scientist (Nov. 1964); A. Watson and J. B. Dirlan, "The Impact of Underdevelopment on Economic Planning," Quarterly Journal of Economics (May 1965), pp. 167-194; T. Morgan, "The Theory of Error in Centrally Directed Economic Systems," Quarterly Journal of Economics (August 1964).

57. For discussion of responsiveness of export crop farmers to price changes, see E. Clayton, Economic Planning in Developing Agriculture (Heddley Bors, 1963); for inelasticity of world demand for African exports see summary in Green and Seidman, Unity or

Poverty? pp. 38-41 and 45 ff.; for limitations of export crop production, see A. M. Kaarck, The Economics of African Development (New York: Praeger Publishers, 1966), pp. 150-153. Mining firms may restrict their output to hold prices up, aggravating unemployment among the African labor force by reducing tax revenues obtained by the African government: Barber, The Economy of British Central Africa, pp. 123 ff.

58. While African exports grew over 75 percent in the decade after the mid-1950s, African imports grew about 80 percent. See Green and Seidman, Unity or Poverty? Ch. 2; and U.N. Department of Economic and Social Affairs, U.N. Economic Survey of Africa Since 1950 (New York, 1960), pp. 149-151.

59. See current issues of International Monetary Fund, Annual Report, for terms of trade data.

60. ECA, Economic Bulletin for Africa IV, no. 1, Part A, "Current Trends," especially Table A. 11.1, p. 4.

61. S. D. Neumark, "Foreign Trade and Economic Development in Africa, An Historical Perspective," Food Research Institute (Stanford: Stanford University), especially Ch. 10; and D. Johnston, "Change in Agricultural Productivity," Economic Transition in Africa, Ch. 8.

62. This appears to be a subject of debate, cf. contra: Johnston, "Changes in Agricultural Productivity," but it may actually reflect different stages of development; see Seidman, Ghana's Development Experience, 1951-1965, Ch. XI.

63. Cf. M. Bronfenbrenner, "The High Cost of Economic Development," Land Economics (August 1953); also D. Seers, A Theory of Inflation and Growth; and W. Baer, "The Economics of Prebisch and ECLA," Economic Development and Cultural Change.

64. Cf. A. I. Bloomfield, "Monetary Policy in Underdeveloped Countries," in Betz, Choudhry, and Morgan (eds.), Readings in Economic Development, pp. 375-384.

65. Hunter, The New Societies of Tropical Africa, p. 62.

66. ECA, Industrial Growth in Africa: A Survey and Outlook; and G. Hunter, The New Societies of Tropical Africa, p. 61. For the Nigerian experience, see Aboyade, Foundations of an African Economy, pp. 133-140. For East African Experience, see Seidman, Comparative East African Development Strategies, Ch. VI.

67. W. A. Lewis "Unemployment in Developing Countries," lecture to Mideast Research Conference, Oct., 1964 (mimeo), University of Wisconsin Library; also Lewis, Development Planning, p. 7 ff.; for implications for African economies, see G. Arrighi, "International Corporations and the Labour Aristocracy and Economic Development," to appear in Horwitz (ed.), The Corporation and the Cold War (London: Blond, 1973), passim.

68. Cf. Church, "Some Problems of Regional Economic Development in West Africa," op. cit.

69. E.g., Seidman, Ghana's Development Experience, 1951-1965, Ch. 10.

2

THE EXTERNAL LIMITS
OF EXPORT EXPANSION

A major strategy, stemming from orthodox economic theory and still recommended by some foreign experts for African countries, is the expansion of primary product exports as the only possible "engine for development." African governments are urged to create a "hospitable investment climate" for foreign firms to invest in mineral export production and to encourage African peasant producers to enter into export crop production on the assumption that resulting expanded incomes will create the necessary conditions for some sort of multiplier effect to begin to spread development throughout the economy.

This chapter provides detailed evidence as to the characteristics of the markets for the five major exports of sub-Saharan Africa to substantiate the hypothesis, suggested by the model of underdevelopment proposed in Chapter 1, that reliance on export expansion is likely to culminate, not in sustained development, but stagnation. This is not to argue that African governments should ignore export production; given that it provides a fourth or more of the Gross Domestic Product and all the foreign exchange earnings of most African countries, that would obviously be extremely unwise. Rather this evidence is presented to underline the necessity of reducing dependence on fluctuating world markets for raw materials by refocusing development plans and plan implementation machinery toward capturing the investible surpluses produced in this trade, and redirecting it to the attainment of a balanced, nationally integrated, self-reliant economy.

This process cannot be left to the "free play" of market forces, as suggested by some theorists.[1] The export markets for African primary markets are far from being characterized by even the modified competitive forces assumed by modern proponents of traditional theory. The consequences that may be anticipated when oligopoly reigns in export markets were aptly described by Myint himself in the 1950s:

. . . in the typical situation where foreign enterprises in the backward countries are large enough to be monopolistic buyers of labor and peasant produce, their behavior may depress the terms of trade. Thus they may meet the pressure of competition in the world market by cutting prices rather than output and by pressing down on the internal incomes of the backward countries while maintaining their "normal" profit on an unreduced volume of output.[2]

No better explanation appears necessary as to why African governments seriously concerned with attainment of development cannot afford to rely on free trade. What appears needed is state action to reshape the pattern of national participation in foreign trade to insure that it contributes to, rather than undermines, plans to restructure the national economy.

Where possible, African state action to insure that foreign trade contributes to national economic reconstruction should be strengthened by participation with other producing countries in efforts to attain international agreements to stabilize world market prices. Such agreements should be designed to avoid the competitive expansion of output, which reduces the returns obtained from the expenditure of real resources. At the same time they should provide steady foreign exchange earnings as well as tax and profit revenues to be devoted to implementation of long-term national plans.

The five commodities analyzed below constituted roughly half of the sub-Saharan African countries' exports at the time they attained independence. The overseas markets for these products are characterized by a slow rate of increasing demand and a high degree of foreign olipolistic domination.

The rate of growth of demand for four of sub-Saharan Africa's five main exports is estimated to be less than 3 percent a year—barely enough to permit export expansion to keep up with population growth rates. The expected rate of demand growth for the fifth and most important African export, copper, is only slightly higher.

These projected rates of growth (see Table 1) do not deal with the possibility that competition among producing countries may lead to further world price reductions.[3] Nevertheless they suggest the futility of formulating development policies that rely heavily on export expansion. They reflect long-term trends:[4] (1) the expansion of demand in developed countries for food items like coffee, cocoa, and tea is unlikely to exceed population growth rates by much if at all; (2) the introduction of new technologies and the increased share of world trade devoted to consumer durable goods requires a lower proportion of agricultural raw materials; (3) the development of synthetics is slowing the expansion of demand for natural raw materials such as

TABLE 1

Projected Rates of Growth of the Value of the Major
Exports of Sub-Saharan Africa

Export	Projected Rate of Growth (percent per year)		Percent of Total Exports of Sub-Saharan Africa, 1965
	Low	High	
Cocoa	3.0	3.3	8.6
Coffee	2.1	2.3	11.9
Tea	2.2	2.6	—
Oilseeds	2.6	2.6	8.3
Sugar	1.4	2.8	—
Cotton	1.7	2.5	7.1
Rubber	0.8	1.9	1.3
Sisal	0.4	1.0	1.3
Timber	3.3	4.4	3.3
Aluminum	6.6	7.0	—
Tin	1.1	1.3	2.2
Copper	3.9	4.4	14.6
Iron	5.6	6.2	3.5
Petroleum	minimum	6.0	4.9

Source: D. Wall, Tables II, IV, pp. 29, 36, based on UNCTAD
Document No. T.D./34 App. A (New York, 1968); and Yearbooks of
International Trade Statistics, 1965 and 1966, United Nations (New
York, 1967), cited in R. F. A. Gardiner, "Development and Trade in
Africa," African Affairs, no. 65 (January 1966): 1-14.

cotton and sisal; and (4) the policies of developed countries, like the
imposition of taxes and quotas, have tended to restrict imports of
traditional African exports.

Examination of the major African agricultural exports suggests
that their expansion in the World War II and postwar era has, at least
in part, taken place at the expense of other developing countries. This
is particularly notable in the case of coffee, but is also true of oilseeds
and tea. African cotton exports have grown in recent decades partly
because the U.S. has reduced its cotton exports considerably. There
are signs that European imports of cotton are likely to expand at slower
rates or even to contract as synthetic fibers become more widely used.

The world markets for the major African agricultural exports
are dominated by a handful of giant, increasingly multinational and

multicommodity corporations. There is still a degree of competition among these firms, but it is unlikely to be beneficial to African producers, since all seek to utilize their far-flung marketing networks to obtain the lowest possible raw materials prices. Given the slowly growing world demand, these firms may be expected to take advantage of the rapidly expanding export production of competing developing countries to lower the costs of their raw materials. This already appears to have been a major factor underlying the tendency of the world prices for sub-Saharan Africa's major export crops to decline over the last decade, and the reluctance behind consumer country governments—especially that of the United States—to support international price stabilization agreements.

This chapter aims to examine some of the evidence for these propositions.

AGRICULTURAL EXPORTS

Limited Demand

The output of most individual African countries is marginal to world production in the case of the continent's four major export crops. The major exceptions are Ghana's cocoa and the UAR's cotton. Nevertheless, expansion of continental African production—stimulated by extensive efforts of national and international agencies in recent years to encourage African peasants to increase output—has been an important factor contributing to the general conditions of oversupply that have increasingly tended to prevail on the world market. Hundreds of thousands of African peasants are entering cash crop production for the first time. They grow most of their own subsistence crops, viewing export crops as a supplementary source of cash to augment their meagre living standards. As a result, they have been able to accept relatively low prices for their output.

The output of Africa's most important agricultural export, coffee—increasingly produced by African peasants on small farms— has almost quadrupled in the postwar era (see Table 2). Expanding African coffee exports are particularly suitable for instant coffees that are widely replacing ground coffees in developed countries. They have contributed to a growing oversupply on the world coffee market, a major factor leading to reduced world coffee prices. As a result, serious economic problems plague those countries, particularly in Latin America, that have long depended on coffee for a major share of their export earnings.

TABLE 2

Output of Africa's Major Coffee-Producing Countries,
1952-56 and 1968

	1952-56		1968	
Country	Metric Tons (in thousands)	Percent of World Total	Metric Tons (in thousands)	Percent of World Total
Angola	663	2.5	1860	4.9
Cameroon	129	.2	637	1.6
Congo (K)	278	.6	600	1.6
Ethiopia	470	1.9	1650	4.4
Guinea	81	—	108	.2
Ivory Coast	752	2.9	2040	5.4
Kenya	151	.2	280	.7
Madagascar	421	1.7	670	1.7
Rwanda	54	—	120	.3
Tanzania	185	.1	610	1.6
Uganda	487	1.9	1890	5.0
Africa Total	3,927	16.0	11,313	30.1
World Total	25,211	100.0	37,488	100.0

Source: FAO Annual Yearbook, 1969.

Africa has traditionally been the world's major producer of cocoa, the second most important African export crop. African cocoa production has almost doubled in the postwar decade (see Table 3), outpacing growth of output in other cocoa growing areas. In the 1960s, falling cocoa prices had serious consequences for the African producers, particularly Ghana, which depends on cocoa for two-thirds of its foreign exchange.

Among oilseeds, Africa's third most important agricultural export, groundnuts, oil palms, and copra are the most important in export trade[5] (see Table 4). They may be used for a variety of end purposes, including foods and table uses, soap, and industrial requirements particularly for paints and tinplating. World War II stimulated major changes in the world market for oilseeds, partly by forcing changes of habit in Europe, the major importing area, partly by accelerating invention of new processes that have tended to increase the substitutability of fats and the introduction of synthetic products. The

African countries' exports to Europe expanded with the decline of Asian output so that by the 1950s they produced over 10 percent of world exports, compared to under 9 percent in the 1930s. On the other hand, changed consumption patterns in Europe and the rapid development of synthetics imposed narrow limits on continued expansion of overseas African sales to their main customers. Oilseed prices have in recent years tended to move together because of their increased substitutability. A study of oilseeds production and marketing for the Organization for European Economic Cooperation has emphasized that "The sensitivity of oilseed prices to changes in the economic outlook is a source of weakness for the countries or territories which are economically dependent on these products, and it affects producers who sometimes rely on them for their sole livelihood."[6]

By the end of the 1950s, the main oilseed producers in Africa were Nigeria, which produced about a third of Africa's output; the French West African colonies, particularly Senegal (all together about 13 percent); the Congo (about 13 percent); and Egypt and South Africa (about 5 percent each). The remaining African producers produced about 30 percent of the total African output.

TABLE 3

Output of Africa's Major Cocoa-Producing Countries,
1952-56 and 1968

Country	1952-1956		1968	
	Metric Tons (in thousands)	Percent of World Total	Metric Tons (in thousands)	Percent of World Total
Cameroon	605	7.3	1030	8.2
Equatorial Guinea	197	2.3	380	3.0
Ghana	2446	29.5	3387	27.1
Ivory Coast	648	7.8	1445	11.5
Nigeria	1060	12.8	1865	14.9
Sao Tome	78	0.9	106	0.8
Sierra Leone	17	0.2	50	0.4
Togo	52	0.6	200	1.6
Africa Total	5,172	62.0	8,614	68.9
World Total	8,280	100.0	12,485	100.0

Source: FAO Annual Yearbook, 1969.

34

TABLE 4

Output of Africa's Major Oilseed-Producing
Countries, 1968

Country	Metric Tons (in thousands)	Percent of World Total
Palm kernels and oil		
Nigeria	5,433	22.7
Congo-Kinshasa	3,489	14.6
Sierra Leone	1,064	4.4
Dahomey	977	4.0
Cameroon	901	3.7
Ghana	630	2.6
Ivory Coast	580	2.4
Liberia	552	2.3
Angola	473	1.9
Total: Africa	15,028	63.0
World	23,841	100.0
Groundnuts		
Nigeria	13,750	9.1
Senegal	8,280	5.5
Niger	2,680	1.7
South Africa	2,270	1.5
Uganda	2,000	1.3
Sudan	1,970	1.3
Upper Volta	1,330	0.8
Malawi	1,310	0.8
Cameroon	1,250	0.8
Congo-Kinshasa	1,150	0.7
Chad	1,100	0.7
Mali	1,000	0.6
Total: Africa	44,650	29.6
World	150,340	100.0
Copra		
Mozambique	598	1.8
Tanganyika	140	0.4
Zanzibar	120	0.3
Total: Africa	1,171	3.6
World	32,232	100.0

Source: FAO Production Yearbook, 1969 (Rome, 1969).

Prior to independence, the British consumed almost the entire output of their colonies' oilseeds. During the initial postwar oilseeds shortage, the British Government made long-term contracts with the colonies for their entire output. In 1954 these were for the most part replaced by private contracts between the overseas marketing boards—then still governed by colonial authorities—and private British buyers. The surplus was sold on the free market. The French Government, on the other hand, provided a guaranteed market for the companies buying and/or producing oilseeds in French West Africa by restricting imports from other sources. As a result, the French prices tended to be higher than the world market prices.*

After independence, British private firms continued to buy through the national marketing boards, still consuming a major share of the oilseeds output of their former colonies. France, on joining the European Common Market, pledged to reduce the price differentials in its trade with its former colonies and to permit extension of sales to the rest of Europe.

In the case of cotton, African output has expanded to about 10 percent of the world total. United States production, in contrast, was a third of the world total in the 1950s and dropped to barely more than 20 percent in the 1960s. (See Table 5.) European nations rely heavily on imported cotton for their textiles industry. The desire to diversify the sources of raw cotton historically played an important role in British colonial policies. The United Kingdom textile industry was founded on imported raw cotton, so that maintenance of adequate supplies has "always been a matter of concern both to the industry and the government."[7] In the mid-nineteenth century when the United States provided 75 percent of the United Kingdom's cotton, the United Kingdom's government sought to broaden the sources of supply by distributing seed and cotton gins in the Near East, India, and South America. The defeat of the Southern slave states in the U.S. Civil War accelerated these efforts, particularly leading to encouragement to Egypt to expand its output. In 1902 the British Cotton Growing

———————

*The available data in the case of palm oil suggest that the percent received by the African producers tended to be low; a significant share of the difference tended to go directly to the companies. High prices of company imports tended to offset the slightly higher producer prices, so it is doubtful they benefitted much by the differential. The price paid by the companies to African palm oil producers in the Congo, on the other hand, appeared to be a significantly smaller proportion of the final sales prices than in either French or British West Africa. (The prices paid to the African producers are not reported for Portuguese Guinea or Angola.)

TABLE 5

Output of Africa's Major Cotton-Producing Countries,
1952-56 and 1968

	1952-56		1968	
Country	Metric Tons (in thousands)	Percent of World Total	Metric Tons (in thousands)	Percent of World Total
Central African Rep.	13	0.1	22	0.2
Chad	21	0.2	57	0.5
Congo (K)	49	0.5	12	0.1
Mali	2	—	15	0.1
Mozambique	32	0.3	44	0.3
Nigeria	25	0.2	27	0.2
South Africa	6	—	16	0.1
Sudan	87	0.9	184	1.6
Tanzania	18	0.1	52	0.4
Uganda	64	0.6	76	0.7
United Arab Republic	354	3.8	437	3.8
Africa Total	671	6.77		100.0
World Total	9,227	100.0	11,336	
U.S. Total	3,193	34.6	2,384	21.0

Source: FAO Annual Yearbook, 1969.

Association was established to foster cotton production throughout the British Empire. Uganda's cotton production dates back to that period. After World War I, the Empire Cotton Growing Corporation, consisting of industry and government representatives, began to carry on research and other nontrading activities. The Sudan's Gezira scheme was initiated by a private British firm with substantial government encouragement.

By the 1950s, the British African colonies had become an important source of raw cotton for British industry. But British cotton textiles production had begun to decline, reflecting Britain's decline as a major cotton textiles exporter, as well as a growing shift to noncotton textiles production.[8] The European Common Market countries, producing about 70 percent of the OECD countries' cotton textiles output, imported almost two-thirds of their cotton from non-U.S. sources. By the late 1960s, they were importing about 80 percent of their raw cotton from non-U.S. sources, but had also begun to reduce their cotton imports, in part reflecting the growing trend toward non-cotton textiles.

Oligopolistic Buyers

African countries, competing to expand their exports to limited world markets for their four main export crops in order to augment foreign exchange earnings, confront a relatively small number of increasingly interlinked multinational corporations. To disentangle the multitude of strands and interconnections between these oligopolistic enterprises would require volumes. A few examples must here suffice.

Consider the case of coffee, the largest single African export crop in the 1960s. The largest world importer of coffee is the United States, which imports about four times as much coffee as the next largest consumer, West Germany.[9] Four companies, the General Foods Corporation, Standard Brands, Inc., a Coca-Cola subsidiary, Tenco, and Nestles, handle about 80 percent of all U.S. coffee imports and sales.[10] These firms are engaged in a wide range of businesses related to foods. They have been rapidly expanding their ties with European firms as well as those in other areas of the world in the postwar era. General Foods acquired a British food manufacturer and processor in 1947; a major interest in a Stockholm coffee processor in 1963; a 51 percent share of a Spanish instant coffee producer in 1965. It owns subsidiaries in Mexico, Italy, Australia, Spain, Sudan, Canada, United Kingdom, West Germany, Japan, Denmark, South Africa, France, Brazil, and Venezuela. Its 1969 income before taxes was $216 million. This exceeds the combined 1969 current and development budget of Uganda, one of Africa's biggest coffee producers, which sells most of its coffee to the United States.[11] Standard Brands, while not as big as General Foods, also has an extensive business in foods and allied products. It owns subsidiaries in fifteen countries, including Latin America, the United Kingdom, Asia, and South Africa, and it owns major shares in a French coffee processor, a Portuguese food manufacturer, and firms in Germany, Italy, and Spain. Nestles is a Swiss holding company with extensive interests in food industries including milk, chocolate, soluble coffee, soups, diabetic products, and frozen foods. It owns 820 factories, sales branches, depots, and operating units throughout the world. In 1970 it merged with Unilever to operate a joint foods business throughout Germany, Australia, and Italy.

The linkup between Nestles and Unilever directly ties a major purchaser of African coffee and cocoa with the company that has been buying a predominant share of African oilseeds and other agricultural produce. Unilever itself is a holding company, the second largest firm in Great Britain, excluding oil companies. It has long dominated African agricultural exports, particularly from West Africa, through the United African Company.[12] It owns subsidiaries in Cameroon, Congo (Zaire), Ghana, Ivory Coast, Kenya, Malawi, Nigeria, Rhodesia, Sierra Leone, South Africa, and Zambia. Its Zairien subsidiary, Huilieries de Belges, owns hundreds of thousands of acres of plantations in that country. It manufactures a range of goods for household consumption in 70 countries, has over 200 operating companies, and operates 150 factories. Its 1969 world sales totaled $7.4 billion, not much less than the total value of all African exports—about $8.5 billion—in 1967.[13]

The same expansion of the range of business and the merger of existing giants in unrelated fields appears to be taking place among firms handling all of Africa's major exports. Hershey Chocolate Corporation—long one of the "big three" along with Nestles and British Chocolates in the cocoa buying business—recently changed its original name to Hershey Foods Corporation to reflect its expanding range of food business including macaroni and spaghetti, biscuits and crackers, coffee brewing equipment, air treatment appliances, and "convenience foods."

Recently Hersheys reached a joint agreement with another firm, Anderson Clayton and Company, to sell chocolates in Latin America.[14] Anderson Clayton, which at one time characterized itself as the "world's biggest cotton merchandizer," has also expanded its own business into handling coffee, cocoa, oilseeds, and general foods. Anderson Clayton's expansion into other fields apparently reflects a desire for increased flexibility and broadened profit opportunities in the face of a narrowing market for cotton. This expansion has been paralleled by growing concentration among textiles manufacturers.[15]

The British cotton textile industry, the main consumer of cotton from the English-speaking African countries, had already become relatively concentrated by the end of World War II, with the ten largest companies handling over half of the exports and the five largest spinning firms controlling almost 40 percent of the output. Immediately after the war, the British government established a monopoly to buy raw cotton "to obtain whatever benefits there were to be derived from bulk buying."[16] When the Conservatives came to power, the Liverpool market was reopened, but a higher degree of integration of spinning and weaving firms began to take place, in part because expansion into the production of noncotton textiles required higher capital investments.

Examination of these trends suggests that the postwar merger movement in the developed countries has tended to strengthen the marketing power of the firms dominating the sales of African produce. They no longer find it convenient or necessary to risk actual investment in African agricultural production as they sometimes did in the days of outright colonial rule. With their governments' support they encourage African governments and peasants to expand their own investments to produce more export crops, taking advantage of the consequent competition to buy the output at the lowest possible prices. The resulting fluctuations and overall downward trends in the prices of sub-Saharan Africa's major exports has already sharply reduced the contribution that these exports might have made to African development (see Table 6).

At the same time, the profits of the resulting conglomerates have tended to rise (see Table 7). The shift of emphasis from actual overseas investment to marketing control appears to have been a factor

TABLE 6

Prices of Some Major African Export Crops
($ per kilo)

| Year | Coffee | | | Cocoa | | | Cotton |
	France (Ivory Coast)	Germany	U.K.	U.S. (Ghana)	London (Ghana)	France (Ivory Coast)	U.K. (Egypt)
1955	0.89	1.30	—	82.4	83.2	96.6	1.43
1956	0.84	1.35	—	60.2	61.1	62.7	1.60
1957	0.89	1.31	—	67.5	66.2	70.8	1.09
1958	0.92	1.17	0.74	97.7	92.5	106.2	0.78
1959	0.70	0.89	0.62	80.7	75.1	86.3	0.98
1960	0.70	0.85	0.44	62.6	60.4	70.1	1.03
1961	0.67	0.83	0.40	49.8	48.2	55.0	0.95
1962	0.68	0.83	0.45	46.3	45.4	53.5	0.91
1963	0.62	0.81	0.60	55.8	55.8	65.1	1.01
1964	0.79	1.07	0.77	51.6	51.0	59.0	1.15
1965	0.62	1.02	0.66	38.1	37.9	42.2	1.10
1966	0.78	0.93	0.73	53.8	52.7	58.4	1.13
1967	0.77	0.91	0.72	64.0	63.2	69.3	1.23
1968	0.74	0.90	0.74	75.8	74.2	84.0	1.38

Source: FAO Production Yearbook, 1969. By design this table starts with a year of relatively high prices to indicate the extent of world market fluctuations for these major sub-Saharan export crops.

TABLE 7

Net Income of Some Major Foods Firms, 1963 and 1969
(in millions of dollars)

	1963	1969
General Foods	78.5	103.3
Standard Brands	21.5	35.3
Unilever	60.0	67.2
Coca-Cola	52.0	110.0

Note: Net income is usually calculated after costs, depreciation, and taxes. Because each company uses its own accounting methods, the data cannot be considered strictly comparable. They are only indicative of trends.

Source: Moody's Industrials (New York, 1970).

contributing to these rising profit margins. The way this works is illustrated by the case of the British firm of Brooke Bond, initially a tea producing and marketing firm, now merged with Leibig meatpacking interests, which was reported not to have suffered as a result of recent declines in tea prices.[17] The depressed prices reduce plantation profits, on which local taxes tend to be high, as in the Indian case; but the "wholesale end can make up much of the deficit." Brooke Bond controls about 38 percent of the United Kingdom market, which consumes about 40 percent of the world's tea exports. The company reportedly did not separate out the tea turnover or profit in its overall accounts—"possibly because of politically sensitive relations with tax-hungry primary producing nations"—but its overall accounts showed a 3 percent rise in its pre-tax profits in 1969.

The Difficulties of Attaining International Agreements

International agreements to stabilize the agricultural prices of developing country exports have been suggested as a partial solution to these problems. Although they may secure a degree of stability of returns, however, they cannot contribute significantly to changing the world patterns of demand for African agricultural exports, and hence cannot alter the fact that continued export dependency is unlikely to attain adequate rates of development. International efforts to attain and maintain such agreements, furthermore, have confronted continual opposition by the multinational buying firms.

The International Coffee Agreement—currently the only one affecting major African agricultural exports that seems to be working—suggests the limitations of this approach. First, coffee prices are still relatively low, although providing a better return to coffee growers than prevailed before the agreement. Second, the quotas are not large enough to accommodate the existing output of producing countries, so a significant share (at least 6 percent*) is sold in nonquota markets, sometimes to be resold in competition with quota coffee. African countries, in particular, have complained that their quotas have not taken into consideration the existence of coffee trees already planted but not yet bearing, so their quotas are not large enough. Third, the agreement rests in large part on political considerations in the United States, rather than the self-reliant, united actions of the producers. For example, the coffee buying countries—and particularly the United States, which is by far the largest—have argued that the agreement constitutes a form of "aid" that, going mainly to coffee producers, does not contribute to diversification of developing country economies. The U.S. Comptroller-General, in a report to the U.S. Congress,[19] argued that from 1964 to 1967 total U.S. coffee "aid" totaled $601 million a year; he raised the question as to whether this was the "best form" of providing aid. In 1971 the U.S. Congress arbitrarily refused to ratify the next scheduled renewal for a time because of an argument with Brazil over off-shore fishing rights.

Fourth, the buying companies have sought to influence the quota system to exclude the import of processed instant coffees into "their" markets. Since instant coffees are cheaper to ship, labor costs in developing countries are less, and the domestic price of beans in the developing countries are considerably lower than the ICA price, the big U.S. firms have argued that they are at an "unfair" competitive disadvantage. In response, others have suggested[20] that the less developed countries should be permitted to benefit from their comparative advantage to expand their processed coffee sales, and that the big companies should shift into other products. Nevertheless, in 1967 the Brazilian delegation to the ICA was apparently forced to agree to tax Brazilian manufacturers an amount equivalent to the advantage gained from lower cost domestic beans, in order to secure the support of the United States delegation for the renewal of the agreement.[21]

---

*In Uganda's case, in 1969/70, nonquota sales were almost 40 percent of the quota.[18]

Whereas the coffee agreement has encountered problems, the producing countries have been unable to get the companies and their governments to reach any kind of agreement in the case of other major African agricultural exports. In the case of cocoa, for example, the "self-interested lobbying" of the cocoa dealers is reported to have determined the United States stand on the proposed cocoa agreement, including opposition to increased processing in less developed countries into cocoa butter and other produce.[22] It appeared initially that an agreement was about to be reached in 1967 for the establishment of a buffer stock that would purchase cocoa whenever the cocoa price fell below £160 a ton and sell it whenever the price rose above £230 a ton. But a "howl of opposition" arose from cocoa traders in the United States and Europe, accompanied by concentrated lobbying in Washington and London. They argued that the price limits were too narrow (although they allowed for 50 percent fluctuations) and that the minimum was too high, although the proposed range was clearly on the low side of the actual postwar price range. It has been suggested that United Nations cocoa conferences have repeatedly failed to overcome the few remaining hurdles to attain an agreement because of "pressure" from U.S. trade representatives on the U.S. delegation.[23]

MINERAL EXPORTS: THE CASE OF COPPER

Oligopoly in Mineral Production and Sales

Although sub-Saharan Africa's minerals at present constitute a smaller share of the area's total exports than agricultural produce, their projected rate of growth is much higher (see Table 1). Copper, which already makes up the largest percentage of the value of exports of any single commodity (14.6 percent), is projected to expand at 3.9 to 4.4 percent annually. The export of aluminum, which is increasingly being substituted for copper in a range of final outputs, is projected to expand at 6.6 to 7 percent annually. Iron ore exports—some of the biggest mines in the world have recently been opened in West and South Africa—are expected to grow at 5.6 to 6.2 percent a year. Petroleum exports, as a result of extensive exploration—stimulated perhaps by the tension and growing nationalism in the Middle East, as well as Latin America—are expected to expand at a minimum rate of 6 percent annually.

The foreign firms engaged in minerals extraction have in the past invested directly in the mines in Africa and elsewhere in the Third World. The largest of them have direct links with the parent companies processing the crude exports in the metropolitan area. Because their

total investments at home and abroad are so vast, there has historically tended to be a far higher degree of concentration among firms
engaged in minerals production than in agricultural produce manufacturing. Thus, for example, two iron and steel firms, Bethlehem
and United States Steel, dominate the entire steel industry in the United
States. These are the U.S. firms that have joined with European firms
in opening new iron ore deposits in Liberia and Gabon in the postwar
era. Krupp, by far the biggest German iron and steel firm, has opened
a mine in Angola. In aluminum, three firms, Alcoa, Kaiser, and
Reynolds, are the dominant producers in the United States and in the
world market. Kaiser has shown considerable interest in Africa. It
built a smelter using Ghana's cheap hydroelectric power to smelt
alumina imported from the West Indies (though Ghana, as well as other
African countries, has bauxite that could be processed into alumina).

In oil, Shell-BP, the biggest British firm, and a handful of the
biggest United States oil firms have joined the widespread exploration
for oil throughout the African continent, and are already pumping oil
out of several countries including Nigeria, Angola, Libya, Gabon, and
Algeria. Although this section will concentrate on an analysis of copper
because it is sub-Saharan Africa's main mineral export, oligopolistic
power is far more pervasive in oil production, which is expanding
rapidly in both independent and still-to-be liberated Africa. Gulf Oil,[24]
just to illustrate with one example, is the tenth largest U.S. corporation
and the fourth largest oil company in the world. In sub-Saharan Africa
it is pumping oil from Nigeria as well as the Portuguese colony of
Angola. Gulf's annual revenue is about ten times the national budget
of Nigeria. With 219 subsidiaries spread throughout the world, Gulf
has its own worldwide marketing system, its own marine fleet, and
through one of its subdivisions is engaged also in uranium mining and
production of reactors, nuclear fuels, and nuclear power systems.
Gulf is involved in what is essentially an oil cartel—probably the most
powerful private international arrangement of its kind with ramifications
throughout the Western and Third World—which has been amply described elsewhere.

The Structure of the Copper Industry

The structure of the copper industry,[25] which buys the largest
share of all African exports, may not be as concentrated as that of
iron and steel, aluminum, or oil, but the evidence suggests that a
handful of firms nevertheless dominates the market. New discoveries
of copper deposits are continually being made, and new technologies
are opening up old deposits for further exploitation. In the last fifteen
years Canada has expanded output very rapidly, and Japan and South

Africa have increased their output significantly from negligible amounts (see Table 8). Nevertheless, Chile and Zambia remain among the leading world copper mine sources, next to the United States and the USSR. Zaire is the sixth source following Canada. A new mine being opened up in Mauritania is said to be among one of the largest in the world, and another is planned for Botswana.

Although 60 to 70 percent of the costs of refined copper have historically been mining costs, the major controls in the industry rest in the ownership of the smelters and associated refineries established by the biggest copper companies, for the most part in the developed countries. The top four firms, which produced about half of the world output in 1956, have remained substantially the same since before World War I, based on their integrated mining-smelting-refining business in the United States.[26] They are Kennecott, Anaconda, Phelps Dodge, and American Metal Climax. Sometimes fourth place has been contested by Union Minière de Haute Katanga (Congo) and International Nickel, both of which have extensive holdings in African minerals.

The extensive intertwining of the structures of these giant companies has had direct consequences affecting their investment and development policies in Africa. Anglo-American of South Africa,[27] although initially engaged in production of gold, has over the decades expanded its holdings, not only into copper— it is one of the two big

TABLE 8

Copper Production of the Countries That Are the
World's Major Sources of Copper in 1953, 1963 and 1968
(in thousands of metric tons)

Country	1953	1963	1968
Australia	38.1	114.8	108.6
Canada	229.7	410.6	562.5
Chile	361.1	601.5	666.7
Zaire	214.1	271.3	326.0
Japan	58.9	107.2	119.9
Peru	33.6	201.4	194.5
South Africa	35.9	54.8	127.7
USSR	305.0	600.0	800.0
U.S.	840.5	1,100.6	1,092.8
Zambia	372.7	588.1	684.9

Source: UN Statistical Yearbook, 1969, p. 172.

companies that owned mines in Zambia—but also into diamonds (it owns the deBeers Diamond operations), iron ore, uranium, tin, coal, and a range of industrial and financial interests throughout southern Africa and in some politically independent African countries as well. It has ties with U.S. Kennecott Copper Corporation.

Although in 1960 Kennecott sold its interests in South African gold mining companies to C. W. Englehard of Rand Mines (an Anglo-American affiliate), it did so in exchange for a 20 percent share of the profits. Kennecott continues to carry on exploration for rich metals deposits in southwest Africa. It has an interest in Kaiser Aluminum.

The second big firm with interests in Zambia's mines is American Metal Climax ("Amax") a forerunner of which began investing in Zambian copper through the Roan Selection Trust (RST) back in 1929.[28] American Metal Climax is allied with Patino (copper, tin, and other metals) and the French interests in the Société des Minerals et Métaux in a combination known as COFRAMET. In the postwar period, American Metal Climax has been expanding into other fields, purchasing Tsumeb Corporation with its mines in southwest Africa, Bikiti Minerals, which owns lithium-beryllium properties in Rhodesia, and, in 1962, aluminum interests as well as other alloys in the United States and West Germany. Amax and Kennecott have proposed a joint operation to mine copper in Puerto Rico. By 1969 two-thirds of Amax' sales were aluminum, molybdenum and special metals, chemicals, and petroleum. In 1969 it agreed to turn over 51 percent of its mine ownership to the Zambian government, continuing to provide management, and to sell the produce through its marketing affiliate. At the same time, it maintained a controlling interest in a proposed new copper-nickel mining venture in Botswana. An American Metal Climax marketing affiliate, the Ametalco Group, sells the produce for twelve companies outside the RST group; RST group companies' output accounts for barely over half of its total sales.

Union Minière de Haute Katanga,[29] originally established to implement the Belgian government's policies of exploiting Congo's* rich mineral wealth, extended its interests over the last half century into a wide range of financial and business activities in that vast Central African country. When the Congo achieved political independence, it was the world's leading producer of cobalt and a major source of uranium, as well as one of the world's largest copper producers. Several Union Minière affiliates had connections with Anglo-American Corporation directly or by way of Tanganyika Concessions. Union Minière owned the Lubumbashi copper refinery, the world's third

_____

*Congo (Kinshasa) changed its name to Zaire in 1972.

largest smelter, and completed a 100,000 ton electrolytic copper plant in Luilu in the 1960s. Prior to independence, the company had been able to set aside for dividends, reinvestment, and depreciation about a third of its gross income, which appears to mean a net profit rate of 15 to 20 percent after taxes. Tanganyika Concessions, which built the copper export railway from the Katanga mines to the Angolan Port of Benguela, owned some 14 percent of Union Minière's shares and had directors on its board. Tanganyika Concessions is in turn controlled by major international financial groups, including Tanganyika Holdings in London, Lazard Frères in Paris, and Société Générale in Brussels.*

Prior to World War II, the big U.S. copper firms made several overt efforts to shape the world copper market. In the 1920s, with U.S. government sanction under the Webb-Pomerene Act, they formed first the Copper Export Association and then the Copper Exporters, Inc., through which they were estimated to control directly or indirectly about 85 percent of the market. In the 1930s, after intensifying their domestic coordination with U.S. government assistance under the National Recovery Act, the U.S. firms joined with foreign firms to form an international cartel, setting worldwide quotas and regulating trade practices of the members. These links were extended and tightened during World War II. In the postwar years, although there appeared to be no such overt coordination, the copper prices on the London Metal Exchange appeared significantly different from the U.S. prices, indicating that fabricators contrived to maintain fixed relations with producers. It has been suggested[30] that this might be because during crises like the Korean war, those who did not have such ties paid a very high price to obtain blister copper.

In the postwar period the major copper companies began to diversify their interests to increase their own flexibility in maximizing their profits. Their price and output policies were adjusted in view of their global holdings, rather than their impact on individual producing countries. As the African countries began to attain political independence, for three years until mid-1964 the copper companies appeared to be running production at between 80 and 85 percent of capacity to hold prices up; the consequences for the host countries were additional numbers of unemployed. By 1965 the copper companies were selling Zambian crude copper at £260 a ton, £240 a ton below the London price, allegedly to keep their share of the European

---

*Société Générale's agricultural affiliates produce perhaps 35 to 40 percent of Zaire's export crops; together with a Unilever subsidiary, Huileries du Congo Belges, it dominates the entire agrobusiness of the Zaire.

market.[31] This, of course, reduced the share of value attributable to the Zambian production, and hence the share that the newly independent government might tax.

In the latter 1960s, as Rhodesian-Zambian disputes, Congolese uncertainty, and Chilean demands for nationalization of the U.S.-owned mines appeared to threaten major traditional sources of supply, world copper prices mounted rapidly. Major copper users began to reduce their imports, substituting aluminum and plastics where possible since copper price increases had resulted in raising their costs. The copper companies began shifting their investments into aluminum, the main competitor for copper, as a hedge against further reductions in copper sales. This option was, of course, not easily available to the African producing countries, who had neither the natural resource deposits nor the capital to make the shifts.

The existence of market control by a handful of big copper firms apparently has influenced their reactions to the efforts of the politically independent African Governments to obtain greater benefits from their rich copper resources. When the Congolese Government tried to take over a major share of the ownership of its mines, it discovered that the companies blocked the sale of its copper in Europe.[32] The upshot of affairs was that the Congolese gave the Union Minière a lucrative management and sales contract for twenty-five years with compensation running in the area of $800 million for the mine assets. Meanwhile, the Union Minière formed a separate Canadian subsidiary with Tanganyika Concessions and Sogemines participation and an Australian subsidiary to take over its assets in those countries. In 1968 the Union Minière reported a net profit from its reorganized business—minus ownership of its former Congolese mining assets—of $25 million.

When the Zambian Government sought in 1969 to take over a 51 percent share of the business of its copper mines—which produced about 95 percent of the country's exports—it found the companies more cooperative. They were reported to have learned that they could "still have a tolerably profitable operation in Central Africa and one that is less vulnerable to political pressure."[33]

The Zambian government's deal, described as looking as though it would leave the shareholders "better off than they expected,"[34] provided $316 million in compensation, including interest and free of Zambian taxes, over a ten-year period, and a ten-year management and sales arrangement. American Metal Climax' RST was to receive $6.24 million a year as a management fee, out of which it was to pay overhead.* In other words, while African countries have paid

---

*In 1973, the Zambian Government took steps to pay for its shares of ownership in full, in part borrowing on the Euro-dollar

TABLE 9

Net Income of Selected Copper Companies in
1963 and 1969
(in millions of U.S. dollars)

Company	1963	1969
Kennecott	56	165
Phelps Dodge	38	89
American Metal Climax	37	69
Anglo-American (holding company)	na	42 (1968)
Union Minière	na	25 (1968)

Source: Moody's Industrials and Financials (New York, 1970).

Note: Net income is usually calculated after costs, depreciation, and taxes. Because each company uses its own accounting methods, these data cannot be considered strictly comparable. They are only indicative of trends. Net income may be arbitrarily influenced by company decisions as to allocation of funds between costs, as well as among branches and affiliates. Three Anglo-American affiliates, for example, reported net income totaling $53.1 million, considerably more than Anglo-American itself. More important than the actual amounts would appear to be the trends of the data, which suggest that from 1963 to 1969 those copper companies for which data are available actually almost doubled and in some cases more than doubled their net profits.

considerable sums in compensation to acquire nominal ownership of a majority of the shares of their national copper resources, multinational corporations retain the management and make critical decisions affecting price and output in light of their own profit-maximizing requirements.

The mine companies' stock on the London stockmarket recovered fairly quickly from an initial fall. The loss of foreign confidence that would result in reduced foreign investment was counteracted by the expansion of investor interest in new copper deposits outside the

Market at high (floating) interest rates, in order to attain greater control of the mines as well as the right to tax the companies at higher rates.

previously staked-out copper belt. The flexibility of the options open to the companies is suggested by the fact that the big copper companies have already made major new investments in Botswana and Mauritania, which are expected to begin producing by the mid-1970s, providing new sources of copper in countries apparently more amenable to company control.

The Zambian government granted four-year permits to explore to companies other than the Anglo-American or RST, as long as they would provide capital investment in which the Zambian Government could take a majority of shares, for which it would eventually pay through its share of profits.

Significantly, the biggest copper firms have shown steadily increasing profits despite seminationalization measures adopted in the Third World (see Table 9).

By the end of 1971, world copper prices had again fallen sharply. The companies, which had been able to hedge by diversification into aluminum, began to call for reduced copper production to hold world prices up. Chile and Zambia, both suffering serious shortfalls in their foreign exchange earnings, found it necessary to purchase offsetting funds from the International Monetary Fund. This was Zambia's first purchase from the Fund.[35] This new exigency underlines once again the necessity for Zambian planners to stress the implementation of a self-reliant development strategy aimed at reducing the nation's dependence on copper.

CONCLUSIONS: THE NEED TO REFOCUS NATIONAL PLANS

In sum, examination of the characteristics of the world market for sub-Saharan Africa's major exports holds out little hope that expanded export production alone will lead to higher levels of living for the broadest masses of the population. The expansion of world demand for Africa's major agricultural exports is barely keeping pace with African population growth. Moreover, the giant marketing and processing firms that purchase the major African agricultural crops appear to be becoming increasingly interlinked, strengthening their power to bargain with the many competing producing countries to obtain low-priced raw materials. Efforts to achieve international price and output stabilization agreements have encountered well-organized company opposition. African countries' efforts to expand export crop production by African peasants—stimulated by Western national and international economic aid and advice—have been rewarded by fluctuating prices frequently exhibiting a general downward trend. As a result, many African nations' real output has risen dramatically—doubling and tripling in the postwar era—but their real incomes have stagnated and in some cases have actually fallen.

In the case of minerals exports, where the growth of developed country demand is likely to be more favorable, the domination of the market by a few larger firms is even more pronounced. In the case of sub-Saharan Africa's largest single export, copper, the largest firms are consolidating their control over the world markets through their smelting, refining, and fabricating facilities, exploring for new copper deposits in order to broaden their sources of raw materials, and acquiring interests in production of competing materials like aluminum. Any single producing country seeking to become "too" independent may discover that it has lost the traditional market for its major mineral export.

These facts underline the argument that an African nation seeking higher levels of living for the broadest masses of its population, will need to restructure its entire economy to reduce its dependence on exports. Its planners will need to formulate a development strategy directed to achieving an internally integrated, balanced national econ- omy in which increased productivity in every sector, industry, agri- culture and trade, is matched by expanding internal demand.

This is not to suggest that exports would play no role in such a development strategy. Careful analysis of export possibilities would be essential to maximize foreign exchange earnings for the purchase of essential capital equipment and machinery. Producing countries should seek to cement international agreements as to prices and out- put in order to insure stability of their foreign exchange earnings. But as rapidly as possible, new investments and efforts to increase productivity should be refocused toward meeting the needs and ex- panding the incomes of the broader masses of the people in all sectors of the economy, not just those producing for export.

NOTES

1. H. Myint, Economic Theory and the Underdeveloped Countries (London: Oxford University Press, 1971), esp. Ch. 13; see also Chs. 6, 7.

2. Ibid., p. 98.

3. Cf. R. K. A. Gardiner, "Development and Trade in Africa," African Affairs 65 (January 1966): 1-14.

4. Ibid., and R. H. Green and A. Seidman, Unity or Poverty? The Economics of Pan-Africanism (Harmondsworth: African Penguin, 1968), Part 1.

5. For following background data, see Organization for Economic Cooperation, The Main Products of the Overseas Territories—Oilseeds (Paris: Organization for European Economic Cooperation, 1957.)

6. Ibid., p. 42.

7. For background relating to British cotton textiles industry, see R. Robson, The Cotton Industry in Britain (London: MacMillan and Co., Ltd., 1957).

8. For postwar trends in European cotton consumption, see Organization for Economic Cooperation and Development, Textile Industry in O.E.C.D. Countries, 1967-1968 (Paris, 1969).

9. United Nations, Department of Economic and Social Affairs, Yearbook of International Trade Statistics, 1967 (New York: United Nations, 1969), pp. 284 and 310.

10. For the following information relating to these companies and their relations with others, see Moody's Investment Manual, Moody's Industrials, 1970 (New York, 1970).

11. Republic of Uganda, Statistics Division: Ministry of Planning and Economic Development, Background to the Budget, 1970-1971, 1970, Ch. IX.

12. P. T. Bauer, West African Trade, A Study of Competition, Oligopoly and Monopoly in a Changing Economy, rev. ed. (Routledge and Kegan Paul, London, 1963), esp. pp. 68-75. See also Moody's Industrials, 1970, p. 3037.

13. UN, Yearbook of International Trade Statistics.

14. Moody's Industrials, 1970, pp. 2539 ff.

15. Robson, The Cotton Industry in Britain, esp. pp. 149, 188.

16. Ibid., p. 260.

17. "Brooke Bond-Leibig: No Stir in the Tea Leaves," Economist, November 22, 1969.

18. Republic of Uganda, Background to the Budget, 1970-71, p. 12.

19. "Foreign Aid Provided through the Operations of the United States Sugar Act and the International Coffee Agreement—Report to the Congress by the Comptroller-General of the United States," Inter-American Economic Affairs 23 (Winter 1969); 82-96.

20. "Price of Instant Coffee," Economist, Feb. 3, 1967.

21. "Instant Coffee: A Bad Precedent," Economist, Feb. 24, 1970; "Price of Instant Coffee," Economist, Feb. 3, 1967.

22. "Cocoa: Cry Wolf," Economist, Nov. 18, 1967.

23. "Cocoa: Hope Died," Economist, Dec. 23, 1967.

24. Africa Group, Committee of Returned Volunteers, Gulf Oil, A Study of Exploitation (262 West 26th St., New York, New York); see also Moody's Industrials, 1969.

25. For discussion of the historical development of copper industry structure, see O. C. Herfindahl, Copper Costs and Prices: 1870-1957 (Baltimore: Johns Hopkins Press, published for Resources for the Future, 1958).

26. For information relating to their holdings and income status, see Moody's Industrials, 1970.

27. For current data regarding Anglo-American, which is a holding company, see Moody's Bank and Financial Manual (New York, 1970). For background information, see K. Nkrumah, Neo-Colonialism: The Last Stage of Imperialism (London: Nelson, 1965), esp. Ch. 9.

28. For detailed current information see Amax, 1969 Annual Report (New York, 1969); Roan Selection Trust, Ltd., Annual Report, 1969, (Lusaka, 1969); Roan Selection Trust, Ltd., Explanatory Statement for Meetings of Shareholders to Be Held on 6th August 1970 and Appendices to Explanatory Statement of Roan Selection Trust Ltd. for Meetings of Shareholders to be Held on 6th August 1970.

29. For background, see Nkrumah, Neo-Colonialism, pp. 94, 104, 196; and Green and Seidman, Unity or Poverty? esp. pp. 102-105.

30. Herfindahl, Copper Costs and Prices, p. 195.

31. "Zambia's Two-Way Pull," Economist, May 8, 1965.

32. Economist, Oct. 25, 1969.

33. "Zambia: Foreigners Needed—on Our Terms," Economist, Oct. 25, 1969.

34. "Zambian Copper: Richer but Not Wiser," Economist, Nov. 22, 1969. For detailed analysis of the positions of the Zambian government and the companies, see M. L. O. Faber and J. G. Potter, Towards Economic Independence (Cambridge: Cambridge University Press, 1971).

35. International Monetary Fund, Financial News Survey XXIII, no. 49 (Dec. 15, 1971).

CHAPTER

3

CLASS STRUCTURE AND
ECONOMIC DEVELOPMENT

DEFINITION AND ROLE OF CLASS

The model of underdevelopment proposed in Chapter 1 underlines a conclusion, widely accepted in Africa, that the state must be
the prime mover in formulating and implementing national development plans. At the same time, however, the model exposes the fact,
commonly ignored by standard economic theorists, that the state
bureaucracy itself is enmeshed in a web of conflicting interests that
is spread throughout the entire inherited institutional structure. If
national planners overlook this reality, they may, unwittingly, propose
policies that, far from attaining broad development goals, merely
perpetuate the status quo.

Schumpeter once observed[1] that economists had given sustenance
to the view that economics was merely a "device" for bolstering political programs. This may be just as true in Africa as anywhere
else in the world.

Research in social sciences other than economics has provided
significant insights into the way in which, in the very process of its
formation as a formal bureaucratic structure, a given state apparatus
may come to represent a set of interests of a dominant class or classes
rather than the harmonious homogeneous interests of the entire community.[2] The characteristics of human beings as individuals and
as members of social groups have, historically, led to conflicts between power groups over surpluses produced as a result of technological advance. As the amounts of surpluses involved have increased,
the dominant power groups have utilized the machinery of state—
initially in some cases by exercising its monopoly of violence; in
the longer run in all cases through more subtle measures of ideology
and institution-creation—to capture the major share of the surpluses

54

for themselves. Once in control of state power, the dominant groups have tended to hinder the further development and spread of technological advance.

In other words, extensive sociological evidence suggests that the state bureaucracy is likely to pursue policies designed to strengthen the power of dominant groups that may accumulate a major share of the investible surpluses.[3] There seems to be plenty of evidence that these groups will seek to exercise their control of state machinery to perpetuate the status quo, irrespective of its potential constricting effect on overall production and consumption. National planners who overlook this possibility may well find that their proposed policies advantage entrenched interest groups rather than contribute to attainment of broader development goals.[4]

Recognition of this danger has led more and more social scientists concerned with problems of development to emphasize the necessity of altering the entire set of political-economic institutions in a way calculated to increase the participation of the vast majority of the populations, who stand to gain from changes to be made in the decision-making process.[5] These kinds of considerations might well encourage national planners to examine the possibilities and problems involved in altering the entire complex of political-social-economic institutions that may be required to facilitate this kind of participation.

If the hypothesis is valid that the state inevitably represents specific class interests when it makes critical development decisions, then examination of the nature of those interests may illuminate the extent to which they may be expected to contribute to or hinder the implementation of measures designed to foster development as thus defined. Once the potential role of different classes is defined vis à vis the development process, it should be possible to formulate additional fruitful hypotheses as to the essential institutional changes needed to insure that the state represents, not those whose perceived interests are linked to maintenance of the status quo, but those who stand to gain from changes that must be made if development is to take place.

It is of course essential to define the operational characteristics of "class" in order to test this hypothesis against the facts of the existential situation. Some social scientists define interest groups or classes in terms of "objective" indices such as income differentials;[6] others define them in terms of relative power and privilege;[7] still others argue that the functional relationship of groups of individuals to the process of production is critical.[8]

In the African case, it seems useful to define classes in terms of their functional relationship to the production process for several reasons. Monetary income, per se, is not a valid index of the relative power and privilege of different groups in the African context, since significant sectors of the population are by no means fully integrated into the modern monetized economy.[9] The relative power and privilege of different groups are fundamental attributes of different classes, but these are precisely what must be explained. The question is, what is the basic source of power and privilege acquired by some classes as opposed to others? The answer appears to lie in the functional relationship of specific groups, that is, classes, to the production process itself. It is the control over productive resources—initially land, and with the spread of specialization and exchange, access to improved tools and equipment and trade channels—that enables some classes of individuals and families to exercise power and privilege vis à vis the remainder of the community. In the African context the state has historically been the instrument by which a class or allied classes have established and maintained their control over the productive process in order to enhance their own power and privilege.

The problem of attempting to analyze emergent class relationships in Africa is complicated by the existence of wide variations from country to country and region to region because of widely differing historical experiences. Major differences in stages of development of productive processes and associated class structures existed in the various regions of precolonial Africa. These both influenced and were altered by the colonial experience in differing ways.

This chapter seeks to examine the predominant characteristics of the classes that have emerged in differing historical contexts, particularly in areas colonized by the British, with a view to assessing their potential role in postindependence development. It should be emphasized that a careful, detailed study would need to be made in each country, and even in each region within each country, to determine how any particular complex, emergent class structure would be likely to influence the participation of differing groups in a given development program. This chapter attempts only to consider the broad outlines of the available evidence, relating primarily to what has been broadly characterized as English-speaking Africa, which tends to substantiate the hypothesis that the relative power and role of differing classes in the state apparatus will significantly influence national planning. The argument is that the hypothesis, if valid, provides a fruitful heuristic guide for further research into the role and consequences of class formation for development programs in specific newly independent countries.

In brief, this chapter seeks to outline the range of class structures that had already emerged prior to the imposition of colonial rule and to indicate the way British colonial rule influenced and was affected by these diverse structures in different areas of the continent. On this basis, an effort will be made to generalize from some of the fragmentary evidence as to the way classes thus shaped have influenced decisions affecting postindependence development programs in the former British colonies. Finally, the chapter will outline some of the basic principles relating to institutional changes suggested by this evidence that have or might be made to insure that those who stand to gain from development proposals may participate more effectively at all levels in decision-making affecting the development process.

CLASSES IN THE TRADITIONAL
POLITICAL-ECONOMIC INSTITUTIONAL SETTING

Prior to the outright imposition of colonial rule, a wide range of divergent political-economic institutional structures had emerged in different regions of the vast African continent. These were shaped by widely differing geographic, climatic, and above all historical circumstances. Almost every historical stage of development was represented, from simple, almost communal societies, through slavery and feudalism, up to city states engaged in trade extending throughout entire regions as large as the present continental United States.[10]

Nomadic tribes and those engaged in shifting cultivation spread across parts of the vast dry plains and in some rain forest areas. They produced barely enough for subsistence, using very simple tools. They essentially remained dependent on the vagaries of the climate and weather. They typically stored only limited surpluses against recurrent droughts and famine: a few extra head of cattle or a little grain preserved in simple storage bins constructed of mud or sticks. They commonly supplemented their cattle or few crops by hunting. A rough division of labor tended to emerge within the extended family or tribe, fundamentally characterized by allocation of work according to sex and age: for example, the men might confine their activities mainly to hunting and defense, and clearing land if crops were sown, while women cultivated the crops and cared for the children and the house. They participated relatively little, if at all, in exchange of produce with other groups, producing almost all their own necessities. Their social structure was characterized by a kind of rough democracy within the framework of working rules designed to insure that the minimum needs of all participants would be met, given the sharp constraints imposed by scarce resources. Commonly, each group functioned in accord with a consensus arrived at through discussion among the elders. The group norms, evolved over time through a kind of trial-and-error process, tended to be reinforced by religious sanctions. Individuals might aquire recognition and status as a result of age or religious functions, but all participated in the production process essentially in accord with their ability and accustomed norms.

In other areas of the continent, powerful centralized states emerged, governed by strong ruling classes that lived in part or entirely on surpluses extracted from subordinate classes in the form of tribute or taxes of various kinds. In some cases, such a state might be created when a militarily powerful group, perhaps a predominantly nomadic hunting tribe, conquered a more sedentary tribe engaged in agricultural production. The history of Central Africa[11] is one of the rise and fall of successive kingdoms established by a combination of military strength, organizational ability, a supporting religious ideology, and control of trade routes over which gold, ivory, cloth, iron and copper, slaves, and cattle were exchanged, some to distant coastal trading stations for trade with Arabia and even India and China. Agricultural productivity was sufficient to provide adequate surpluses constituting the tribute necessary to support these ruling groups.

Ethiopia's history[12] is characterized by the emergence of militarily strong groups that established their rule by force, demanding tribute from weaker tribes; its political-economic structure, backed by the weight of the ancient Christian Church, may even today be characterized as essentially feudal.

Elsewhere, trading states[13] emerged when specialization and exchange had developed sufficiently to permit production of surpluses of such items as cloth, tanned leather goods, and pottery. These could be sold to relatively distant consumers. In the trading states agriculture was required to produce enough surplus to support fairly large urban areas. Irrigation works were sometimes built to insure essential steady water supplies. The ruling groups sometimes used prisoners of war as slaves to run farms. In other cases, peasants turned over surpluses to landlords as tribute or in taxes, part of which was passed along to the central government. Such trading states as the ancient kingdoms of Mali and Ghana, or the more recent Hausa and later Fulani city states in what is now Northern Nigeria, had trading links across the Sahara that extended north into southern Europe and as far south as what is now the Zaire.

THE IMPACT ON COLONIALISM ON
CLASS FORMATION

Colonization by the European powers introduced a new pattern of specialization and exchange, linking African colonies—arbitrarily carved out by rival European powers—to the markets and factories of Europe and America. At first the European traders, looking primarily for gold, ivory, and spices, established coastal trading stations. Then, as the demand grew for cheap labor power to produce raw materials in the Americas for their burgeoning industries at home,

Europeans created an expanding market for the mass sale of human beings. Millions of African slaves, many of them captured in battles between African tribes, were shipped out of the continent to provide a labor force for the production of cotton, tobacco, and sugar in the Americas for the factories of England and, later, New England.*

New military states were built in West Africa to conduct raids to capture and sell neighboring peoples to the European slavers.[15] The Ashanti, Dahomey, and Yoruba kingdoms emerged primarily as powerful middlemen states, engaging directly in capturing and selling slaves, or profiting by buying them up-country and selling them to European slave ships. When the slave trade was finally suppressed, some of the profits thus accumulated among these African traders provided the initial capital for development of trade in "legitimate" produce like palm nuts and oil and cocoa. At first this trade was carried on up-country by powerful African traders who made not a few efforts—including the use of military force—to exclude European trading companies.

In the nineteenth-century "scramble for Africa," the colonial powers provided the necessary sanctions and, where necessary, armies to enable expanding European trading firms to establish up-country trading posts in direct competition with the existing African middlemen.[16] When, for example, one African trader—King Eyo Honesty—chartered a boat to ship palm oil directly to England, the British consul, in cooperation with Liverpool interests, used his judicial powers, backed by superior military force, to prevent the ship from setting sail.† Political deals dividing one group of Africans against another, backed when necessary by factory-made guns, led ultimately to the defeat of even the more powerful African kingdoms by the early twentieth century.[17] Simultaneously, the chauvinist ideology of African inferiority was spread throughout Europe to rationalize governmental support for the private colonial interests.[18]

Eventually, outright colonial rule was established as an umbrella under which private colonial companies could continue to expand their operations.

---

*E. Williams[14] describes the way this trade emerged and how it differs from the slavery then prevailing in Africa. In not a few cases in Africa, an able slave might become a member of a ruling family and eventually even a chief. In the Americas, in contrast, the Africans provided a continually renewed cheap labor force, condemned to toil from dawn to sunset for the rest of their lives, bought and sold like cattle, without regard to family ties.

†Honesty himself was jailed for failure to pay for the ship—which of course he could not do unless the oil was sold in England.

Lord Lugard, one of the initiators of the "dual mandate," quite
frankly described the goals of the British colonizers: the growing
population of Europe, together with its industrial expansion, he said

> . . . led to the replacement of agriculture by manufactur-
> ing industry, with the consequent necessity for new mar-
> kets for the product of the factory, and the importation of
> raw materials for industry, and food to supplement the de-
> creased home production, and feed the increased popu-
> lation.[19]

Sir Harry Johnstone, another of the architects of British colonial
policy, explained[20]—in an argument which still rings familiar today—
that these goals could be achieved "if the European capitalist can be
induced by proper security to invest his money in Africa and if native
labor can be obtained by the requisite guarantees of fairplay towards
native rights." What he meant by "proper security" for European
investment he made quite clear: "The White capitalist . . . must
have something conceded to him. The native must be prepared to
guarantee a fairly handsome return for money hazardously invested."
What he meant by "fairplay" to the African he had spelled out many
years earlier:

> All that needs to be done is for the Administration to act
> as friends of both sides, and introduce the Native labourer
> to the European capitalist. A gentle insistence that the
> Native should contribute his fair share to the revenue of
> his country by paying his tax is all that is necessary on
> our part to ensure his taking a share in life's labour which
> no human being should avoid.[21]

The differences in the political-economic-social structure that
had emerged prior to the outright imposition of colonial rule both
influenced and were altered by the colonial policies. In the eastern
and southern regions, where the climate was more favorable, the
British established settler rule, excluding the Africans from the best
land and cutting them off from all opportunities to earn cash except
by working in the foreign-owned mines or on settler estates and
plantations.[22] The Africans were forced to live in "reserves" where
their pre-existing forms of rule were distorted to facilitate the maintenance of law and order as well as a steady flow of labor to the export enclave. Typically, Africans were expressly prohibited from
selling cash crops in competition with settler farms. In Tanganyika,
which, as a League of Nations trusteeship, was viewed by the British
as less secure for their own investments than Kenya and the Rhodesias,

individual Africans were permitted to grow coffee and cotton for sale.*

Where the African social structure was characterized by powerful and militarily strong ruling classes, and the settlers were weak or nonexistent, the British administrators relied more heavily on indirect rule through pre-existing traditional institutions. In Buganda[23] and Northern Nigeria,[24] they entrenched cooperating ruling groups, giving them a stake in the expansion of export-import trade. They granted the Bugandan nobles title to "mailo estates"—so called because they were measured in miles—and the tenants were required to pay rent in return for their right to use the land to produce cash crops. In Northern Nigeria, the traditional but not always certain rule of the emirs was solidified with the backing of British bayonets; it became more difficult for dissatisfied citizens to utilize traditional channels to replace them. In areas like Southern Nigeria[25] and Ghana,[26] the colonial administration ruled through cooperating chiefs where they existed. If the customary institutions did not involve chieftancy, as in Ibo territory, or if the existing chief refused to cooperate, they attempted to establish new chiefs who would maintain law and order to enable the big British companies to carry on their prospering trade. As cash crops expanded, and customary tribute was changed to monetary forms similar to rent, cooperating chiefs accumulated considerable wealth along with and reinforcing their power.[27]

In the contexts of these varying colonial policies, the handful[28] of giant, predominantly British trading, mining, and in some cases settler interests expanded their prosperous trade in the export of cheap raw materials in exchange for manufactured goods. A whole set of associated political-economic institutions emerged to facilitate their activities:[29] a monetary system hinged to their foreign exchange earnings; commercial banks run from London offices with which they had various links; and shipping and insurance firms that they either owned or with which they had close ties.

Conflicts occasionally emerged between European settlers, trading companies, and colonial administrators, reflecting the differing interests of each. These conflicts were, typically, not over basic issues of colonial strategy, which was directed to fostering the profitable expansion of the export enclave and associated institutions, but rather over the ways in which that strategy should be implemented. The trading firms[30] sought to maximize their profits by purchasing

---

*Coffee estate owners sought to eliminate this competition as they had in Kenya, complaining about lowered quality and attempting to inhibit marketing of African coffee.

low-cost raw materials and selling back higher-cost manufactured goods, regardless of whether Africans or settlers owned the land on which the raw materials were grown.

The big mining companies and settlers sought to maximize their profits by employing Africans at wages a tenth to a twentieth of what they would have had to pay in the United States or Europe.[31] The fact that Africans could sometimes, as in Uganda and West Africa, sell their own crops tended to create shortages of laborers willing to work such low wages; so wherever they could, the settlers and miners exercised their influence on the colonial governments to prohibit Africans from producing cash crops.[32] When the world market prices collapsed in the 1930s the settlers in East and South Africa established complex systems of regulatory marketing boards and cooperatives[33]—from which Africans were, of course, systematically excluded—in an effort to control output and obtain better prices vis à vis the home-based trading companies.

The colonial administrators' goal,[34] in general, was to create the framework for enclave development directed to expanding the profitable export-import trade at a minimum cost to the British taxpayers. They utilized existing traditional institutions to maintain order except where new "modern" institutions were required to facilitate development of that peculiar pattern of overseas specialization and exchange that fostered the growth of the British Empire. They tended to prefer hut and poll taxes and the establishment of up-country recruiting stations, rather than the exercise of military might, to "persuade" Africans to produce cash crops or work in the mines and on settler estates. They might on occasion use a punitive force to wipe out an offending village, but more frequently they sought to engage the support of powerful African individuals or groups and even, on occasion, to curb settler excesses in an effort to insure peace and the prosperous expansion of export enclave activity.

It should be emphasized that these apparent differences between the private and governmental colonial interests did not constitute basic disagreement regarding the aim of expanding the export enclave as an appendage of the metropolis. Rather they reflected conflicting views as to how that goal might best be attained and how the profits should be shared.

The educational system established under colonialism tended to reinforce the power and privilege of groups of Africans cooperating with the colonial administration. In some cases, the colonial government or missionaries consciously selected sons of cooperating chiefs to attend schools. In consequence they acquired the new skills required to manipulate the machinery of the modern state, if only on a local level, in their own interests as well as those of the colonial power.*

In other areas, the missions, unable to obtain the cooperation of the chiefs, provided education to the children of formerly disadvantaged groups, who then were able to obtain relatively more prestigious jobs as clerks or teachers.

In general, education became perceived as a means of self-advancement in the colonial context. It emphasized rote memorizing and British classics, designed to foster skills required of clerks. Critical analysis and an understanding of the necessary link between theory and practice was seldom encouraged. This type of education contributed to a widespread rejection of rural life by primary school graduates, which is today commonly cited as a major factor stimulating migration to the cities despite the unemployment of as much as 20 to 30 percent of the urban labor force.

Colonial administrators commonly restricted African efforts to become entrepreneurs in productive sectors outside of agriculture, seeking to reduce or avoid African competition with British enterprise. Legislation or administrative directives frequently curbed Africans' entry into major sectors of the economy. The foreign-owned commercial banks typically refused to provide would-be African entrepreneurs with essential credit. The prevailing educational system was never designed to provide necessary entrepreneurial and technical skills.

Colonial policies restricting African entrepreneurs varied from region to region, however, depending in large part on the relative strength and demands of the trading companies, the settlers, and the mining interests, as well as the Africans themselves. Although on the West Coast and in Uganda, small African traders might be permitted to act as up-country agents for the big foreign trading companies, Lebanese and Asian traders were given greater encouragement in wholesale trade. African traders were almost entirely excluded from engaging in direct export and import trade. Efforts to develop modern industry that might in any way compete with goods shipped from factories in Britain itself were sharply discouraged. The British trading companies, selling broadly consumed items like cheap factory-made textiles, fairly quickly replaced local craftsmen in the export enclave and even in the hinterland, where migratory laborers sometimes spent their meager cash earnings to buy "modern" imported goods.

---

*In Northern Nigeria the existing rulers refused to let Christian missions or the colonial administration establish schools; but the sons of the rulers often were sent to schools or tutored in the skills required to rule.

Significant African entrepreneurial groups did, nevertheless, emerge in West Africa. Some individuals invested the surpluses they had accumulated in the precolonial trade in slaves as well as more "legitimate" items in land and further expansion of trade. Larger farmers, employing hired and/or sharecrop laborers, accumulated additional surpluses that they typically invested in trade, transport, speculative real estate, and money lending. By the mid-1950s, for example, 25 percent of the Ghanaian cocoa farmers—those hiring labor, investing in trade and speculative real estate, and engaging in money lending—received about 55 percent of the incomes of the cocoa belt.[35] More recent studies in the Nigerian cocoa areas indicate that the concentration of land ownership and wealth increased rapidly in the 1960s, apparently primarily due to the greater access of larger farmers to marketing, credit, and farm inputs.[36]

Expansion of internal trade and transport became the foundation for the emergence of fairly large African capitalist interests in West Africa.[37] Azikewe in Eastern Nigeria, for example, accumulated sufficient funds to establish a newspaper and a bank. Others, not so well known, also carried on substantial private businesses, accumulating large amounts of capital. In Kumasi, in Ghana, alone some sixty large African traders were identified as carrying on business with an annual turnover valued at several hundreds of thousands of dollars.*

This nascent African entrepreneurial class was from the outset linked to the emerging intellectual elite. Its members had money to educate their sons, even sending them overseas for a university education. Together, the two groups played a significant role in movements to demand national independence which, in their view, would enable them to end colonial restrictions on the expansion of their own political-economic power and privilege.

In East and Central Africa (excluding Uganda), where the settler and mining interests were particularly powerful and Africans were perceived primarily as a cheap labor force, would-be African entrepreneurs were far more sharply restricted in their activities than in West Africa. Licensing acts explicitly limited the size and scope

---

*Unfortunately, few studies have been made of the sources or extent of the wealth and power of these entrepreneurial groups. In fact some studies, like household budget surveys of farmers and their sources of income in Ghana cited above (see note 35), explicitly excluded absentee landowners, and even excluded farmers with incomes significantly above the average, hence vitiating any insights such studies might have provided as to the way wealth and power were accumulated.

of African traders, favoring Asians, who were viewed as convenient middlemen throughout East and Central Africa. Lord Lugard rationalized that the climate in most parts of Africa rendered it "impractical" for Europeans to perform necessary supervising roles at every level, and he maintained that "white and colored labor have not learned to work side by side on equal terms." The Asian trader, on the other hand, he asserted, was not affected by these disadvantages and hence could open up new markets:

> As a merchant his standard of living, his assiduity, and his frugality enable him to reduce his establishment charges to a minimum, and undersell the European.[38]

Only as independence neared in East Africa and parts of Central Africa did the British permit and even encourage Africans to participate more fully in trade and associated activities in the export enclave.* Sir Michael Blundell, a long-time settler and former head of the Agricultural Ministry, explained[39] that, given the expense of putting down the guerrilla movement in Kenya in the 1950s, it was necessary to "make our position safe by other means." He argued for including a few select Africans among the "haves," especially those in the governing circles. This, he pointed out, would insure their interest in maintaining the status quo, perpetrating, only in slightly altered form, a context in which the settlers, trading companies, and associated interests could continue their activities. In addition to the high salaries a few Africans obtained when they stepped into the shoes of the departing British administrators, government loans were granted to African civil servants and politicians to enable them to purchase large farms, establish trading firms, and even acquire a few shares and sit on local boards of directors of the few manufacturing companies that had come into being. Blundell himself forecast that this would contribute to a realignment along class lines in Kenya:

> As African political thought becomes more experienced in the actual practice of government, there will be a regrouping on economic lines if democracy continues in Kenya; one party will be socialist and revolutionary in

---

*In South and Central Africa, outside of Malawi and Zambia, in contrast the settlers have rejected the African independence option and are further restricting Africans, backed by military force. The outcome there, as guerrilla warfare spreads throughout the region, remains in balance.

concept, looking to the landless and lower paid workers
for support, while the other will increasingly be a progressive evolutionary alliance of property owners and
'haves' as distinct from the 'have nots'.[40]

As a result of almost a century of outright British colonial
rule, the vast majority of Africans barely earned or produced enough
on which to subsist at the time of independence. This was the sum
consequence of policies of the British that resulted in the African
case, as elsewhere, in what Myint so accurately described as "the
'fossilization' of the backward peoples in their conventional roles of
undifferentiated cheap labor and unspecialized peasant producers."[41]
Many Africans continued to farm, using little more than a hoe, in
traditional areas. Their contribution to the "modern" export enclave
was a constant stream of cheap labor. Hundreds of thousands of able-
bodied young men still migrated to work on the foreign-owned mines
and plantations and smaller African-owned farms (as wage or sharecrop labor) to produce the raw materials for the overseas sales on
which the new nations still depended.
    Only those who worked in the mines, factories, plantations, and
railways, as well as in the handful of modern factories, could be
characterized as members of a modern "proletariat." The lower
their wages and the less skills they required, however, the less likely
were even these workers to view themselves as permanent members
of the wage-earning labor force.[42] Most of them continued to maintain ties with their families in the areas from which they came, including their rights to obtain usufruct land where it was available
despite population growth.
    Rail and dock facilities were essential for shipping crops and
raw materials out of the colonies, so that everywhere rail and dock
workers constituted a considerable segment of the wage-earning
population. Railway employment requires a considerable degree of
skill; so these workers were usually a better paid and relatively more
permanent element of the working force.
    Mine workers constituted another important segment of the
modern work force in countries like Zambia, Ghana, parts of Nigeria
and Sierra Leone, as well as South Africa. Often they were hired
as contract workers, agreeing to stay only for a fixed period of months
or years. In South Africa the more skilled jobs were reserved for
Europeans, who organized unions not only to advance their own interests, but explicitly to exclude Africans. In West Africa, in contrast,
where Africans were able to take more skilled jobs and, especially
in the postwar period, as they organized unions and won some improvement in their working conditions, they began to perceive their employment as relatively more permanent.

The hundreds of thousands of workers employed on foreign-owned plantations in Eastern, Central, and Southern Africa were—and still are—recruited from remote areas to work on a contractual basis for six months or a year. Wages were generally very low* and few skills were acquired. On settler-owned estates, some received the right to own small plots of land to supplement their inadequate cash earnings, and began to live there more permanently with their families.

Tens, probably hundreds of thousands more peasants† migrated regularly into the export enclave to participate in cash crop production, in some form of sharecropping or hired labor arrangement with African landowners in Ghana, Nigeria, Uganda, Tanzania, and so on. Sharecroppers in Ghana's cocoa belt and on Ivory Coast's coffee farms have been known to travel from as far away as Upper Volta and Mali. Typically, the cropper received a third, the landowner two thirds of the crop income. Where wages have been paid, as in Tanzania's coffee and maize areas, they have tended to be very low; even to this day they may be as little as the equivalent of five to six dollars a month. Increasingly, however, many of these migratory workers, like the mine workers, came to consider their sharecrop farms as their homes, marrying and raising families there.‡

In contrast to the far larger number of workers engaged in the railways and plantations as well as the mines in direct production for export, wage earners in manufacturing constituted a tiny portion of the total national labor force (see Table 10).

Despite the relatively small size of the wage-earning labor force, many of its members felt the necessity of organizing to protect themselves from pressures to reduce wages as well as from insecurity of urban life. Commonly, at first, efforts to organize took place along ethnic lines. Ethnic groups from homogenous cultural and linguistic backgrounds in the traditional sector created ethnic associations in the urban centers that maintained ties with the participants' home community.[46] Eventually, as urban employment was perceived as

---

*"The ratio of average earnings of white and African miners in SA increased from 11.6:1 in 1936 to 17.6:1 in 1966. Even allowing for the value of food supplied to African workers and leaving aside the benefits accorded to white workers, the gap widened from 10.7:1 to 15.2:1. The gap increased further since 1966."[43]

†Their numbers are undoubtedly great, but the statistical evidence is woefully inadequate.[44]

‡Not a few of the thousands of Africans uprooted and returned to their "home countries" by the Busia government's ejection of "non-Ghanaians" in 1969 were sharecroppers and other laborers who had been in Ghana for a generation or more.[45]

TABLE 10

Manufacturing Employment as Percent of
Total Active Labor Force for Selected
African Countries[a]

Country	Manufacturing Employment[b] (in thousands)	Percent of Total Active Labor Force[c]
Ghana (1967)	40.2	1.1%
Kenya (1963)	49.8	1.1
Malawi (1967)	16.9	0.8
Nigeria (1967)	75.8	0.2
South Africa (1963)	832.0	10.3

[a]This is at best a rough estimate that only indicates relative orders of magnitude.

[b]The manufacturing employment estimate as reported varies somewhat from country to country, in some cases including workers for establishments of less than ten, in others not; but the precise method of estimation is not here known.

[c]The estimated total active labor force has been taken as half the total population on the assumption that anyone over 15, including women, who works in the fields and as traders as well as in the homes, is a member.

Source: United Nations Statistical Yearbook, 1969.

more permanent, and more effective organization of the workers required unity without regard to ethnic background, many wage earners began to organize in trade unions, especially in the postwar periods.* Typically, the rail, dock, and where mines were important, the mine workers built the most powerful and militant unions. The numbers of manufacturing workers were usually too small to enable them to play as significant a role. Government workers' rights to organize were usually prescribed. The organization of plantation workers was hindered by continual turnover and close surveillance by employers Little or no effort was made to organize the migrant laborers on African farms. Yet general strikes swept across many African

*See below, pp. 246.

countries in the face of rising prices in the immediate postwar period, and trade unions were active participants in the ensuing demands for national independence.[47]

THE ROLE OF CLASSES IN RESTRUCTURING THE INHERITED POLITICAL-ECONOMIC STRUCTURE

It is self-evident that the pattern of resource allocation and associated institutions in Africa prevailing at the end of the colonial era were not favorable to increased productivity and higher levels of living for the broad masses of the population. That African per capita incomes, characterized by a sharply skewed distribution* remained among the lowest in the world, is eloquent testimony to this fact. Since independence, almost every African government—spurred by recognition that the state alone is capable of exercising sufficient power to mobilize national resources for a more favorable pattern of development—has formulated some kind of development plan to raise per capita output. Precisely what changes in resource allocation and institutions are required to redress the imbalance inherent in the externally dependent dual economies continues to be the subject of constant debate. But available evidence suggests that the post-independence African states have for the most part been unable to alter the prevailing resource allocation pattern to contribute significantly, not only to increased productivity, but also to higher levels of living for the broad masses of the population. On the contrary, there is evidence showing that, despite significant increases in production of export crops, falling world prices and rising costs of imports and domestic prices have actually tended to reduce the real levels of living of major sectors of the population in not a few countries.[48]

The fragmentary evidence available tends to substantiate the hypothesis that in most countries the state failed to change the inherited set of economic institutions to implement national plans designed to attain a more beneficial resource development pattern. In large part this was because in few instances was a network of channels created to insure that the state would respond to the demands of those who would gain, particularly the vast majority of the populations who still labor as unskilled wage earners or peasants. As indicated by the above review of class relationships and institutions shaped in the colonial era, those channels did not yet exist at the time independence was attained. Although traditional institutions varied widely, reflecting differing historical experiences, they were primarily

---

*See pp. 350.

69

designed to facilitate dispute settlement among relatively limited
ethnic groups or to maintain the power and privilege of ruling classes—
not infrequently the more powerful ethnic groups. Some of these were
reshaped during the colonial rule, when they were used for the purposes of indirect rule, but they became, if anything, less responsive
to the demands of the broad masses of the population. Few were
apt for insuring full participation of all citizens in the process of
building a modern, nationally integrated, balanced economy.

The colonial rulers had designed their administrative apparatus
to facilitate the emergence of powerful foreign private trading-mining-
settler interests. These continued after independence to make the
critical investment decisions, which tended to perpetuate the externally dependent resource allocation pattern of the dual economy
with only marginal changes.

The postindependence importation of Westminster-type parliamentary or Washington republican forms of democracy was incapable
of altering this underlying economic structure—nor were these forms
designed to attain that goal. They were originally conceived in Europe
and North America on a philosophical foundation that presumed that
economic decisions should be left primarily to private "market forces"
in accord with doctrines enunciated by Western economists since the
days of Adam Smith.

But more than that, the postindependence experience of several
former British colonies suggests that imposition of this kind of political
structure served to aggravate inter-African conflicts, while at the
same time deflecting attention from the necessity of restructuring
the fundamental economic institutions that perpetuated the inherited
dual economies. Those elected to the newly established legislatures[49]
have typically been teachers, "businessmen," well-to-do farmers,
traders, or real estate speculators. A considerable number have
held chiefly positions. All have tended to be imbued with the theories
and values fostered under colonialism, particularly the ideology that
self-advancement is the key to "national" development. Given the
severe resource constraints embedded in the foreign-dominated export enclaves, the ensuing competition among the elites for the limited
opportunities that existed in the political arena became the source
of mounting conflict: they quarreled among themselves as to who
"deserved" the "fruits" of independence. Many perceived "their"
ethnic group as a natural base for mass support in this conflict; so
the competitive struggle for their own advance tended increasingly
to be pictured as a broad-based ethnic competition.[50] Notions of
restructuring the national economic institutions tended to become
submerged in the ensuing mounting tensions, spurred by increasingly
vivid vituperation between members of ethnic groups at all levels.

Nigeria is the tragically classic case: the newly independent nation was divided along lines of the major ethnic groups* into a federation in a way that prevented both the regions and the federal government from formulating unified national plans to meet national needs. Basic investment decisions remained in the hands of private interests, still dominated by the large foreign firms and associated financial institutions. Small African entrepreneurs lacked the know-how and the capital to make essential major investments directed to restructuring the economy—even if they had had the understanding and interest in doing so. The divided state governments lacked the most elementary powers to take essential steps to alter the inherited institutional and resource pattern; the enshrinement of federalism in the constitution rendered it difficult even to levy taxes on the most important wealth-creating assets of the nation.[51] The ruling elites of each region, apparently blinded by the notion that federation insured some kind of "decentralized democracy," tried to win support of "their" region, and more particularly "their" ethnic group, as opposed to all others,[52] in the prevalent competition over the limited investible surpluses remaining in the country. Eventually the mounting conflict broke out in a prolonged civil war. The post-civil war establishment of twelve still less viable individual states appears, if anything, even less likely to contribute to attainment of a united national effort to make the deep-seated institutional changes required to implement a nationally planned program to capture and redirect the major investible surpluses to increasing productivity and higher levels of living throughout the nation.

The postindependence frustration of national plans to achieve development, coupled with growing ethnic frictions in several countries, argues for a new approach. It hardly seem adequate to expect the state to play a major role in restructuring the entire political economy if the state machinery rests in the hands of those classes—loosely termed the "elite"—that emerged in and benefitted from the status quo shaped during the colonial era. It appears essential, rather, to create a network of channels directed to the mobilization of the vast majority of the populations who remain disadvantaged by the status quo; to involve them in the process of restructuring; and to provide feedback as to the consequences of measures to restructure crucial institutions at every level of government.

It is not the purpose of this chapter to explore in detail the way such mobilization, participation, and feedback mechanisms should be structured in any given country. Rather it is to call attention to

---

*It should be noted that the interests of many minority ethnic groups wtihin these regions were overlooked entirely by this decision.

the fact that, unless adequate attention is directed to these mechanisms and institutions, plans and plan implementation machinery, inevitably resting heavily on state participation in the economy, are likely to be warped to benefit those historically shaped interest groups or classes that at all levels, stand to gain from maintenance of the status quo—and development as here defined is likely to be thwarted.

Postindependence African experience suggests at least three hypotheses as to institutional changes needed to enable those who stand to gain to participate more effectively in restructuring the political economy. First, despite a widespread emphasis on rural development, particularly the expansion of marketing cooperatives among existing and potential cash crop farmers, the governments of the former British colonies have for the most part failed to involve the small peasant in critical decision-making, even on a local level, and far less on the national level. Evidence from almost every country suggests that rural institutions like marketing cooperatives have tended to be dominated by "big men," those who have accumulated wealth and power as larger farmers and/or traders in the past; or those who have not hesitated to use their control of state machinery to expand their power and accumulate wealth and power since independence.[53] Smaller farmers have typically had little opportunity to exercise any form of countervailing power. The tens upon tens of thousands of sharecroppers and seasonally hired laborers working for African landholders in particular have been excluded, not only from decision-making processes but even from the minimal protection afforded by national minimum wage legislation.* To the extent that this systematic exclusion of the smaller peasants and the growing numbers of landless workers and tenants persists, it appears probable that rural institutions will not be directed to increasing the levels of living of the broad masses of the rural populations—no matter how necessary central planners may consider it to be to create broader internal markets for new industries designed to contribute to a more balanced national economy.

To the extent that "big men" engage in various forms of corruption to twist rural development institutions to their own advantage, furthermore, peasants may refuse to support establishment of those institutions altogether. Thus, for example, the peasants may refuse to participate in marketing cooperatives, although these have been widely perceived as essential means of augmenting rural involvement

---

*This is still the case even in Tanzania, although it appears contrary to the official ideology of Ujamaa, which explicitly opposes the growth of divisions between wealthy farmers and hired laborers in the countryside.

and benefits resulting from the spread of national specialization and exchange.*

If rural institutions like marketing cooperatives are to contribute effectively to involving peasants in helping to reshape the national economy, attention should be directed not only to the training of competent managers, bookkeepers, and accountants to reduce mismanagement, but also to devising working rules to enable the mass of smaller peasants to participate in decision-making to insure more equitable distribution of the returns from increased output.

Second, to date only limited efforts have been made in most countries to involve the broad mass of the wage earners in national reconstruction efforts. Few trade union representatives have had an opportunity to continue to participate in decision-making at all levels of government activity. One rationale for this failure appears to be the widely adopted argument that wages must be restrained to insure the availability of surpluses for investment in national development; it is apparently feared that worker representation would create undue pressure for increased wages. Creation of a narrow high-income group of workers, an "aristocracy of labor," could, it is true, aggravate the prevalent urban-rural dichotomy inherent in every dual economy, as well as consume surpluses that might be directed to more balanced national growth. Yet careful examination of the available data reveals the average workers' wages in Africa are still typically barely sufficient to support the worker, let alone his family, given mounting urban living costs.[55] If, on top of that, the line is held on wages while high government officials indulge in conspicuous consumption, workers will almost inevitably become alienated, undermining the very support required if the government is to pursue measures required to restructure the economy.† To maintain workers' support, policies designed to augment profits must be accompanied by careful planning

---

*After the 1966 coup in Ghana, a report showed the farmers themselves to be opposed to the continuation of any form of marketing cooperatives, which had previously been made compulsory, because of alleged mismanagement and corruption. A note of caution in interpreting this report appears necessary. Those issuing it had an interest in criticizing the previous regime to justify the coup. Furthermore, the farmers' attitudes may have reflected their desire to find a convenient scapegoat for the sharp cut in producer prices that followed the fall in world cocoa prices.[54]

†In Ghana, where a wage freeze in 1961 was followed by an 80 percent increase in domestic foodstuff prices in the next four years, workers appeared apathetic if not antagonistic in the face of the 1965 coup.

and institutional measures to ensure that those profits are in fact invested to implement essential development projects which may be visibly seen to contribute to the improved welfare of lower income urban and rural populations. An important means of ensuring this might be the institutionalization of unity between representatives of the urban wage earners and the peasantry in influential positions at all levels of government.*

Third, in the context of this perspective it would appear logical that new political institutions, rather than dividing the population along ethnic lines, should be consciously directed to uniting the masses of the working people, the peasants and wage earners, behind a national program to restructure the inherited political economy. Tanzania's TANU, with its ten-house units in almost every village, might serve as a model of such a mechanism that could create a two-way channel between rural and urban working populations and the various levels of government. But studies[56] indicate that the leaders of these units frequently lack both understanding of the broader issues and the technological know-how needed to provide essential leadership. This suggests that ways need to be devised to help these leaders in particular, as well as the general population, to understand and act on development matters. To assist in this process, the entire educational system, formal and informal, needs to be revised: the curriculum at all levels of schooling, in the past designed primarily to fulfil the requirements of indirect rule, would need to be reoriented to meet manpower needs within the context of the national development program. Every possible means of communication—radio, newspapers, meetings of villagers and cooperatives, trade unions, and womens' and youth organizations should be engaged in educational activities to bring key development issues to the broad mass of the citizenry. Simultaneously, new institutions may need to be devised, perhaps along the lines of Tanzania's constitutionally enshrined Commission of Inquiry, to provide a channel for complaints if any individual or group seeks to twist new development institutions to advantage themselves directly or indirectly.

SUMMARY AND CONCLUSIONS

This chapter has attempted to outline the evidence substantiating the hypothesis that, in the context of the conflicting class interests that have emerged in Africa over time, the kind and degree of post-independence development actually attained is likely to be significantly

---

*See further discussion of incomes policy, chapter 13.

influenced by which classes have been able, through their control of state machinery, to exercise critical decisions affecting development. The varied patterns of class and governmental structure that had emerged in the precolonial era were primarily those of relatively classless tribal groups whose members cooperated to wrest a sub- sistence living from a harsh climate; or the emergence of more power- ful ruling groups, or classes, not infrequently ethnically distinct, that extracted agricultural surpluses in some form of tribute from the weaker peasant masses, who engaged in productive activities. The development of the slave trade, particularly in West Africa, to provide a cheap labor force for plantations in the Americas tended to augment the wealth and power of the most militarily successful rulers. Out- right colonial rule, rationalized by an ideology of racial inferiority, was eventually made possible primarily because of the superior mili- tary might of the Europeans, armed by guns produced by the industrial revolution, as well as political-ethnic divisions among the Africans. Once in power, the colonialists created a political system of indirect rule either through existing ruling groups, or, if necessary, by re- placing them; in either case, the goal was to create a sufficient degree of law and order to permit private colonial firms and settlers, assisted as needed by the colonial government, to establish a hegemony over the emerging externally dependent pattern of specialization and ex- change that provided them with cheap raw materials, markets, and profitable investments.

The attainment of political independence by the African countries did not alter the fundamental class relations or the dominant set of private institutions that had emerged during the colonial era. More- over, the educated African "elites" who assumed political power were, more often than not, members of those very classes that had benefitted most from the colonial reign. Neither the reams of paper used to print plan documents nor the establishment of Western political insti- tutions were capable of altering this underlying reality. It has become increasingly evident that, if real changes are to be made to end the domination of the national economy by giant foreign trading and as- sociated interests, the state machinery will increasingly need to represent the classes that stand to gain from those changes: the vast majority of the populations, who at independence remained as poor peasants and wage earners. This argues that, if the state is to play its essential role in planning and implementing development policies in the newly independent nations of Africa, more is required than paper documents proposing new resource allocation patterns. A new set of political-economic institutions must be devised to create a network of two-way channels to mobilize, unite, and involve the broad masses of the population in decision-making at every level to insure that essential economic reconstruction actually does take place.

NOTES

1. J. Schumpeter, History of Economic Analysis, edited from manuscript by E. B. Schumpeter (New York: Oxford University Press, 1954), p. 19.

2. Cf. G. Lenski, Power and Privilege, a Theory of Social Stratification (New York: McGraw Hill, 1966), chs. 2-4.

3. For data showing distorted patterns of income distribution in Africa, see UN Economic Survey of Africa since 1950, Table I-LIV, "Annual Personal Income, African and Non-African, in Selected Countries," p. 94; D. Ghai, "Some Aspects of Income Distribution in East Africa" (mimeo), Nov. 24, 1964; G. Hunter, The New Societies of Tropical Africa, p. 135; R. Gullet, K. Caldwan, and L. Dina, Nigerian Cocoa Farmers (London: Oxford University Press, 1966), passim; C. C. Wrigley, "African Farming in Buganda" (East African Institute of Social Research Conference, 1953).

4. Cf. B. F. Hoselitz, "Social Implications of Economic Growth," Economic Weekly (Feb. 14, 21, 1959), cited in Morgan et al., Readings in Economics, pp. 78-94; H. O. Schmitt, "Two Economists, the World Bank and El Salvador," lecture to Workshop on Economic Development, Sept. 19, 1967, University of Wisconsin. See also Higgins' summary of other economists' evaluation of the relationship between attitudes and economic change in Economic Development; E. E. Hagan, "The Traditional State of Societies," in On The Theory of Social Change, pp. 55-85, for discussion of interest group conflicts in less developed countries.

5. E.g., E. Owens, "Development" (mimeo, 1971), devotes several chapters to the necessity of organizing people, devising a policy for involving farmers, and the significance of nonformal education, all conceived by him as necessary features of the new concept of "broad based development" that should form the foundation of the new approach to U.S. foreign assistance.

6. For list of such objective indices, see H. M. Johnson, Sociology: A Systematic Introduction (New York: Harcourt, Brace & World, Inc., 1960), p. 503.

7. Lenski, Power and Privilege, pp. 74-77.

8. K. Marx, Communist Manifesto, argued for this definition, which since has been adopted by a range of other scholars. For comparison of Marxian and other sociological concepts of class, see Johnson, Sociology, p. 505.

9. The significant division of the economy into a monetized export enclave and a traditional, low-productivity sector characterized by predominantly low-productivity subsistence production is a critical aspect of underdevelopment. It has given rise to one-sided theories of sociological dualism (cf. J. H. Boeke, Economics and Economic

Policy of Dual Societies [New York, 1963]) and technological dualism
(cf. B. Higgins, "The Dualistic Theory of Underdeveloped Areas,"
Economic Development and Cultural Change, Jan. 1956). For an effort
to examine the pervasive interrelated characteristics and consequences
of dualism in the African context, see A. Seidman, "The Key Variables
in a Model for Development—The African Case," paper presented to
Rural Sociology Conference, Denver, August 28-31, 1971.

10. See H. S. Lewis, "African Political Systems: A Bibliographical Inventory of Anthropological Writings," University of Wisconsin,
Mar. 1971 (mimeo).

11. E.g., T. O. Ranger (ed.), Aspects of Central African History
(London: Heinemann, 1968), esp. chs. 1-6.

12. R. Greenfield, Ethiopia, A New Political History (London:
Pall Mall Press, 1965).

13. B. Davidson, The Growth of African Civilisation: A History
of West Africa 1000-1800 (London : Longmans, 1965).

14. E. Williams, Capitalism and Slavery (Chapel Hill: University of North Carolina Press, 1944).

15. E.g., M. Crowder, A Short History of Nigeria (New York:
Praeger Publishers, 1962), esp. chs. 3-7.

16. Ibid., chs. 9-11.

17. E.g., D. O. Okonkwo, History of Nigeria in a New Setting,
from the Earliest time to 1961 (Aba: International Press), esp. ch.
19.

18. P. Curtin, The Image of Africa, British Ideas and Action,
1780-1856 (Madison: University of Wisconsin Press, 1964).

19. Lord Lugard, The Dual Mandate in British Tropical Africa
(London: Frank Cass & Co., 1965), p. 614.

20. Harry Johnstone, "The Importance of Africa," J. African
Society 17 (1918): 179m.

21. Harry Johnstone, Trade and General Conditions Report
(Nyasaland, 1895096.)

22. M. W. Forrester, Kenya Today, Social Prerequisites for
Economic Development (S. Gravenhage: Mouton & Co., 1962), describes
the impact of this system on the African population in Kenya.

23. K. Ingham, The Making of Modern Uganda (London: Allen
& Unwin, 1958); see also H. Fearn, An African Economy, A Study of
the Economic Development of Nyanza Province of Kenya (Nairobi:
Oxford University Press, 1961); and International Bank for Reconstruction and Development, Economic Development of Uganda (Baltimore: Johns Hopkins, 1962), pp. 235-6.

24. Okonkwo, History of Nigeria in a New Setting, ch. 15; and
Crowder, A Short History of Nigeria, ch. XII.

25. Okonkwo, History of Nigeria in a New Setting, pp. 198-9.

26. D. Kimble, A Political History of Ghana, The Rise of Gold Coast Nationalism, 1850-1928 (Oxford: At the Clarendon Press, 1963).

27. E.g., D. Austin, Politics in Ghana, 1946-1960 (London: Oxford University Press, 1964), pp. 271-2.

28. E.g., P. T. Bauer, West African Trade, A Study of Competition, Oligopoly, and Monopoly in a Changing Economy, revised (London: Rutledge & Kegan, Ltd., 1963), passim.

29. E.g., W. T. Newlyn and D. C. Rowan, Money and Banking in British Colonial Africa (Oxford, 1964); W. Barber, The Economy of British Central Africa, a case study of economic development in a dualistic society (London: Oxford University Press, 1961); Study of the Role of Public Agencies in the Economic Development of British West Africa in the Period 1947-1955 (New York: Bookman Associates, 1961), passim.

30. C.f. Bauer, West African Trade, passim.

31. E.g., compare Commerce and Industry (Pretoria, South Africa June 1963), pp. 612-614; and Statistical Abstract of the United States, 1962 (Washington D.C.: Government Printing Office).

32. E.g., Forrester, Kenya Today, passim.

33. E.g., Kenya Colony and Protectorate, Committee on the Organization of Agriculture, Report (Nairobi, 1960).

34. Lord Lugard, The Dual Mandate in British Tropical Africa (London: Frank Cass & Co., 1965), esp. pp. 43, 614. For various colonial policies, see Crowder, Short History of Nigeria, esp. chs. VII-XI; Okonkwo, History of Nigeria in a New Setting, esp. ch. 9; D. Kimble, A Political History of Ghana, passim; Ranger, ed., Aspects of Central African History, esp. chs. 3-9. For material relating to colonial labor policy, see Forrester, Kenya Today, pp. 127-131; W. Elkan, Migrants and Proletarian Urban Labour in the Economic Development of Uganda (London: Oxford University Press, 1960); H. Kuper, ed., Urbanization and Migration in West Africa (Berkeley: University of California Press, 1965), p. 65.

35. Survey of Cocoa Producing Families in Ashanti, 1956-57 (Accra: Office of the Government Statistician, Dec. 1960).

36. H. V. Driesen, "Patterns of Land Holding and Land Distribution in the Ife Division of Western Nigeria," Africa (London: Oxford University Press), XLI, no. 11 (Jan. 1971); see also S. M. Essang, "The Distribution of Earnings in the Cocoa Economy of Western Nigeria: Implications for Development," Unpublished Ph.D. Thesis, Michigan State University, 1970.

37. G. Hunter, The New Societies of Tropical Africa, A Selective Study (London: Oxford University Press, 1962), ch. VII.

38. Lugard, Dual Mandate, p. 482.

39. M. Blundell, So Rough a Wind, The Kenya Memoirs of Sir Michael Blundell (London: Weidenfeld and Nicolson, 1964), p. 263.

40. Ibid., p. 287.

41. Myint, Economic Theory and the Underdeveloped Countries, p. 88.

42. Forrester, in Kenya Today, shows that in preindependence Kenya the subsistence sector in effect subsidized the wage earners in Nairobi.

43. Financial Mail (Johannesburg), Mar. 26, 1970.

44. For estimates of Ghana cocoa farmers, e.g., J. C. Caldwell, "Migration and Urbanization," in Birmingham, Neustadt, and Omaboe (eds.), A Study of Contemporary Ghana, Vol. II: Some Aspects of Social Structure (London: George Allen & Unwin, 1967), esp. pp. 122 ff. For general discussion of migration, see W. A. Hance, Population, Migration and Urbanization in Africa (New York: Columbia University Press, 1971).

45. Cf. Legon Observer, Jan. 2, 1970; West Africa, Dec. 20, 1969, Jan. 1, 1970.

46. E.g., C. Baylies, Ethnic Associations in Nigeria, MA thesis, University of Wisconsin, 1971.

47. I. Davies, African Trade Unions (Harmondsworth: African Penguin, 1966).

48. E.g., in Tanzania, some 30,000 sisal workers were laid off when world sisal prices plummeted in the 1960s; and in Ghana it was estimated that when producer prices were cut after cocoa prices plummeted in 1965, their real incomes were below 1938 levels (data on file in the Planning Commission, Accra, Ghana).

49. Hunter, The New Societies of Tropical Africa, tables XIII, XIV, p. 285.

50. M. Staniland, "The Rhetoric of Centre-Periphery Relations," Journal of Modern African Studies 8, no. 4 (1970): esp. 634-6.

51. Cf. A. Adedeji, Nigerian Federal Finance (New York: Africana Publishing Corp., 1969), esp. ch. 11.

52. I. Enwemnwa, unpublished paper on ethnic groups and politics in Nigeria, University of Wisconsin, 1971.

53. E.g., Report of the Commission of Enquiry into Trade Malpractices in Ghana, W. Abraham, Chairman (Accra: Government Printer, 1965); United Republic of Tanzania, Report of the Presidential Special Committee of Enquiry into Cooperative Movement and Marketing Boards (Dar es Salaam: Government Printer, 1960); and C. Widstrand, ed., Cooperatives and Rural Development in East Africa (New York: Africana Publishing Corporation, 1970).

54. Report of Committee of Enquiry on the Local Purchasing of Cocoa, de Graft Johnson, Chairman (Accra: Government Printer, 1966); compare to Commission on the Marketing of West African Cocoa, Report, W. Nowell, Chairman (London: Cmnd. 5845, 1938).

55. Cf. Central Statistical Bureau, Household Budget Survey of the Wage Earners in Dar es Salaam (Dar es Salaam, 1967); in contrast the top 10 percent of all employees, managerial and clerical staff, earned 40 percent of all employee income (Central Statistics Bureau, 1965 Industrial Survey [Dar es Salaam, 1966]), Table 16.

56. E.g., S. F. O'Barg and S. Samoff, co-chairmen, "Cell Leaders in Tanzania: Agents of Change," papers from African Studies Association Conference panel, No. C4, Denver, 1971.

80

4

BASIC REQUIREMENTS
FOR PLANNING
IN AFRICA

Up to this point, Part I has attempted to provide an explanation of the problem of underdevelopment in Africa as an alternative to that commonly suggested by orthodox economic theory. A model has been proposed to suggest that the source is the inherited institutional structure and lopsided resource allocation pattern that have emerged as integral features of, and continue to perpetuate, the externally dependent dual economy of the typical ex-colony. Given slowly expanding world demand and the domination of the world markets by oligopolistic multinational corporations, the African nation that remains dependent on overseas sales of crude materials is likely, over time, to be condemned to economic growth rates that barely keep pace with population expansion. This underscores the necessity for state action to formulate and implement national plans designed to change the institutional structure and resource allocation patterns to attain a balanced, nationally integrated economy capable of achieving increased productivity and higher levels of living for all inhabitants. Examination of the conflicting classes that had emerged at independence further emphasizes the added requirement that the institutional changes made must include channels enabling those who may expect to benefit from this kind of development to exercise a sufficient degree of influence over the machinery of state.

The first section of this chapter will briefly summarize the colonial and postindependence planning experience that led some African political leaders in the former British colonies to conclude that fundamental institutional changes must be made to implement national plans to reallocate resources for development. The second section will outline some of the critical features that appear to be essential for more effective national planning.

THE FIRST ROUND

The Limits of Colonial Planning

Planning of a kind is not new in Africa. The governments of the British colonies, particularly after World War II, drew up a variety of plans for development. These were, however, particularly limited. For the most part they consisted essentially of "departmental shopping lists,"[1] indicating the kinds of projects and the funds needed to implement proposals strung together by the various governmental departments. Wedded to the idea that for the most part only private enterprise should invest in productive activities, the plans provided the social and economic infrastructure needed to encourage private firms— of necessity mainly foreign—to make those investments. The net result was that the colonial plans, if anything, served primarily to further the expansion of the export enclave and the increased external dependence of the colonies.

The First Postindependence Plans

Upon attainment of independence, the first round of African plans publicly proclaimed the goal of augmenting the per capita incomes of the African populations. In reality, however, they continued to prescribe policies not unlike those adopted by the colonial government planners. True, a greater emphasis was placed on social as well as economic infrastructure: many more schools and hospitals, as well as roads and ports, were to be built. But private enterprise was still expected to provide the main motor for development in the productive sectors. The underlying assumption apparently continued to be that government's expanded efforts to construct infrastructure and create an "hospitable investment climate" would attract the necessary private investment to achieve proposed production targets.[2]

The targets incorporated in the plans were "guestimated" with the help of data on past activities. These data, gathered by colonial government statisticians, were almost entirely confined to exports and imports. The data were commonly extrapolated to set new targets on the basis of rather simplistic assumptions about capital-output ratios. In some cases more sophisticated techniques were utilized in an effort to manufacture some kind of input-output table. Lack of any accurate information about whole areas of the economy rendered these tables little more than not-so-very-educated-guesses about essential coefficients. The lack of backward and forward linkages in many areas of the economy left many of the "boxes" virtually empty.

As the end of the Development Decade neared, it became increasingly self-evident that the first round of national plans had achieved little notable success in spreading productivity and raising the levels of living of the broad masses of the population in any African country. What effort had been made to expand production—much of it still concentrated on exports—appeared to have been vitiated by falling world prices. Balance of payments crises had spread as governments sought to increase the import of capital goods and equipment to meet plan targets.

Ghana, the first sub-Saharan nation to win independence, doubled its output of cocoa in the decade from 1955 to 1965; but, when world cocoa prices plummeted from £500 a ton to £90 a ton in the latter year, the nation confronted an economic crisis that was by no means resolved by the military coup in 1966.[3] Tanzania's economists estimated[4] that falling world prices for that country's major exports from 1962 to 1967 had resulted in a loss of $22 million—roughly two times the inflow of all foreign funds in the same period.

Foreign finance anticipated in the plans for development did not appear to be forthcoming in the amounts anticipated.* Some nations, notably Ghana and Nigeria, began to utilize high-cost suppliers' credits in an effort to build promised social and economic infrastructure and, in Ghana's case, some import-substitution type industries. The required repayments of interest and principal increased the burden on the future balance of payments.

Given the realities of the circumstances confronting the newly independent African governments, it should have surprised no one that their initial plans turned out to be little more than paper documents. One observer suggested, in addition, that "men and organizations can easily become captives of rite and ritual, thus reducing planning activities to little more than formal, symbolic exercises."[5] Sometimes this was justified by the experts: after all, it was said, the purpose of planning was merely to provide some sort of propaganda tool to arouse African populations to necessary development efforts.[6] Others concluded that there was really no point in planning at all. The best that could be hoped for under the circumstances, they held, was a kind of year-to-year effort to evaluate progress and suggest next steps.[7]

The Theoretical Underpinning

That national planning had been to a considerable extent reduced to a formalistic ritual with little impact in attaining development was

---

*See Chapter 14

83

due in no small part to the fact that for the most part the government planners—like their colonial predecessors—adopted uncritically the prescriptions and techniques built on the foundations of standard theory. This theoretical underpinning was peculiarly unsuited for guiding national planning, given the African circumstance, for three reasons.

First, the plans typically assumed that private enterprise could provide the necessary motor for growth in the productive sectors within the inherited, institutional framework. This assumption is based on the premise embodied in standard theory that a sufficient degree of competition exists to enable the interaction of private "market forces" to achieve a relatively advantageous allocation of resources.[8] In contrast, as suggested by the model proposed in Chapter 1, a fundamental aspect of reality in Africa is the pervasive presence of major imperfections built into the institutional structure that dominates both external and internal markets. These cannot, given the imperatives of modern technology and the limited distorted markets shaped by skewed income distributions, simply be removed so as to restore anything like the competitive conditions needed to lead to an improved allocation of resources. As the model shows, the major share of the investible surpluses produced in Africa are, because of the peculiar features of the inherited institutional structure, either siphoned out of the country or concentrated in the hands of a narrow high-income group associated with export enclave activities. Economic plans based on the assumption of anything resembling the required degree of competition will, in this context, inevitably fail to achieve broader development goals.

Second, the analytical tools of standard theory have, implicitly or explicitly, assumed that economies always tend to move toward conditions of static equilibrium. The explanatory model proposed in Chapter 1 suggests that attainment of development in Africa requires fundamental changes in the institutional structure to eliminate the dual economy and attain balanced, nationally integrated economic growth. Several economists have emphasized that such structural-institutional change cannot be adequately encompassed by the static framework assumed by standard theory.[9]* If national planners are to contribute more effectively to the formulation of national development plans, they

---

*The dynamic approach being incorporated into current standard theory, seeking to trace the path of change from one state of static equilibrium to the next,[10] appears unlikely to meet this objection, since it is based on essentially the same set of assumptions. Leontief, whose input-output tables have done so much to build empirical foundations for general equilibrium theory, has caustically commented, "Seldom in modern positive science has so elaborate a theoretical structure been erected on so narrow and shallow factual foundations."[11]

can no longer rely on paradigms with fixed parameters assuming a return to equilibrium within a given institutional context. They need, instead, to focus on implementing on-going structural changes in the crucial institutions that shape the patterns of resource allocation.

Third, mathematical tools of the kind today being designed to describe the structure of resource allocation in developed economies are inherently of limited utility for explaining and guiding the kind of institutional changes needed to attain development in Africa. Mathematical models may describe quantitative variables and fixed relations between them. (This, of course, assumes the appropriate data are available, which is in itself a major problem in most developing countries.) But the existence of a mathematical relationship between two variables does not explain the nature of the causal relationship that may exist between them; that is, it does not explain how changes in one may affect another, or whether both are, in fact, influenced by a third (perhaps unknown) variable.* Sole reliance on mathematical tools, which by their nature exclude consideration of needed institutional changes, must therefore inevitably, in the context of less developed countries, obscure the basic causes of underdevelopment.

This is not to argue that mathematical tools, like input-output tables and linear programming, will not be useful for planned allocation of resources—assuming the appropriate statistical data are available— once the necessary institutional changes have been made to implement such resource allocation plans. After the necessary institutional changes have been made so that national planners may control and direct national resources more effectively, and as soon as the essential statistical data have been accumulated, the mathematical tools now being devised in developed countries will, without doubt, have an invaluable role to play in the formulation of plans leading to a more rational allocation of resources.[14]

---

*This is true, incidentally, for models of phenomena encountered in the physical as well as the social sciences.[12]

Georgescu-Roegen[13] goes beyond this to argue that what he terms the "arithmomorphic" concepts of which mathematical models are constructed are incapable of encompassing the kinds of institutional changes required to achieve development. He defines "arithmomorphic" concepts as those that do not overlap, such as numbers. In contrast, he holds, the penumbras associated with "dialectical," nonmeasurable concepts, such as institutions, do overlap. Change takes place as a continuum through the penumbra of one such concept into another. Mathematical models, built of "arithmomorphic" concepts that are incapable of encompassing this kind of change, are, he holds, incapable of even describing, let alone explaining, the kinds of qualitative institutional changes that are required if development is to take place.

CRITICAL ASPECTS OF MORE EFFECTIVE PLANNING

The experience with the first round of planning in Africa led the political leaders of several countries to begin to search for a new approach to national planning. In particular, more careful consideration is beginning to be given to five essential aspects, including the possibilities and problems of control of the "commanding heights"; the formulation of a long-term development strategy designed to reallocate resources to attain a balanced, nationally integrated economy; the implementation of coordinated, self-reliant financial planning; decentralization of planning to involve the broad masses of the population; and the institutionalization of an on-going process of evaluation of the entire planning activity.

Control of the "Commanding Heights"

Among the former British colonies, Tanzania's government leaders took the lead in 1967 by proclaiming the Arusha Declaration.[15] Self-reliant development could be attained, they claimed, only if the national government assumed control of the "commanding heights"— basic industries,* export-import and internal wholesale trade, and the financial institutions. These were held to be the critical areas of the economy that, dominated in the past by oligopolistic foreign interests, had been shaped primarily to provide profitable sources of raw materials and markets for the industries of Europe and North America, not to facilitate the spread of productivity and higher levels of living throughout the rural areas. The Tanzania government began to direct attention to the kinds of changes in the working rules governing these institutions to generate a more appropriate pattern of industrial growth and to draw the long neglected rural populations into the orbit of national development.†

Other nations began to follow Tanzania's lead. Zambia's government took over a majority of shares of the main manufacturing industries and big mines that had for so long dominated the economy.[17] Former President Obote proposed that Uganda should "move to the left"[18] and his government began to negotiate to purchase 61 percent of the ownership of firms in the key areas of the economy; but these

---

*Insofar as they existed; in Tanzania's case they still for the most part remained to be built.

†Despite talk of "socialism" in Nkrumah's Ghana, only limited steps had been taken in these areas before the 1966 coup; and these were reversed wherever possible afterwards.[16]

negotiations were halted by still another in a lengthening list of military coups.*

Simply taking over a majority of the shares ownership in critical sectors of the economy could not, of itself, resolve the host of problems confronting African national planners and political leaders. As Chapter 3 emphasizes, the interests of the different classes that had emerged by the time of independence were by no means always in harmony. At worst, increased state control might actually increase the opportunities for some government ministers, highly placed civil servants, and politicians to utilize the machinery of state to advance their own interests. At best, on the other hand, it might create the preconditions necessary to enable government political leaders and planners sincerely desiring to plan for the needs of the broad masses of the African populations to begin to take appropriate steps to reallocate resources to increase productivity and raise the levels of living of the population throughout the nation. To realize the latter possibility, however, it became increasingly apparent that new kinds of political institutions must be created to insure that the broad masses of the population, who would gain from restructuring the economy, were sufficiently educated about the critical issues and that they would have adequate opportunity to influence governmental decision-makers to reallocate resources in a way designed to meet their needs.

It would require another volume to examine in depth the manifold problems involved in building appropriate political institutions to insure that state action really reflects the needs of the broad masses of the population. The remainder of this book will, of necessity, assume that efforts are being made to solve these problems. It will seek only to evaluate the probable consequences of the kinds of changes that have been or might need to be made in the sets of institutions dominating the commanding heights that more directly determine how resources are allocated: those institutions that directly control the pattern of investment in the productive sectors, industry, and agriculture and those shaping the way trade and finance influence the spread of specialization and exchange throughout the national economy.

The Necessity of a Long-Term Development Strategy

Once a government has asserted greater control over the "commanding heights", it must immediately begin to formulate a long-term

---

*These coups threatened to make postindependence African history resemble that of Latin America, which remains underdeveloped despite almost 160 years of "independent" political rule.

development strategy designed to achieve a gradual but steady increase in the material well-being of the broad masses of the population over a period of twenty or twenty-five years. In particular, as Tanzanian planners have declared, it is essential to formulate an industrial strategy[19] to insure that industrial growth stimulates rural development and the growth of internal trade. The growth of industrial productivity is required to contribute to rising incomes, generating a domestic market for local foodstuffs and employment opportunities outside agriculture. At the same time, industrial growth must center around the introduction of improved tools and scientific farming techniques in agriculture, gradually releasing rural labor from traditional low-productivity, low-income occupations as more productive higher-income employment becomes available in other sectors. (See Chapter 5 for a detailed discussion.)

Adoption of a long-term development strategy should make it possible at the end of, say, twenty-five years for at least the larger of the former British colonies here considered to attain a self-reliant, nationally integrated and balanced economy characterized by rising productivity and incomes in all sectors. It should be emphasized that "self-reliant" as here used is not meant to imply autarchy, cutting off the African economy from world trade. What is implied, instead, is that decisions as to the pattern and pace of growth will no longer be dependent either on the fortunes of a few raw material exports to an uncertain world market or the decisions of a handful of powerful multinational corporations. The changes in the institutional structure and resource allocation patterns made over this longer-term period must be designed by national planners to insure that internal specialization and exchange will continue to facilitate the spread of increasingly productive technology to all sectors of the economy.

If the individual nations of Africa could unite their markets, national resources, and capital, they would undoubtedly be able to achieve a more rapid rate of development throughout entire regions.[20] Realization of this possibility depends on attainment of a degree of joint control of the commanding heights by the participating state governments that requires a long-term political commitment as well as economic policies designed to restructure the regional economy. It is likely to be thwarted in the future—as it has in the decade since independence was achieved[21]—if the state machinery of the participating nations remains dominated by groups who perceive their interests to be linked to the status quo. Essentially, this is a political issue. Despite its crucial importance, it cannot be adequately dealt with here. It must suffice to stress that government leaders seeking self-reliant development should make every effort to achieve the necessary joint political agreement with neighboring governments to implement joint regional plans if at all possible. At the same time, they must make

a realistic political assessment of the possibilities and avoid entangle-
ments that might undermine their own efforts to implement a long-term
development strategy designed to restructure their own economy.

The formulation of a long-term development strategy will provide
the framework within which shorter-term plans, covering periods of,
say, four to six years, could be worked out in much more concrete
detail. As the Tanzanian planners have pointed out, shorter-term plans
must necessarily be shaped by the perspectives set forth in the longer
term strategy:

> Successful industrialization is achieved through a success-
> ful choice of the appropriate sequence of steps; if the
> foundations are not correctly laid in the coming decade,
> then industrialization will seem even more difficult in 1980
> than it does today.[22]

Specific physical features of the major industrial and infrastructural projects and their associated linkages, designed to set off
chains of growth throughout entire areas of the economy, should constitute the cornerstones of each of the shorter-term plans. The plans
themselves should cover a time-period long enough for such major
projects to be completed and to begin to function in reshaping the
structure of resource use in the economy.

Given the initial scarcity of adequate statistical data, it is probable that shorter-term plans would, at the outset, be able to provide
details, based on careful feasibility studies, only of the most important
projects and their expected impact in reallocating resources in accord
with the proposed long-term perspective. The required physical inputs and outputs will probably only be roughly balanced. Only as data
improve and critical linkages are worked out in greater detail over
time will more sophisticated input-output tables be likely to be helpful.

Essential institutional changes should also be explicitly provided
for in these shorter-term plans. The plans should, from the outset,
indicate explicitly how government direction of the critical sectors
of the economy may be expected to facilitate the proposed construction
of essential major projects and associated linkages. This will require
careful evaluation and revision of the inherited sets of working rules
governing these institutions so that they do in fact play the role anticipated.

The Financial Plan: A Dual of the Physical Plan

The shorter-term physical plans should, in addition to incorporating the detailed concrete physical features of proposed major projects,

spell out explicitly how the necessary financing for each major project is to be obtained. In a sense, the resulting financial plan should be a dual of the physical plan: it should be designed to show how investible surpluses from all sources are to be redirected to the new physical projects through the appropriate sets of policies relating to taxes, credit, and prices. The danger of creating inflationary pressures that may distort plan perspectives must be avoided. The working rules of the entire set of financial institutions affecting taxes, credit, and prices should be re-evaluated and revised in the context of the national financial plan to insure that they reinforce, rather than inhibit, each other in contributing to implementation of the national plans.

Decentralized Planning

Accumulating experience in Africa tends to support the hypothesis that local participation in planning and carrying out activities to facilitate the spread effects of major projects can best be stimulated in the context of government control of the commanding heights directed to implementing a long-term development strategy to restructure the economy. At the same time, stimulating participation requires the development of new institutions to foster two-way communications between local groups and national political leaders and planners to insure that their efforts mutually reinforce each other in attaining national development goals.

African planners have begun to emphasize the necessity of decentralized planning with a view to uncovering potential investible surpluses hidden in underemployed rural labor supplies or neglected possibilities for increasing the sales of agricultural produce. Given adequate price incentives, there is ample evidence that the African peasant family will increase its output.[23] This suggests the importance of insuring that the national plan provides adequate market facilities, as well as essential farm inputs and sufficient credit to enable the peasants to take advantage of new market opportunities. There are many African examples that prove, too, that when community members are convinced of the necessity of building new feeder roads, or the possibility of financing a new school or clinic by increasing their crop sales, they are willing to participate in cooperative self-help efforts directed to these ends.

Widespread reliance on a policy of local finance to stimulate local initiatives should be weighed against the danger that it may foster growth of inequalities among localities. From the point of view of creating a nationally integrated economy characterized by growing demand as well as supply, it would seem essential for all sectors to participate in the spread of productivity and higher levels of living.

90

This suggests that the central government probably should direct a greater share of centrally accumulated funds to provide market facilities and the necessary inputs to stimulate productivity in less developed areas of the country.

Different African governments have sought to stimulate local initiatives in different ways. Regional and district planning groups have been established in several countries. In Kenya, for example, foreign teams of experts have been imported to formulate plans for each of several districts. These plans, like those of their national counterparts, have tended to assume the institutional context as given; as a result, the district plans, too, have typically listed hoped-for projects, rather than focusing on the institutionalized involvement of local citizens in planning and implementing local projects to increase their own productivity and gain greater material benefits for themselves.

Jackson describes planning in Kenya "at the grassroots level" as "still largely a formal exercise which has not yet involved local citizens to any extent or significantly affected development activities which take place in spite of planning." He adds:

> And this situation will not likely change until planners themselves gain greater influence on the allocation of public goods and services in rural areas and invite the preferences of local groups to guide allocation decisions.[24]

Without greater national control and direction of resources to the rural areas, however, it seems unlikely that the Kenyan planners can insure that the necessary marketing facilities and inputs are available as a precondition for greater involvement of the citizens in local decision-making. Jackson suggests that, under the present circumstances, to invite rural inhabitants to participate in planning discussions

> . . . may open a pandora's box of rural instability caused by excessive political claims and too few public goods and services to satisfy these. Perhaps planners and other public officials know this and perhaps this is why decision making may not get beyond the stage of rhetoric in Kenya.[25]

Holmquist, after making a case study of local efforts to build cattle dips in Kissi, in Kenya, noted[26] that the lack of "strong alternative institutions such as parties linking the administrative-political 'top' with its counterparts at the 'bottom'" rendered it probable that the central government might attempt to take even the existing limited planning functions out of the hands of local participants. This conclusion appears to underline the necessity of creating new sets of political institutions if national planning is to create the necessary framework within which local participation can be encouraged.

Tanzania's political leaders have asserted that involvement of the broad mass of the citizens must be given priority in national planning:

> To us development means both the elimination of oppression, exploitation, enslavement and humiliation, and the promotion of our independence and human dignity. Therefore, in considering the development of our nation and in preparing development plans, our main emphasis at all times should be the development of the people. If development is to benefit the people, the people must participate in considering, planning and implementing their development plans.[27]

In Tanzania, where there is both greater national control of the commanding heights and a more unified political party with roots in remote rural areas as well as the cities, the conditions would seem to be more appropriate for increased local participation in plan implementation. Trained Tanzanians have been appointed as regional planning officers, and a rural development fund has been created to give local planners a degree of flexibility in implementing proposed projects. The implementation of the "ujamaa" village programs, discussed below, is perceived by the government as a way of involving peasants in cooperative activity designed to augment productivity and raise their own levels of living in the context of the national development strategy. Tanzania's political leaders argue that the political party, TANU, must play a key role in involving people in decision-making about the plans:

> The duty of our Party is not to urge the people to implement plans which have been decided upon by a few experts and leaders. The duty of the Party is to insure that the leaders and experts implement the plans that have been agreed upon by the people themselves. When the people's decision requires information which is only available to the leaders and the experts, it will be the duty of leaders and experts to make such information available to the people. But it is not correct for leaders and experts to usurp the people's right to decide on an issue just because they have the expertise.[28]

Institutionalization of an On-going
Process of Evaluation

The institutional changes required to implement national plans can only be made by altering the sets of working rules or laws that determine the behavior of the individuals or groups involved. Adoption of a problem-solving orientation requires that every such change in working rules must be continually evaluated to determine whether in fact the changed behavior induced really does contribute to attainment of long-term development goals.

This process itself should be institutionalized at every level of the planning process, from the national center to the most remote village. Quantitative and qualitative data are needed as to the unanticipated side-effects, as well as the expected consequences of changes in the working rules that may stimulate or hinder initiatives required on the national, district, or local level to implement complementary aspects of the plan. The results of the evaluation process should continuously be reincorporated into revision of shorter-term plans to insure that they contribute more effectively to desired longer-term goals.

The changes in working rules or institutions necessary to implement national plans typically seek to prompt new patterns of behavior on the part of citizen-role occupants who fulfill various roles in the community: peasants, artisans and entrepreneurs, trade union members and school teachers, industrial managers, and so forth. The formulation and implementation of new working rules also self-evidently require supportive activities on the part of lawmakers and bureaucrats in national and local government agencies. There is inevitably extensive interaction between these various actors that is likely to influence the outcome of any particular changes in working rules.

Sociological studies[29] have shown that the behavior of any individual, or "role occupant," affected by a given set of working rules, is the function of the entire "field" in which he operates: the normative and institutional structure; the ideologies; the technological and resource constraints of the society; the class structure; the myths and traditions of the community; the values held—all these, and a host of other forces, tend to shape the individual's area of choice, frequently within relatively narrow limits, in his response to changed working rules.

A fairly comprehensive research agenda is suggested by a simple paradigm for examining the consequences of existing or proposed working rules in terms of the behavior of the various actors involved.[30] This paradigm may be depicted in a diagram like Figure 2. A two-dimensional diagram cannot illustrate all the possible interactions of

FIGURE 2
A Paradigm of Law and Development

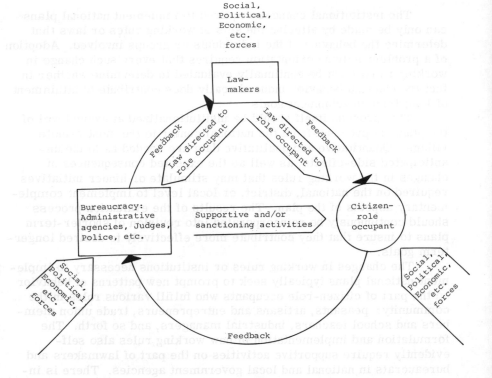

FIGURE 2
A Paradigm of Law and Development

Source: R. B. Seidman, "Law and Development: A General Model,"
Law and Society Review, Winter, 1972.

the different sets of social forces that affect different actors in the context of the national political economy. Nevertheless, it suggests the kinds of interactions that must be considered in evaluating the consequences of specific institutional changes.

The desired development activity of the citizen-role occupant is typically induced by activities of bureaucrats, acting pursuant to rules addressed to them, rather than by criminal sanctions on the citizen himself. That laws are, in this sense, directed primarily to bureaucrats with a view to requiring them to take actions designed to alter the activities of the citizen-role occupants is indicated in the diagram by the use of dotted lines for the arrow directed to the latter.

A number of middle-level hypotheses have been formulated that suggest the kinds of political, social, and economic forces that may influence an individual role occupant's behavior in response to a new working rule or norm designed to facilitate attainment of development. These hypotheses provide heuristic guides for the systematic evaluation of what may be crucial factors influencing the way an individaul responds to an existing or changed working rule.* The results of such an evaluation may lead to conclusions as to further changes in the working rules to obtain more suitable behavior.

Given the importance of the bureaucracy in implementing laws designed to alter institutions, the paradigm emphasizes the necessity of considering how the bureaucrats in particular may be expected to respond to a proposed change in working rules. The individual bureaucrat may, in general, be placed in the position of the role occupant for the purposes of study. The fact that bureaucrats are organized into complex organizations, however, suggests an additional line of hypotheses beyond those relating to role occupants in general. These are largely drawn from the sociology of complex organizations.

In the same way, it is possible to examine the role of the lawmaker by considering (1) the content of norms defining the lawmaker's role, the subject matter of much of administrative and constitutional law; (2) the forces operating upon him, which have been extensively canvassed in the political science literature; and (3) the various institutions (usually vague and diffuse, consisting of unwritten customary procedure as well as explicitly stated norms) for sanctioning his activity.

Any law designed to attain institutional change is itself subject to a constant process of change either by formal amendment, or as a result of the way the bureaucracy acts. This is because the social,

---

*In the process of the evaluation, new middle-level hypotheses may be formulated providing still more useful guides to this kind of systematic evaluation activity.

economic, and other forces operating on the various actors are changing; and the actors themselves—the citizen-role occupant, the lawmakers, and the bureaucracy—react to the law and the changing forces operating on them. These reactions are delineated by the lines showing feedback. The extent to which the feedback channels from the citizen-role occupant to the lawmakers and the bureaucrats are kept open, as well as the actual way in which the latter respond to specific feedback, may affect the range of social, political, and economic forces in the community. A sufficiently unpopular law, vigorously enforced in the face of citizen opposition, may lead to loss of governmental legitimacy and even threaten the stability of the government itself. On the other hand, to the extent that citizen-role occupants are involved in making decisions, as well as evaluating their consequences, they are more likely to be willing to cooperate in implementing them. Given the conflict of interests described in Chapter 3, it appears particularly important to involve the majority of the populations, the peasants and wage earners, in the decision-making machinery. Special attention to this aspect is warranted, furthermore, by the fact that those benefitting from the status quo, well-to-do traders, farmers, and businessmen, tended also to be those who dominated the political areas at independence. Unless new institutional channels are created, the vast majority of the populations appears likely to continue to be excluded from crucial planning decisions.

All of these interactions need to be considered in an on-going evaluation process designed to assess the success of institutional changes in facilitating plan implementation. It is important that the evaluation agency not be too closely associated with the government, in view of the fact that the necessary objectivity is difficult to achieve when the plan formulators are the evaluators. Perhaps it would be preferable to locate the evaluative machinery in the national university with a sufficient degree of autonomy to draw conclusions as to plan failures as well as successes. Recognition of the probable conflicts of interest suggest, furthermore, that special efforts need to be made to encourage members of organizations like peasant cooperatives and trade unions to participate in the evaluation process, which is itself, properly conceived, a crucial aspect of decision-making. Whatever the particular form of institutionalization of the evaluative process, it should be perceived as a necessary feature of the entire national planning exercise.

SUMMARY

The failure of the first round of national plans to contribute significantly to broadly defined development goals has led some

African political leaders to search for a new approach to planning. Several governments have begun to direct greater attention to five aspects that seem crucial in the implementation of national plans. These include: (1) greater national control of the "commanding heights"— basic industries, export-import and internal wholesale trade, and financial institutions—to create the essential preconditions for directing resources to plan implementation; (2) formulation of a long-term development strategy, covering twenty to twenty-five years, outlining the basic changes in institutions required to reallocate resources to increase productivity and raise the levels of living of the broad masses of the population in the context of an increasingly integrated, self-reliant economy; (3) coordination of all sources of funds in a national financial plan to insure that projects critical to attainment of the long-term development perspectives are adequately financed; (4) decentralization of planning mechanisms within the context of the national plan to involve the broad masses of the population in decision-making; and (5) institutionalization of an on-going process of evaluation to insure that institutional and resource allocation changes do in fact contribute over time to the desired development goals.

The remainder of this book attempts to examine in more detail the consequences of the alternative policies that have been introduced in various countries in the critical areas dominated by what have come to be called the "commanding heights". Part II examines the productive sectors, with a view to determining the critical features of balanced industrial and agricultural growth, and outlines some of the evidence as to the probable consequences of some of the alternative institutional changes in the productive sectors themselves that have been proposed to attain it. Part III outlines the extent to which the trading institutions that emerged during the colonial era have hindered the spread of productivity throughout the national economies, and again seeks to consider some alternative institutional innovations proposed to overcome these problems. Part IV is devoted to consideration of the essential ingredients of an appropriate national financial plan, including the formulation of an appropriate national incomes policy. It attempts to outline some of the necessary institutional changes that might be required to achieve a coordinated financial program in which taxes, price, and credit policies reinforce each other in implementing the long-term development strategy.

NOTES

1. R. H. Green, "Four African Development Plans: Ghana, Kenya, Nigeria, and Tanzania," Journal of Modern African Studies 3, no. 2 (1965).

2. Cf. R. Lacey, "Foreign Resources and Development," in G. Hyden, R. Jackson, and J. Okuma (eds.), Development Administration: The Kenyan Experience (Nairobi: Oxford University Press, 1970), p. 71. See also the various plan documents of the countries themselves.

3. The 1972 coup was aimed to overcome symptoms of the same crisis, now further aggravated by six years of failure to make essential structural changes. See A. Seidman, Ghana's Development Experience (Nairobi: East African Publishing House, 1972) Postscript; and West Africa, Jan. 7, 21, 28, 1972; also "Ghana: Popular Moves," Africa Confidential, Feb. 18, 1972.

4. A. S. Nkwabi, "Self-Reliance and Foreign Trade," Dar es Salaam, a panel, Economic Society of Tanzania, Sept. 11, 1968.

5. R. Jackson, "Planning, Politics and Administration", in Hyden et al., Development Administration, p. 172.

6. Cf. Discussions by participants at the Conference of International Economists on Ghana's Seven Year Development Plan, Legon, 1963, attended by the author.

7. A. Waterston, Development Planning: Lessons of Experience (Baltimore: Johns Hopkins Press, 1965), after summarizing the negative planning experiences of many Third World nations, tends to reach this conclusion, which he stated more explicitly in a talk at a University of Wisconsin in Workshop on Development, 1967.

8. For a standard current discussion of the underlying assumption of competition and suggested limited modifications of it, given imperfect competition, see, e.g., J. J. Bailey, National Income and the Price Level, A Study in Macrotheory (New York: McGraw-Hill Book Company, 1962), esp. pp. 131-2. It should be noted that even as modified in this discussion, imperfect competition as described does not correspond to the case presented in the model of underdevelopment in which control of the export enclave by a handful of large (in the African case, foreign) firms and associated interests dominates the political-economic institutional structure of entire less developed economies.

9. W. F. Barber, The Economy of British Central Africa, p. 175.

10. E.g., P. A. Samuelson, "The Stability of Equilibrium: Comparative Statics and Dynamics" and "Dynamic Process and Analysis," The Collected Papers of Paul A. Samuelson (Cambridge: MIT Press, 1966); see also J. R. Hicks, Value and Capital, An Enquiry into some Fundamental Principles of Economic Theory (London: Oxford University Press, 1965, reprinted), Ch. IX; for comment regarding failure of dynamic model to show how to turn a stagnant economy into a prosperous one, see Higgins, Economic Development, Principles, Problems and Policies (New York: Norton, 1959), pp. 209-213.

11. W. Leontief, Theories and Theorizing, p. 33; see also Georgescu-Roegen, Analytical Economics, p. 107; and J. Schumpeter, History of Economic Analysis, p. 1161.

12. Cf. A. Inkles, What is Sociology? An Introduction to the Discipline and Profession (Englewood Cliffs, N.J.: Prentice-Hall, Inc., 1964), p. 42; Hanson, Patterns of Discovery, p. 72; and Black, Models and Metaphors, pp. 225-226.

13. Essentially, Georgescu-Roegen here appears to be building on the Hegelian method. See Georgescu-Roegen, Analytical Economics, Part I, esp. pp. 22 ff., 42, 120.

14. Cf. A. Brody, Prices, Proportions and Planning (New York: North Holland, 1971).

15. "The Arusha Declaration: 29 January 1967," in J. K. Nyerere, A Selection from Writings and Speeches, 1965-1967 (Dar es Salaam: Oxford University Press, 1968), pp. 231-250.

16. A. Seidman, Ghana's Development Experience, 1951-1965, Ch. 7.

17. K. D. Kaunda, Address at the Opening of the Second National Convention, Kitwe, Zambia Information Services, Dec. 12, 1969.

18. M. Obote, The Common Man's Charter (Krampala: Milton Obote Foundation, Adult Education Center, 1971).

19. United Republic of Tanzania, Second Five Year Plan for Economic and Social Development, 1st July, 1969-30th June, 1974, Vol. 1: General Analysis (Dar es Salaam: Government Printer, 1969), Ch. 4.

20. These possibilities have been examined in some detail in R. H. Green and A. Seidman, Unity or Poverty? (Harmondsworth: African Penguin Library, 1969).

21. A. Seidman, Comparative Development Strategies of East Africa (Nairobi: East African Publishing House, 1972), Ch. 10.

22. Tanzania, Second Five Year Plan, p. 59.

23. This is the basis of Myint's acceptance of the theory of a "vent-for-surplus" ("The 'Classical Theory' of Trade," in Economic Theory and the Underdeveloped Countries, Ch. 5).

24. Jackson, "Planning, Politics and Administration," p. 199.

25. Ibid., p. 176.

26. F. Holmquist, "Implementing Rural Development Projects," in Hyden et al., Development Administration, p. 228.

27. Tanganyika African National Union TANU Guidelines, 1971 (Dar es Salaam: Government Printer, 1971), p. 9.

28. Ibid.

29. Landberg and Lansing, "The Sociography of Some Community Relations," American Sociology Review 2 (1937): 318 ff.

30. R. B. Seidman, "Law and Development: A General Model," Law and Society Review, No. 6 (Winter, 1972).

5

TOWARD BALANCED
INDUSTRIAL AND
AGRICULTURAL GROWTH

The notion that either agriculture or industry can or should be developed without regard to the other is here rejected at the outset. That they are of necessity related seems undisputable; the real issue is what is the nature of that interrelationship. This part aims to examine in some detail the hypothesis that the formulation and implementation of an appropriate industrial strategy is essential to attainment of a balanced, nationally integrated economy capable of providing full employment and higher levels of living for the broadest masses of the population throughout the rural areas for several major reasons.[1]

First, the establishment of carefully planned industries is needed to provide a domestic market for agricultural raw materials and foodstuffs produced in the expanding agricultural sector. In this sense they would contribute to expanding internal specialization and exchange and reduce the relative importance of overseas crop sales to the national economy. At the same time, industrial processing of exports could increase national foreign exchange earnings, significantly increasing the national capacity to import essential capital equipment and machinery needed to increase productivity in all sectors of the economy. This, of course, assumes a market could be found for manufactured goods either in developed countries or by reciprocal agreements for manufactured goods trade between developing countries.

That such markets will not be easily obtained is illustrated by the resistance of the African nations' major trading partners in Europe and the United States to proposals made at the United Nations Conferences on Trade and Development. The pervasive monetary crisis confronting the Western developed nations has tended to strengthen their resistance to such proposals. Confronted by their own monetary and balance of payments problems, they—particularly the United States and Britain—have not hesitated to impose further tariff and other restrictions on imports from developing areas. Manufactured imports have been especially affected. Devaluation of their currencies was specifically designed to reduce all imports still further. On the other hand, the expansion of trade in manufactured goods among developing countries appears to require a level of cooperation and planning that few have as yet achieved. Nevertheless, increased processing of agricultural materials for domestic consumption is of itself a worthwhile goal, and where possible it should be combined with projects to increase foreign exchange earnings.

Second, new industries could produce appropriate farm inputs that, over time, could contribute to expanded agricultural productivity. It has been argued[2] correctly that too rapid expansion of agricultural production through introduction of imported capital-intensive machinery and equipment is likely to reduce employment opportunities in rural areas, creating a dilemma for the future of agriculture: the faster agricultural output expands, the more rapidly the number of unemployed may be expected to drift into the urban centers of the export enclave. Widespread experience suggests, too, that the attempt to introduce machinery and equipment into agriculture too rapidly has resulted in extensive waste of capital because of the lack of skills and knowledge relating to its use. Hence it may be argued that the establishment of domestic industries producing somewhat more labor-intensive tools in the first stages would contribute to expanded productivity at a pace more in keeping with the current characteristics of the agricultural labor force. Over time as agricultural productivity, skills, and purchasing power expand, industries producing farm implements of a more advanced character will begin to be justified.

Third, appropriately planned industries, linked to the needs of the rural populations, could provide new jobs for underemployed agricultural workers. Relatively labor-intensive industries in rural areas for processing agricultural produce or turning out simple consumer necessities and farm inputs could be operated on a seasonal basis, providing employment during off-season periods. This would contribute to the expansion of specialization and exchange without the extensive family and social dislocation required for workers to migrate to major urban industrial areas. It would permit peasants to acquire some of the necessary skills for building up rural industries over time. In other words, as agricultural output per man expands, appropriately planned rural industries could be designed to absorb the surplus agricultural labor force, providing them with new skills and employment.*

---

*In Poland expansion of industry in rural areas has absorbed surplus labor to such an extent that it has become necessary to introduce

Fourth, carefully planned industries could set off chains of development in rural areas that could contribute to restructuring the entire economy. Higher rural incomes resulting from steadily expanded agricultural sales to the growing domestic industrial sector could contribute to a greater demand for industrial products, which in turn would raise rural living standards. This would help to equalize opportunities between urban and rural areas, reducing the drift of rural dwellers to urban areas.[4]

The social anthropologists' argument that industrialization must disrupt the rural economy and traditional life is, it has been said, "permeated with romanticism."[5] It might be added that a dismal picture has been justifiably painted of industrial life in Africa, primarily as a consequence of the distorted way industrialization has been introduced on that continent. The potential positive growth impact of a rationally planned industrial strategy is considerable.

It is the underlying hypothesis of this book that only by careful planning and implementation of an appropriate industrial strategy, carefully related to increased expansion of agricultural productivity, may the benefits here outlined be attained. To substantiate this hypothesis, this part seeks, first, to examine the limitations of the existing pattern of industry in Africa, shaped by the set of political-economic institutions inherited from the colonial experience; the main ingredients that should be considered in developing a strategy more likely to contribute to a balanced resource allocation; and the institutional changes needed to implement such a strategy.

Second, this part aims to explore the way agricultural development could contribute to and benefit from implementation of the proposed industrial strategy, first, by analyzing the constraints in the existing agricultural resource pattern and its implications for efforts to augment productivity and raise rural levels of living; and, second, by considering the way alternative institutional developments might affect realization of the possibilities for improved agricultural resource use.

NOTES

1. The importance of modern industry to development of rural is not a new idea; cf. R. K. Das, The Industrial Efficiency of India (London: P. S. King and Son, 1930). For the modern argument, cf. W. A. Lewis, "Unemployment in Developing Countries," World Today,

_____

new methods in agriculture to expand output per man in order to meet the needs of the expanding internal market.[3]

no. 23 (January 1967): 13-22; for Africa, R. H. Green and A. Seidman, Unity or Poverty? The Economics of Pan Africanism (Harmondsworth: African Penguin Library, 1968), especially Part III, Chapter 2.

2. See B. F. Johnston and P. Kilby, Agricultural Strategies, Rural-Urban Interactions and the Expansion of Income Opportunities (Stanford: mimeo, 1971; to be published by OECD Development Center, Paris); and C. Eicher, et al., Employment Generation in African Agriculture (Michigan State University, Institute of International Agriculture, July 1970). Mounting unemployment has been cited as a growing problem in both Lagos (cf. P. C. W. Gutkind, The Energy of Despair: Social Organization of the Unemployed in Two African Cities: Lagos and Nairobi [Montreal: Centre for Developing-Area Studies, McGill University, Reprint Series No. 8, 1970]) and Ghana (cf. data showing decline in employment in Republic of Ghana, Economic Survey, 1966 [Accra: Government Printing Office, 1967], p. 9).

3. Conference "Optimal Model for Development of Traditional Agricultural Areas" Department of Research on Industrialized Regions, Polish Academy of Science, 1969. (herein cited as "Polish Studies"); see also A. Rajiweca, "Industrialization and Structural Changes in Employment in Socialist Countries," International Labour Review, September 1966, No. 94, pp. 286-302.

4. R. J. Harrison Church, "Urban Problems and Economic Development in West Africa," Journal of Modern African Studies, December 1967, No. 5, pp. 511-20.

5. W. Smith, "Industrial Sociology in Africa: Foundations and Prospects," Journal of Modern African Studies, May 1968, Vol. 6, pp. 81-95.

6

**CREATING A
NEW PATTERN OF
INDUSTRIAL GROWTH**

It is all too evident that the inherited pattern of industry—insofar as any industry exists at all in most newly independent African countries[1]—is incapable of contributing much to a balanced, nationally integrated economy. What little industry has been built has led only to marginal changes in the export enclave carved out during the colonial era, changes that have if anything tended to reinforce the lopsided characteristics of the inherited dual economy.

This chapter seeks, first, to examine the limitations of the inherited industrial sector and, second, to explore the possibilities of creating a different pattern of industrial growth that might contribute more significantly to the spread of productivity to all sectors of the economy, creating the necessary preconditions for raising the levels of living of the broad masses of the population.

THE CHARACTERISTICS OF INHERITED INDUSTRY

The literature is full of examples of the problems inhering in the industrial pattern in Africa that duplicate those encountered in other developing areas.[2] First, the industries established are predominantly of three main types: (1) first-stage processing of agricultural and/or mineral exports primarily to reduce bulk and/or transport costs; these processing plants are seldom integrated into the national economy in a manner calculated to set off chains of growth in any significant direction;[3] (2) last-stage processing of luxury items for the relatively high-income elite associated with the export enclave (for example, beer and cigarettes and, in more advanced stages, assembly of private automobiles), which constitutes a disproportionate share of industrial output;[4] and (3) a few more broadly consumed necessities like textiles and soap. In East Africa, projects like cement plants were constructed in Uganda, mainly to save the 1000-mile haul from the sea, and in Kenya, where the settler market was larger than in any sub-Saharan country that attained independence.[5]* For the most part, in other words, the kinds of industries extant reflect the fact that decisions to establish them have been governed by profit-maximizing goals rather than the need to insure that they contributed to increased productivity in all sectors.

Second, those industries that have been built, with the exception of first-stage mineral and agricultural processing (which ordinarily took place near the initial production area), have usually been concentrated in the urban centers in the export enclave.[8] Thus about 60 percent of the employment and manufacturing establishments in Kenya are located in Nairobi and Mombasa, a percentage that increased in the decade prior to independence.[9] A similar pattern of concentration has emerged in all the sub-Saharan countries as a limited range of industries was built to take advantage of the existing market and emerging external economies.[10]

This concentration of industry aggravates the imbalance characteristic of the dual economy. The numbers of landless and underemployed agricultural workers have grown as agricultural production for export has expanded and population pressures have mounted in traditional areas. As elsewhere in the world,[11] the rural underemployed and landless have tended to drift into city slums looking for work. Statistics are grossly inadequate, but estimates suggest that in cities like Lagos, Accra, Nairobi, and Abidjan as much as 30 percent of the labor force may be unemployed.† Mounting urban unemployment has tended to contribute to tribal conflict as ethnic groups have accused each other of usurping the available jobs.[13]

Third, those few modern industries that have been constructed tend to use relatively capital-intensive technologies, reducing their

---

*Kenya's industrial sector, linked to the settler economy and selling within the protected East African Common market, produced 13.8 percent of Gross Domestic Product at independence,[6] a larger share than in any other independent sub-Saharan country, although significantly less than Chenery's study suggests for the average country, given its per capita income and population.[7] Rhodesia's and South Africa's industrial sectors, likewise linked to settler economies, still produce a considerably larger share of total GDP than those in any of the independent sub-Saharan countries.

†Gutkind describes the conditions and psychological impact resulting from their persistent unemployment, as well as how they have tended to organize.[12]

potential for providing employment.[14] On the one hand, these industries have in some cases undermined the few handicrafts industries that had survived the competition of imported manufactured goods. For example, modern shoe and sandal factories have reduced the market for the small handicraftsmen who formerly made shoes of leather or worn-out rubber tires.[15] These handicraftsmen have had little alternative but to join the ranks of the unemployed. On the other hand, construction of modern industries requires the import of expensive capital equipment and machinery, and often, in addition, semiprocessed parts and materials.[16] This tends to mesh these African economies more securely into overseas manufacturing-marketing complexes, actually heightening their external dependency.[17]

Fourth, this pattern of industrial expansion has contributed to growing balance of payments problems. The import of capital equipment and machinery, linked with the subsequent import of semiprocessed parts and materials, has not significantly reduced the value to imports, but only marginally altered their form. Insofar as these industries have actually replaced local producers using locally produced raw materials and implements, they may have increased the national economy's reliance on imports. It should be noted, too, that last-stage industries that have replaced the direct import of consumer goods have reduced government revenues in not a few cases where tariffs have been levied on final goods, since capital equipment and machinery and intermediate goods are imported duty free.[18] Heavy payments in the form of profits and interest* have aggravated balance of payments difficulties still further.

Finally, large-scale modern industries tend to be oligopolistic, if not monopolies, in the African circumstance. There is seldom room for more than one or two near-optimum-sized projects in any given field of industrial output in the limited markets existing in most African countries.[20] Even some of the larger countries like Kenya or Ghana have populations smaller than New York City or London. The notion underlying Western economic theory that competition will operate to insure the best allocation of resources is, under these conditions, reduced to a pathetic joke. Producing behind government-erected tariff barriers that exclude potential competitive imports, it is common for industrial firms to raise their prices to maximize profits, an added burden for low-income consumers as well as the entire domestic economy.[21]

_____

*Interest rates frequently run as high as 7 percent for capital equipment and machinery supplied under Western supplier credit arrangements, and principle is frequently to be repaid in five to seven years.[19]

Johnston and Kilby[22] argue that these lopsided features typical
of the industrial sectors of "late developing" countries stem primarily
from the inadequacies of pricing, taxing, and foreign exchange policies.
It is the underlying hypothesis here, in contrast, that these policies
serve only to aggravate consequences that might be expected as long
as crucial decisions relating to investment in industry are made by
private, mainly foreign, firms in the context of the narrow distorted
markets characteristic of the inherited dual economy. The objective
constraints affecting short-term profit-maximizing possibilities are
determined by those market and economy-of-scale factors built into
modern industry. They may be influenced, but not fundamentally
altered, by changing government policies affecting prices, taxes, and
foreign exchange rates. Small domestic entrepreneurs do not have
either the capital or the know-how to build modern industrial projects;
for the most part, insofar as they are not primarily involved in agriculture, they engage in trade and speculative real estate.[23] Only a
few—typically "big men" in government—participate in the industrial
sector as "token" African representatives on boards of directors of
foreign firms.[24]*

The pattern of foreign private investment in African industry
may be illustrated by the case of the United States firms that have
been expanding their investment in the newly independent countries
of Africa if anything more rapidly than those of the former colonial
powers. For the most part, United States firms, alone or as participants in multinational corporations, are primarily engaged in independent Africa in extracting raw materials:[25] pumping out oil (for
example, in Nigeria, Libya, Algeria, as well as the Portuguese colony
of Angola); digging out iron (for example, in Liberia, Gabon), manganese
(for example, in Gabon, as well as South Africa), copper (for example,
in Zambia, Zaire), and uranium (for example, in Zaire, as well as
South Africa); and growing crops like rubber (for example in Liberia
and, since the coup, in Ghana), bananas (for example, in Somalia),
and pineapples (for example, in Kenya).

The major industrial investments of United States firms in
industries outside the United States are not in Africa, but in Canada
and Europe, with some spilling over into Latin America. Where they
have invested in manufacturing in Africa, they have tended, like the

---

*In exceptional cases, like that of the former Finance Minister
Okotie-Eboh of Nigeria, Africans may amass enough funds through
their manipulation of state machinery to invest in such projects as
a sandal factory. In that particular case, since Okotie-Eboh also was
in a position to impose a protective tariff, the price of sandals was
immediately raised for the domestic consumer.

British firms, to invest in South Africa, where they may take advantage of the relatively large market of the high-income whites and the exceedingly low-cost labor of the African workers, sustained by the racist doctrines of apartheid.[26]

Where they have invested in the limited industrial sectors of independent African countries, foreign firms have sought—as they do in their own countries—to maximize profits under the existing market conditions. Firms extracting raw materials have sometimes found it necessary to process them before export to reduce costs, but, confronted by limited markets, political uncertainty, and shortages of skilled and managerial labor[27] they have tended not to build integrated industries in competition with their own plants back home.*

As newly independent African countries have erected tariff barriers to encourage industry, foreign firms have tended to locate last-stage assembly and/or processing plants in existing urban centers in African countries to take advantage of existing external economies and insure control of the limited internal markets.[29] They have shown a great reluctance to move to the hinterland, where the risks are greater and returns smaller. Since their aim is primarily to expand markets for their own goods produced in their home factories, foreign firms tend to fund projects utilizing their own capital equipment and machinery as well as, after completion, their semiprocessed parts and materials imported from their own initial processing facilities elsewhere. This tends to promote capital-intensive technologies, since their machinery and equipment is designed to meet factor supply conditions in their own countries, not Africa.[30] At the same time, since tariffs are not infrequently designed to protect even the higher-cost local handicraftsmen,[31] foreign firms are insured of profits significantly higher than they might anticipate at home. The average rate of profit of U.S. manufacturing firms in Africa was, according to reports to the U.S. government, 19.11 percent, the highest in any area of the world.[32]†

---

*This tendency is reinforced by the erection of tariff barriers by the industrialized countries against manufactured goods imported from developing countries, which, despite all declarations of good intentions to the contrary, remain and, in some cases, have even been increased in recent years.[28]

†That such reports may underestimate the real rates of profit is suggested by the fact that in East Africa the general experience is that foreign firms require profit rates of 20-25 percent if they are to invest at all.[33] This may be compared with the profit rates of 30 percent or more obtained by foreign firms investing in Latin American industry[34] or the 16.54 percent obtained by firms in the United Kingdom.[35]

The efforts of independent African governments to use such devices as tax incentives, licensing, tariff manipulation, and erection of industrial estates have to date not been sufficient to offset this pattern of industrial investment.[36] Foreign firms, with a choice of over forty African countries in which to locate their operations, may always move elsewhere if government requirements in any one country prove too onerous.

Inherited financial and trading institutions, basically those that emerged in the colonial era to finance export enclave activities, tend to reinforce the pattern of industrial investment decisions made by private investors. The financial institutions dominated by two or three foreign commercial banks through direct and indirect ties[37] mainly provide credit for commerce associated with export-import trade.[38] In recent years they have loaned some funds to the large foreign industrial firms, often accompanying loans made with the establishment of interlocking directorates,[39] but seldom to small, domestically owned projects. Numerous studies substantiate the assertion that "conventional credit institutions have . . . not paid adequate attention to the small industrial sector and suitable and adequate credit facilities have generally been lacking."[40] (This is discussed in Part IV.)

The large foreign trading firms that handle the bulk of the export-import trade could hardly be expected to pursue policies designed to build up African industries in competition with manufacturing firms back home with which, in many cases, they have direct ties through boards of directors and various financial arrangements. Some firms, like the United African Company, have built last-stage processing plants to protect their hold on African markets while avoiding payment of tariffs on their semiprocessed imported materials. They have been encouraged, if not required, to do this primarily by the imposition of tariffs by the host country; without those tariffs, there is considerable question as to whether they would invest at all. They do not, however, seek to integrate these projects into restructured African economies, for this would cut off their own profitable activities of importing parts and materials from their associated enterprises elsewhere. Furthermore, they exhibit few tendencies to pioneer in purchasing either locally produced items or those imported from lower-cost supply areas (which might be linked to opening new markets for African exports), because this again would tend to undermine their own profitable trade and links with firms back home.[41]

The companies often advance the argument that the alternative sources of supply are inferior and that their customers prefer their own brands. This may be so insofar as members of the higher-income elite associated with export activities have come to associate prestige with these brand names; but from the point of view of national development, to permit the sale of these old brands in competition with the domestic output can hardly be justified, even on grounds of a slight real (or imagined!) superiority.

The potentially serious negative consequences of leaving import decisions in the hands of foreign trading firms is illustrated in the case of the automobile importers, whose profit rates have run as high as 50 percent of investment.[42] These firms tend to utilize a considerable amount of scarce foreign exchange to import automobiles for private use, reducing funds available for the import of capital machinery and equipment needed to restructure the national economy. In Kenya, for example, the foreign exchange cost of importing private automobiles in 1968 equaled about three-fourths of the total investment in manufacturing in that year.[43] There is little incentive for such firms to shift the pattern of imports to foster domestic industrial growth. While this example is, perhaps, extreme, it illustrates the way foreign decision-makers may influence investment patterns in a manner contrary to the national interest of the African state.

In sum, the inherited pattern of industry in Africa has been far from conducive to attaining a balanced, nationally integrated economy capable of achieving increased productivity and higher levels of living for the broad masses. The kinds of industries established have tended to be limited to first- or last-stage processing of luxury items for the high- income elite and a very few broadly consumed necessities. They have generally been concentrated in the export enclave, aggravating the imbalance characteristic of the dual economy. Utilizing imported capital-intensive machinery and equipment, they have been incapable of accelerating the rate of employment in the modern sector; and instead, in some cases, have actually contributed to unemployment by undermining existing handicrafts industries. Dependent on imports not only for initial capital and equipment, but also for materials and parts, they have tended to contribute to growing balance of payments problems. Finally, large-scale modern manufacturing plants have tended to become oligopolistic, if not monopolistic, in the narrow markets of individual African countries, taking advantage of protective tariffs to maximize profits by raising prices; without those tariffs, however, there is no assurance that they would have invested at all.

Investment decisions by private entrepreneurs, both foreign and domestic, backed by associated financial and trading institutions, have tended to reinforce this distorted pattern of industry. Government efforts to use tax incentives, licensing, tariff manipulation, and industrial estates to offset it have been relatively unsuccessful in Africa, as elsewhere, because the major foreign investors could always adopt the option of moving to other African countries or even to other continents. Yet, as Johnston, Kilby, and others have amply demonstrated, such a pattern of industrial growth has contributed little to the spread of meaningful development.

AN ALTERNATIVE INDUSTRIAL ALLOCATION
PATTERN

There is considerable agreement on the need to reshape the existing distorted pattern of industry and related urban growth in Africa. As Church, a noted geographer, has declared:

> By restraining the top-heavy expansion of large cities,
> urban growth can be properly related to African society,
> agriculture, internal trade, regional development, crafts
> and industries serving real indigenous needs; rather
> than by relating urban growth, as hitherto, to European
> concepts, external trade, and largely expatriate industry.[44]

It is not too difficult to outline the ingredients of an industrial allocation pattern that might contribute more successfully than the prevailing one to increasing the productivity and the levels of living in all sectors of the national economy.[45] The details would, of course, need to be worked out carefully in terms of the constraints inhering in the particular resource patterns of each African state. Nevertheless, these broad outlines are set down here to suggest the possibilities in contrast to the distorted pattern of industry fostered by the dual economy type of growth. The critical features of an adequate industrial allocation pattern relate to the kinds of industries, their location, and the appropriate technology to be introduced in order to insure that industry and agriculture expand in a mutually reinforcing manner within the context of an increasingly integrated, balanced economy.

Kinds of Industries

A more appropriate pattern of industrial investment should be designed to foster the growth of industries capable of contributing to increased productivity in all sectors of the economy. At the same time, industrial output should contribute directly to the improvement of the material levels of living of the broad masses of the population.

1. <u>Farm inputs to increase agricultural production</u>: These should include fertilizers and farm implements designed in terms of the current level of farmers' skills and available capital, as well as the peculiar characteristics of tropical soils. Initially, for example, a country might produce locally a standard animal-drawn plough* and

---

*It has been reported that in Upper Volta many different types of animal-drawn ploughs were imported so that, even in the case of

such obvious tools as cutlasses, shovels, and wheelbarrows.* As the
farmers' levels of skill and capital are increased over time, simple
standard tractors might eventually be introduced. First, the basic
machine might be imported, and only some of the parts produced
locally. Later the entire machine might be produced for a larger
country, or, preferably, for several countries in a region, building on
the pre-existing base of parts production established earlier.

Some of the possibilities of this kind of industrial development
have been detailed in Johnston and Kilby's excellent monograph[47]
describing the historical experiences primarily of India, Pakistan,
Taiwan, Japan, the United States, and Mexico. The establishment of
the appropriate kinds of farm implement factories and repair shops,
they argue, should be based on a careful on-going research as to the
real constraints relating to labor, land, and capital in each country.
The appropriate technical innovations should be spread to all farmers
through carefully designed supplementary farm extension, trading,
and credit institutions to insure that they are widely used by all farmers,
rather than enabling a narrow set of larger commercial farmers to
expand their output through capital-intensive mechanization programs
that oust their smaller competitors from the market, aggravating
problems of rural unemployment and inequality.

2. Transport equipment to facilitate the expansion of internal
specialization and exchange: Bicycles and simple wooden carts could
reduce the prevalent arduous headloading that so sharply limits the
possibility of selling agricultural surpluses even in neighboring markets. The introduction of simple rugged standard trucks could broaden
the network of transport of agricultural surpluses for sale in more
distant consuming areas. Initially a single type of standard truck
should be imported in order to facilitate local production of bodies
and parts until such time as the national industry can produce the
entire truck. It is economically wasteful to perpetuate the import of
a variety of trucks simply to maintain the myth of competition in the
African circumstance. Public buses might also be produced, using
simple converted truck motors and frames with locally built bodies.†

---

these relatively simple implements, once one was broken, it was almost impossible to obtain the requisite type of spare parts without
a prolonged wait and the associated waste of capital.[46]

*In Ghana, when the world cocoa price plummeted in 1965, the
country confronted a drastic shortage of cutlasses, the basic tool of
all farmers, since there was not enough foreign exchange available
to continue to import them.

†The well-known "mammy-lorry" of West Africa might serve
as prototype.

These would facilitate greater internal mobility of the labor force as well as the sale of small agricultural surpluses and even manufactured consumer goods in more distant markets. Simultaneously, there should be a sharp reduction in the import of private automobiles to save foreign exchange for needed industrial and transport machinery and equipment.*

3. Construction materials to improve low-cost housing as well as to contribute to the many other types of building projects required to expand production: Utilization of local materials, including bricks, tiles, and lumber, could contribute to a reduction of imports of steel and concrete. Where cement is already being produced using local raw materials, as in Nigeria, Uganda, Kenya, and Tanzania, the importation of, or, if feasible, the domestic production of simple equipment, including hand-mixing machines and wheelbarrows, would facilitate use in local construction throughout rural areas. Timber could be processed to meet a wide range of construction requirements if local handicraftsmen could be given adequate hand tools, including saws, planes, and hammers. Attention would need to be given to utilization of appropriate wood preservatives. Local brick works, such as the open-air firing operations using local clays near Iringa in Tanzania, could provide cheap bricks that might considerably increase the longevity of local private housing, as well as schools and other community buildings, to improve rural living conditions.

4. Simple consumer necessities to meet the needs of the expanding internal market accompanying increased rural incomes: Textiles, processed foods,† and simple consumer durables, including wooden furniture, dishes, cups, pots and pans, could easily be produced locally. Some already are being produced by local handicraftsmen using very limited kinds of tools. Production of simple improved tools in domestic factories—for example, planes and saws as well as hammers, chisels, and axes—and eventually the introduction of simple power tools would facilitate the expansion of output.‡ A sharp reduction

---

*It has been suggested[48] that second-hand motors and bodies from developing countries might reduce the cost of providing transport, but given the difficulty of providing the needed range of spare parts, as well as the rugged use such transport facilities face, this possibility seems frought with difficulties in the African circumstance.

†These might be put up in returnable glass jars, permitting the establishment of small-scale food processing operations in rural areas without the heavy capital expenditure required for canning factories.

‡A study of consumer durables in 1,400 low-income households in East Africa showed that most of the furniture, baskets, and pots

of imported competing items would save foreign exchange and permit the expansion of these relatively labor-intensive projects to meet the needs of the internal market.

5. Depending on the rate of expansion of the population and the internal market, it should eventually be possible to build basic industries producing iron and steel, chemical products, glass, and so on. Initially, these would need to be designed to be at the lower end of optimum-scale projects producing a range of simple items that could contribute most directly to providing for the needs of and facilitating the expansion of the emerging industrial complex. Steel reinforcing rods and beams for heavy construction, for example, might provide a starting point for an iron and steel industry. Chemical fertilizer plants might contribute by-products that could be used in other processes. A glassware plant might produce the reusable glass jars needed for food processing on a small-scale rural level, as well as bottles and simple panes of glass for improved housing. The future potential of such industries needs to be considered seriously at every point to insure that each project, using local raw materials, contributes significantly to the rest of the growing industrial and rural sectors. This requires careful physical planning of the proposed linkages based on a detailed analysis of resources, available labor skills, and markets, as well as investment funds.

It is evident that a number of the tiny, balkanized countries of Africa—for example Togo, Dahomey, Lesotho, Swaziland, Sierra Leone, Liberia, République Centrafricaine, Chad, Gambia, Gabon—could not by themselves create the necessary markets or amass sufficient funds to create such basic industries on anything like even a minimal optimal scale. Even larger African countries, like Tanzania, Ghana, Kenya, Uganda, Madagascar, Somalia, and Sudan, are still smaller in terms of population and gross domestic product than New York City, Paris, London, or Tokyo. Herein lies the strongest argument for African unification on a regional and, if possible, a continental scale.[50] If Africa, as a whole, could unite, it would present a formidable political-economic unit of some 300 million citizens in a land area exceeding that of Western Europe and the United States combined, with some of the world's most valuable mineral resources. This would make possible a far more rapid introduction of basic industries, thus facilitating more rapid implementation of an industrial strategy designed to achieve increases in productivity and higher levels throughout all areas of the continent, including the most underdeveloped.

---

were produced by local "fundis" (handicraftsmen) working part or full time in establishments of less than three persons, using very simple hand tools.[49]

117

Unfortunately, however, this goal does not appear immediately realizable. In southern Africa, the required unity cannot conceivably be attained without first winning national liberation. Even in independent Africa, unification requires a major reorientation of the inherited political-economic structure. Given the existing political-economic divisions, it appears probable that independent African countries, particularly the larger ones, seeking meaningful development will have to begin to implement national industrial strategies to provide the kinds of industries needed to increase productivity in all sectors of their own economies on a more limited scale. At the same time, they should be working realistically to realize the broader possibilities inherent in greater political-economic unity with their neighbors, so that it will eventually be possible to unite their resources, capital, and markets to build the optimal-scale basic industries essential to more advanced levels of modern development.

Location of Industries

Many studies in both developed and developing areas have shown the necessity for more careful location of industries to avoid over-crowding of existing urban areas as well as to contribute to growth in less developed rural areas. Even developed nations like England have been seriously concerned with the necessity of spreading industries to stimulate growth in less developed areas.*

In the African context W. A. Lewis has maintained that the external economies emerging from the size of towns are probably "exhausted well before one reaches a city size of 300,000."[52] This suggests that efforts should be made to initiate pole-of-growth industries in smaller urban centers in less developed areas, rather than continuing to concentrate industries in major urban centers linked with export enclave growth. This would help to reduce the impact of past industrialization—where it has been introduced at all—in aggravating the lopsided development of African economies.

---

*It has been estimated[51] that each new manufacturing job created in an underemployed area in the United Kingdom creates one extra job in nonmanufacturing employment; that is, the total employment effect is doubled. On the other hand, if one person leaves an under-employed area, the loss of his purchasing power contributes to additional unemployment among those who remain; thus if 10,000 persons leave Scotland, probably little is changed in the picture of unemployment among those remaining.

The concept of a pole-of-growth relates to the establishment of an industrial project large enough to stimulate the spread of specialization and exchange in several directions simultaneously.[53] For example, the erection of a sugar processing plant might provide a market for local farmers to produce sugar cane as well as some food-stuffs for the workers taking jobs in the factory itself. This could increase the farmers' incomes and purchasing power for the output of other manufacturing projects in the area or elsewhere in the country. It could provide employment for underemployed farm workers without necessitating that they leave the area altogether. Flexible employment schedules in the plant could be designed to complement seasonal agricultural requirements. Domestic sugar production could reduce national imports of sugar, releasing foreign exchange to buy capital equipment and machinery for other projects. Bagasse, a by-product of sugar production, might be used to make paper and fairly durable cardboard. The chemical by-products of sugar production might contribute eventually to development of simple chemicals industries.*

Just what kind of pole-of-growth industry needs to be built in each region requires analysis and planning within the framework of the national plan designed to spread specialization and exchange to every sector of the rural economy. The selection of the particular type and scale of project to be located in a given area would, of necessity, be determined primarily by the character of available natural and manpower resources.

It has been argued[54] that the concept of poles of growth is of limited applicability in underdeveloped nations because market limitations, transport and communication deficiencies, and a primary structure of production "all make difficult the implantation of precisely those industries likely to serve as a leading or propulsive element." This argument hinges on the notion that pole-of-growth industries must generally be "capital-intensive, operate under increasing returns to scale, and cannot produce economically at low levels."† The counter-hypothesis here introduced is that planned poles of growth in remote regions may be relatively smaller scale as required by existing resource constraints in given contexts. A relatively small flour mill established in the 1950s in Iringa, Tanzania, for example, had major effects in stimulating cash crop production of maize, laying a foundation for further introduction of other small-scale industries as farmer incomes expanded. The establishment of such a "natural" pole of

---

*For a discussion of some of the problems, see pp. 122ff.
†See discussion on range of technologies available even for relatively capital-intensive pole-of-growth projects, pp. 120-126.

119

growth needs to be followed by consciously and carefully planned linkages within the framework of a national plan of development if continuing chains of growth are to spread throughout an entire area. Eventually, new, larger pole-of-growth projects might be introduced that could stimulate the spread of specialization and exchange throughout the region on a more advanced technological level.

African countries may be able to take advantage of "permissive" locational features that have emerged in recent years;[55] that is, modern industry may be more flexible in its locational requirements than in the past. Improved transport and greater mobility of labor appear to be essential aspects of this "permissiveness" needed to insure the availability of necessary inputs and markets as well as an adequate skilled labor supply. This suggests that initial pole-of-growth projects started on a fairly small scale may be expanded as transport and labor skills grow, tending over time to greater specialization and exchange.

Modern technology may make it possible to develop arid and semiarid areas for urban industrial purposes if adequate attention is given to essential requirements and the population has adequate skills and ability to participate effectively in the expanding resource use.[56] Since semiarid conditions characterize large areas of rural Africa, these possibilities should be explored extensively. It should be kept in mind, however, that unless essential prerequisites are considered, projects in semiarid areas may lead to the serious deterioration of the geographical features of the region. Hence careful planning is a prime necessity.

Although the particular pole of growth appropriate for each region cannot be specified prior to careful analysis of the existing resource possibilities, it is crucial that every region should have one. The national planners should incorporate these regional industrial projects into a national plan designed to stimulate greater participation by each region in the specialization and exchange spreading throughout the nation. These could be integrated into proposals for the establishment of smaller townships that would absorb some of the rural-urban flow that today crushes into the crowded slums of big cities throughout Africa.[57]

Capital- vs. Labor-Intensity

An industrial allocation pattern designed to contribute to restructuring the economy would need to incorporate appropriate technologies for specific projects, depending on their anticipated role in the context of the overall national plan as well as regional resource constraints. Lewis has made a useful distinction[58] between the substitution of capital-intensive machinery for labor to move things and capital-

intensive processes that can <u>transform</u> raw materials into manufactured products. Probably the biggest wastage of available resources
is incurred by replacing labor with capital equipment to handle materials in factories or to move earth in mining and/or construction.
These tasks only require unskilled laborers, who, if replaced by machinery, will be forced to join the ranks of unemployed. On the other
hand, where capital equipment contributes directly to the transformation of raw materials into manufactured goods, as in the case of a
sugar cane factory, or spinning cotton into yarn and weaving it into
fabrics, or smelting ores into ingots, then a fairly large expenditure
on capital may be required for the process to be introduced on an
extensive scale.

The fact remains, however, that given African resource constraints, many processes can and should be carried on using relatively
more labor-intensive, smaller-scale techniques than would be optimal
in developed countries.[59]* Planners should evaluate the probable contribution of the range of available techniques to the stimulation of
essential industrial growth.[60] In deciding the technological requirements for specific projects, they will need to weigh the relative increase in value added and the interest charges and foreign exchange
costs, as well as possible employment creation, the costs of training
skilled labor, and problems of marketing the final product.[61]

Many of the arguments concerning the necessity of utilizing the
most labor-intensive technologies in industry parallel those relating
to infrastructural projects. Studies of the latter have shown that
several alternative possible technologies are available for building
infrastructure, including feeder roads and small bridges as well as
larger trunk roads; but there is mounting evidence that "technologically
culture-bound" foreign experts—sometimes influenced by considerations other than the welfare of the African states involved—have tended
to design roads far exceeding initial requirements.[62]† National

---

*Even in England a movement has emerged calling for simple,
less expensive techniques, an "intermediary technology," to produce
relatively small quantities of certain kinds of goods for limited local
markets to avoid the excessive urbanization accompanying creation
of gigantic modern factories.

†The construction of a four-lane highway from Accra to Tema
in Ghana, with telephone booths at intermittent posts in case of accident, is only one example of this type of wasteful excessive construction.[63] The road was built several miles from the many local villages
that already existed along a pre-existing road, which therefore remains overcrowded while the truck highway is barely used. There
appears to have been an element of corruption involved here, since

planners have begun to learn of the necessity of scrutinizing available alternative technologies for constructing infrastructural projects to select the one drawing on the best possible combination of (abundantly available unskilled) labor and (severely short) capital supplies in order to meet the minimum requirements. This lesson is equally applicable in the case of industrial technologies.

It may be postulated that, given their anticipated role in the national economy, certain kinds of industries should be more capital-intensive than others. Pole-of-growth projects, certain basic industries, and export processing in particular, should probably employ relatively capital-intensive technologies, the first two because of their intended impact in increasing productivity in entire regions, the third because of the competitive requirements of the world market. Furthermore, it is evident that certain industries cannot be rationally dispersed except at considerable cost; perhaps the most evident example of attendant wastage is the attempt to split Nigeria's iron and steel project among three different states to satisfy political demands.[65]

Planners must examine the alternative technological possibilities for pole-of-growth projects with great care in terms of the availability of labor, markets, and capital in given regions as well as the requirements of the national plan. Dumont[66] has pointed out that large sugar plants suggested as potential pole-of-growth pole projects (see p. 119) are sometimes introduced too early in African countries, leading to considerable losses of funds due to the inability of the peasants to expand cane output rapidly enough, as well as difficulties in making the project work efficiently given the prevailing levels of skilled labor, and so on. In Tanzania, for example, the Kilombero Sugar Project[67] was started by a private British-Dutch consortium in the early 1960s when world sugar prices soared to £100 a ton, about twice the fixed internal East African price.* The project involved building road, rail, and air communications into the isolated Kilombero valley. About 7,000 acres were cleared to grow cane under overhead irrigation.

---

the foreign construction company that built the road admitted to bribing government officials to gain contracts. The company's own advantage, in this as in other cases, lay in gaining a higher profit as a percent of the more costly project. The government established in 1972 canceled the debts owed to this and other companies accused of having used corrupt methods to obtain contracts.[64]

*The world price increase was due to the United States ban on imports of sugar from Cuba. Until then, East African sugar interests had succeeded in maintaining the fixed £46 a ton ex-factory price— about twice the world price. The consumer paid about 50 percent more due to costs of transport, marketing, and so on.

Some 3,000 acres more were cultivated by outgrowers. A new town was built to house the 3,500 employees and their families. The plant added 30,000 tons to Tanzania's sugar output, including a sufficiently refined product for use in soft drinks, canning, and processing, thus ending all sugar imports into the country.

The project encountered serious problems after it was established, particularly in obtaining a regular supply of cane from the isolated valley where it was established. The cost of operating the machinery and equipment ran higher than had been anticipated—a problem commonly encountered in early stages of large-scale mechanized farming in Africa; yellow wilt caused crop losses and the necessity of replanting a resistant strain of cane; and unusual rains obstructed early harvests. About half of the initial investment was made in the form of supplier's credit from foreign interests; this had to be paid off, including a 7-percent interest—about £600,000 a year—before any dividends could be declared. About £200,000, 16 percent of direct costs, was also set aside annually for depreciation. As a result, management reported that the project had operated at an accumulated book loss that by 1968 totaled about £500,000.*

Dumont concluded from several experiences of this kind that sugar projects should initially be started on a smaller scale, producing somewhat less refined sugar at lower costs for broader consumption by the population. This is precisely the kind of issue that requires very careful study as to the appropriate pole-of-growth project that should be built given circumstances surrounding each region in the context of the national plan. Among the competing factors for consideration would be the potential scope of the chains of growth to be engendered by taking advantage of economies of scale, including the production of by-products as opposed to more immediate returns from an initial investment in several smaller projects.

The range of technologies available for various kinds of industrial projects varies significantly. Johnston and Kilby provide evidence[68] that suggests that industrial projects required to produce more labor-intensive farm and transport equipment—hoes and bicycles, for example —are themselves likely to create more industrial employment for funds invested than are projects producing more capital-intensive farm inputs like tractors. They are also likely to utilize a wider range of locally produced parts and materials, increasing the possibility of greater internal linkages and spread effects.

---

*The government purchased £300,000 worth of Kilombero shares, about 14 percent of the total, in 1968. It acquired full ownership in 1969, paying the former owners a total sum of £3.1 million over sixteen years for a present value of £2.4 million at 7 percent interest.

123

Johnston and Kilby also raise the question whether, given the high capital and foreign exchange costs of establishing an optimally sized modern fertilizer plant, it might not be economically preferable for a considerable period to import low-cost fertilizers produced by excess capacity now being established in metropolitan areas. The answer to this question must lie in a careful study of the technological and market possibilities, including the resource base, in given African countries. Certainly if regional projects could be established utilizing Africa's extensive natural deposits of fertilizer base materials, they would more likely be viable. If that is not feasible, research should be directed to the possibility of establishing technologically less complex fertilizer plants appropriate for individual countries.

Even factories producing the same kinds of items may vary extensively in levels of capital-intensity. In Tanzania,[69] for example, two integrated textile mills were constructed, both producing 24 million square yards of fabric annually. One was built near Dar es Salaam with an interest-free loan from China for Shs. 50 million and, at capacity, employs 3,000 persons. This project also produces 1,000 tons of yarn to be woven into cloth in other factories. The second plant was built in Mwanza at a cost of Shs. 80 million, of which Shs. 60 million was loaned by two French banks at a 7-percent rate of interest. At capacity it employs only 1,000 persons. Clearly the first project is relatively more labor-intensive than the second and, given the relative factor availabilities prevailing in Africa, would appear to have been preferable.*

Even for basic heavy industrial projects, the kinds and costs of technologies vary widely. The newer oxygen plant method of making steel, for example, is not only about nine times as efficient as the open-hearth converter (measured in hours required to produce an ingot of steel), but also less than half as expensive to install (measured in terms of capital cost for equivalent productive capacity).[70] On its face, it would appear worthwhile utilizing the oxygen method in Africa, unless other constraints are overwhelming. These kinds of examples argue for extensive feasibility studies before selecting any particular capital-intensive technology for a pole-of-growth, basic industry or export-processing projects.

Industries established to produce domestically consumed goods and to provide backward and forward linkages from poles of growth throughout the economy may well, at least initially, be considerably more labor-intensive.[71] Evidence is accumulating that the emphasis

---

*The Mwanza plant, using raw materials produced in the immediate region and providing industrial employment in a predominantly agricultural area, would appear to have been in a preferable location.

on increasing productivity through introduction of capital-intensive technologies may contribute to serious problems of unemployment and reduced sales even in developed countries.[72] In Africa the need to increase employment in rural areas of underemployment, as well as to spread incomes and broaden markets for expanding output of manufactured items, underlines the necessity of developing more labor-intensive projects wherever possible. This would appear to be particularly true in the case of consumer goods, like furniture and processed foodstuffs, as well as local construction.

Efforts to develop appropriate labor-intensive technologies for smaller projects, however, also require careful research into alternative possibilities. In India,[73] for example, the government invested significant amounts of money to subsidize the introduction of a hand-spinning technique that on first sight appeared somewhat more advanced than the traditional one. More careful examination showed that the subsidized technology maximized neither additional output nor employment nor reinvestment. Comparisons showed that the privately established modern capital-intensive textile industry more successfully maximized reinvestment funds. The traditional hand-spinning techniques maximized additional output and employment more successfully than the subsidized innovation, and even yielded higher reinvestment funds if the hand-spinners' average propensity to save was assumed to be positive. Clearly, while every effort should be made to encouraged local handicraftsmen to increase output through introduction of simple improvements in technology, the government should not plunge ahead to subsidize new innovations without very careful research as to available alternatives. Furthermore, it should be noted that government efforts devoted to expanding credit, transport, and marketing facilities to insure provision of the necessary inputs as well as broader outlets for goods produced may in some cases be more important than direct subsidization in stimulating artisans to adopt new ways to increase their output.[74]

Numerous studies have emphasized the necessity of providing education for local artisans and unskilled labor to enable them to operate the somewhat more advanced, but still labor-intensive technologies introduced.[75] Employment on smaller-scale projects provides peasant labor with the opportunity to learn more skills, contributing to the necessary creation of a more flexible labor force.[76]*

---

*In Poland,[77] for example, where industrial output has increased fourteen times in the last two decades, and industrial employment three times, special efforts were initially made to locate large projects in rural areas. Sociological studies there have underlined the necessity to provide vocational training at all levels to enable former

Planned Balanced Industrial and Agricultural
Growth

As available skills, markets, and reinvestment funds expand
through the spread of more advanced (still relatively labor-intensive)
technologies in the context of long-term plans for restructuring the
national economy, they will over time build the essential foundation
for the planned introduction of still more advanced, more capital-
intensive industries linked to increased productivity in both the industrial and the agricultural sectors of the economy. Planning is
essential to maintain the balance between expanding industrial and
agricultural output to insure the steady and balanced expansion of
incomes and employment.[78] The development of industries capable
of producing more advanced farm inputs and consumer items for the
rural sectors must be matched by the rural sectors' ability to employ
these new inputs at capacity in order to increase essential inputs of
raw materials for factories as well as foodstuffs for the growing industrial workforce. Expanding productivity per man and per acre leading to increased incomes for some in agricultural pursuits will eventually lead to reduced agricultural employment opportunities for others.
Expanding industrial employment must be capable of providing new
employment and income for those displaced.
Studies[79] indicate that planned industrialization may in a relatively short time lead to a considerable change in the entire traditional
outlook of peasants, who have been willing to commute long distances
to take advantage of new job and income sources in order to acquire
some of the manufactured consumer goods being made available for
the first time. This experience may be contrasted with the destruc-
tive consequences of industrialization in the racist context of South
Africa that has been explicitly designed to hinder the acquisition of
skills by African labor force participants.[80] The spread of planned
industrial growth throughout the national economy may contribute
to profound changes in the levels of living of rural populations without
the forced uprooting of major segments and the growth of urban squalor
in a few enormous cities.

---

peasant laborers to enter the industrial workforce. Significantly,
too, the process of introducing industrial projects has of itself apparently stimulated a considerable desire on the part of Polish peasants, both men and women, to acquire new vocations through more
advanced education.

SUMMARY

The inherited pattern of industry in Africa is narrow, directed
to a range of outputs primarily to meet the needs of the limited higher-
income groups associated with export enclave expansion, and to a considerable extent dependent for parts, materials, and finance on foreign
firms.
    There is fairly widespread agreement on the need to develop
new industry allocation patterns in Africa to attain more balanced,
nationally integrated development. The ingredients of a more desirable
pattern are not too difficult to identify, although undoubtedly considerable research is essential to work out specific details. In particular,
attention needs to be directed to insuring that the kinds of industries
established contribute to increased productivity within the context
of the spread of specialization and exchange to all sectors of the economy; that they are located in a manner designed to stimulate participation by all regions in the growth process; and that specific projects
are carefully designed to insure that the best available combination
of labor and capital is achieved to contribute to restructuring the
national economy. This argues for careful, on-going research and the
incorporation of the results in physical plans designed in view of
existing resource constraints to maximize their contribution to the
attainment of a nationally balanced economy.

NOTES

1. For a survey of the level and overall characteristics of industry in the African states at the time they were attaining independence, see UN Economic Commission for Africa, Industrial Growth
in Africa—A Survey and Outlook (E/CN.14/INR/I), December 1962.
2. Church, "Urban Problems and Economic Development in
West Africa," and Lewis, "Unemployment in Developing Countries,"
describe many of the general problems in the African circumstance.
For problems in other countries, see W. Baer and M. E. A. Herve,
"Employment and Industrialization in Developing Countries," Quarterly
Journal of Economics, no. 80 (May 1966): 88-107; P. Bairoch, "Révolu-
cion industrielle et sous-dévelopment," reviewed by J. Marczewski
in The Economic Journal no. 75 (September 1965): 611-13, R. R.
Nelson, "A 'Diffusion' Model of International Productivity Differences
in Manufacturing Industry," American Economic Review 58 (December
1968): 1219-48; M. Paglin, "Surplus Agricultural Labor and Development: Facts and Theories," American Economic Review, 55 (September 1965): 815-34; P. P. Karan, "Changes in Indian Industrial Location," Association of American Geographers, Annals 54 (September
1964): 336-54.

3. The limited degree of linkage between processing industries and the rest of the economy, even in Ghana, which has a relatively high income per capita (around $200), is described by R. Szereszewski, "The Performance of the Economy, 1955-62," in W. Birmingham, I. Neustadt, and E. N. Omaboe, A Study of Contemporary Ghana—Vol. 1, The Economy of Ghana (London: George Allen and Unwin, Ltd., 1966), Ch. 3.

4. In Kenya about 15 percent of the total value added by manufacturing was produced by the spirits, beer, malt, soft drinks, and tobacco industries (cf. Republic of Kenya, Census of Industrial Production, 1963, [Nairobi: Ministry of Economic Planning and Development, Statistics Division, 1965]), whereas in Ghana these same industries produced about a third of the value added by manufacturing as recently as 1968 (see Republic of Ghana, Two Year Development Plan, 1968-70 [Accra, 1968], especially pp. 50-52.). In Zambia the beverages and cigarette industry produced 40 percent of the value added by manufacturing as late as 1972 (Central Statistical Office, Monthly Digest of Statistics [Lusaka: July, 1973] p. 54).

5. For information relating to manufacturing projects at time of independence in Kenya and Uganda, see the International Bank for Reconstruction and Development, Economic Development in Kenya (1963) and Economic Development in Uganda (1962) (Baltimore: Johns Hopkins Press).

6. Republic of Kenya, Development Plan, 1966-1970 (Nairobi: Government Printing Office), p. 17.

7. Cf. H. B. Chenery, "Patterns of Industrial Growth," American Economic Review 2, no. 4 (September 1960): 624-55.

8. Church, "Urban Problems and Economic Development in West Africa," and "Some Problems of Regional Economic Development in West Africa," Economic Geography, no. 45 (January 1969): 53-62.

9. Compare data in Republic of Kenya, Industrial Production Survey, 1957 (Nairobi) and Census of Industrial Production, 1963 (Nairobi).

10. Church, "Urban Problems and Economic Development in West Africa," and Seidman, Comparative Development Strategies in East Africa, Part I.

11. Cf. Lauchlin Currie, Accelerating Development: The Necessity and the Means (New York: McGraw-Hill Book Company, 1966), for Latin American case.

12. P. C. W. Gutkind, The Poor in Urban Africa: A Prologue to Modernization, Conflict and the Unfinished Revolution, and The Energy of Despair, Social Organization of the Unemployed in two African Cities: Lagos and Nairobi (Center for Developing-Area Studies McGill University, Montreal, Canada).

13. Gutkind, The Energy of Despair: Social Organization of the Unemployed in two African Cities: Lagos and Nairobi, pp. 385-6.

14. Seidman, Comparative Development Strategies in East Africa, Ch. 6, and Ghana's Development Experience, 1951-1965, Ch. 10; for parallel experience on other continents, see Nelson, "A 'Diffusion' Model of International Productivity Differences in Manufacturing Industry," and Baer and Herve, "Employment and Industrialization in Developing Countries."

15. P. Raikes, Report on a tour of regions in Tanzania, Economic Research Bureau Seminar, 1969; and for other countries, cf. Nelson, "A 'Diffusion' Model of International Productivity Differences in Manufacturing Industry."

16. Cf. D. Seers, "The Role of Industry in Development: Some Falacies," Journal of Modern African Studies, December 1963, p. 464; and for other continents, see "The Economic Growth of ECAFE Countries," Economic Survey of Asia and the Far East, 1961, UN ECAFE, pp. 21-38; Nelson, "A 'Diffusion' Model of International Productivity Differences in Manufacturing Industry."

17. E.g., Uganda Government, Background to the Budget, 1969-70, pp. 15-16. The Latin American experience with import substitution exemplifies this problem still more sharply; cf. Nelson, "A 'Diffusion' Model of International Productivity Differences in Manufacturing Industry."

18. Uganda Government, Background to the Budget, 1967-68, section on manufacturing industry.

19. Cf. W. A. Lewis, Development Planning, The Essentials of Economic Policy (New York: Harper and Row, 1966), p. 142, for discussion of this problem. The terms of provision of suppliers' credit caused serious problems for the Ghana government's industrialization program in the early 1960s; see Seidman, Ghana's Development Experience, 1951-65, chs. 10 and 12.

20. Cf. Working Party, National Christian Council of Kenya, Who Controls Industry in Kenya? (Nairobi: East African Publishing House, 1968), esp. Ch. 12 and Part Two, for consideration of these issues in Kenya.

21. Ibid., Ch. 14, for Kenya case; and see Nelson, "A 'Diffusion' Model of International Productivity Differences in Manufacturing Industries," for parallel experience in Latin America.

22. B. F. Johnston and P. Kilby, Agricultural Strategies, Rural-Urban Interactions, and the Expansion of Income Opportunities (Stanford: Mimeo draft, 1971; to be published by OECD Development Center, Paris).

23. For Kenyan case, see Republic of Kenya, Economic Survey, 1969, p. 91; National Christian Council of Kenya, Who Controls Industry in Kenya? passim. For Ghana case, see Seidman, Ghana's Development Experience, 1951-1965, Ch. 10.

24. National Christian Council of Kenya, Who Controls Industry in Kenya? Ch. 13.

25. F. T. Ostrander, "U.S. Private Investment in Africa," Africa Report, no. 68 (January 1969): 38-41; and U.S. Department of Commerce, Survey of Current Business, current issues (Washington, D.C.: Government Printing Office).

26. U.S. Department of Commerce, U.S. Business Investments in Foreign Countries, A Supplement to the Current Survey of Business, current issues (Washington, D.C.: Government Printing Office).

27. A. O. Hirschman, Strategy of Economic Development (New Haven: Yale University Press, 1958), pp. 145-7; H. Myint, Economics of Developing Countries (New York: Praeger, 1965), p. 137; and, for reasons for locational decisions, G. Krumme, "Toward a Geography of Enterprise," Economic Geography, no. 45 (January 1969): 30-40.

28. See R. H. Green, "UNCTAD and After: Anatomy of a Failure," Journal of Modern African Studies 5, no. 2 (1967), for analysis of difficulties in attaining agreement on reduced tariffs by developed countries.

29. Hakam, "The Motivation to Invest and the Locational Pattern of Foreign Private Industrial Investments in Nigeria"; and Church, "Urban Problems and Economic Development in West Africa."

30. Cf. M. I. Kanien and N. L. Schwartz, "Optimal 'Induced' Technical Change," Econometrica, no. 36 (January 1968): 1-17.

31. Nelson, "A 'Diffusion' Model of International Productivity Differences in Manufacturing Industry."

32. Measured as the net returns of U.S. branches and subsidiaries as a percent of investment: see J. H. Adler (ed.), Capital Movements and Economic Development (New York: St. Martin's Press, 1967), Statistical Appendix, Table 6h.

33. National Christian Council of Kenya, Who Controls Industry in Kenya? Ch. 14.

34. Nelson, "A 'Diffusion' Model of International Productivity Differences in Manufacturing Industry," pp. 124 ff.

35. J. M. Samuels and D. J. Smyth, "Profits, Variability of Profits and Firm Size," Economica, no. 35 (April 1967): 348-55.

36. For two countries where this approach has been most explicit, see Republic of Kenya, Economic Survey, 1969, Table 1.6, p. 17, regarding Kenyan industrial growth pattern; National Christian Council of Kenya, Who Controls Industry in Kenya? Part II; J. Oser, Promoting Economic Development with Illustrations from Kenya (Evanston: Northwestern University Press, 1967), pp. 212-17. Regarding Ghanaian industrial growth since 1965, see Seidman, Ghanaian Development Experience, 1951-1965, postscript to Ch. 16.

37. National Christian Council of Kenya, Who Controls Industry in Kenya? Ch. 15; W. T. Newlyn and D. C. Rowan, Money and Banking

in British Colonial Africa (Oxford: Clarendon Press, 1954), passim;
A. R. Roe and M. J. H. Yaffey, "Money and Banking," in Svendsen
(ed.), Economic Problems of Tanzania (Dar es Salaam: University
College, mimeo, 1968); J. Loxley, "Financial Intermediaries and Their
Role in East Africa," University of East Africa Social Science Con-
ference, December 1966.

38. Cf. Report of the British Economic Mission on the Tanzania
Five Year Development Plan, C. R. Ross, Chairman, December 1965;
H. H. Binhammer, "Financial Infrastructure and the Availability of
Credit and Finance to the Rural Sector of the Tanzanian Economy,"
Dec. 30, 1968-January 3, 1969, University Social Science Council
Conference, Makerere; Republic of Uganda, Background to the Budget,
1969-70, p. 51; J. H. Garvers, "Preliminary Results of a Survey on
the Financing of Large-Scale Enterprise in Uganda," EDRP No. 122,
Mar. 17, 1967; G. R. Rosa, "Results of a Survey of Financial Demand
by Small-Scale Enterprise in Uganda," EDRP No. 111, Oct. 28, 1966;
and D. Hunt, "Some Aspects of Agricultural Credit in Uganda," EDRP,
No. 106, Aug. 8, 1966.

39. Cf. National Christian Council of Kenya, Who Controls
Industry in Kenya? Ch. 13.

40. H. M. Mather, Industrial Economy of a Developing Region,
p. 199.

41. The current relative profitability of that trade is suggested
by the fact that in 1969 Unilever reported lower profits for many products, attributed to inflationary costs, that were partially offset by
the profits of the United Africa Group (The New York Times, Nov. 5,
1970).

42. E.g., Cooper Motors report to the Nairobi Stock Exchange,
1967.

43. Kenya, Economic Survey, 1969, Table 1.10, p. 17.

44. Church, "Urban Problems and Economic Development in
West Africa," p. 520.

45. For a detailed examination of the possibilities of regional
industries by the United Nations Economic Commission for Africa
see Industrial Growth in Africa, E/CN.14/INR/1/Rev 1, 1962; Iron and
Steel in Africa E/CN.14/27, 1963; Iron and Steel in West Africa, E/CN.
14/IS/2, 1963; East and Central Africa Industrial Mission, E/CN.14/247,
1963; West African Industrial Mission, E/CN.14/246, 1963; Algeria,
Libya, Morocco, Tunisia, Industrial Mission, E/CN.14/248, 1964; and
Report of ECA Mission for Economic Cooperation in Central Africa,
1965; Industrial Coordination in East Africa: A Quantified Approach
to First Approximations, E/CN.14 INR 102, 1965. These reports and
some underlying principles are summarized in Green and Seidman
Unity or Poverty? pp. 232-262. Given that these regional industries
require major political-economic agreement and institutional coordination, these regional proposals are not likely to be implemented rapidly

(see A. Seidman, "Problems and Possibilities of East African Economic Integration," World Order Models Project (Makerere, 1970). The requirements of an industrial strategy and the consequences of alternative approaches on a national level have been considered in Seidman, Comparative Development Strategies in East Africa, Ch. 6, and Ghana's Development Experience, 1961-1965, chs. 10, and 15. See also R. Dumont, False Start in Africa (Washington, Praeger Publishers, 1966), Ch. 8. The possible consequences in terms of stimulating rural development are considered in Food and Agricultural Organization, Progress in Land Reform, Fifth Report (United Nations, New York, 1970), esp. Part V.

46. M. Patton, based on two years' effort to introduce animal-drawn ploughs in Upper Volta, in interview, 1970.

47. Johnston and Kilby, Agricultural Strategies, Urban-Rural Interactions, and Expansion of Income Opportunities.

48. J. R. Meyer, "Economic Development: Advanced Technology for Poor Countries—Transport Technologies for Developing Countries," American Economic Association, Papers and Proceedings, no. 56 (May 1966): 83-117.

49. I. Livingstone, Results of a Rural Survey: The Ownership of Durable Goods in Tanzanian Households and Some Implications for Rural Industry, Economic Research Bureau Paper 70.1 (Dar es Salaam: University College, 1970).

50. This argument is considered at length in Green and Seidman, Unity or Poverty? Some of the difficulties in attaining even regional unity are considered in Seidman, "Possibilities and Problems of East African Economic Integration."

51. D. Jay, "Distribution of Industry Policy and Related Issues," The Economic Journal, no. 75 (December 1965): 740.

52. Lewis, "Unemployment in Developing Countries," p. 16.

53. Green and Seidman Unity or Poverty? pp. 72, 239-40; see also H. Myint "Infant Industry Arguments for Assistance to Industries in the Setting of a Dynamic Trade Theory," in International Trade Theory in a Developing World; Hirschman, Strategy for Development, Ch. 6; and F. Perroux, "Note sur la notion de 'pole de croissance,'" Economie Appliqué, January-June 1955, pp. 307-20.

54. H. Tolosa and T. A. Reiner, "The Economic Programming of a System of Planned Poles," Economic Geography 46, no. 3 (July 1970): 45.

55. Krumme, "Toward a Geography of Enterprise," p. 38.

56. P. H. K. Amiran, "Arid Zone Development: A Reappraisal Under Modern Technological Conditions," Economic Geography no. 41 (July 1965): 189-210.

57. Church, "Some Problems of Regional Economic Development in West Africa," p. 62.

58. Lewis, "Unemployment in Developing Countries."

59. Dumont, False Start in Africa, Ch. 8.

60. "Strategy for Development," Economist, Sept. 12, 1964, p. 10.

61. "Economic Development, Employment and Public Works in African Countries," International Labour Review no. 91 (January 1965): 14-46.

62. Meyer, "Economic Development: Advanced Technology for Poor Countries.

63. Seidman, Ghana's Development Experience, 1951-1965, Ch. 8.

64. "Ghana: Popular Moves," Africa Confidential 13, no. 4 (Feb. 18, 1972).

65. Church, "Urban Problems and Economic Development in West Africa."

66. R. Dumont, False Start in Africa.

67. Cf. Kilombero Sugar Co., Ltd., Annual Report, 1967-1968; United Republic of Tanzania, The Annual Economic Survey, 1968 (A Background to the 1969-70 Budget) (Dar es Salaam: Government Printer, 1969), p. 76; and C. R. Frank, "The Production and Distribution of Sugar in East Africa," proceedings of EAISR Conference, January 1964.

68. Johnston and Kilby, Agricultural Strategies, Rural-Urban Interactions, and the Expansion of Income Opportunities, esp. Ch. V.

69. National Development Corporation, Third Annual Report and Accounts, 1967-68 (Dar es Salaam, 1968), p. 55.

70. W. Adams, and J. B. Dirlam, "Big Steel, Invention and Innovation," Quarterly Journal of Economics, no. 80 (May 1966): 167-89.

71. Cf. Church, "Urban Problems and Economic Development in West Africa"; Rajiewicz, "Industrialization and Structural Changes in Employment in Socialist Countries"; and R. K. Das, The Industrial Efficiency of India.

72. "The Productivity Myth," Economist, May 25, 1968, pp. 81-2; Baer and Herve, "Employment and Industrialization in Developing Countries"; and "Technical Progress and its Social Consequences in the French Textile Industry," International Labour Review, no. 92 (July-December 1965): 51-62.

73. A. S. Bhalla, "Investment Allocation and Technological Choice—A Case of Cotton Spinning Techniques," The Economic Journal, no. 75 (September 1964): 611-22.

74. Cf. I. Livingstone, The National Small Industries Corporation of Tanzania: An Examination of Current Plans and Prospects, ERB, Restricted Paper, 70.1 (Dar es Salaam: University College, 1970); and, for parallel with agricultural case, A. Mosher, lecture

133

to Economic Development Workshop, University of Wisconsin, April 11, 1967, regarding necessity to raise the "economic ceiling" through introduction of adequate marketing facilities.

75. Cf. "Economic Development, Employment and Public Works in African Countries."

76. T. Morgan, "Trends in Terms of Trade," in R. Harrod and D. Hague (eds.), International Trade Theory in a Developing World, Proceedings of a Conference held by the International Economic Association (New York: St. Martin's Press, 1964).

77. Polish studies.

78. FAO, Progress in Land Reform, Fifth Report, pp. 282-87.

79. Polish studies.

80. See summary of studies, W. Smith, "Industrial Sociology in Africa: Foundation and Prospects," especially pp. 87-89.

IMPLEMENTING THE
INDUSTRIAL STRATEGY

THE NEED FOR INSTITUTIONAL CHANGE

It is far more difficult to implement proposals for a new pattern
of allocation of industry to attain a more balanced, nationally-integrated
economy than it is to formulate them. Not a few plans for industrial
growth have been drawn up in Africa—and the record of achievement
is indeed dismal.[1] Both the logic of the situation, spelled out in the
model of underdevelopment, and a decade of experience in the newly
independent countries of Africa argue that a more integrated industrial and agricultural development pattern can only be achieved by
changing the inherited institutional structure governing decision-
making in the industrial sector.

This conclusion appears to be substantiated by the experience
of several countries outside of Africa. In India, for example, with a
much larger population and market than any individual African economy, governmental efforts (through licensing, tax incentives, and
so on) to persuade private entrepreneurs to locate industries in less
developed rural areas have generally failed: existing locational patterns there, too, have been reported to be self-reinforcing and will
probably continue to be so "unless concerted efforts are made by
government to intercede and alter the direction of growth."[2] In Australia, where six state governments have vied with each other to attract industry to their less developed areas (using techniques not
unlike those currently employed by the more balkanized states of Africa), results have been no less encouraging; in some instances, efforts to persuade private firms to locate outside overcrowded capital
cities have apparently caused them to move away from Australia
altogether.[3] Even in England a President of the Board of Trade concluded that only the exercise of public authority could assure the

distribution of industry in a manner required to insure full employment of labor and industrial capacity.[4]

There is plenty of evidence to substantiate the conclusion that the economic conditions for diffusion of industry to stimulate national development are no more favorable in Africa than in other less developed areas. In Africa, as elsewhere, these factors have been reinforced by elements imbedded in the inherited institutional structure, which shapes industrial investment decisions in a way that perpetuates the externally dependent characteristics of the inherited dual economies. Given the prevailing constraints imposed by shortages of skilled manpower and capital, a government strategy to implement the proposed industrial allocation outlined in Chapter 6 should focus on changes in the institutions governing critical investment decisions relating to industry. Only the central government has the capacity to mobilize essential skilled manpower (if necessary, hiring foreign management until African managers can be trained) and funds to invest in such projects. Furthermore, if these projects are to stimulate essential chains of growth, contributing to balanced development throughout entire regions, they need to be carefully planned and integrated into the overall economy in a manner that only the government can accomplish. Short-term profit maximization cannot be the primary criterion for establishing such projects. The government is the only agency fully capable of taking into consideration such crucial variables as employment and income creation, markets for local raw materials, and other linkage effects.[5]

The importance of state action to stimulate industrial growth in Africa is widely agreed.[6] What policies the state should pursue, however, remains a matter of debate. The aim of this chapter is to survey briefly the consequences of the postindependence efforts of governments of some of the larger African countries to make the necessary institutional changes to implement an industrial strategy directed at restructuring the inherited dual economy. In particular, an effort will be made to consider the kinds of industries over which the central government has sought to exert direct controls; the institutional forms through which the central governments have attempted to exercise that control; the potential role of trade unions in representing the interests of the workers in decision-making at national and plant levels; and the creation of institutional techniques for stimulating local initiative to build labor-intensive industries to provide essential linkages throughout the rural areas.

WHAT INDUSTRIES SHOULD BE CONTROLLED BY THE CENTRAL GOVERNMENT?

It is fairly widely agreed that the government should assume control over some sectors of industry in Africa, given private enterprise failure to develop an industrial sector capable of contributing to the spread of development. There is little agreement, however, as to which industries should be included in the central government sector.

The British initiated a degree of government control over some industries in its African colonies with the stated view of stimulating more development. These efforts were most pronounced in Uganda, where The Uganda Development Corporation (UDC)[7] was established in 1952 to stimulate the growth of import-substitution industries in an effort to overcome the heavy costs of the long haul from the sea. Among the most significant of the UDC manufacturing projects established in the preindependence days were the Uganda Cement Industry at Tororo; the Nyanza Textiles Industries (Nytil), at Jinja, purchased from private investors in 1957 after they had operated for three years at a loss; and the Tororo Industrial Chemicals and Fertilizers Plant, managed by an affiliate of Imperial Chemical Industries and Anglo-American with an American and a Canadian firm as partners. UDC controlled, through subsidiaries, a number of tea estates, a cattle ranch, and a chain of hotels and participated, in association with overseas firms, as a minority shareholder in hire-purchase, banking, mining, food-processing, and production of specialized building materials.

By 1966 the UDC had over twenty subsidiaries, assets with a book value of £21.3 million, and a gross turnover of £22 million. It employed over 20,000 workers, receiving wages and salaries totaling £3.9 million, and reported a profit of £2 million before taxes.

While still under colonial rule, Ghana's government invested some £7 million in industry, about three-fourths of it in brick and match-making, boat building, and timber and engineering projects.[8]

In Tanganyika the government acquired shares in a meat-packing plant and a cement factory, as well as the diamond mines, before the Arusha Declaration.

Once independence was attained, African governments had somewhat greater freedom to determine for themselves what industries should be brought into the public sector. The widely varied policies they adopted reflected both the lack of consensus on this issue and the varying circumstances of each country.

Ghana's government, for example, purchased the least profitable of the foreign-owned gold mines when their owners insisted they could not afford to pay the newly established minimum wages and keep the mines open. The most profitable mine, Ashanti Goldfields, remained in the hands of a foreign private firm. The Ghanaian Seven Year Development plan proposed a greater emphasis on export-processing as well as construction of basic industries, including a small steel plant, an oil refinery, technical engineering products, chemicals, and fertilizers. These proposals were not linked into a carefully developed overall strategy; rather they appeared to be based on some generalized notions about the potential role of a basic industries. In the event, the implementation of the plan was hampered by the financial crisis caused by the collapse of world cocoa prices, and the plan itself was terminated by the 1966 coup.

Kenya's government, after independence, issued its White Paper on African Socialism, which maintains that the government should only nationalize companies where the security of the nation is involved; productive resources are being wasted; private firms operate them to the detriment of the nation; or other "less costly" means of control are ineffective.[9] A Development Finance Corporation was established with funds provided by the Kenyan government, United Kingdom, and West Germany, later joined by an official Dutch agency. Its primary purpose was to encourage large-scale private investments. In the first years of its operation, it claimed to have induced over £7 of private, mainly foreign, investment for every £1 it had invested. The private partners managed the firms as well as putting up some of the capital. In addition, the government established an Industrial and Commercial Development Corporation to promote African industrial and commercial enterprise by lending funds to small African entrepreneurs and establishing industrial estates. In neither case, however, was it anticipated that the government would exercise direct control to insure that the projects would conform to roles explicitly formulated in the national plan. Once established, the projects, managed by the private partners, were to function essentially like any other private enterprise.

Following the Arusha Declaration, Tanzania's government took over all the major grain milling firms and a majority of the shares of the local affiliates of several foreign companies: the two large breweries, the tobacco monopoly, and the only big factories producing shoes, metal containers, and pyrethrin extract. By 1969 Tanzania's National Development Corporation held investments totaling about £18 million and employed about 20,000 people[10]—still less than Uganda's Development Corporation. The government staked out the areas restricted to outright government ownership to include the major grain milling establishments and the arms industries. The industrial sectors to be controlled by the central government—though not necessarily through full ownership—were defined as the major means of production, including land, forests, mineral resources, water, oil, electricity, communications, transport, steel, machine tool, automotive, cement, fertilizers, textiles, and "any other big industry upon which a large section of the population depends for its living or which provides essential components for other industries and the plantations." All other industries, not covered by the first two categories, could be financed by private firms with or without government participation, depending on their own desire, as long as they conformed with laws regarding employment conditions and so forth.

Zambia, like Tanzania, sought to extend state control over its industrial sector in the late 1960s. The Zambian government's efforts to formulate self-reliant policies were, in part, accelerated by the desire to reduce the nation's economic dependence on Rhodesia and South Africa, whose private financial and industrial interests had long exercised a dominant influence on the Zambian economy. As a significant feature of the Mulungushi reforms, a government development corporation, Indeco, acquired 51-percent ownership in twenty-four major nonmining firms. This action gave INDECO shares in assets far exceeding that of any of its East African neighbors. In 1970 Indeco reported its group assets to be worth almost $200 million.[11] The management of these firms remained in the hands of the private foreign partners, as it did in most of the other countries. Zambia's manpower training program, though sharply accelerated after independence, could not yet provide personnel to manage these projects.

In addition to its Indeco holdings, the Zambian government took over 51 percent of $980 million worth of assets of the two big mining companies, Roan Selection Trust (affiliated to American Metal Climax) and Anglo-American Company, which controlled its big mines. These were placed under the control of Mineco, the government mining corporation. Here too management remained in the hands of the foreign partners.

It is, perhaps, dubious whether the mere act of government acquisition of 51 percent of the shares of a brewery or a cigarette plant could be expected to contribute much to creation of a new pattern of industrial growth. In Africa these are relatively capital-intensive projects established in accord with profit-maximizing criteria for sale primarily to the higher-income groups associated with export enclave production; and to the extent that the sales of "European" beer, for example, spread into rural areas, they are likely to put small, more labor-intensive local drinks producers out of business. But the particular industries that the new governments took over in this fashion were, in part, predetermined by what already existed in the truncated industrial sector that had emerged in the context of the dual economy by the time of independence. As President Nyerere explained, the list of firms affected in Tanzania was short because "you can't nationalize nothing."[12]

In the African context, it appears probable that far more significant than the initial industrial plants taken over by the central government will be the new industries built to set off chains of growth throughout the countryside. Analysis of the possibilities and constraints inherent in the underdeveloped economies, along the lines of that in Chapter 6, suggests that the most important of these are industries producing the tools and equipment needed to increase productivity in all sectors of the economy; poles of growth; and relatively capital-intensive projects to process traditional exports to increase foreign exchange earnings as well as to produce additional inputs for local and regional consumption.

The Tanzanian Second Five Year Plan proposed four criteria for judging proposed projects designed to implement a long-term industrial strategy. These included:

1. The net foreign exchange effect: Specific projects must contribute to a positive balance of payments after adding the cost of importing capital equipment, materials, and supplies.

2. The real net contribution to domestic product: Projects should contribute significantly to national output by broadening the range of real local resources employed.

3. The budgetary impact: Account should be taken of the fact that the substitution of domestic for imported manufactures might result in a loss of import duties usually not fully matched by direct and indirect taxes on domestic output.

4. The social impact: Such factors as greater regional balance, as well as other possible social benefits of specific projects, including employment, should be considered in selecting given projects.

Critical examination of these criteria in light of the kinds of considerations introduced in Chapter 6 might lead to the objection that they remain too vague; they do not provide adequate guidelines for establishment of industries to change the pattern of productivity throughout industry and agriculture, nor do they put enough emphasis on the importance of regional growth and employment and income expansion. These criteria, and any others that might be proposed, should be rigorously tested and revised to insure that new industries built with scarce central government funds and draining the limited supply of high-level personnel really do contribute to implementing an appropriate long-term development strategy designed to increase productivity and raise the levels of living of the broad masses of the population throughout the nation.

CAN DEVELOPMENT CORPORATIONS DO THE JOB?

Once the decision has been made as to which industries to incorporate into the central government sector, both through acquisition and through new investments, the appropriate institutional arrangements must be designed to enable government control to direct further industrial development along the desired path.

The British Model

Most African governments, either before or upon attainment of independence, had established some form of development corporation, typically along the lines of a model established by the British. The Uganda Development Corporation, taken over directly from the British by the independent Ugandan government as its main instrument for fostering industrial growth, has been characterized as "a compromise between private enterprise and full state control."[13]

In a like manner, the Zambian government had taken over the preexisting Industrial Development Corporation upon attaining independence, and following the 1968 Mulungushi Economic Reforms, empowered it to spearhead the government industrial development policy. The corporation had first been established as the Northern Rhodesian Industrial Development Corporation in 1960 as a joint venture between the government, the British Commonwealth Development Corporation, and the interests that controlled the copper mines: Anglo-American, British South Africa Company, and the Roan Selection Trust. In 1964 the government took over 100-percent ownership, and in 1968 the corporation, entitled Indeco, became a 100-percent-owned subsidiary of the Zambian Industrial and Mining Corporation (Zimco), formed to hold the government's total mining and industrial portfolio. Indeco's sister subsidiary, Mineco, Ltd., was formed to hold 51 percent of the shares of the mining companies.

The typical development corporation is itself essentially a kind of holding company. It may invest in various large industrial projects by itself or jointly with private interests—usually foreign, since domestic private investors have neither adequate capital nor know-how. Once a project is operating profitably, the corporation charter usually provides that it should be sold to private investors in order to reinvest the funds in another project. Each particular enterprise, functioning under the umbrella of the development corporation, is usually organized as a public corporation, a form initially introduced in England to permit firms in the public sector to function as much as possible like private enterprise outside the state civil service bureaucracy.[14] This would seem particularly inappropriate in many African countries, where the most competent educated personnel may be state employees. The system hardly seems designed to provide adequate controls by the state planning and financial agencies over the public sector in terms of insuring implementation of the plan goals.

Problem of Control

1. The Ghanaian Case

Ghana's experience illustrates some of the problems that African governments have encountered when they have sought to gain

141

greater control over public enterprises through the typical development corporation. Direct government investment in Ghana was initiated by the colonial government, which created the Industrial Development Corporation (IDC) to help establish industrial projects. Once
they were going concerns, these were to be sold to private firms.[15]
Under the preindependence national government, the IDC established
small-scale import-substitution factories, supposedly designed to use
local resources. By 1960, of an authorized £8 million in government
advances, the development corporation was reported to have invested
some £7 million, often in partnership with foreign interests. An outside consultant agency commented that these projects were:

> (1) Usually small, (2) frequently irrelevant to any basic
> economic development goal, (3) sometimes unsuccessful
> as business enterprises, (4) occasionally involved in seg-
> ments of the economy in which nongovernmental business-
> men are its competitors or could supplant it, and (5) some-
> times continued after the IDC has completed its develop-
> mental purpose instead of being sold and the proceeds used
> for development rather than administration.[16]

Private partners, holding less than a majority of the capital,
were apparently able to obtain voting control of IDC-aided projects,
since government participation was often in the form of nonvoting
shares or loans.[17]
    In 1962-63, Ghana's Seven Year Development Plan called for
accelerated investment in the productive sector, particularly industry.[18]
The plan asserted that the government would continue to encourage
private investment, both foreign and domestic, but it would itself shift
a share of its investment to production in order to stimulate more
rapid economic development. Annual government investment was
to expand under the plan from £G9.5 million in 1963-64 to £G26.7 million in 1969-70, totaling some £G109.3 million for the entire period.
Private investment was expected to average £G17 million annually,
totaling about £G119 million for the plan period.
    The IDC, having sustained major losses, was dissolved under a
barrage of severe criticisms and investigations of corrupt practices.
Its projects, said to include twenty-two subsidiaries and nine associated companies,[19] were taken over by the Ministry of Industries and,
in 1964, handed over to a newly formed State Enterprises Secretariat.
The declared aim of this latter body was to create an organization
that would assume full responsibility for control and evaluation of
operating enterprises.
    The role of the State Enterprises Secretariat was still not com-
pletely clear in 1965,[20] however, and there appeared to be conflicts

between its functions and those of other ministries. Its policy, like that of its predecessor, was not to interfere with the day-to-day operations of affiliated enterprises; these were left to the boards of directors, typically consisting of politicians, private businessmen, and civil servants. It aimed primarily to assist in relations with government, to establish standardized accounting and statistical records, and to help overcome bottlenecks.

By 1965 only eleven state corporations reported profits, while six more had incurred losses. The steel project,[21] built and managed by a British contracting firm that later admitted to having given bribes to obtain contracts, was never profitable. Careful analysis suggests several reasons for the failure of state enterprises as a whole to make major contributions to the economic reconstruction of the country: (1) many were established without adequate feasibility studies; (2) most plants were large-scale and capital-intensive, exerting severe pressures on limited government savings and foreign exchange while creating relatively little employment; (3) most operated at less than capacity; (4) many relied in large part or entirely on imported parts and materials; (5) lower-level managerial personnel lacked adequate training; (6) excess numbers of workers were hired, apparently to contribute to employment targets; and (7) none had sufficient working capital.

These shortcomings are similar in several respects, with the exception of overemployment, to those exhibited by private industrial projects built behind tariff walls; but they appear to be aggravated by the lack of institutionalized checkup and controls that must, in the public sector, be substituted for the profit-conscious private entrepreneur. Apparently little or no attention was directed to planning how each project and its associated linkages would contribute to restructuring the economy.

In 1966 Ghana's Finance Minister called[22] for further measures to improve the management of state enterprises, including what would appear to have been a bare minimum: the requirement that they report on their accounts for the year. This indicates a critical lack of the kind of government control over the public-sector firms that is essential to insure implementation of plan goals. An interview by the author with one of the officials of the State Enterprises Secretariat in 1966 indicated that its top personnel, pressed with immediate problems, still had not thought out the organization's responsibilities. Each state enterprise was still encouraged to operate on its own along lines similar to those of private firms.

After the 1966 coup, the military government returned to the philosophy that the less government intervention in the productive sectors the better. It sought to sell as many of the state enterprises to the private sector as possible. Some efforts were initially made to tighten up on the audits of enterprises left in the state sector. Charges were made that deals were being negotiated to sell assets at less than their real value.[23]

In all, the Ghanaian experience tends to substantiate the hypothesis that the autonomous public corporation, a form initially designed for the British private enterprise economy, is not a sufficiently effective instrument for insuring adequate operational or financial control in the context of attempts to implement national physical plans to restructure the economy.

2. Tanzania's Efforts to Develop New Working Rules

Tanzania's government originally established the Tanganyika Development Corporation in 1962, in line with the recommendations of a World Bank Mission and later a U.S. consulting firm financed by U.S. AID.[24] Both had argued that such corporation might be expected to stimulate private enterprise in a manner similar to that of the Uganda Development Corporation.

The Tanganyika Development Corporation received a capital of £500,000 in addition to the already existing government holdings in the Williamson Diamond Mines (50 percent), the Tanganyikan Packers (51 percent), and the Nyanza Salt Mines (81 percent). In 1965 its name was changed to the National Development Corporation. It expanded to take over the assets of the Tanganyikan Agricultural Corporation, created earlier by the colonial government to take over the assets of the ill-fated Groundnut Scheme. Essentially, its structure was like that of Ghana's IDC or Uganda's UDC.

The Tanzanian government, in line with its post-Arusha Declaration policies of self-reliance, began to revise the working rules governing the National Development Corporation. It had, it should be remembered, gone considerably further than Ghana's government under Nkrumah in taking over export-import and internal wholesale trade, as well as the commercial banks,* so that it was in a position to re-examine the National Development Corporation's policies within a broader context of direct government controls.

Several issues emerged as important in the process of reorganizing the National Development Corporation. The first concerned the relationship of the National Development Corporation to the entire ministerial structure of government. The ministerial system, inherited from the British, has tended to perplex the independent government of every former British colony. Each minister is a politician, jealous of his prerogatives and responsible primarily for his own area

---

*See parts III and IV for discussion.

of government. In the past, the Tanzania Treasury had a sort of veto power over projects proposed by each ministry through its control of the purse strings. In 1964 Devplan had acquired overall direction of economic policy subject to final control by the cabinet. The fact that six ministers sat on the board of the National Development Corporation was expected to provide for adequate coordination of its role as the instrument for industrial development with the other ministries' activities. Each minister was fully engaged with his own area of responsibility, however, which left him little time to devote to the complexities of NDC policy. All of this created the possibility that inadequate consideration might be given to potential linkages of specific industrial projects within overall development strategy. In 1969 the authors of Tanzania's Second Five Year Plan (1970-1974) proposed a more careful delineation on the role of the various ministries in planning and implementing proposed industrial projects.[25]

The second issue related to the fact that the management of almost all NDC affiliates and subsidiaries was carried out by private foreign partners. Their aim was—as it must be expected to be—the maximization of their own profits.* Possible conflicts of interest might be envisaged here. For example, in the case of Tanganyika Packers, originally established jointly by the colonial government and Leibig to process Tanganyikan livestock for export, the relatively low rate of return over turnover could reflect the fact that the overseas firm of Leibig has a monopoly over the purchases of the final product; a low price—including only a relatively low profit on the local product—might reduce the share of investible surplus retained by the government. If this were so, Leibig's international returns would have been enhanced by higher profits accumulated by its overseas associates.

When the Tanganyika Packers experienced a loss in 1967 due to the spread of hoof-and-mouth disease, the government, with a majority of shares, bore the major burden of the loss. Leibig's international profit picture suffered relatively less since it could simply shift to another source of supply.

---

*Helleiner remarked, "Management contracts undertaken. . . may involve costs that are every bit as heavy as the costs to the economy would be if the corporation in question were fully under direct foreign ownership. . . . [Tanzania's] bargaining strength is so weak that the cost of the servicing of human capital may well have risen considerably. . . . Research upon the present terms of management contracts is urgently required. It is extremely difficult, however, to obtain information about them. Both parties to these contracts guard their terms so carefully that this alone is grounds for suspicion."[26]

In the case of the Dar es Salaam Portland Cement Plant, the management recommended building a second plant near the first to double output to meet growing national demand. It is possible that a preferable location might have been in northeastern Tanzania, but the plant management, with interests also in its Kenya plant, may have wished to reduce competition with Kenyan supplies imported by rail. Furthermore, the cement project does have a fairly high rate of return in relation to turnover, but this appears to be because a relatively high price has been set for the cement output. While the high price maximizes profits for the shareholders, including the foreign partners, who own 49 percent of the shares, it also raises the cost of this important construction item for local development projects, a major share of which are built by government. It is conceivable that national welfare would in this instance dictate a lower price and lower profits to reduce the costs of development in Tanzania itself.

These illustrations are introduced only to show that potential conflicts may exist between the interests of the private managements of projects and national welfare despite state ownership of the majority of the shares. They pose the question as to whether the institutional arrangement for management of the government industrial sector through NDC provided for adequate consideration of overall policy matters such as location, profits, and pricing in relation to national requirements.

A third issue concerned a National Development Corporation subsidiary, the Tanzania Finance Co., Ltd. (Tafco), which appeared to constitute something of an anomaly in a country declaring a perspective of increased socialization. Tafco held National Development Corporation shares in Tanganyika Packers, Tanzania Breweries, Sisal Enterprises, Nyanza Salt Mines, and others.[27] Industrial Promotion Services (T), as the main private participant, held a small percent of Tafco's total share capital of £2 million. The Tanzanian government has taken a 20-percent share of the Industrial Promotion Services (T) stock. The remainder of Industrial Promotion Services (T)'s £2.5 million investment in Tanzania was in a variety of projects producing cotton and rayon piece goods, blankets, sisal cordage, hosiery and knitwear, shirts, nails, suitcases, primus stoves, and pharmaceuticals. Planned projects included a major tourist development program, a rubber sheeting and strap factory, an office block in Dar es Salaam, and a real estate company. Mr. Paul Bomani, speaking as Chairman of both Devplan and the National Development Corporation, described Tafco as the instrument through which the government intends "to sell off part investments of our equity to the people of Tanzania and to use the proceeds for investment in new projects."[28] This sounds much like the approach typically adopted by British-type development corporations, but how it fits into the socialist perspective is unclear.

146

In short, the Ghanaian and Tanzanian experiences illustrate the serious problems confronted by African governments in attempting to adapt the development corporation, originally designed for a predominantly market economy, to implement an appropriate industrial strategy. Government planners seriously concerned with restructuring the national economy need to re-examine the entire set of institutions and working rules governing the central government's industrial sector to insure that it does play its anticipated role in implementing long-term development plans.

TRADE UNIONS AND THE WORKERS' ROLE
IN LARGE-SCALE INDUSTRY

Discussion of the kinds of institutional changes required to insure that industries held in the central government sector play their essential part in restructuring the economy would not be complete without some consideration of the role of trade unions. It has been posited above that the new political-economic institutions created in Africa should be designed to insure participation at all levels of decision-making by those who may be expected to gain from the economic development. This includes the wage earners increasingly employed in the relatively modern, large-scale industries likely to predominate in the central government sector as the transformation of the economy takes place. Their rights and interest must also be represented in those industries still managed and owned in part or wholly by private firms in the mixed economy.

There is not space here to deal with this issue, despite its importance; but the parameters of the problem should at least be outlined in any discussion of reshaping the institutions designed to implement an appropriate industrial strategy.

Colonial Trade Union Policy

The role of the trade unions in postindependence Africa has been significantly influenced by their preindependence history. Prior to World War II, the British colonial governments, for the most part, endorsed company and settler opposition to any form of trade unionism. After the war, the British policy changed somewhat under the direction of the Labour Party. In part the changes constituted a response to a ground swell of strikes among African workers all across the continent. Some of them were general strikes, which spread to all sectors of the wage economy. Not only did the workers demand wage increases to match soaring postwar prices. The more militant workers' organizations provided a real impetus and a mass base for the national independence movements in which members of the African elites were beginning to show interest.

A two-pronged policy was adopted by the British in response to growing demands for trade union rights. On the one hand, the most outspoken leaders of striking workers were jailed, and efforts were made to dismantle their organizations. On the other, a system of official government registration was established to force recognized unions to conform to certain requirements. Registered unions had to provide lists of their members and annual reports on their finances. They were expected, too, to refrain from outright political activity. The effect of these policies was to weaken the more militant unions, opening the path for more "cooperative" elements to organize the workers.

The consequences of this two-pronged British policy is illustrated by the Kenyan experience described by Sandbrook.[29] The East African Trades Union Council was formed in May 1949 to provide organized workers with a channel for achieving political as well as collective bargaining goals. Predictably, the Kenyan government refused it the right to register. It was denied permits for mass meetings and its leaders were arrested. When it called a general strike in Nairobi in response to the arrests, a massive show of force by the army as well as the police and the arrest of some 300 more workers led to its demise.

The Kenyan Labour Department's Annual Report of 1950 declared that with the disappearance of the East African Trades Union Council the "field was left clear for . . . this policy of the gradual growth of trade unions pursuing narrow industrial goals . . . [and] 'simpler' alternative forms of employee representation than trade unions."

The Regulation of Wages and Conditions of Employment Act in 1959 provided for formation of wages councils for various industries in a further effort to discourage broader trade unionism. In 1952 the Registrar of Trade Unions was given discretion to determine when unions might be registered and who would be allowed to assume union office. Compulsory arbitration was extended to almost all the major industries in the early 1950s. Measures taken following the proclamation of a state of emergency in 1952, designed to defeat the guerrilla forces mobilizing in the forests, reduced the trade unions "to mere shells, with few members weakly led." Only the Kenya Federation of Registered Trade Unions, formed in June 1952, later the Kenya Federation of Labour, was able, with financial backing from the International Confederation of Free Trade Unions (ICFTU), to survive to play a moderate political role. Led by Tom Mboya, and with the support of American and British unions from abroad, the federation managed to retain the right of registration privileges throughout the 1950s. As independence neared, the federation leaders, Mboya in particular, were given an opportunity to participate in the new Kenyan government.

The colonial government's policy of containing the Kenya trade unions, despite particular features related to the antiguerrilla warfare policies of the 1950s, was not fundamentally dissimilar from that adopted elsewhere in Africa.[30]

The colonial governments sought to confine the wage earners' movements to "bread and butter" unionism, collective bargaining for higher wages and better working conditions within fairly narrow limits. This approach was fostered by training and financial support provided by the colonial government and by the International Confederation of Free Trade Unions. It was almost inevitable that such policies would influence the role trade union leaders would seek to play after independence had been won.

Trade Unions After Independence

Upon attainment of independence, the new governments confronted the necessity of making a host of decisions as to the appropriate role to be played by the trade unions. Three main questions have emerged:

1. What role should trade unions play in mobilizing workers to increase productivity in the mixed economies typical of African, characterized by private as well as public ownership of significant sectors of the economy?
2. To what extent should trade unions exercise their bargaining power to raise wages when this might reduce available surpluses for investment in restructuring the economy?
3. To what extent should trade union leaders, representing the interests of the workers, participate in the crucial decisions directing the national plan and the government instruments—like the development corporations—for implementing it?

Each independent government has wrestled with these questions in its own way. In each case, the final outcome has inevitably been influenced by the extent to which the government really seeks to restructure the economy in the interests of the broad masses of the population. It has been influenced, too, by the degree to which the trade unions and their members are themselves fully cognizant of the issues and support the government in its efforts to implement that perspective. Attainment of worker understanding of the issues is probably rendered more difficult because of the lack of formal education on the part of the union members. It has also been hindered by the existence of a union bureaucracy carefully nurtured to adopt a narrow ideology of bargaining over wages without responsibility for national problems and politics.

149

Most government leaders have urged trade union members to augment their productivity, and have sought by various means to reduce labor disputes and work stoppages. In most countries the predominant conflict has been over the appropriate wages policy; this has inevitably plagued the issue of the role trade unions should play in mobilizing workers to increase productivity. The wages issue will be considered in the context of the discussion of the formulation of an appropriate incomes policy and national financial planning.* Here it is intended to deal primarily with the third question, that is the extent to which workers and their representatives have been involved in decision-making concerning the plan and its implementation in a manner calculated to convince them that it really is designed to contribute to their benefit.

In few African countries have trade unionists been incorporated in top-level government positions and political posts. Even where they are, questions have been raised as to whether they actually do represent the workers' interests. This may again be illustrated in the case of Kenya, where several trade union leaders have been appointed to a number of governmental boards—including some public corporations—where they "participate together with members of the political and economic elites."[31] But their mere presence may not be sufficient to insure that the workers' interests are represented, particularly if they are not firmly committed to trade unionism, "but view it as a convenient 'springboard' into politics."

To evaluate whether this charge is true in any given instance would require careful scrutiny of the system of organization, communication, and feedback between the union leaders and their members.[32] Analysis of the postindependence policies of the Kenyan government toward unions suggest that they have been increasingly designed to control the unions to insure conformance with government perspectives, rather than to represent their members' concerns. A wave of strikes spread throughout Kenya in the early sixties, mainly wildcat strikes on farming and plantation industries as workers in these sectors sought to realize the economic benefits of "uhuru." An effort was made to set up a second trade union federation with an outright socialist perspective. The parliamentary majority passed a series of laws to enable to government "to safeguard national unity and to avoid unnecessary damage to our economic development." The two national trade union federations were deregistered and a new one, the Central Organization of Trade Unions (COTU), was established under close government supervision. The President of the Republic appointed the top officials, and informal rules required that the

---

*See pp. 248-255.

Registrar of Trade Unions' office should examine COTU's expenditures. In 1969 the Minister of Labour announced that the salaries and allowances paid to COTU officials were to be cut by varying amounts and certain administrative posts were to be abolished. The right to strike was restricted, at first informally, and then formally, by the requirement that unions would only call strikes with the approval of the national center. Politically, a firm though informal rule requires that COTU leaders must not only be loyal to the government but must support the governing party. Several union leaders have been detained for allegedly "subversive" activities. At the same time, the government has granted the trade unions a compulsory "checkoff" system permitting them to collect dues from the employers before the workers are paid, thus reducing the workers' potential control.

This history of Kenyan trade unions after independence leads Sandbrook to conclude that the participation of union leaders in government positions and on the boards of public corporations does not imply that they represent the interests of the workers: the Kenyan government has "operated on the principle that trade unionists, if allowed to share in the confraternity of power, are less likely to regard themselves as having distinctive interests conflicting with those of the political elite."

The role of trade union leaders on the national level may be evaluated from a second angle: to what extent may it be said that the government policies do in fact contribute to restructuring the economy to meet the needs of the broad masses of the population, including both workers and peasants? It is difficult to involve trade union members in national economic planning, at least in initial stages, because of their lack of information and understanding of the relatively complex economic issues involved. Furthermore, to the extent that they have been trained to view their role from the narrow perspective of their own wage advantage, they may overlook the crucial importance of restructuring the economy to involve the vast rural populations in the spreading national pattern of specialization and exchange. Hence it would appear vital that evaluation of the role of trade union leaders on the national level include analysis of the extent to which government policies, which trade unionists have been in a position to influence, are designed to attain these broader goals.

By this yardstick also, the Kenyan trade union leaders' participation in governing bodies may be said to fall short of desired performance. It has been remarked that "the direction of Kenya's economic progress and its long-term socio-political implications are the source of some disquiet," adding up to "the unfortunate and politically explosive perpetuation of existing distribution inequities."[33] If this is true, it suggests that the trade union leaders' presence on Kenya's government boards has not contributed significantly to formulation of appropriate policies. Hence one might indeed subscribe to the view that they had been "coopted."

Not many efforts have been made in former British colonies to provide for worker participation in the management of the plants in which they work. Nkrumah's Ghana, in the early 1960s, and Tanzania, in the early 1970s, announced plans to attain this goal. In the Ghanaian case, these efforts ended after the 1966 coup; and the increasing antagonism between postcoup governments and the "workers," expressed in growing numbers of strikes and lockouts, culminated in the dissolution of the trade union congress just before the second military coup in 1972. In Tanzania the political party, TANU, issued Guidelines in 1971 that stressed that only through workers' involvement in plant management could the workers be made to feel the necessity of working harder to fulfill national plans. Attainment of this goal, the Guidelines emphasized, required revising inherited work patterns in all fields:

> The truth is that we have not only inherited a colonial governmental structure but have also adopted colonial working habits and leadership methods. For example, we have inherited in the government, industries, and other institutions the habit in which one man gives the orders and the rest just obey them. If you do not involve the people in work plans, the result is to make them feel a national institution is not theirs, and consequently workers adopt the habits of hired employees.[34]

The attempt to involve workers is rendered more difficult not only by the historical exclusion of workers from the entire management field, but also the workers' lack of information needed to enable them to make useful contributions to appropriate decisions. For such proposals to be worth more than the paper on which they are written requires an extensive education campaign among the workers, involving them at all levels in discussions of the issues and their relationship to overall national plans. Initially, worker participation might most successfully relate to in-plant production possibilities and improved labor relations. Gradually, over time, it might be extended to broader issues of the relationship of the plant's production and pricing policies to national economic reconstruction.

The growing involvement of workers in decision-making appears to necessitate a two-way education process involving both workers and managers. Management, usually expatriate or Africans educated by expatriate predecessors or elitist institutions, also needs to be re-educated to encourage worker participation. The Tanzanian Party Guidelines argue that the Party itself must play a central role in this process: It "has a duty to emphasize its leadership on this issue."[35]

It has been possible only to attempt to outline the main issues of the participation of trade unions and their members in national and local economic decision-making. Nevertheless, it appears crucial that the entire set of institutions and attitudes be reviewed if wage workers are to play a constructive role in implementing plans to re-structure the national economy.

LOCAL INITIATIVES TO BUILD RURAL INDUSTRIES

It has been emphasized that usually only the central government is capable of exercising adequate control and mustering the capital, high-level manpower, and markets to create huge, relatively capital-intensive projects to provide poles of growth, basic industries, and export processing. Nevertheless, planners need to formulate new working rules to stimulate local initiative to insure that more labor-intensive, small-scale industries spread throughout the rural areas in the context of the national plan. The range of small-scale industrial activities that might be established in rural areas includes: local processing of agricultural produce for domestic consumption as well as for export; repair and eventually the production of simple farm tools; and the output of locally consumed household items and con-struction materials.

A base already exists for this kind of expansion in most rural areas in Africa, where local handicraftsmen are still producing con-sumer necessities despite the inroads of mass-produced commodities in urban and some rural markets in cash crop areas. A survey of consumer goods used in rural Tanzania showed that local handicrafts-men, using little more than chisels and knives, still produce a range of wooden household items such as stools, doors, and cocoa-nut shred-ders. Others use local clay to produce pottery. Some weave mats of locally grown fibers for various household uses.

Studies made in Uganda likewise show that small private entre-preneurs have tended, more than big foreign enterprises, to locate away from export enclave urban centers, but they lack access to credit facilities needed to expand.[36] An analysis of Ghana's industrial struc-ture shows that private domestic entrepreneurs, producing locally consumed items like vegetable oils, dried fish, furniture, are far more widely dispersed than large, modern capital-intensive projects.[37]

National planners may, in a variety of ways, provide the nec-essary incentives and supporting activities to stimulate rural initiatives to expand labor-intensive industrial activities in the context of the national plan. The national government itself, either alone or in co-operation with local governments, may need to provide major physical infrastructure and centralized marketing, transport, and storage facil-ities. Local groups may be encouraged to supplement these by their own self-help projects to build feeder-roads and local storage facilities.

These are essential to link local villages to national markets and supplies of inputs, enabling local producers to ship their surplus produce to other areas of the country. In a sense, the central government will thus be creating the institutions and infrastructure necessary for the expansion of internal trade parallel to those established in earlier decades by the colonial government and foreign trading firms to create the market outlets that enabled African peasants to use underemployed labor and land to expand their output of cash crops for export; only now they will be directed by government to facilitate internal specialization and exchange. Marketing cooperatives alone or in partnership with state agencies may be encouraged to enter into processing agricultural produce[38] before sale to provide additional jobs for and augment the incomes of local producers. This arrangement is already fairly common for export crops. It might be more widely introduced to increase the possibility of selling otherwise perishable items like fruits and vegetables throughout the national market.

To foster the spread of small-scale rural industries, the national government will probably have to go further, in cooperation with local groups, by providing technical personnel and construction materials to facilitate provision of power, water supplies, education, and health facilities.

Government technical assistance may facilitate the introduction of improved but still relatively labor-intensive technologies. National, relatively more capital-intensive industries will probably have to produce improved tools and equipment to enable local industries to expand their output: even saws and planes would be an advance in some areas; and eventually small power-driven tools should be devised to suit local needs. Individual handicraftsmen and small entrepreneurs may be encouraged to combine their limited funds through some form of cooperative to purchase improved tools and equipment produced by new national industries. Appropriate credit institutions should be devised to enable them to buy the necessary inputs.

Local village governments may contribute to internal specialization and exchange by building simple industrial projects in the context of community self-help plans. In the multipurpose "ujamaa" village cooperatives in Southwestern Tanzania, for example, participants in some fifteen villages involving about 1,500 inhabitants built a combination flour-saw mill in an ingenious operation to get double use out of their small investment in milling machinery.[39] To foster this kind of activity may require that national planners insure that appropriate technically trained personnel are available who are willing to work in cooperation with villagers to solve the organizational, technological, and marketing problems involved in setting up the appropriate kinds of labor-intensive, small-scale industries. In turn, national government programs and policies can and should play a vital role in facilitating the spread of industry into rural areas. On the one hand, such initiatives by the national government will facilitate local efforts to process local produce for national markets; and, on the other, they will provide concrete evidence of the advantages of national and local cooperation in planning by creating the conditions for material improvements in the level of living of local populations.

SUMMARY AND CONCLUSIONS

Institutional changes are essential to implement proposals for creating industry that can contribute to increased internal specialization and exchange, augmenting productivity in all sectors to raise the levels of living for the broad masses of the population. There is plenty of evidence. In Africa and elsewhere, that private enterprise, foreign or domestic, seeking to maximize short-run profits, is unlikely to insure the spread of the appropriate kinds of industry. The state is the only agency capable of making the necessary institutional changes to reallocate resources to achieve the appropriate pattern of industry throughout an integrated national economy.

The primary issue, therefore, revolves around the role the state should play in implementing proposals for a carefully planned industrial strategy. It is probable that it should invest in and exercise outright control over critical relatively capital-intensive projects to provide poles of growth, process exports, and, over time, produce the necessary kinds of machinery and equipment needed to increase productivity in all sectors of the national economy. Once measures have been taken to achieve this goal, however, it is still essential to re-examine the entire inherited set of institutions by which the state seeks to implement the proposed industrial strategy. The British type of development corporation, initially designed to function like a private owned holding company in a market economy, undoubtedly requires reshaping if it is to function effectively as a tool of government participation. This necessity is amply illustrated by the Ghanian and Tanzanian experiences. Major problems appear to involve relations of public-sector industries to the overall government structure and formulation of appropriate working rules and controls to insure that public-sector industry managements pursue day-to-day policies contributing to national economic development. These problems are aggravated by the continued operation of foreign firm managements.

Trade unions may constitute a means of insuring that the interests of workers are represented on national and plant levels in formulating and implementing the proposed industrial strategy. In most former British colonies in Africa, however, trade unions were carefully nurtured during the colonial era to pursue limited wage goals without respect to African national perspectives. In the postindependence era, new approaches and attitudes appear necessary if the unions are to provide instruments through which workers may be involved at every level of production in critical decisions to insure that the industrial strategy carried out does contribute to restructuring the national economy in the interests of the broad masses of the population, including the workers themselves.

At the same time, national planners need to create new sets of working rules to stimulate local initiatives to build small-scale, labor-intensive industries as crucial linkages necessary to set off chains of growth from nationally planned industries throughout the rural areas. Here the national government may provide infrastructure, centralized marketing facilities, improved tools and equipment, technical assistance, education, and credit to stimulate the expansion of activities by small-scale handicraftsmen, cooperatives, and local village communities. All of these should be encouraged to take advantage of the possibilities of broader markets and improved tools to increase their output of locally manufactured goods in the context of the nationally planned pattern of specialization and exchange.

NOTES

1. A. Waterston, Development Planning—Lessons of Experience (Baltimore: Johns Hopkins Press, 1965).

2. P. P. Karan, "Changes in Indian Industrial Location, "Association of American Geographers—Annals, no. 54 (September 1964): 336-54.

3. Linge, "Governments and the Location of Secondary Industry in Australia."

4. Jay, "Distribution of Industry Policy and Related Issues."

5. Cf. Economic Commission for Africa, "Industrialization and Economic Planning," Economic Bulletin for Africa (New York: United Nations, January 1963), III, 63.

6. Cf. Economic Commission for Africa, Conference of Ministries of Industry from 27 African countries, May 4-9, 1971, Addis Ababa.

7. Y. Kyesimira, "The Public Sector and Development in East Africa," Makerere Institute of Social Research Conference Papers, January 1968; see also International Bank for Reconstruction and Development, The Economic Development of Uganda (Baltimore: Johns Hopkins Press, 1962), regarding industry; and E. J. Soutjesdijk, Uganda's Manufacturing Sector, East African Studies No. 28 (Nairobi: East African Publishing House, 1967).

8. Industrial Development Corporation, Annual Report 1960 (Accra: Government Printer, 1960).

9. KPU Manifesto, 1966, pp. 3-4.

10. National Development Corporation, Third Annual Report (Dar es Salaam: National Printing Corporation, 1969).

11. Republic of Zambia, Financial Statistics of Public Corporations, 1965-1969 (Lusaka: Central Statistical Office, 1969), pp. 60-61; see also T. Homes, "Zimco—Still More in the Pipeline," Zambia Six Years After African Development: Economic Survey, 1970.

12. National Development Corporation, Jenga, no. 1 (1968): 2-3.

13. Kyesimira, "The Public Sector and Development in East Africa."

14. Cf. Gold Coast, Government Proposals in Regard to the Future Constitution and Control of Statutory Boards and Corporations in the Gold Coast (Accra: Government Printer, 1956), esp. p. 5.

15. Industrial Development Corporation, Annual Report XI, p. 3. Hotels, among its more successful endeavors, appear to have been included in the industrial category.

16. G. H. Wittman, Inc., The Ghana Report (New York: G. H. Wittman, Inc., International Economic Consultants, 111 Broadway, 1959), p. 26.

17. Ibid., p. 30.

18. Seven Year Development Plan, op. cit., passim; E. N. Omaboe, "The Process of Planning," in Birmingham et al., The Economy of Ghana, op. cit., pp. 454-455.

19. From the Files of the Planning Commission, Accra 1966.

20. H. P. Nelson, A Report on the Administration and Operation of State Enterprises under the Work Schedule of the State Enterprises Secretariat for the Period 1955-1965 (Accra, Dec. 1, 1966), pp. 5, 14, 18 (mimeo). Hereinafter referred to as "State Enterprises Report."

21. Visited by the author, January 1966. The British officials in charge would release no figures on the plant's operations. This was one of the companies whose contracts were cancelled by the new Ghanian government in 1972: see "Ghana: Popular Moves," Africa Confidential 13, no. 4 (Feb. 18, 1972).

22. K. Amoako-Atta, "Budget Speech, 1966," reported in Ghana Daily Gazette, Feb. 23, 1966.

23. West Africa, April 1, 1969.

24. International Bank for Reconstruction and Development, Economic Development in Taganyika (Dar es Salaam: Government Printer, 1960); and Arthur D. Little, Inc., Tanganyika Industrial Development, A Preliminary Study of Bases for the Expansion of Industrial Processing Activities, on behalf of the Ministry of Commerce and Industries of Government of Tanganyika under contract with the U.S. Agency for International Development, 1961.

157

25. United Republic of Tanzania, Second Five Year Plan for Economic and Social Development, 1st July 1969-30th June, 1974 (Dar es Salaam: Government Printer, 1969) Vol. I, Ch. XVII.

26. G. K. Helleiner, "New Forms of Foreign Private Investment in Africa" (Dar es Salaam: Economic Research Bureau, Paper #67.12, Dec. 9, 1967).

27. National Development Corporation, Third Annual Report, 1968.

28. Ibid., p. 15.

29. The data and citations related to this case, unless otherwise cited, were reported in R. Sandbrook, "The State and the Development of Trade Unionism," in G. Hyden et al., Development Administration—The Kenyan Experience (Nairobi: Oxford University Press, 1970), pp. 251-295.

30. For details of parallel experiences in other countries, see R. H. Bates, Unions, Parties and Political Development, A Study of Mineworkers in Zambia (New Haven: Yale University Press, 1971); A. Seidman, Ghana's Development Experience, 1951-1965 (Nairobi: East African Publishing House, 1972); and T. M. Yesufu, Introduction to Industrial Relations in Nigeria (London: Oxford University Press, 1962).

31. Sandbrook, "The State and the Development of Trade Unionism," is again the source of these materials relating to trade unions unless otherwise indicated.

32. For an analysis of this aspect in Zambia, see Bates, Unions, Parties and Political Development.

33. R. H. Jackson, "Planning, Politics and Administration," in G. Hyden et al. Development Administration, pp. 180-1.

34. Tanganyika African National Union, TANU Guidelines, 1971 (Dar es Salaam: Government Printer, 1971), p. 4.

35. Ibid., p. 4.

36. F. I. Nixson, "Some Results of a Survey of Industrial Location in Uganda," University College of Makerere, EDRP No. 108, Aug. 7, 1966.

37. M. Darkoh, "Industrial Location in Ghana," unpublished Ph.D. thesis, University of Wisconsin, 1971.

38. For history of rapid postindependence growth in East Africa, for example, see Seidman, Comparative Development Strategies in East Africa, Ch. 8.

39. L. Cliffe and G. Cunningham, "Ideology, Organization and the Resettlement Experience in Tanzania," Rural Development Research Committee, Paper No. 3 (Dar es Salaam: University College, 1968).

CHAPTER

8

LAND TENURE AND
RURAL INSTITUTIONS

The necessity of formulating and implementing an industrial strategy should not be permitted to obscure the equally pressing requirement of reshaping rural institutions to insure that increased productivity and higher levels of living spread throughout the rural areas. Foremost among rural institutions likely to be of critical importance are those governing land tenure. This is true not merely because land tenure systems determine who may use and develop particular pieces of land, but because, as emphasized in Chapter 3, the control of land as the primary productive resource in rural Africa has, historically, shaped the essential relationships of power and privilege that determine how rural populations or segments of them are integrated into or excluded from the spread of specialization and exchange within the nation. They affect the extent and the pace of the introduction of new productive techniques; the impact of expanding markets and credit; and whether the peasants obtain the higher incomes necessary to create an internal market and the higher levels of living that constitute the primary goal of development.

This chapter will first briefly summarize the characteristics of the land tenure systems that had emerged as a result of the imposition of colonial export agriculture on traditional land use arrangements. Second, it will outline the objectives and constraints that might be expected to influence the formulation of more appropriate land tenure systems to insure that the broad masses of the rural population do benefit from the planned spread of specialization and exchange throughout the national economy. Third, it will consider the probable consequences of the two main alternative approaches to land tenure reform under consideration in sub-Saharan Africa today. And fourth, it will explore some of the implications of these alternative approaches for associated rural institutions affecting the spread of new agricultural techniques, credit, and marketing.

EXISTING LAND TENURE SYSTEMS

The newly independent African countries inherited such a wide range of land tenure systems that it would be impossible to describe them all in the limited space here available.[1] It is, nevertheless, possible to outline their main characteristics to indicate the extent to which they may foster or hinder the necessary integration of rural populations into national development plans. This section seeks to indicate the predominant characteristics of the main traditional systems and those introduced with the expansion of export crops under colonialism to set the stage for considering how reformed tenure systems might contribute to increased productivity and higher levels of living for the broad masses of the African population.

Traditional land tenure patterns tended over wide areas to reflect the constraints imposed by near-subsistence agriculture, given the particular characteristics of the environment.[2]* What has been widely characterized—perhaps misleading—as "communal tenure" has tended to be associated with the development of shifting agriculture.[4] The head of the community (which might vary in size from an extended family to a fairly large tribe) was empowered to give a group member the rights to use a given land area (usufruct rights) for purposes of growing the crops required by his family. The farmer and his family cleared the land, frequently by some form of "slash and burn" technique, and farmed it for several years until it began to become exhausted. Then it was allowed to lie fallow for a period of five to ten years or longer; since it was out of use, the usufruct lapsed and the land returned to the common pool. Meanwhile, the farmer obtained rights to another piece, or pieces, and began the process over again. For the most part his tools were simple—a hoe and a cutlass. A man and his family could cultivate about three to five acres a year. They produced almost all their own needs, including their food, their clothing, and their housing. Occasional markets provided the opportunity to exchange a few items, notably salt, some vegetables, simple handicrafts like pots, stools, and cloth, and perhaps some small livestock like chickens or goats. The farmer did not have the right to sell the land or alienate it in any way. This reflected the circumstance that there was plenty of land available, as well as the political-economic relationships inherent in the traditional system. Land had no cash value.

---

*A substantial body of anthropologists maintain that the very use of English terminology, shaped as it has been by English experience, distorts the characteristics of traditional land tenures.[3] There is no space to deal with this argument here, but one needs to be sensitive to the linguistic problem.

In widespread areas of the semiarid continental plains, cattle complexes emerged in which cattle, rather than land itself, was the scarce resource.[5] Cattle became a form of "walking bank" for the community, providing food, clothing, and even materials for house-building. A family's status in the community reflected, to a significant degree, the number of head of cattle it owned. These groups tended to migrate according to season in search of fodder and water for their cattle, covering vast areas of range land. Ordinarily they undertook little stable cultivation of the land itself. Extensive burning over of the ranges traditionally utilized by specific groups was considered essential to enable the cattle to graze on the best new grass. Some of these groups tended to be more settled than others, but cattle remained a major source of wealth and prestige.

As land areas became crowded, some nomadic herders engaged in shifting cultivation too and moved on to new areas, contributing to widespread migration movements across the continent. In other cases the tribes settled permanently, sometimes participating in the creation of larger political economic units, remaining settled even when population pressures reduced land availability.

As emphasized in Chapter 3, prior to colonialism the establishment of larger political states, either for military or trade purposes, led to the accumulation of agricultural surpluses in the hands of powerful rulers. In places like Ethiopia, Northern Nigeria, and parts of Central Africa, the actual peasant producer was reduced to the status, essentially, of a tenant at will. The ruling groups acquired control of landed areas, and the peasants could continue to use them only upon payment of various forms of tribute, taxes, or tithes. The surpluses thus accumulated by the rulers tended to be expended on various forms of conspicuous consumption and military activities. They were seldom directed to investment in technology designed to augment agricultural productivity.

The imposition of outright colonial rule introduced major changes in land tenure in the export enclaves established to produce agricultural raw materials for European industry. The pattern of ownership of the productive agricultural units varied widely, however, depending on a variety of factors. In North, East, South, and Central Africa, the European colonizers created large-scale, relatively modern settler estates and plantations for production of crops for export.[6] Africans were simply pushed off much of the best land onto "reserves," and settlers or plantation companies were allocated giant tracts for little or nothing in the way of cash payment.* In some cases outright forced

---

*The land was not always owned outright. In East Africa the settlers held land under long-term lease, which in theory at least

161

labor was introduced. In others, hut and poll taxes were imposed to compel Africans to work; since Africans were prevented from selling export crops, the only way they could pay the tax was to work on the estates or in the mines. Hundreds of thousands of young men migrated hundreds of miles from their homes annually in search of work. This had serious and lasting effects on the social, political, and economic systems in areas from which they came.[7]

In West Africa and Uganda the British encouraged the African peasants themselves to produce export crops for sale to the colonial trading firms.

A British colonial officer explicated the economic rationale for this policy:*

The agricultural industries in tropical countries which are mainly, or exclusively, in the hands of the native peasantry (a) have a firmer root than similar enterprises when owned and managed by Europeans, because they are natural growths, not artificial creations, and are self-supporting as regards labor, while European plantations can only be maintained by some system of organized immigration or by some form of compulsory labor; (b) are incomparably the cheapest instruments for the production of agricultural produce on a large scale that have yet been devised; and (c) are capable of a rapidity of expansion and a progressive increase of output that beggar every record of the past, and altogether unparalleled in all the long history of European agricultural enterprises in the tropics.[8]

In these regions the colonial government encouraged private British interests to provide the markets and credit necessary to

---

was subject to being taken over by the Colonial Administration in the event that it was not developed in accordance with specific criteria. Usually, however, they obtained such long-term concessions that, to all intents and purposes, they exercised ownership rights.

*It is perhaps also significant that in West Africa the Africans mounted military opposition against the colonizers until just before World War I, suggesting that had the British granted large landholdings to Europeans there, they might have faced further military expenditures, which would have rendered the colonies uneconomic. In Uganda, where the Bugandan King represented a potentially powerful political and military opponent, the British gave the Bugandan notables themselves large land areas, on which cotton and later coffee were introduced through their tenants.

facilitate expansion of African peasant production export crops. Private British trading firms financed up-country buying stations. The African farmers, sometimes doing the work themselves, sometimes hiring (or using sharecrop) labor, planted and harvested the crops for sale to the big firms. The governments used taxpayer money to build the essential roads, railroads, and ports to transport the crops out of the country. As the growth of export crops spread in these areas, traditional land tenure systems were gradually transformed. Land itself, once cleared and especially when planted with valuable tree crops, began to acquire a cash value. More successful individual farmers, not able to hire migratory labor to do the work, sought to buy more land from their less prosperous neighbors in order to increase their profits. "Indeed," one scholar has observed, "one of the criticisms of customary land law . . . has been of its over-successful adaptation to the business of making money rather than keeping alive!"[9]

Gradually new land tenure systems emerged, reflecting the spread of cash cropping for export and the growing scarcity of land. The chiefs eventually discovered they could obtain large amounts of cash for sale of rights in land to "strangers," those not members of the clan.[10] Farmers, seeking loans, pledged their crops, sometimes even the rights to harvest crops from their lands. Despite traditions of "communal" ownership, conditions increasingly approaching individual ownership and sale of land began to emerge. Colonial courts, in dealing with the endless litigation that came before them concerning land rights, tended to make decisions reinforcing the rights of individual ownership, although maintaining the fiction of inalienability.[11] Banks, mostly foreign-owned, but also government-sponsored lending agencies, provided credit either through trading firms or, in East, Central, and South Africa, to larger farmers (almost entirely non-African), whose rights to their land provided security. In Kenya, in the midst of the guerrilla warfare waged by Africans seeking to regain their land, the Colonial Administration devised the Swynnerton Plan to consolidate each farmer's separated pieces of land into one unit, registering the title to formalize his ownership. One aim, among others, was to create a politically stable yeoman class of farmers that would support government efforts to defeat the guerrilla fighters.[12]

Upon obtaining independence, the new African nations had thus inherited sets of working rules from the colonial era that functioned to support the expansion of export enclaves as a source of raw materials and to provide markets for the metropolitan countries. The legal structure[13] was designed to import, at least into these areas, the admixture of public and private institutions similar to that prevailing in Europe: the government provided the infrastructure and administration; private—mostly foreign—firms and individuals owned the farms and mines, the trading companies, the banks, shipping companies, and insurance firms. The working rules served to reinforce the expansion of individualized land tenures in cash cropping areas, even where African farmers themselves carried on production. Production and trade were carried on through contracts between private buyers and sellers, enforceable at law. The giant foreign trading firms advanced funds to up-country buyers and through them to individual farmers on export crops that they would acquire when harvested. Farm workers worked for settlers under contracts enforceable by criminal procedures under colonial rule, agreeing to work for a given period for a fixed wage. As cash crop farming extended to African farms, farm laborers made similar contractual arrangements (verbal or written) with private African farmers. Thus the legal system provided the essential sanctions to insure that the larger private farm owners could hire labor.

Outside the export enclaves, traditional agricultural practices and associated tenures tended to persist, only marginally changed. In some areas, as population expanded, population pressures began to mount. This reduced the fallow time required for shifting agriculture to succeed,[14] and tended to lead in some cases to fragmentation of land as fathers divided their parcels among their sons (or whoever traditionally inherited). Land shortages were particularly aggravated in eastern, central, and southern territories, where Africans had been forced into restricted reserves. Increasing numbers of young men began to leave their homes in the less developed rural areas to seek employment in the urban areas, mines, or the larger farms of the export enclave.

Women, in particular, together with their children, increasingly carried the main burden of sowing and harvesting food crops to maintain their families. Low productivity in these areas and lack of adequate marketing channels hindered the expansion of the foodstuffs needed to sustain the growing urban populations; increasingly the export enclaves came to rely on imported foodstuffs, particularly for the higher-income group.[15]

By the time of independence, then, land tenure systems and associated institutions tended to reflect and reinforce the dualistic characteristics of the national economy. Attainment of a balanced, nationally integrated economy, capable of achieving increased productivity and higher levels of living in all sectors of agriculture as well as industry, required fundamental revision of these and the entire set of associated rural institutions.

OBJECTIVES AND CONSTRAINTS RELATING TO LAND REFORM POLICIES

National planners need to consider the appropriate system of land tenure and associated rural institutions which will stimulate the peasants—the vast majority of the populations in most cases—to increase their productivity in the contest of national development goals. Parsons has argued[16] that:

As the productive capacity of agriculture is increased and development supported by the integration of science, technology and capital into the farm economy, with the correlative conversion of agriculture into a market oriented economy, so have the customary tenure systems to be modernized by bringing the powers of the state to bear upon the system of tenure relations.

Some Criteria for Evaluating Land Tenure Systems

Several criteria have been proposed for consideration in formulating appropriate land tenure systems.[17] Among these, the following appear to be the most important:

1. Economic size and layout of the farm: Tenure systems should foster establishment of farms that, in terms of size and layout, facilitate the use of technologies and labor in relation to their relative availability in the economy as well as geographical conditions.
2. Incentives and opportunities: The system adopted should create the incentives and opportunities to induce the farm operators to use the most efficient productive methods, given the availability of unskilled labor and shortages of skilled manpower and capital.
3. Capital investment: If productivity is to increase over time, the tenure system must create the conditions needed to encourage the farmers to invest a significant share of the surpluses produced in improved technologies[18] as skills improve and planned new job opportunities are made available in other sectors of the economy. Over time, these conditions include the establishment of productive units involving a single area large enough to accommodate the use of increasingly modern cultivation and reaping machinery.
4. National development perspectives: The tenure system should insure that as rural populations expand their productivity, their incomes also grow sufficiently to create the internal market necessary for domestic industrial growth as well as to provide them with the higher levels of living that constitute the primary aim of development.

The Issue of Scale and Productivity in Africa

Given the small size of the typical traditional African farm, the issue of the size of holding needed to permit expanded productivity

165

has been the subject of considerable debate and experiment. Initially, given shortages of skill and capital, considerable increases in productivity may be achieved by introducing labor-intensive improvements to increase yields per acre: for instance, the use of improved seed varieties, inexpensive fertilizers, appropriate simple technologies for eliminating diseases and pests, and small irrigation projects. Over time, and land tenure system adopted should probably facilitate peasant participation in larger irrigation schemes and the investment of surpluses accumulated in improved machinery and equipment to increase the land area utilized as well as output per acre. The issue of whether large-scale productive units will eventually be required to attain these goals has been extensively debated. There is, however, sufficient evidence to argue that land units considerably larger than the traditional African farms of three to five acres will be necessary.*

Repeated experiences in both East and West Africa have, on the other hand, led to the conclusion that to attempt immediately to increase agricultural productivity by simply introducing large-scale productive units with capital-intensive productive equipment like tractors and combines is unlikely to contribute to creation of the conditions necessary for balanced national development. In the short run, and with only a few exceptions, such projects consume large amounts of scarce capital resources with relatively low returns and in some respects significant negative consequences for national

---

*It has been argued, particularly in the Latin American context,[19] that available evidence suggests that large-scale farms may be less productive than smaller ones. There is evidence[20] that the largest farms in Latin America consist of very large holdings on which large areas may be left fallow, and whose owners—usually latifundistas—accumulate surpluses from low labor costs rather than increased productivity. Smaller, more commercialized farms between 40 and 100 hectares—still considerably larger than the typical African peasant farm—are more productive, but they are in fact essentially more capitalistic and profit-motivated than the latifundistas. There is similar evidence that large Kenyan settler farms were not as productive as those of the middle-sized African peasants who took over in the low-density schemes on the highlands.[21] But, again, these farms tend to be larger than the typical African farm, and the owners were carefully selected with a view to their educational qualifications and other factors that might be expected to contribute to their output. This evidence tends to support the contention here made that as managerial skills spread, the requirements of efficiency are imposed by increased labor costs, larger units are likely to be required to take advantage of economies of scale.

development. This is true for several reasons relating to economic factors.[22] First, the lack of research concerning the appropriate techniques to use in tropical soils has led to expenditure of huge sums of money on the wrong kinds of equipment. Second, lack of appropriate skills on the part of the typical peasant leads to inappropriate use and frequent breakdowns of equipment. Third, difficulties of obtaining spare parts for machines has resulted in large amounts of capital being tied up in idle equipment while new parts are imported; the initial importation of a wide variety of makes of equipment has aggravated this problem by requiring many different types of spare parts, which are expensive to keep on hand. Fourth, the utilization of scarce capital in agriculture does not contribute to employment of the growing numbers of underemployed rural workers. Instead, as tractors substitute for labor, numbers of younger peasants crowd into urban slums seeking employment, while the shortage of capital for implementation of a planned industrial strategy hinders the construction of factories in which they may be employed.* Fifth, the initial high capital and wage costs per unit of output of this pattern of agricultural production render it incapable of competing in the domestic market with crops produced by peasant families who use their own (unpaid) labor and provide for their own subsistence, and limits the competitiveness of its output on the world market unless heavy government subsidies are introduced.[24] Finally, the vast majority of peasants must, because of capital scarcity, remain outside the resulting limited modern sector; their incomes will remain inadequate to provide the internal market needed to permit expansion of an industrial sector producing a broad range of farm inputs and consumer goods.

In addition to these economic factors, there are important sociological factors that have tended to be neglected.[25] Among the most important of these have been the failure of planners and managers to adequately consider the needs and desires of the peasants. Markets have not been organized, on the assumption that settlers could set them up without assistance. Scheme budgets have been drawn up without consideration of local needs. Repayment schemes have been heavy. Settlers have been expected to handle new crops and new grades of livestock without previous experience or adequate training. Attitudes of settlers toward new crops and techniques have tended to be ignored. Managers have been drawn from different cultures, often from abroad, and not infrequently have been unable to inspire settlers with confidence or mobilize them for more effective productive activity.

---

*Eicher, et al., have pointed out that foreign aid tied to the sale of specific agricultural machinery has been a significant factor contributing to unemployment in Africa.[23]

This last shortcoming may be aggravated by the provision of expensive housing and facilities for the management, with the result that they are further set apart from the peasants as some kind of a bureaucratic elite.

The Gezira scheme in the Sudan has been held to be an outstanding exception to the record of failures of large-scale projects in Africa.[26] Based on initial plans dating back to 1907 to pump Nile waters for irrigated cotton, a British company gradually expanded the project until it was finally taken over in 1950 by the Sudan Gezira Board, an autonomous public authority. The scheme now involves over 2 million acres and is operated on a partnership basis: the government provides the water and land; the board administers the scheme and does the research, allocates the tenancies, supervises and finances the tenants, mechanically cultivates the land, provides seed and fertilizer, undertakes pest control, and transports, gins, and markets the cotton; the tenants provide the labor. The proceeds are divided 44:40:10 between the tenants, government, and the board. Of the remaining 6 percent, 2 percent goes to the local government, 2 percent is spent on social development by the national government, and 2 percent goes into a reserve fund held by the board against possible crop failures. The land is under cotton only a quarter to a third of the time, depending on the area; other crops grown belong entirely to the tenants. In recent years tenants have numbered about 75,000. Their average annual share has been around $500 per family. In addition, the board employs 10,000 workers, and the tenants themselves hire about 250,000 migrant laborers.

The following have been identified as critical variables that might contribute to the success of large-scale projects like that of Gezira:

1. Productivity can be markedly increased, as, for example, through irrigation, greatly improved farming prices, or introduction of a saleable crop.

2. A high-value crop should be grown, providing means of obtaining returns on investment (tea, cotton, rubber).

3. Economic crops should be capable of control through sale, processing, or both (for example, cotton at gin, tea at processing factory) to avoid illegal marketing or consumption and proper division of returns among participants.

4. Specialist technical and/or managerial skills should be required.

5. Capital investment should be required that the farmers themselves cannot provide.

6. Control of farming practices should protect the soil, assure adequate production of cash crops, improve quality of the product, and prevent unnecessary damage by plant pests.

Little evidence has been gathered, however, on the extent to which the success of the Gezira scheme tenants depends on their ability to hire a much larger number of low-cost migrant laborers, who are excluded from the real benefits of the project. It would, perhaps, be worthwhile to make a study of the more far-reaching consequences of such a pattern of income distribution for national development perspectives.

In some places state farms have been introduced for the purpose of agricultural experiment and to educate the peasants as to the possibilities of expanding production through the use of more modern techniques. Given the shortages of capital and highly skilled manpower needed to make such farms function effectively, it would seem prudent to implement such a policy sparingly. The experience with more than one hundred state farms established in a few years in Ghana[27] before the 1966 coup is instructive. In the case of tree crops, and perhaps for the introduction of crops new to the area, large-scale plantations that the state alone can organize and finance (unless foreign capital is used) appear to be economically justified. After the coup in 1966, the Ghana government sold the state-owned rubber plantations to a private U.S. firm, which suggests that it was viable. The government continued to operate the Russian- and Israeli-initiated rice projects, which apparently became viable once redundant labor supplies were laid off.

Those state farms that attempted to produce crops like maize in competition with domestic peasant farmers, on the other hand, were unable, in the short years of their existence, to surmount the economic and sociological problems cited above.

The African experience suggests that initially for most crops, relatively labor-intensive agricultural techniques should be developed, utilizing more efficiently existing relatively abundant supplies of underemployed rural labor. This would contribute to the gradual expansion of specialization and exchange and increased productivity depending on the pace with which more and more peasants gained new skills and the ability to utilize scientific methods and manage larger, more productive units; the expansion of the rural market in the framework of an appropriate industrial strategy directed to producing appropriate improved agricultural tools and equipment; and the accumulation of investible surpluses needed to permit acquisition of more modern machinery and equipment throughout the agricultural sector. This suggests that the land tenure policy formulated should be so designed that, over time, as the constraints are gradually eliminated, larger land units may be created in which all the potential economies of scale may be realized. The choice of land tenure policy selected to attain these objectives would seem to have implications for overall national development perspectives.

THE CONSEQUENCES OF ALTERNATIVE
LAND TENURE SYSTEMS FOR
NATIONAL DEVELOPMENT

Two broad categories of approaches to land tenure seem to be emerging as aspects of post independence efforts to involve the broad masses of African peasants in commercial agriculture. One is the extension of individualized private ownership of land, in which the rights in land acquired by individuals are mortgageable and saleable.[29] The other centers on some form of cooperation among groups of producers, perhaps building on traditional communal tenures to expand output.[30]*

These two categories are dealt with here in the sense of ideal types. In reality, there is a continuum between them. The purpose of setting up the ideal types of models here is to single out the key variable that may have significant consequences for development in the long run and that should therefore be taken into consideration by planners even in formulating short-run approaches to tenures systems.

Individualized Tenures

Perhaps the most significant argument in favor of individualized tenures is that it relies on the individual farmer's own initiative: he risks his own labor (initially; later he may hire others) and capital (if he has any; in any event, he may create capital in the form of cleared land and, in some cases, the planting of palm, rubber, or cocoa trees).[31] There is no need for heavy governmental expenditure or imported management skills; the farmer does his best with what he has, taking advantage of government assistance if it is forthcoming and he deems it worth his while.

In the early stages of efforts to draw farmers into an increasingly monetized system of increased specialization and exchange with gradual increases in productivity, this approach appears to have something to recommend it. Government assistance in the form of extension advice, establishment of marketing institutions (perhaps through cooperative marketing, which has become widely spread, especially for

---

*In addition, governments supporting both categories of approach have invested in state-owned agricultural projects for experimental, research, and sometimes pole-of-growth effects. As indicated above, lack of managerial and technological skills at all levels in the early stages has tended to limit the initial spread effects of such projects, even in countries committed to an expanding public sector.

sale of export crops, in most African countries), and provision of credit may be provided relatively easily with only slight modifications of existing institutions to aid African (as opposed to foreign settler) farmers.

In the longer run, this approach may have less desirable consequences for the national development. As internal markets expand and capital and skills accumulate—creating conditions necessary to introduce more advanced technologies requiring larger productive units—more "progressive" farmers are likely to expand their acreage, perhaps at the expense of their less fortunate neighbors, and hire laborers to work it.

This was clearly anticipated in the Kenyan case, where individualized tenures were introduced in part to offset the Mau Mau claims for recovery of land from the white settlers during the prolonged guerrilla warfare of the 1950s.*

President Nyerere of Tanzania maintains that the emerging pattern of individualization of tenure typified in export crop production in Africa has led to abandonment of the old traditions of living and working together and sharing the proceeds. On the other hand, the resulting increases in productivity have, he admits, increased the national output, but they have been accompanied by increases in the relative wealth of the man who owns, manages, and initiates the larger farm. On the other hand,

> . . . the moment such a man extends his farm to the point
> where it is necessary for him to employ laborers in order
> to plant or harvest the full acreage, then the traditional
> system of ujamaa has been killed. For he is not sharing
> with other people according to the work they do, but simply
> paying them in accordance with a laid out minimum wage
> . . . the result is that the spirit of equality between all
> the people working on the farm has gone—for the em-
> ployees are the servants of the man who employs them.
> Thus we have the beginnings of a class system in the
> rural area.[32]

The creation of a balanced, internally integrated economy depends critically on the continuing expansion of an internal national market as productivity increases; otherwise, inevitably, the only market available for expanded output, both agricultural and other, will be limited to the uncertain export market and the high-income elite in the associated export enclave. If the incomes of the broad masses

---

*See above, Chapter 3, p. 65.

of peasants are restricted in the manner indicated by the Swynnerton planners[33] to low wages or thinly spread shares of export crops, then perpetuation of an externally dependent dual economy appears to be probable. Furthermore, the consequent emergence of what Sir Michael Blundell has characterized as a society of "haves" and "have nots"[34] is likely to be politically unstable.

Producer Cooperation

The other approach to land tenures that has emerged in Africa has been centered on the possibility of building some form of producer cooperation, perhaps on the foundation of existing traditional tenures.* Fundamentally, the notion seems to be that traditional tenures did provide for a degree of community effort as well as joint ownership of the land. If agricultural development policies could contribute to expansion of productivity by building on this presumably pre-existing cooperation, some African leaders have argued that it will be possible over time to move toward larger units of production that could take advantage of economies of scale without the emergence of a pattern of "haves" and "have nots," which is both economically undesirable and politically potentially explosive.

President Nyerere, for example, holds that

> To make our socialism and our democracy a reality we should . . . adapt to modern needs the traditional structure of African society. We must, in other words, aim at creating a nation in which ujamaa farms and communities dominate the rural economy and set the social pattern for the country as a whole.[36]

Supporters of producer cooperatives argue that, over time, they will contribute more effectively than individualized tenures to a nationally integrated, balanced pattern of internal specialization and exchange, insuring that increased productivity and higher levels of

---

*These have frequently been associated with the concept of "African socialism," although that term has remained so vague and undefined as to contribute little as an analytical device for evaluating the consequences of proposed policies. Some Africans espousing a socialist perspective, however, argue that individualization of tenures may be essential to breaking down resistence to new forms of social and economic development necessary before socialism can be established in Africa.[35]

living do reach the broad masses of peasants in rural areas. As groups of peasants learn to work together to plan the division of labor and improve farming methods through joint efforts using increasingly large land units and invest the resulting surpluses to buy more advanced equipment and machinery as their skills increase, all participants are expected to benefit directly in terms of increased incomes. On the one hand, this will lead to the continued expansion of the internal market required to insure an adequate demand for the output of new industrial projects. On the other, it should provide incentives for all members of the group—not only the owner of the land, as would be the case with individualized tenures—to exercise their ingenuity to the utmost to continue to increase productivity for the benefit of all.

Various attempts have been made to achieve a degree of producer cooperation, ranging from block farms, on which individual peasants share in the use of mechanical equipment on blocks of land (frequently owning their own small plots in addition), to outright collective ownership of the land and productive facilities. Experience suggests a considerable degree of caution in attempting to implement this approach in the short run. Block farms and similar schemes have encountered problems of management and misuse of equipment[37] not unlike other large-scale projects cited above.

Experience to date in Tanzanian ujamaa villages—attempting a higher degree of cooperation and common land ownership utilizing relatively more labor-intensive techniques by building on presumed cooperative traditions—has not been notably successful; in fact the widespread endorsement of the President's approach has led to numerous attempts to build ujamaa projects, but to date only a fairly limited number are reported to have been able to implement the ujamaa principles suggested.[38]

There appear to be several difficulties that need to be overcome if producer cooperation is to be achieved among large groups of peasants. First, research is required as to the extent to which traditional practices really can contribute to effective cooperative activity in modernizing agriculture.[39] Such research should focus on the extent to which substantial class differentiation that may hinder cooperative productive efforts has already emerged. Where a few large commercial landholders come into being, as they have in most of the export crop areas in Africa, there is already evidence that they may act covertly or overtly to sabotage government policies designed to increase cooperative efforts.[40] Building cooperative production activities would appear to require special attention to the involvement of landless and poor peasants as well as middle peasants, whose efforts to expand production are already restricted by their limited resources.

Second, shortages of adequately skilled leadership and managerial and technical manpower may lead to serious difficulties.

173

Instances of mismanagement of group production activities have, in the past, discouraged some peasants from all desire to participate in further cooperative efforts.[41] Left to their own devices, and utilizing family labor to take advantage of improved techniques and expanded market opportunities, they might have contributed to increased production. The kind of leadership required to promote cooperative endeavor does not merely require managerial or technical skills, but ideological insight and commitment as well as the ability to work with and mobilize peasant participation in cooperative activities. It takes time to develop this kind of leadership.[42] There is a danger that mismanaged cooperative projects may undermine peasants' interest and willingness to participate in future projects even when qualified leadership becomes available.

Third, working rules must be carefully devised to insure that individual participants have adequate incentives to contribute to cooperative production activities. These involve careful consideration as to appropriate schemes for payment for work done, as well as sanctions for those who fail to do their tasks.[43] This third point is related to the second, for good leadership must be exercised to involve the participants themselves in formulating and evaluating the necessary working rules for joint productive activities to insure that they will live up to them.

Fourth, there is a severe scarcity of the capital necessary to acquire the modern machinery and equipment that might provide an important incentive as well as the requirement for more effective immediate resolution of the three problems outlined above. In one sense, this may be an advantage, for it may well be that efforts to achieve cooperative production can best be implemented gradually as skilled leadership and capital, as well as technical know-how, are built up. Perhaps a government seeking to foster a cooperative approach to land tenure could, in early stages, while leadership cadre and capital are still scarce, encourage individual peasant families to augment their output and sell their surpluses on expanding internal markets. While means should be found to encourage peasant families to invest in appropriate improved methods and equipment to augment production, these should not be provided by enshrining previously nonexistent individualized ownership of pieces of land through legal devices that may hinder greater cooperation at later stages. Cooperative productive activities could be encouraged wherever appropriate circumstances prevail. Small-scale irrigation projects, for example, might be built by cooperative efforts, permitting double cropping on communally held property; this might be an important aspect of cooperative endeavor in some of the relatively dry plains areas characteristic of large areas of sub-Saharan Africa. Limits might also be set to the size of land unit an individual family might own or to the number of laborers it might hire, so that attainment of economies of scale in production beyond a specified size might require resort to cooperation with neighbors.

As the pool of trained leadership grows with expanding educational opportunities,* and the amount of investible surpluses is increased, areas of cooperation could be expanded to take advantage of economies of scale, including the use of appropriate mechanical equipment. The cooperative division of labor might also extend from agricultural activities to the introduction of simple labor-intensive industries to provide new employment opportunities for seasonally unemployed workers. These industries should be built within the framework of the national industrial strategy to process agricultural produce and provide essential farm inputs, construction materials, and consumer necessities, so that they not only raise the incomes of the workers directly employed, but also contribute to the greater material welfare of the broader rural community.

In some cases, short cuts may be possible. For example, large settler farms or estates, with large accumulations of land and capital, may be taken over to be run as producer cooperatives or state farms with increasing worker participation in decision-making. There is, however, a danger that producer cooperatives thus established may continue to advance (perhaps with extensive government assistance), raising the output and incomes of those lucky enough to be participating "owners,"[45] while the rest of the economy stagnates. This appears particularly probable where the "owners" are permitted to hire land-less laborers for low wages on a seasonal or permanent basis. Such an approach hardly appears likely to foster the creation of the broad internal market required to attain national development. Nor is it like-ly to avoid the growth of the gap between the "haves" and "have nots".

In sum, it appears that land tenure policies are in the short run likely to be conditioned by constraints imposed by inherited conditions relating to land, manpower skills, and capital. Long-run approaches are, however, likely to differ significantly, depending on the pattern of national development desired. A long-run approach such as that recommended in Kenya by the Swynnerton Plan, leading to the emer-gence of wealthy commercial farmers and low-income landless laborers, appears likely to contribute to perpetuation of the inherited dual econ-omy, with its built-in external dependence. Alternative efforts to build

---

*Obviously the educational system would need to be overhauled to insure that it contributed to skilled committed leadership that will work to reshape agricultural institutions, rather than generating an elite that seeks to remove itself as rapidly as possible to the supposed delights of urban life.[44]

on traditions of cooperation require careful research relating to the
scope and potential of those traditions and conscious mobilization of
the mass of the poorer and middle peasants to expand their productivity
and incomes through increased joint cooperative efforts. Initially
such policies should avoid fostering individual land ownership while
seeking to encourage increased investment and output, widespread
appropriate education of leadership-manager cadre capable of helping
to build producer cooperatives over time, and formulation of new sets
of working rules that would in the long run foster increased cooperative
productive activity to take advantage of the technological possibilities
of scale as existing constraints of manpower and capital are overcome.

RESHAPING ASSOCIATED RURAL INSTITUTIONS

Government policies relating to land tenure extend beyond the
issue of the ownership and control of land to include associated institutions that are essential to overall rural development.[46] This broader
system will both affect and be affected by the national plan, particularly
as it shapes industrial strategy, as well as the range of working rules
relating to marketing, farmer education, and credit and taxation. These
latter will be discussed briefly here in an effort to place them in the
context of the considerations of the appropriate land tenure system
and its consequences for national development perspectives, but they
will be examined much more fully in later chapters in the broader
framework of the overall national plan.

It has already been emphasized that agricultural and industrial
development must be planned simultaneously so that they mutually
support and reinforce each other. This is true in terms of both the
resource allocation pattern and the new institutions being introduced.

In this context, careful attention needs to be directed to insuring
that marketing, farmer education institutions, credit and tax policies
perform the required supportive role for the land tenure system
adopted to implement national plan perspectives. In the first place,
accumulating evidence suggests that no agricultural development policy
will be successful unless adequate attention is given to building appropriate marketing institutions.[47] To those who argue that African
peasants do not respond to economic incentives, the obvious answer
is to point to the rapid expansion of export crops in all parts of Africa
once the farmer has been assured of a market and an adequate price.[48]
This experience also tends to prove that a prime prerequisite for
African development is to insure that the old marketing institutions
are reshaped and new ones created to provide an assured market at
reasonable prices for the farmers' output and an adequate supply of
reasonably priced manufactured farm inputs and consumer goods to

176

the farmers in return.[49] Improved road and transport systems are, of course, required as the foundation on which any expansion of a national marketing system must rest; but examination of the existing set of marketing institutions in Africa suggests that this, by itself, is unlikely to be sufficient.

In the colonial era, foreign trading firms established the new marketing institutions to insure that African farmers could sell their produce on the world market for cash.[50] Now, however, the evidence suggests they constitute major institutional features perpetuating the external dependency characteristic of the inherited dual economies of Africa; they seem unlikely to pursue policies of broadening sources of supply and overseas markets, or selling increasingly processed agricultural exports, because of their existing linkages with overseas manufacturers.

In internal trade, available evidence suggests that a small portion of the more powerful private traders in Africa seek, where possible, to corner the market in order to lower prices to farmers, while raising them in urban areas. On the one hand, this has tended to constitute a disincentive to farmers to enter cash crop production; in a few cases, surpluses produced in one year may be left uncollected, rotting, so the next year the farmers logically refuse to do the extra work needed to produce the surplus. On the other hand, rising urban food prices and even shortages of foodstuffs have led to increased importation of foodstuffs and contributed to the inflationary pressures that to one degree or another characterize most African cities.

A range of institutional innovations has been introduced in various independent African countries, including marketing cooperatives and various types of parastatals in an effort to provide a more effective internal marketing system.[51] From the outset, these institutions seem to have been plagued by shortages of skilled, dedicated manpower. There seems to have been a widespread tendency for larger, more powerful farmers to manipulate marketing cooperatives for their own advantage, occasionally contributing to disrepute for marketing cooperatives in general.

The experience with efforts to reshape internal and external marketing institutions needs to be evaluated in terms of its consequences for the overall rural development. The critical issue is to what extent do the new marketing institutions contribute to the spread of industry and agricultural productivity, as well as higher levels of living for the broad masses of the population? This should be viewed in the framework of national plans designed to shift from dependence on the export of agricultural raw materials to an internally balanced economy supported by a new pattern of foreign trade.

Part III seeks to provide an analytical framework for such an evaluation and to consider some of the evidence available.

Second, careful attention needs to be directed to formal and informal educational programs to encourage peasants to adopt new agricultural techniques. In the colonial era, extension education was typically geared to encouraging individual farmers to adopt more scientific methods and improved technology for export production. Experience in Africa, as elsewhere, furthermore, indicates that this approach tended to lead to provision of greater amounts of assistance to larger, more well-to-do farmers, thus fostering the emergence of a skewed pattern of distribution of rural incomes.[52] If the goal is to gradually build toward cooperative farming practices as skills and capital are accumulated, farm extension education programs need a thorough overhauling to insure that they provide essential leadership and skills to foster this approach.[53] In particular, the extension workers would themselves need to adopt a new set of attitudes directed toward seeking opportunities for and encouraging group activities at every conceivable point in the production as well as the marketing process. In a like manner, the entire national system of education, as well as the system of recruiting and educating extension workers, needs revision to overcome the bias introduced prior to independence that tended to denigrate agricultural pursuits.[54]

Third, the existing financial institutions and their credit policies need to be re-examined to insure that they too contribute to desired rural development policies. Experience suggests that the existing set of private foreign-owned commercial banks are unlikely to innovate in the direction of stimulating small African farmer production, far less in encouraging producer cooperation.[55] Loans, when made to African farmers at all, have mostly been for actual crops, using the crops themselves for security, rather than for longer-term development investments. What is required is to insure that credit institutions direct more credit to small peasant farmers for the type of capital investment needed to increase productivity, especially if individual African farmers are to be encouraged to expand production.

If the goal is to work gradually toward increased cooperation in production, several credit practices should probably be revised.

It would seem necessary to seek other forms of security than individual land titles—a common requirement of private commercial banks.[56] Where banks have provided credit to larger farmers to hire labor, this appears to have acted as a disincentive to farmers' continued or increased participation in any form of producer cooperation.[57] Attention should be directed to creating incentives for farmers to invest as groups in the long-term improvements required to enhance productive capacity. For this approach to succeed, however, it appears probable that the leadership and working rules of cooperative projects need to be carefully formulated to insure effective operation to insure repayment; otherwise it may turn out that the government will have

to use tax powers (or create money with attendant inflationary potential) to subsidize such projects. All this suggests that if it is desirable
to support some form of group tenure for production purposes, then
a considerable amount of research and evaluation needs to be directed
to creating appropriate supporting credit institutions and policies.

Fourth, the government seeking to restructure the economy will
need to work out appropriate tax policies.[58] These will be influenced
by the governmental philosophy regarding the best way of implementing
the national plan. If private enterpreneurs are to make critical investment decisions in agriculture, careful consideration of taxes on income,
exports, imports, sales, and possibly land is required to insure that
they do not discourage and if possible encourage individual farmers
to make appropriate decisions. If it is concluded that in the long run
group productive enterprises in agriculture are more likely to contribute to national economic reconstruction, tax policies may be reshaped
to stimulate developments in these directions. If such a perspective
is to be implemented only over time, it may be essential, in the shorter
term, to avoid discouraging individual farmers from increasing productivity and selling their surpluses on the market, as long as they
do not hinder advancement along the lines of producer cooperation.
Only recently have tax policies begun to receive the scrutiny they
deserve as critical development instruments in the African context.
Extensive research is required to see that they play their part within
an overall financial plan designed to insure adequate funds to implement the national development strategy. Credit and tax policies are
considered in more detail in Part IV.

SUMMARY AND CONCLUSIONS

This chapter has attempted to outline a conceptual framework
for evaluation of alternative land tenure systems and associated institutions and working rules in Africa. It has presented a brief overview
of the land tenure systems inherited by the newly independent states
of Africa within the framework of the externally dependent dual economies shaped in the colonial era. These consisted of individualized
tenure systems in the relatively modern export enclave, supported
by the institutions and working rules established under the umbrella
of the colonial administration, and a wide variety of traditional systems,
which have tended to persist outside of the sector devoted to export
crop production.

In the context of this inherited pattern, the two broad categories
of land tenure systems generally fostered by African governments
since independence have been tentatively evaluated in terms of their
potential consequences for the incentives and opportunities of the

peasants, capital investment, and overall national development perspectives. On the one hand, individualized tenures, initiated in the colonial era in the export enclave, provide conditions in which the individual small peasant farmer exercises initiative at his own risk to expand production. If this approach is pursued, attention needs to be directed, on the one hand, to avoiding fragmentation through inheritance rules and, on the other, to insuring a sufficiently permanent interest in the land to encourage the peasants to make long-term investments to increase productivity. In the long run there appears to be a considerable probability that continued expansion by individual peasants seeking to take advantage of economies of scale may lead to acquisition of large amounts of land by a few wealthy farmers from their less fortunate neighbors; the former will then seek to hire the resulting landless laborers at the lowest possible wages. This is likely to lead to the emergence of landed and landless classes. In addition to the probable political and social tension arising from such a division, the accompanying skewed income distribution is likely to limit the market for expanded industrial production, and hence to hamper creation of a nationally integrated, balanced economy.

The alternative of attempting to build producer cooperatives to take advantage of economies of scale while avoiding the emergence of "haves" and "have nots" also appears likely to encounter difficulties in the early stages. Shortages of capital initially render the rapid acquisition of modern machinery and equipment impossible except in a few limited cases, so that initially at least the expansion of the size of units of production is not a primary requisite for expanded output. The lack of ideologically committed and technically qualified leaders who can help to shape the new institutions and working rules to weld the masses of traditional peasants into modern producer cooperatives appears to be an equal if not more serious problem. This suggests that countries pursuing this alternative approach to land tenures should encourage attainment of the essential preconditions of producer cooperatives—in particular training cadres of leaders and developing attitudes and activities fostering cooperation wherever possible—while avoiding any rigidification of individualized tenures, which might hamper the creation of cooperatives at the stage when emerging economies of scale require larger production units. Introduction of small-scale industrial projects as part of an expanding regional specialization and exchange may arise from and contribute to expanding areas of producer cooperation. As productivity expands, and capital and manpower skills accumulate, the gradual emergence of producer cooperation may then insure the more equitable distribution of resulting increased incomes, laying the essential foundation for internally balanced and integrated national economies.

The government will need to evaluate the entire complex of associated institutions to insure that they contribute to the implementation of whatever approach to land tenures it adopts. Both agriculture and industry need to be planned to expand simultaneously to insure creation of an internally balanced economy, reducing dependence on the inherited export enclave. At the same time, the associated institutions and working rules providing for marketing, farmer education, and credit and taxation need to be reviewed to insure that they are supportive of national plan perspectives. The inherited set of institutions and working rules in the export enclave tends to foster individualized tenures. If, however, a government adopts an approach designed to build producer cooperation over time, it seems evident that it will be necessary to re-evaluate and alter these basic institutional structures and working rules to implement this approach. Again, careful research is required to insure that measures introduced will work; and adequate feedback is essential so that once new institutions and working rules are adopted, they may be altered if their initial operation proves unsuccessful.

NOTES

1. For an extensive bibliography on land tenures and possible reforms, see Food and Agriculture Organization of the United Nations, Rural Institutions Division, Bibliography on Land Tenure in Africa, ESR/MISC:70/23 (Rome, 1970).

2. Cf. A. M. Karmarck, Economics of African Development (New York: Praeger Publishers, 1967), Ch. V.

3. P. Bohannan, "'Land' 'Tenure' and 'Land-Tenure,'" in Biebuyek (ed.), African Agrarian Systems (1963), pp. 101-111; V. Ayoub, "Review: The Judicial Process in Two African Tribes," in M. Janowitz (ed.), Community Political Systems (New York: Free Press of Glencoe, 1961), pp. 237-250; M. Gluckman, Politics, Law and Ritual in Tribal Society (Oxford: Basil Blackwell, 1965), pp. 182, 185.

4. W. Allan, African Husbandman (Edinburgh: Oliver & Boyd), passim, for description of various kinds of shifting agriculture.

5. Cf. O. Bremand and J. Pagot, "Grazing Lands, Nomadism and Transhumance in the Sahel," in Arid Zone Research No. 18, Problems of the Arid Zone: Proceedings of the Paris Symposium (Paris: UNESCO); pp. 311-324; R. Capot-Ray, "Problems of Nomadism in the Sahara," International Labour Review 90, no. 5, (Geneva: International Labor Organization, 1964), pp. 472-487; and M. El Filall, "The Economic and Social Development of Nomadic Populations before and after They Have Become Settled," in M. R. El Ghonomy (ed.), Land Policy in the Near East (Rome, FAO), pp. 38-52; D. Chirot,

"Urban and Rural Economies in the Western Sudan: Birni N'konni and Its Hinterland," Cahier d'études africaines 8, no. 4 (32) (1968); 547-65.

6. For description of land holdings of settlers and Africans, see B. Floyd, "Land Apportionment in Southern Rhodesia," Geographical Review, 52, no. 4 (1962); 566-582; Central Statistical Bureau, The Treasury, Census of Large-Scale Commercial Farming in Tanganyika (Dar es Salaam, November, 1963); C. M. N. White, "Note of Land Policies in the Belgian Congo, Mozambique and Madagascar," FAO, Development Center on Land Policy in East and Central Africa, Uganda (Rome, 1960). For an analysis of the consequences of the policies summarized for the Africans in Kenya, see M. W. Forrester, Kenya Today, Social Prerequisites for Economic Development (The Hague: Mouton & Co., 1962).

7. E.g., J. Wayne, "The Development of Backwardness in Kigoma Region," seminar paper, University of Dar es Salaam, June 15, 1971.

8. Governor of Nigeria, Sir Hugh Clifford, Address to the Nigerian Council, 29 December, 1920 (Lagos, 1920), p. 186, cited in H. A. Oluwasanmi, Agriculture and Nigerian Economic Development (Ibadan: Oxford University Press, 1966), pp. 124-5. The consequences of this policy are summarized in A. Seidman, Comparative Development Strategies in East Africa, Part 1, and Ghana's Development Experience, 1951-65, Ch. IV. An illuminating analysis of the Ghana case from a legal point of view is that of S. K. Asante, "Interests in Land in the Customary Law of Ghana—A New Appraisal," Yale Law Journal 74 (1965).

9. Allott, "Legal Development and Economic Growth in Africa," in Anderson (ed.), Changing Law in Developing Countries, 1963.

10. I. Ofori, "Land-Man Relationships in Ghana," Seminar, Land Tenure Center, August 19, 1970. See also D. Austin, Politics in Ghana, 1946-1960 (London: Oxford University Press, 1964), esp. pp. 271-272.

11. S. K. B. Asante, "Interests in Land in the Customary Law of Ghana—A New Appraisal," Yale Law Journal 24 (1965): 848-885.

12. For an analysis of this policy, see M. P. K. Sorrenson, Land Reform in the Kikuyu Country: A Study in Government Policy (London: Oxford University Press, 1967).

13. For an examination of the role of British law as it has affected development, see R. B. Seidman, "Law and Economic Development in Independent English-Speaking sub-Saharan Africa," in T. W. Hutchison (ed.), Africa and the Law: Developing Legal Systems in African Commonwealth Nations (Madison: University of Wisconsin Press, 1968), pp. 3-74.

14. Cf. H. Ruthenberg, Agricultural Development in Tanganyika (Berlin, 1964), esp. p. 19.

15. The value of food, drink, and tobacco imports into Kenya, for example, tripled from 1956-1966. Republic of Kenya, Economic Survey, 1967 (Nairobi: Ministry of Planning and Development, 1967), p. 24. In Ghana, as cocoa output has spread, mounting imports of foodstuffs have continued to be a major burden on the balance of payments (cf. Republic of Ghana, Central Bureau of Statistics, Quarterly Digest of Statistics, March 1968, Table 18 p. 16) and the inadequacies of foodstuff marketing has been the subject of repeated debates (e.g., "Ghana's Agriculture, 2: Sorting Out the Legacy," West Africa June 13, 1968). The problems of marketing institutions are summarized in Seidman, Ghana's Development Experience, 1951-65, esp. section three of Ch. IV.

16. Parsons, Land Reform in Nigeria, p. 9.

17. Food and Agricultural Organization, United Nations, Africa Survey: Report on Possibility of African Rural Development in Relation to Social and Economic Growth (Rome, 1962), p. 18; and cf. T. F. Carroll, "Appraising Adequacy of Land Tenure Systems," pp. 585-587.

18. Cf. W. Allan, The African Husbandman (Edinburgh: Oliver & Boyd, 1964), p. 470; and, for discussion of implications for land tenures, see Seidman, "Law and Economic Development."

19. P. Dorner and D. Kanel, The Economic Case for Land Reform: Employment, Income Distribution, and Productivity, prepared for AID Spring Review, June, 1970.

20. D. Stanfield, "Economic Strata and Dependency as Determinants of Innovativeness and Productivity in Rural Brazil," Rural Sociological Society Meetings, August 1970.

21. Farm Economics Survey Unit, Ministry of Economic Planning and Development, Survey of 1965-66 Crop Year, reported in Republic of Kenya, Development Plan, 1966-1970, p. 152.

22. For some postindependence experiences, see M. Miracle and A. Seidman, State Farms in Ghana (Land Tenure Center, 1968); R. Apthorpe (ed.), Land Settlement and Rural Development in Eastern Africa (Kampala: Nkanga Editions, Transition Books); D. Forbes Watt, Mechanized Group Farming in Uganda, Land Reform No. 1 (FAO, 1968); and M. Hall, "A Review of Agricultural Mechanization in Uganda" (Makerere: 1969, mimeo); and C. Eicher, T. Zalla, J. Kocher, and F. Winch, Employment Generation in African Agriculture, Institute of International Agriculture, College of Agriculture, Research Report No. 9, Michigan State University, East Lansing, July 1970, passim; CSNRD No. 33, "Strategies and Recommendations for Nigerian Rural Development, 1969/1985" (East Lansing, Michigan, July 1969) describes Nigerian settlement schemes in East and West Nigeria; E. H. Whetham, Co-operation, Land Reform and Land Settlement (London: Plunkett

Foundation for Cooperative Studies, 1968), pp. 49-50; Food and Agricultural Organization, United Nations, Agricultural Development in Nigeria, 1965-1980 (Rome: FAO, 1965), p. 347.

23. Eicher et al., Employment Generation in African Agriculture, p. 14.

24. E.g., both Tanzania and Kenya still subsidized exports of surplus maize in the late 1960s, although they hoped to eliminate these subsidies in the 1970s. (See Republic of Kenya, Development Plan, 1970-74, and United Republic of Tanzania, Development Plan, 1969-1974, Vol. 1).

25. Apthorpe (ed.), Land Settlement and Rural Development in Eastern Africa, esp. articles by Apthrope and J. Morris; see also J. O. Akinwoiemiwa, "The Farm Settlement Scheme in Western Nigeria, and Assessment of the Problems Involved and Evaluation of the Results Achieved to Date," World Land Conference, (Rome: RU:WIR-C/66/2, May 1966).

26. UN, FAO, "Land Reform in the Republic of the Sudan," Country Paper (Rome: RU C/66/36, May 1966); and W. A. Hance, African Economic Development (New York: Praeger Publishers, 1967), Ch. 2.

27. Miracle and Seidman, "State Farms in Ghana," passim.

28. For discussion of the ingredients of an industrial strategy and the consequences of alternative policies, see Seidman, Comparative Development Strategies in East Africa, esp. Ch. 6, and Ghana's Development Experience, esp. Ch. X and Part III.

29. This approach, as indicated above, was introduced in the colonial era and since independence has been consciously fostered in particular in Kenya; cf. Sorrenson, Land Reform in the Giku Areas, passim; and Seidman, Comparative Development Strategies, Ch. 7.

30. FAO Africa Survey: Report on Possibilities of African Rural Development in Relation to Social and Economic Growth, (Rome, 1962).

31. For an effort to estimate the creation of capital through the planting of tree crops, see R. Szereszewski, Structural Changes in the Economy of Ghana, 1891-1911 (London: Watson and Viney, 1965), p. 137.

32. J. Nyerere, Socialism and Rural Development (Dar es Salaam, 1967), p. 7.

33. Swynnerton Plan.

34. M. Blundell, So Rough a Wind: The Kenya Memoirs of Sir Michael Blundell (London: Weidenfeld and Nicolson, 1964), p. 287.

35. S. Amin, "The Class Struggle in Africa," Africa Research Group, Reprint #2, pp. 42 ff.

36. J. Nyerere, Socialism and Rural Development (Dar es Salaam, 1967), p. 15.

37. E.g., M. Hall, "A Review of Agricultural Mechanization in Uganda" (Makerere, 1969, mimeo); M. Miracle and A. Seidman, "Co-operatives and Quasi-Cooperatives in Ghana, 1951-1965," Land Tenure Center, University of Wisconsin, 1968; and L. Cliffe and G. Cunningham, "Ideology, Organization and the Settlement Experience in Tanzania," Rural Development Research Committee, Paper No. 3, University College, Dar es Salaam, 1968.

38. For summary, Thirteen Rural Africans (Michigan: African Studies Center, Rural African, 1971).

39. Ibid., L. Cliffe, "Class Struggle and Ujamaa Vijijini," pp. 5 ff.; for additional research efforts undertaken on this issue, see also L. Cliffe and G. Cunningham, "Ideology, Organization and the Settlement Experience in Tanzania"; D. Feldman, "An Assessment of Alternative Policy Strategies in the Agricultural Development of Tanzania and their Application to Tobacco Farming in Iringa," ERB Paper 68.21, UCDSM, 1958; D. Feldman, "The Economics of Ideology, Some Problems of Achieving Rural Socialism in Tanzania," Economic Research Bureau, UCDSM, Seminar Paper, Nov. 1, 1968; R. W. Kates, J. McKay, L. Berry, Twelve New Settlements in Tanzania: A Comparative Study of Success, University Social Sciences Council Conference, Makerere, Dec. 30, 1968-Jan. 3, 1969. There is need for more, as emphasized in United Republic of Tanzania, The Economic Survey and Annual Plan, 1970-71, p. 25. Other research includes W. J. Argyle, "The concept of African Collectivism," Mawazo (Makerere) 1, no. 4 (December 1968): 37-43.

40. A regional commissioner was assassinated in southwestern Tanzania by a large landholder who apparently feared his efforts to foster "ujamaa" (L. Cliffe, Talk to Sociology of Economic Change Program, University of Wisconsin, Feb. 15, 1972.)

41. The problem of the inadequacy of managerial skills as well as the inappropriate attitudes of many managers is discussed in Cliffe and Cunningham, "Ideology, Organization and the Settlement Experience in Tanzania." See also Tanzania, The Economic Survey and Annual Plan, 1970-71, p. 25; M. Miracle and A. Seidman, "Cooperatives in Ghana, 1951-1965," African Urban Notes (Michigan: African Studies Center, Fall, 1970), pp. 59-94.

42. That neither Tanzania's typical ten-cell party leaders nor the traditional extension agents have the insights or commitment to achieve this kind of leadership has been indicated by several studies: e.g., I. K. S. Musoke, "The Establishment of Ujamma Villages in Bukoba Rigazi (Nyerere) Village: A Case Study" (March 1970) and "A Collection of Essays on Ujamaa Villages" (March 1971) (Dar es Salaam: University of Dar es Salaam, Political Science Department). See also F. DuBow, "Legal Development in Tanzania: The Cell Leader as a Para Legal Agent," A. Nimtz, "Ten House Cell Leaders as an

Index of Political Change: The Case of Bagamoyo," J. F. O'Barr,
"TANU Cells and Their Leaders: The Pare Case," and J. Samoff,
"Agents of Change-Cell Leaders in an Urban Setting," papers presented
to African Studies Association, 14th Annual Meeting, Nov. 3-6, 1971,
Denver, Colorado.

43. The differences in working rules among ujamaa settlements
existing in Tanzania, for example, was illustrated by a report of a
student to the author's class in the University College, Dar es Salaam,
who said that, in one village of former sisal workers, a worker absent
without adequate excuse was fined not only for the day lost, but also
for an additional day's pay; in a village of more traditional farmers,
sanctions were far less onerous.

44. For an interesting analysis of the problems of developing
an appropriate extension education program, see B. Harris, "Survey
of Agricultural Training Institutes: Implications for Producing Ujamaa
Vijijini Extension Workers," Rural Development Paper No. 2, Sixth
Annual Symposium of East African Academy, University College, Dar
es Salaam, September 1968.

45. Cf. Simons, "Land Reform in Tunisia," and Foster, "Land
Reform in Algeria," Agency for International Development, Spring
Review, 1970. This appears to be a possible problem in the case of
Chile's assentamientos (D. Stanfield, "Progress Report on Research
regarding Chilean Assentamientos," Seminar, Land Tenure Center,
Madison, Wisconsin, Mar. 1, 1972).

46. Parsons, "Land Reform in Nigeria," p. 39.

47. Cf. A. Mosher, paper delivered to workshop in Economic
Development, University of Wisconsin, April 11, 1967.

48. For discussion of responsiveness of export crop farmers
to price changes, see L. Clayton, Economic Planning and Developing
Agriculture (Headley Bros., 1963); and W. O. Jones, "Economic Man
in Africa," Food Research Institute Studies (Stanford, California:
Food Research Institute, 1960).

49. The importance of reshaping marketing institutions and the
alternative approaches available are considered in A. Seidman, Comparative Development Strategies, esp. Ch. 8.

50. For a detailed examination of the role of these trading
companies in West Africa, see P. T. Bauer, West African Trade, A
Study of Competition, Oligopoly and Monopoly in a Changing Economy,
revised (London: Rutledge and Kegan Ltd., 1963).

51. See A. Seidman, Comparative Development Strategies, Ch.
8, for alternatives and an initial assessment of their consequences
for national development in East Africa; see also African Urban Notes,
Special Issue on Markets and Marketing in Africa, M. Miracle (ed.)
(Michigan: African Studies Dept. 1970).

52. Cf. B. Harris, Survey of Agricultural Training Institutes. Discussions of Rural Sociological Conference in Washington, Aug. 28-Sept. 1, confirm that this has been experienced in the South in the U.S., although an additional factor has been discrimination against blacks; and for Latin America, see M. Brown, Land Tenure Center, University of Wisconsin, 1970.

53. Harris, Survey of Agricultural Training Institutes.

54. Interview with Mr. Kahumbe, Senior Tutor, Institute of Adult Education, Tanzania, at Madison, Land Tenure Center, spring, 1970.

55. See M. P. Collinson, "Agricultural Credit in Tanzania," in Helleiner (ed.), Agricultural Planning in East Africa, for discussion of problems allocating credit to small farmers; also J. Loxley, "Financial Intermediaries and Their Role in East Africa," University of East Africa Social Science Conference, December 1966; for efforts to change the limited role of commercial banks in East Africa, see Republic of Ghana, Economic Survey, 1962, esp. pp. 100-101, 1963, pp. 54-63, and 1964, pp. 52-60.

56. This has been a major argument in Kenya for consolidation and registration of title of farmers in the former African reserves; cf. I. K. Kutuku, Senior Economist/Statistician, Ministry of Economic Planning and Development, "Land Consolidation and Registration—Kenya's Experience," IDEP/MISR Quarter Continent Conference on Experience with Planning Agrarian Change in East Africa, January 1969.

57. Feldman, "The Economics of Ideology—Some problems of Achieving Rural Socialism in Tanzania."

58. Among materials useful for consideration of the tax issue are: D. P. Ghai, Taxation for Development, A Case Study of Uganda, East African Studies No. 23 (Nairobi: East African Publishing House, 1966); J. F. Due, "Reform of East African Taxation," The East African Economic Review 2, no. 2 (December 1964); D. P. Ghai, "Tax Structure for Rapid Economic Growth in East Africa," in Problems of Economic Development in East Africa (Nairobi: East African Publishing House, 1965); R. G. Penner, "Local Government Revenues in Tanzania," Agricultural Economics, Department of Economics, University College, Dar es Salaam, 1968-69. For details of Tanzania's efforts to reduce tax burdens on rural areas, see United Republic of Tanzania, Speech by the Honourable Minister of Finance Introducing the Estimates of Revenue and Expenditure 1969-70 to the National Assembly on 19th June, 1969 (Dar es Salaam, Government Printer, 1969), pp. 22-24. For comments on necessity of examining taxes on agriculture, see Eicher, Research on Agricultural Development in Five English-Speaking Countries in West Africa, esp. p. 40.

9

THE LIMITATIONS OF
EXISTING TRADING
INSTITUTIONS

The materials presented in the preceding chapters underline the necessity for the newly independent nations of Africa to make critical institutional changes to reorient foreign trade from specialization in the export of cheap raw materials produced by low-cost labor toward increasingly processed exports to earn more foreign exchange for the import of capital equipment and machinery required to implement a nationally oriented strategy of industrial and agricultural growth. Internal trading institutions, too, must be developed to stimulate the spread of internal specialization of exchange made possible through planned and integrated expansion of agricultural and industrial productivity.[1]

This chapter seeks to outline the characteristics of the institutions handling export-import and domestic trade in an effort to explain, at least tentatively, why, as presently constituted, they have contributed so little to achievement of nationally balanced, integrated economic development in the former British colonies of Africa. The remaining chapters of Part III will then consider the evidence relating to the consequences of alternative strategies designed to change these trading institutions to insure that they contribute more constructively to the development plans of those newly independent countries.

FOREIGN TRADE

Obstacles to Shifting the Pattern of Exports

To attain their stated development goals, African nations need to increase the value of their exports to earn more foreign exchange in order to purchase essential capital goods and equipment.[2] This means, in the first place, that they need to make every possible effort to expand sales of their existing exports. They need to seek out new export markets, perhaps linking the sales of traditional raw material exports to the import of machinery that they require for their development plans.*

Second, the processing of raw materials before sale will increase their foreign exchange earnings many times over. Timber processed into final products, for example, earns ten to sixteen times as much dollar value as it does in the form of logs.[3] This is true for all African exports: cotton exported as cloth, groundnuts processed as cake or oil, iron ore manufactured into pig iron or steel—all would earn many times the value they now earn exported as crude materials. At the same time, manufacture of raw materials into these kinds of final products before export would contribute essential inputs and consumer goods needed to increase domestic productivity and levels of living in the African countries themselves. In some cases it may be essential, given the small size of the internal market of the typical African country, to create export markets if some essential new industries are to be established at all.[4]

Several possibilities exist for broadening markets to which manufactured goods might be sold. These include (1) sales to existing trading partners who now mainly import crude materials from Africa; (2) sales to neighboring African countries; and (3) exports to new trading partners in the socialist third of the world and other developing areas.

Realization of the possibilities has, however, been hindered not only by resource constraints, but also by the role of the oligopolistic trading firms that dominate African exports. The interwoven ties between the firms that buy sub-Saharan Africa's five major exports have been described in Chapter 2. In a sense such a description sets the parameters of the problem confronting the African nation seeking to change its pattern of export trade.

First, the major channels for handling overseas marketing of exports to the countries' traditional trading partners was, at independence, still dominated by these large companies. The establishment of marketing boards for agricultural produce in most of the former British African colonies prior to or during World War II had done little to alter control by these companies. The boards were introduced by the colonial governments, often with the support of the companies themselves, to reduce the "wasteful effects" of the remaining vestiges

---

*As shown above, the limitations on world demand and the danger that competitive expansion of output will merely lead to reduced prices on the world market argue that these efforts should be made within the framework of international price-output agreements.

of competition among the companies buying produce directly from the producers and, during the war, to assure a steady flow of raw materials to British industry. In some cases the boards themselves purchased agricultural produce through licensed buyers, often the trading companies' representatives, at a pre-fixed price, and auctioned the produce off to the overseas companies, either in London or, where settlers produced the major share of exports, as they did in East Africa, in the African country. In other cases the boards simply licensed particular companies to handle the entire process of purchasing produce from the farmers and selling it overseas.

Thus the companies themselves still handled a major share of the actual raw material exports at independence, providing the shipping facilities and overseas marketing channels in the "traditional trading partner" nations of the former British African colonies. The companies are frequently linked to the industries that do the processing back home. The main business of Unilever, the parent of the United Africa Company that purchases a major share of West African agricultural produce, for example, is to process those raw materials into a range of foodstuffs, soaps, and oils for sale throughout the world.[5] Companies like Unilever are not eager to set up vertically integrated industries to process African raw materials for sale in competition with their own factories' output.

The industrial interests that process African raw materials, furthermore, have not infrequently influenced their governments to establish tariffs and quotas specifically aimed at reducing the competition of imported processed goods with their own manufactured goods industries. Efforts to reduce these obstacles through the United Nations Conference on Trade and Development[6] have encountered resistance, which has mounted when the developed countries have experienced balance of payments problems of the type that have recently plagued both the United Kingdom and the United States. The 1971 unilateral imposition of a 10-percent surcharge on all imports into the United States merely aggravated an already existing problem. The subsequent currency realignment further reduced the real value of not a few African exports. The Mining Journal declared that

> . . . seen in its simplest terms, the industrialized
> nations have revalued and the developing nations,
> dependent on raw materials, have devalued. . . . The
> result is that raw materials will be cheaper for
> Europe and Japan; for the developing nations, their
> mineral wealth, in future, will buy fewer tractors,
> fewer hospitals, less food.[7]

Second, efforts to expand sales of industrial produce to neighboring African countries may encounter different kinds of problems. All African countries seeking to industrialize confront similar resource possibilities and constraints. Hence they are likely to initiate similar types of industries such as textiles, sugar and other foodstuffs, or perhaps more complex industries like the assembly of bicycles and radios. In other words, each may establish industries that cut off the possibilities of sales to one another. Already inter-African trade—never more than 10 percent of all African trade—appears to be declining as African nations seek to attain self-sufficiency.[8]

This is certainly true in East Africa, where each of the three nations has duplicated industries already established in one of the neighboring countries. Relative overproduction and underutilization of capacity is already a problem in the textiles industry. Analysis of experience to date suggests that only if neighboring countries can attain a sufficient degree of political and economic agreement to plan their industrial strategies jointly so that their industrial sectors are complementary (instead of competitive), will they be able to anticipate expanding sales to each other.[9]

Even with top-level political-economic agreement among African governments, the foreign trading firms that conduct the major share of import trade, linked as they are to overseas manufacturers, may be reluctant to shift to new domestic sources of supply in neighboring nations. Their "reluctance" is commonly bolstered by the argument that the customers themselves want the allegedly higher quality of the imported item.*

Third, the expansion of sales of manufactured goods to socialist countries may encounter still another set of difficulties. In recent years African sales to these areas have consisted mostly of raw materials in exchange for capital goods and equipment.[10] If African governments themselves use these sales to obtain capital equipment for augmented industrialization in the framework of their own carefully-formulated strategies for development, this may provide a significant opportunity for advancing plans to restructure their inherited dual economy†

---

*Some Africans—particularly among the elites—sometimes do adopt this argument, but the need to develop African industry underlines the fact that sanctions, as well as education, may be required to alter the pattern of trade to support a regional development plan.

†It should be emphasized, however, that simply to build factories for the sake of building them, without linking them to utilization of domestic resources and provision of essential inputs for further

In some cases, too, socialist countries have been willing to buy a significant share of the output of manufactured goods produced by new plants thus built. For example, the Soviet Union agreed as part of the initial contract with Uganda that it would purchase a major share of the textile output, thus opening a new market for cotton, one of Uganda's two main exports, in a processed form.[12] But many socialist countries are only just emerging from an underdeveloped status themselves. Total socialist imports from Africa are unlikely to exceed 15 percent of all African exports by 1980,[13] though the percentage of particular imports from particular African countries—for example, cotton from the UAR, bauxite from Guinea, cocoa from pre-1966 Ghana—has been and may continue to be much higher. National planners must seek to use such possibilities primarily to implement plans for building more self-reliant, integrated economies.

The reluctance of existing trading firms to shift to new socialist sources of imports is likely, however, to hamper the utilization of even the limited possibilities for expanding export markets. The government of Kenya, for example,[14] was unable to conclude an agreement with the Soviet Union to build a major new paper plant at Broderick Falls. In part this was because the Soviet Union could not consume additional paper, given its own extensive paper industry. But also the existing trading firms were reluctant to import Soviet goods in order to cover the credit advanced by the Soviets for local construction costs.* As a result, the Kenyan government abandoned the Soviet proposal, finding a substitute only several years later when, with funds from the International Finance Corporation and the British government, it agreed to enter a joint venture with a large private Indian firm.

_____

development of an integrated domestic economy, may constitute unwarranted expenditure regardless of the source of the capital equipment and machinery obtained.[11]

*The Soviets were willing to grant credit for the local costs of the project as well as imported machinery and equipment, but they did not want to pay the local costs in gold or foreign "hard" currencies (dollars or pounds sterling, which they themselves must earn through sales of their own produce to the West); hence they proposed what has become a typical socialist solution of financing local costs by selling Soviet goods in the country, lending the funds thus earned to the Kenya government in order for the latter to pay the laborers and cover the costs of local construction materials for the project.

Obstacles to Changing the Package of Imports

African nations need to reorient their import as well as their export policies to support their development programs. In particular, scarce foreign exchange should be allocated to purchase essential capital equipment and machinery, farm inputs, mass transport vehicles and parts, construction materials, and consumer necessities.[15] Expensive consumer imports—automobiles, air conditioners, television sets, liquor, expensive clothing—for the high-income group associated with export enclave activity[16] should be reduced. Even the import of parts and materials for light industries catering to the high-income elite—rayon and nylon textiles, for example[17]—should be curtailed.

The oligopolistic trading firms that dominate import trade have tended to resist efforts to reduce imports of profitable lines. Their links with manufacturing companies in the developed countries constitute an incentive to persist in importing commodities to fulfill the conspicuous consumption desires of the high-income group. Automobile importers earn up to 50 percent on invested capital.[18] It is rather unlikely that they will willingly give up this lucrative trade. Company resistance to shifting to the import of different items is particularly likely to be pronounced if the items are produced by other firms or in other countries, or if machinery and equipment are to be imported to help African countries build up their capacity for consumer goods industries—which may ultimately cut off the markets of the trading firms altogether.

INTERNAL TRADE

Internal trade in sub-Saharan African countries is likewise dominated by oligopolistic institutions, particularly at the wholesale level, which tend to hinder efforts to spread specialization and exchange, particularly into rural areas. Statistics indicate that the larger wholesale firms make up roughly 10 percent of all firms engaged in domestic trade in most African states. They are located, for the most part, in the major cities in the export enclave.[19] The way these firms have contributed to the creation and perpetuation of dual economies was, historically, particularly noticeable in the case of export production developed in the colonial era. The big foreign trading firms, with colonial government support, took steps to establish up-country buying posts both to collect the cash crops and to expand the sales of a limited range of manufactured goods.

The middlemen who collected the export crops from African peasants usually either functioned directly as agents of the big trading firms or received credit from them in order to perform this role.[20]

Typically, the foreign trading companies provided these agents with cheap trade goods to sell to the peasants from whom they purchased the cash crops. Likewise, the inherited pattern of internal wholesale and retail trade in manufactured goods tended to reflect the domination of the economy by foreign trading firms through the export enclave. The many small private retail shops scattered throughout the countryside might enjoy a type of locational monopoly in that there is seldom more than one or two to a village. This has sometimes enabled them to raise prices above those in urban areas, not only to cover increased costs but to augment profit margins. Nevertheless, given that their living and overhead costs tend to be low—they might even grow their own food on a nearby farm—their profit margins might be considerably less than a large modern store might require to cover the cash salaries of hired employees and more extensive overheads.[21] On the other hand, the retailers, in terms of the kinds and prices of the goods they sell, were themselves entirely at the mercy of the handful of large wholesale firms concentrated in the major cities in the export enclave. As noted above, these wholesale firms are often branches of the big foreign trading firms or are associated with them through various financial arrangements. Controlling the storage and transportation facilities, as well as constituting the primary source of credit for the retailers, these firms garnered a significant share of the higher profits made possible by the retailers' frugal way of life as well as any increases in prices of goods sold in rural areas due to locational monopoly.

In the past the retail shop owners or agents of the big companies were consciously introduced from another culture. In East Africa the colonial administration used its licensing practices to introduce Asian traders,[22] to the disadvantage of Africans. In West Africa the Lebanese and other outside groups were also encouraged.[23] In both cases these groups could obtain credit more easily than Africans, either from the big foreign trading firms or associated foreign commercial banks.[24] If an African managed to establish a small retail store, he usually had to seek credit—if he could get it at all—as well as goods from the agents of the foreign firms.

The U.S. firm Sears, Roebuck, which has expanded rapidly in Latin America since World War II, has been held up as a model of the contribution large modern foreign firms might make to retail trade in less developed countries.[25] Sears "forces a revolution in retailing" by introducing store modernization, consumer credit, a different attitude toward the customer, the store clerk, the supplier, and the merchandise, and modern methods of pricing, inventory control, training, and window display. But even those arguing the advantages of the Sears type of foreign investment admit, "Sears is not a 'low-price' merchandiser. It caters to the middle class in the richer of these countries and to the upper class in the poorest of these countries. . . . Sears is not in Latin America for reasons of philanthropy, but because to be there is good and profitable business with extraordinary growth potential". Those who adopt this view do not point out that Sears, with its highly capital-intensive techniques based on its worldwide marketing apparatus, is in reality contributing to the waste of foreign exchange for imported luxuries to meet the whims of the high-income elites and squeezing out of business the small merchants using local products— thus aggravating the growing unemployment plaguing most developing countries.

In general, the dominant set of internal trading institutions tends, thus, to expand trading links that directly or indirectly perpetuate and expand the externally dependent export-import trade sector. Furthermore, they remain largely dependent on the big foreign trading firms for goods, markets, and credit.[26]

It is somewhat more difficult to trace the manner in which internal marketing institutions handling domestic foodstuffs and locally produced items also function to hinder the development of a nationally balanced economy, even in those regions where Africans have been permitted to become traders on their own account. A casual visit to a local market may give the illusion that many African traders—they may be either men or women, depending on where on the continent the market is located—are competing for sales at the retail level. Orthodox economic theory holds that such competition, if it did exist, would contribute to the spread of internal specialization and exchange. Yet more careful analysis[27] indicates that in many African countries, even where the Africans themselves are engaged in trade, various forms of control persist at the wholesale level. Studies of traditional African traders in West Africa,[28] for example, show that guilds, kinship groups, and marketing "rings" play a role in setting the prices paid to farmers as well as those charged to consumers of domestic foodstuffs. Through their control of the limited available facilities for storage and transport, these groups have long been able to maximize profits by increasing the margin between what they have paid the farmer and what they obtain through the retailer from the consumer. The peasants, seeking to sell their surpluses, must often headload their produce many miles to market, or sell it to the collection agent at his offer price.[29] At the other end of the marketing chain, the retailers may face fines, exclusion from the market, and even physical punishment in some cases if they sell below the agreed minimum market price.[30] The greater the margin, the greater the profit of those who control the wholesale operation. In periods of scarcity created by droughts or shortages of foreign exchange required to import essential supplementary foodstuffs, experience shows that these middlemen may hoard produce, profiting from rising prices.[31] These practices have blocked the expansion of internal specialization and exchange sufficiently so that growing urban populations in the export enclave have no recourse but to rely on import of necessities from overseas.

SUMMARY

African countries need to reshape both their foreign and their domestic trade patterns to support the increased internal specialization and exchange necessary to contribute to increased productivity in all sectors of a more nationally integrated economy. The evidence suggests that the inherited pattern of trading institutions has tended to hinder attainment of this goal. This is particularly true for export-import trade, where foreign-dominated firms tend to exercise control of the critical wholesale, storage, and credit functions. It also appears to be true in the markets for internally produced goods, even where, as in West Africa, private African traders have retained control of these facilities.

NOTES

1. The importance of trade institutions in planning and development is stressed in R. J. Halloway and R. S. Hancock, Marketing in a Changing Environment (New York: John Wiley and Sons, Inc., 1968), p. 408; A. A. Sherbini, "Marketing in the Industrialization of Underdeveloped Countries," The Journal of Marketing 29, no. 1 (January 1965): esp. 28; and P. F. Drucker, "Marketing and Economic Development," Journal of Marketing 22, no. 3, (1958): 252-259.

2. Cf. "The Economic Growth of ECAFE Countries," Economic Survey of Asia and the Far East, (UN ECAFE, 1961), pp. 21-38; and D. Seers, "Industry in Development: Some Fallacies," Journal of Modern African Studies (December 1963), p. 464.

3. Economic Commission for Africa, West African Mission, 3/CN. 14/246, p. 57.

4. E.g., E/CN. 14/248, par. 84.

5. For Unilever's holdings, see Moody's Investment Manual, Moody's Industrials, 1970 (New York 1970), p. 3037.

6. R. H. Green, "UNCTAD and After: Anatomy of a Failure," Journal of Modern African Studies 5, no. 2 (1967).

7. Cited in West Africa, Jan. 14, 1972, p. 43.

8. Green and Seidman, Unity or Poverty? Part 1.

9. E.g., A. Seidman, "Problems and Possibilities for East African Economic Integration," Conference on Africa in World Affairs:

The Next Thirty Years, World Order Models Project, Makerere University College, Kampala, Uganda, 1969.

10. V. A. Martynov, "Soviet Economic Aid to the Newly Liberated Countries," University of East Africa Conference on Foreign Aid, Dar es Salaam, September 1964.

11. E.g., A. Seidman, Ghana's Development Experience, 1951-1965 (Nairobi: East Africa Publishing House, 1972,) Ch. 10.

12. Sunday News (Tanzania), Aug. 31, 1969, p. 3.

13. E.g., G. Skorov and V. A. Martynov at Dar es Salaam Conference on Foreign Aid, September 1964; see also M. Dobb, Economic Growth and Underdeveloped Countries (London: Lawrence and Wishart, 1963), pp. 59-69.

14. J. Oser, Promoting Economic Development, with Illustrations from Kenya (Evanston: Northwestern University Press, 1967), pp. 217-219; see also Republic of Kenya, Development Plan, 1970-1974 (Nairobi: Government Printer, 1970), Ch. 10; and Kenya, Economic Survey, 1969, p. 88.

15. Even prior to independence, African countries had begun to increase their imports of capital goods and equipment (see Department of Economic and Social Affairs, United Nations, Economic Survey of Africa since 1950 [New York, 1959], p. 149), and this trend has been accelerated since independence.

16. For discussion of internal market of the typical African country, see Green and Seidman, Unity or Poverty? esp. p. 62.

17. E.g., Kenya's Development Plan, 1970-74, proposes the establishment of rayon and polyester poplin industries based on imported semiprocessed materials, despite the fact that its neighbors are exporting raw cotton and both plan to expand their cotton textiles industries as a critical feature of their industrial plans; even Kenya plans to expand its cotton production.

18. See, e.g., Cooper Motors' report in Nairobi Stock Exchange Report, 1967; for background of automobile companies, see National Christian Council of Kenya, Who Controls Industry in Kenya? (Nairobi: Africa Publishing House, 1968).

19. E.g., Republic of Kenya, Statistical Abstract, 1967 (Nairobi: Government Printer), pp. 102-3; H. C. G. Hawkins, Wholesale and Retail Trade in Tanganyika, A Study of Distribution in East Africa (New York: Praeger Publishers, 1965); see also Republic of Uganda "Work for Progress," Uganda's Second Five Year Plan, 1966-1971 (Entebbe: Government Printer, 1966), p. 112.

20. See G. Hunter, West Africa Trade, passim.

21. This was advanced by Lord Lugard as the argument for encouraging Asian traders, rather than introducing foreign firm branches, in rural areas in the days of outright colonialism (see Dual Mandate, p. 482).

22. E.g., see Lord Lugard, The Dual Mandate in British Tropical Africa (London: Frank Cass and Company, 1965), p. 482.

23. For role of these groups, see P. Garlick, "Levantine Trading Firms in Ghana," Ghana Economic Bulletin 4, nos. 10-192: 15-18.

24. This became the foundation of common complaints against the foreign private commercial banks throughout Africa, and a major cause of widespread initiatives to open state commercial banks in order to provide credit for African businessmen.

25. The following quotations are from J. Z. Kracmar, Marketing Research in the Developing Countries—A Handbook (New York: Praeger Publishers, 1971), pp. 22-3.

26. The way retailers obtain credit from big trading firms is described in detail in Bauer, West African Trade; and in East Africa Bucknall describes the failure of the Kenyan National Trading Corporation to replace the large wholesalers in State Trading in Kenya.

27. M. Miracle, "Market Structure and Conduct in Tropical Africa: A Survey," University of Wisconsin, mimeographed.

28. See Ibid. for summary of these studies.

29. E.g., see R. M. Lawson, "Inflation in the Consumer Market in Ghana: Its Cause and Cure," review article on Report of the Commission of Enquiry into Trade Malpractices, Office of the President, Accra, January 1966, Economic Bulletin of Ghana, no. 1 (1966).

30. Miracle, "Market Structure and Conduct in Tropical Africa: A Survey."

31. E.g., Abrahams Commission Report, passim.

10

ALTERNATIVE APPROACHES
TO ALTERING FOREIGN
TRADE PATTERNS

African governments have, for the most part, accepted as self-evident the fact that only the government itself is in a position to alter the inherited set of working rules that has perpetuated their external dependence in the area of foreign trade.[1] No private African entrepreneur can begin to compete effectively with a company like Unilever, whose world sales almost equal the total value of Africa's exports.[2] Even most of the individual African governments themselves are, in some respects, like David confronting Goliath: their total current and development budgets seldom equal the net income of the larger foreign trading firms that dominate their export enclaves.

Different governments have introduced differing kinds of measures in an effort to alter the pattern of their nations' participation in foreign trade. Careful examination of the various approaches utilized suggest that some have tended to be more successful than others. Such an analysis may also help to identify the difficulties that may arise in attempting to implement alternative policies.

CHANGING THE PATTERN OF IMPORTS

Tariffs, Licenses, and Quotas

Most African governments have made at least some efforts to revise the inherited pattern of import trade, with its overemphasis on luxury and semiluxury items for the higher-income groups.

Increased import tariffs have been a common device. These measures have been designed both to increase government revenues and to shift the composition of imports to include more capital goods and equipment for development purposes.

The general tendency has been to levy fairly high taxes on consumer luxury items while frequently imposing no duties on capital equipment and machinery.[3] The imposition of such duties has tended to reduce consumer luxury imports somewhat, depending on the amount of duty imposed on specific items. It has contributed to increased government revenue and raised the "living costs" of the upper-income urban dweller associated with export enclave activity, including civil servants; in effect, this may be one means of redirecting investible surpluses from this group to national development programs. Given the notoriously large gap between the incomes of the highest-income group and the majority of wage earners and peasants, this measure would seem justifiable both as a revenue measure and a method of reducing consumer luxury imports.

Insofar as import duties have been levied on more broadly consumed necessities, they have also contributed to government revenues, but they have tended simultaneously to raise the living costs of lower-income urban dwellers.[4] Unless the nation can produce such items (or adequate substitutes) domestically, careful analysis would appear to be required as to the impact of such measures in lowering the levels of living of the urban poor.

In general, most governments have not imposed duties on the import of capital goods and equipment, in order to avoid discouraging their import. An unintended consequence of this policy, however, has been the reinforcement of the tendency for large (usually foreign-owned) firms to import capital-intensive machinery and equipment as a substitute for organizing training and adequate supervision for the considerable numbers of available unemployed unskilled laborers.[5] It has been suggested that this tendency might be offset by a policy linking the reduction of the tax burden in some way to increased employment rather than to the import of capital-intensive machinery.[6]

Import tariff policies have had little impact in shifting sources of supply to new nations, including neighboring countries. The foreign-owned trading firms tend to continue to import from their own overseas sources of supply. They can hardly be expected to seek actively to purchase from other, possibly lower-cost, sources of supply in competition with their own overseas affiliates. The exception to this apparent tendency is the case where a large firm has established a last-stage assembly and/or processing plant to retain the market for its imports into a given African country and is eager to expand its sales through its affiliates into other neighboring countries. Such firms frequently support regional common markets to facilitate attainment of this goal. This is typified in the East African case, where large foreign firms have established such plants, usually in Kenya, to take advantage of the external economies historically developed there and to sell the output through their affiliates in Uganda and

Tanzania. This, together with the investible surpluses thus accumulated in the form of profits by these firms, has been a major element in the chronic balance of trade and payments deficits confronted by both countries in their trade with Kenya.[7]

Some African governments have tried to utilize licensing and import quotas in an effort to reduce the import of certain kinds of commodities and, where possible and advantageous, to shift sources of supply. Importing firms have been allocated licenses to import either a total value of imports or, in some cases, quotas of specific commodities. Sometimes the quotas may require purchase from new sources of supply with which the government has made new trade agreements. Experience suggests that this approach may contribute to significant reductions in the quantities of specific goods imported and perhaps to shifting sources of supply. Administration of such measures requires large amounts of high-level manpower, however, which is not extensively available in Africa. As a result, inefficiencies in allocation or inadequate estimates as to future requirements have contributed to serious shortages of essential commodities. For example, Ghana in 1965 allegedly confronted serious shortages, even of such necessary items as cutlasses,* the basic tool required by every peasant farmer. Industries lacked so many essential raw materials and parts that they began to lay off workers. Even essential foodstuffs were said to be in short supply, contributing to the soaring prices of domestically produced foodstuffs.[8] At the same time, wealthy individuals could still buy imported Mercedes-Benz automobiles or air conditioners. While shortages were fundamentally caused by the lack of foreign exchange because of the collapse of world cocoa prices, a more careful analysis of priorities and implementation of the licensing and quota program might have contributed to a more rational import pattern.†

But perhaps as important, or even more so, any system of licensing and quotas may contribute to the spread of bribery and corruption. A large firm desiring to continue or expand its import business may find that a bribe in the right place will ease its way. With a limited supply of highly skilled and dedicated manpower to administer the

---

*After the 1966 coup, the author was present at a durbar at which the United States ambassador presented the villagers with cutlasses, presumably a symbol that the U.S. would help the new government end the shortages of this essential tool.

†Some of the shortages were attributed at the time by the press to efforts of middlemen to hoard goods and speculate on rising prices resulting from the shortages; and there is some evidence that this may have been true.[9]

program, this possibility may be enhanced. In the Ghana case, evidence suggests that the license-granting authority did accept bribes for licenses and enlarged quotas.[10] More than that, these licenses were apparently granted to the private firms traditionally dominating the export enclave to carry on business in the old patterns in direct contradiction to the announced government policy of shifting to new sources of supply that might either be cheaper or help to open new markets for Ghana's cocoa.[11]

The Nigerian experience with strict foreign exchange controls, introduced during the civil war to halt the sharp decline of that federal government's foreign exchange reserves, provides additional evidence as to the difficulty involved in attempting to govern the use of foreign exchange through licensing. Smuggling of imported luxury items developed on a widespread scale, in part because of the ease with which foreign exchange could be obtained on the "black market." Methods of obtaining foreign exchange, in addition to direct sale of smuggled exports like cocoa and groundnuts, have been reported to include[12] sale of Nigerian currency at the airports; purchase of airline tickets for travel abroad that may then be traded in for foreign exchange; illegal use of home allotments by expatriates, who are permitted to ship out 50 percent of their gross salaries; obtaining foreign exchange for the permitted £100 travel allowance from several separately owned private commercial banks, thus multiplying the actual amounts obtained; and transferring unnecessary sums as allotments to students abroad. By 1970 the loss of foreign exchange on the last three of these accounts was estimated to total about £20 million—more than in 1968—an amount almost equal to the total National Development Corporation investment in industry in Tanzania after the Arusha Declaration.

State Trading Corporations

Both import tariffs and licensing-quota arrangements have been fraught with difficulties as measures designed to implement a shift in import patterns. Therefore some countries have attempted to establish state trading corporations to take new initiatives in altering import trade patterns. The declared goals of these corporations have varied significantly from country to country, as have the consequences of establishing them. In some instances these corporations have been directed to try to expand exports as well as change the composition of imports.

Kenya's National Trading Corporation (KNTC), for example, sought primarily to achieve Africanization of trade in Kenya itself.[13] Would-be African traders were granted licenses giving them exclusive rights to sell specific imported items, particularly mass-consumed

goods like blankets and sugar. In some cases the KNTC itself handled
the importing. In other cases it licensed firms to import. At no time
were more than 10 percent of all imports affected. Gradually, the
KNTC's initial policy of lending funds to African traders was eliminated, allegedly because of extensive defaults. By 1970 the KNTC
was reducing the share of imports it handled directly. It began to
appear that attainment of even the limited goal of Africanization of
trade was unlikely to be successful. It has been argued that such efforts
to replace Asian middlemen with Africans in the domestic market
can contribute little to restructuring the nation's participation in external trade in a manner more likely to foster self-reliant development.[14]* This argument appears to be substantiated by examination
of Kenyan trade data, which suggest there has been little shift of sources
or kinds of imports. That the value of imported private automobiles
still equaled three-fourths of the total capital investment in manufacturing in Kenya in 1968[15] indicates a particularly unfortunate allocation of scarce foreign exchange.

Ghana's National Trading Corporation (GNTC) was established
in precoup Ghana with the stated goal of altering import trade patterns
as well as contributing to internal trade expansion.[16] It operated in
competition with the existing foreign importing firms, of which the
United Africa Company remained the largest. Manpower problems
undoubtedly hindered its efforts to attain its goals. The man appointed
as head of the new trading corporation was a retired former head of
the Ghana branch of the United Africa Company itself.† Many of its
employees had formerly worked for UAC as well as other trading
firms, some having apparently been fired by them for inefficiency or
malfeasance.‡ Again, trade data suggest that although the GNTC did
utilize new sources of supply, the alteration in the pattern of import
trade was taking place relatively slowly. This may have been ac-
counted for, in part, by the fact that private competing firms managed
to obtain import licenses from the licensing authorities, apparently
occasionally at the expense of GNTC efforts to expand its purchases
in other areas. After the 1966 coup, the GNTC continued to play a
role in import trade, although more restricted than before. In line
with the new government's stated philosophy of encouraging private
enterprise, it is not surprising that measures to replace foreign private traders were largely abandoned.

---

*The consequences of KNTC policies for internal trade will be
considered below.
  †The United Africa Co. is the main African subsidiary of Unilever,
discussed on p. 40 above. See also pp. 112-13.
  ‡The consequences of the GNTC's internal operations are briefly
considered below.

Immediately after independence, Tanzania's government made several relatively unsuccessful attempts to shift the pattern of trade through state corporations in competition with the existing trading firms.[17] Finally, government and party officials concluded that it would be necessary to take over all import and wholesale trade if the government was to succeed in implementing a development program oriented toward attainment of self-reliance. Following the Arusha Declaration, the government nationalized the five major existing foreign importing and distributing concerns, three of which were in the midst of a triple merger, and joined them with the two existing state agencies engaged in trade in a newly created State Trading Corporation. Some of the nationalized firms were registered in Tanganyika, others were offshoots of companies trading Kenya and Uganda whose East African operations were controlled from Nairobi—and some of the latter were responsible to overseas head offices.[18]

In the first year of its existence, the new State Trading Corporation (STC) management rationalized the operations of the constituent branches, putting all related activities and expertise together to maximize strength and cohesion in particular divisions dealing with broad categories of related commodities. The initial staff of 1,500, including 85 European expatriates, was reduced in size. Savings in rents were made as similar activities in the same areas were combined under one roof. Further savings were made as the STC took steps to eliminate hidden rebates made by former importing houses to manufacturers abroad—said to account for as much as half of the total thirteen-point rise in the 1962-65 Tanzanian import price index.[19]

Despite these visible accomplishments, the process of taking complete control of exports and imports was gradual. While the STC imported about 70 percent of all consumer items, it handled only about 20 percent of all imports by the end of 1968. Much of the remainder was being imported directly through parastatals and government agencies as well as private firms for suppliers' credit. This meant that additional possible savings, as well as standardization of parts and equipment* through coordinated purchases, were not being realized. A variety of consumer durable items, including automobiles, refrigerators, and air conditioners, were still being imported by private firms.

Tanzania's Second Five Year Plan proposed more rapid expansion of the State Trading Corporation's trading activities to attain the goal of complete control of export-import trade as formulated in the Arusha Declaration.[20] To implement the expansion of STC,

---

*It is evident that if domestic industry is ultimately to replace foreign import of supplies of parts, this type of standardization is essential to broaden the potential internal market for it.

207

however, it was held that it would be necessary to clarify a number of issues of principle. Among these was the necessity of determining whether the STC was to function primarily as a commercial organization or to minimize prices to the consumer, and whether it should continue to be required to compete with private firms in both exports and imports or should devise other means to insure continued efficient operation within the framework of its declared purpose of becoming the "authorized body for import trade."[21] The resolution of these issues would seem to be important if the State Trading Corporation is to contribute successfully in the long run to reshaping Tanzania's participation in foreign trade.

EFFORTS TO EXPAND EXPORTS

The expansion of exports, including increasingly processed produce, is just as essential for development in Africa as is reshaping the inherited pattern and role of imports. The extent of institutional changes introduced by the governments of the former British colonies appears to be somewhat less in the case of exports than in the case of imports. In part this may reflect the constraints imposed by the trading companies associated with the manufacturers in the developed country markets to which the countries have traditionally sold their output. It is certainly affected by the persistence of tariff barriers and quotas on processed goods in those countries, despite repeated complaints by all Third World nations. The opening of new marketing outlets in neighboring African countries is hampered because almost all African countries are capable of producing a similar range of produce; unless they can coordinate their development plans to produce complementary, rather than competing products, even existing inter-African trade may be reduced. Establishing new outlets in socialist countries also appears to require the creation of new approaches and new sets of institutions.

Marketing Boards

Most former British colonies inherited marketing boards that handled their overseas agricultural exports. In Central Africa and in East Africa, particularly Kenya, the marketing boards were established primarily to represent the agricultural producers, that is, the settlers who owned the big estates, in their efforts to protect themselves against the collapse of world prices during the Great Depression.[22] African producer representatives were excluded from the boards, just as they were for the most part excluded from export crop production until just before independence.

In West Africa marketing boards were established during World War II primarily to represent the interests of the trading companies as well as the British government in insuring continued supplies of agricultural raw materials during the war.[23] The quota system imposed by the West African produce marketing board has been held to be "a statutory extension and enforcement of prewar produce buying pools and syndicates of West African merchants . . . designed to protect gross and net profit margins of the merchants by restraining buying competition among them."[24]

The marketing boards generally advised the governments on production and price policies. In cases where African farmers were engaged in export crop production, the boards typically set producer prices well below world export prices in order to accumulate "price support" funds. These funds were supposed to be utilized to stabilize producer prices when world prices fell, thus providing an incentive to the African peasants, who had recently entered the cash market, to continue to expand output. Initially, in most cases, the funds—which mounted into millions of pounds sterling[25]—were used to purchase British government securities instead of being added to sorely-needed investment funds in the colonies themselves.[26]

As nationalist pressures mounted and independence neared, aspects of the marketing boards were gradually transformed. The West African produce marketing board, having been divided among the separate colonies, began to include African as well as colonial government representatives.[27] In East Africa, African government representatives began to appear on the boards, although the role of the large settler farmers remained prominent in Kenya.[28] In Tanzania and Uganda more emphasis was placed on including representatives of African marketing cooperatives on the boards. Eventually the price support funds were transferred from England to the African countries to be loaned to governments for utilization in various kinds of projects. It has been estimated[29] that the investments obtained from Uganda's cotton and coffee boards' funds exceeded all the funds made available to that country in the form of grants and loans by the colonial government in the postwar decade.

In the postindependence era, the marketing boards' price support funds were sharply reduced by payment of subsidies to the peasants in the form of stable producer prices when world prices for major exports fell. Eventually, when their funds were exhausted, most boards had to reduce producer payments, thus sharply cutting peasant incomes. The African peasants, lacking extensive understanding of the mechanism of world markets, sometimes viewed this as a form of exploitation by the central government, rather than as the consequence of the decline of world prices. In Ghana, for example, where the cocoa producer price in real terms was reduced in 1965 to a level below that of 1937, this kind of resentment may have been a significant factor contributing to peasant support for the coup that ousted President Nkrumah in 1966.[30]

The fact is, however, that African marketing boards, by and large, have done little on their own to alter the pattern of overseas exports to reduce excessive dependence on the sale of a few raw materials to a few major countries and buying firms. For the most part, they have continued to auction export crops to the same trading companies that purchased them before. The Nkrumah government did transfer the auction of Ghana cocoa from London to Accra[31]—a policy that the Busia government considered reversing[32]—but this of itself did not fundamentally alter the trading patterns. In East Africa most boards had traditionally auctioned their produce in East Africa itself—usually in Nairobi or Mombasa[33]—perhaps reflecting the powerful role played by European settlers. Tanzania, upon independence, established its own auctions for several of its major crops, but otherwise each board initially functioned on its own, much as it had in the past. The location of the auction appears less significant, however, than the fact that, as Bauer and Yamey pointed out in another context, auctions of themselves cannot prevent collusive action among several buyers.[34] The continued purchase of these crops by a handful of large foreign firms that may cooperate in setting prices in relation to supply has given African nations little leeway in their efforts to broaden markets and expand export earnings.

The Special Problems of Selling Minerals

At independence, the sale of the mineral exports produced in Africa's rich mines was almost invariably handled directly by the foreign firms that owned the mines themselves. These firms were often associated directly with the companies that processed the minerals in the developed countries, or else they had established a vast marketing complex to insure their sales directly to those companies. They owned or controlled the necessary shipping and storage facilities, could obtain essential funds from associated financial institutions, and had built up a network of marketing outlets throughout the developed Western world. Not infrequently they cooperated to fix world output and prices of specific minerals. (See pp. 44-50 for copper, Africa's main mineral export, as an example).

African countries seeking to expand their exports of mineral produce confront a somewhat different set of marketing problems than those selling agricultural produce. The cost of establishing processing facilities for minerals for sale to final consumers at home or overseas is usually far too great for any individual African country

210

to undertake alone unless it has a large enough guaranteed external market for the output. Developed countries that have been processing their minerals in their home factories have typically imposed tariffs on competing processed imports. African countries have as yet been unable to arrive at the necessary political-economic agreements needed to build continental markets for the output of such basic industries.[35] This appears to leave the only potential new markets, not already dominated by the marketing apparatus established by the big mining firms and their associated interests, in socialist countries, but these may in some cases already have their own sources of supply.

Zambia, depending on copper sales for over 90 percent of its exports, exemplifies the problems confronting mineral exporting nations. On taking over 51 percent of the ownership of its copper mines, the Zambian government appears to have had no alternative but to leave not only the management, but also the overseas marketing of copper in the hands of the mining companies, Amax and Anglo-American, and their associates. This initially left Zambia still essentially dependent on the decisions of the companies in relation to price and output. (See pp. 47-50). Zambia has encouraged other companies to search for new mines, but at this writing it remains to be seen whether they can compete with the global marketing apparatus already established by the old firms in this extensively cartelized field. And the old firms are busy seeking new sources of copper as well as diversifying into aluminum, which competes with copper for many purposes. The companies have a far greater degree of flexibility in this respect than Zambia, whose main productive sectors have for nearly half a century been tied to the companies' mining activities. Zambia has begun to sell some of its copper to socialist countries, for which it has begun to develop its own marketing arrangements, including shipping and storage facilities.

The Role of State Trading Corporations in Exports

Some countries have attempted to utilize state trading corporations to expand exports to socialist nations.[36] Socialist nations, in particular, seek long-term arrangements at fixed prices enabling them to fit specified amounts of given imports into their own planned economies. They tend to consider participation in competitive bidding at auctions and associated short-term price fluctuations undesirable. Agreements with socialist nations usually require that African countries import goods from the socialist countries in return as a means of payment.* Prior to the 1966 coup, for example, Ghana's government had arranged to sell a third of the cocoa crop to the Soviet Union for several years at £180 a ton,[37] considerably above the then world market price, which had plummeted to £90 a ton. In exchange, Ghana agreed to purchase a wide range of Soviet goods, also at fixed prices. This would appear to have opened a significant new market for Ghanaian cocoa. In the event that the price rose—which it eventually did, although never reaching its postwar peak of £500 a ton[38]—Ghana risked the loss of the difference between the price to the USSR and the new world price. Presumably, on the other hand, it might have been able to expand output to maintain its previous level of sales to its former trading partners, thus significantly augmenting its total foreign exchange earnings.†

Tanzania's Second Five Year Plan,[40] as part of its general proposal for expanding the State Trading Corporation's role to govern all exports as well as imports in line with the Arusha Declaration, directed STC's management to initiate consultations with the marketing boards to explore the possibilities of benefits to be obtained by channeling a greater proportion of their export produce directly through STC. It was suggested that STC might expand the nation's exports more rapidly if it stationed agents in potential new markets, including the socialist countries, to make long-term contracts for fixed prices, perhaps linking them to the purchase of a range of specific imports. The plan also envisaged that STC would play a role in promoting the external sales of expanding manufactured goods production to neighboring countries as well as overseas.

In 1971 press reports indicated that the STC was encountering financial and managerial problems in implementing these directives.[41] Nevertheless, it appeared probable that in the long run a much greater degree of coordination of marketing board activities, the opening of new sales channels overseas, and, insofar as possible, greater export of manufacturing goods remained essential if exports were to contribute more effectively to the needed support for the board's plans for internal development.

SUMMARY

It is widely accepted that only African governments, rather than private entrepreneurs, can make the institutional changes necessary

----

*The International Monetary Fund has typically objected to such so-called "barter" agreements as violating (assumed) international market competition, and not infrequently has required the abrogation of such agreements as a precondition for fund assistance.

†The postcoup government abrogated the agreement, however, in line with International Monetary Fund advice.[39]

to alter the inherited pattern of foreign trade that has linked African economies to uncertain markets for their raw material exports. Tariffs, licenses, and quotas set by governments have been designed to reduce luxury imports and release foreign exchange for the import of capital machinery and equipment. Difficulties in administering these, sometimes aggravated by corrupt practices, have reduced their effectiveness. Some countries have sought to utilize state trading corporations, in some cases to Africanize trade, in others to reshape the entire import sector. Major institutional problems need to be worked out and manpower trained, however, if these corporations are to play an adequate role in restructuring imports.

On the other hand, efforts to expand exports, particularly of manufactured goods, have confronted vast marketing complexes operated by the foreign trading firms that have long dominated African economies. Postindependence agricultural produce marketing boards have provided some governmental control of surpluses produced by local peasants, but have typically continued to sell to the same set of overseas buyers as before. Sales of mineral exports, in the past conducted directly by the firms owning the mines, have been only marginally affected by increased shares of government ownership in the mines themselves; the foreign companies still handle the management of the mines and the overseas sales through the extensive marketing apparatus they have established. If state trading corporations are to contribute to broadening sales overseas, Tanzania, at least, has concluded that they will need to become more vigorously involved in direct export activity. All of these new directions require development of important new institutional approaches as well as the training of highly skilled, committed personnel to implement them.

NOTES

1. Every African national plan incorporates a significant role for the state; see comment by Economic Commission for Africa, "Industrialization and Economic Planning," Economic Bulletin for Africa (New York, United Nations, January 1963), III, 63.

2. See Moody's Investment Manual, Moody's Industrial, 1970, p. 3037; and United Nations, Yearbook of International Trade Statistics.

3. E.g., Republic of Uganda, Background to the Budget, 1967-1968, sections on manufacturing industry and tax revenues.

4. Republic of Ghana, Economic Survey, 1965, p. 100, showed that rising prices were affecting urban wage earners' living costs negatively; taxes on consumer necessities were among the elements causing these price increases.

5. Cf. A. Baryaruha, "Factors Affecting Industrial Employment, Case Study No. 5," Economic Development Research Project (EDRP) No. 89; Madhvani Sugar Works (Kakivo), EDRP No. 100; "Case Study of Nyanza Textiles Industries, Ltd.," EDRP No. 69; "Productivity Analysis and an Attempt on Employment Projection," EDRP No. 76 (Kampala: Makerere Economic Development and Research Project, mimeo.).

6. R. Green, "Wage Levels, Employment, Productivity and Consumption: Some Issues in Social Policy and Development Strategy," EDRP No. 109, p. 36.

7. Republic of Kenya, Economic Survey, 1967, Table 2.1, p. 21. See also Economic Surveys for following years.

8. See Republic of Ghana, Economic Survey, 1961, p. 81; 1962, p. 82; 1963, p. 118; 1964, p. 107; 1965, p. 110.

9. Presidential Commission of Enquiry into Trade Malpractices, W. Abrahams, Chairman (Accra: Office of the President, 1966), p. 54, hereafter cited as Abrahams Commission Report.

10. See Ibid., passim; also, Report of Commission of Enquiry re Import Licenses (Accra, 1964); Ghanaian Times, spring and summer 1966, passim, regarding reports concerning acceptance of bribes by officials.

11. Government memoranda in the files of the Planning Commission, 1966, Accra, Ghana.

12. Afroscope (Nigeria) 1, no. 1 (June 1971): 3 ff.

13. See Bucknall, State Trading In Kenya, esp. Ch. 1.

14. Cf. National Christian Council of Kenya, Who Controls Industry in Kenya? pp. 257-9.

15. Republic of Kenya, Economic Survey, 1969, Table 1.10, p. 17.

16. Information relating to the GNTC was obtained by interviews by the author with a member of the Ghana National Trading Corporation Board of Directors and the merchandizing manager, as well as information in the files of the Government Planning Commission, 1966, some of which appeared in the Abrahams Commission Report, passim.

17. Monck and Wood, Paper on State Trading Corporation; and A. L. Bennett, "Self-Reliance and Foreign Trade, A Panel," Economic Society of Tanzania (Dar es Salaam, September 11, 1968, mimeo).

18. See Bennet, "Self-Reliance and Foreign Trade," for the following information relating to Tanzania's State Trading Corporation, unless otherwise cited.

19. M. J. H. Yaffey, Interview by author, July 20, 1968.

20. United Republic of Tanzania, Second Five Year Plan, 1, 142-3.

21. See Bennett, "Self-Reliance and Foreign Trade."

22. For a summary analysis of these boards as British rule neared its end, see Kenya Colony and Protectorate, Committee on the Organization of Agriculture, Report (Nairobi, 1960).

23. See P. T. Bauer, West African Trade, A Study of Competition, Oligopoly and Monopoly in a Changing Economy (London: Rutledge and Kegan, Ltd., 1963), passim.

24. P. T. Bauer and B. S. Yamey, Markets, Market Control and Marketing Reform, Selected Papers (London: Weidenfeld and Nicolson, 1968), p. 146.

25. E.g., D. A. Lury, "Cotton and Coffee Growers and Government Development Finance in Uganda, 1945-1960," The East African Economic Review 10, no. 1 (1963); H. H. Binhammer, "Financial Infrastructure and the Availability of Credit and Finance to the Rural Sector of the Tanzanian Economy," University Social Science Council Conference, December 30, 1968-January 3, 1969, Makerere; and Gold Coast (later Ghana) Cocoa Marketing Board, Annual Report, 1948 to date.

26. Bauer, West African Trade, passim.

27. See Gold Coast Cocoa Marketing Board, Annual Reports, 1948-1957.

28. Kenya Colony and Protectorate, Committee on the Organization of Agriculture, Report.

29. Lury, "Cotton and Coffee Growers and Government Development Finance in Uganda, 1945-1960."

30. Seidman, Ghana's Development Experience, 1951-1965, Ch. 12, Section 4.

31. Ghana Cocoa Marketing Board, Annual Reports, 1957-1961.

32. For information relating to foreign trade policies introduced by Busia administration in the first months in office, see Legon Observer, Jan. 16, 1970; Ghanaian Times, Oct. 20, 1969; "Commercial News," West Africa, Jan. 24, 1970; Ministry of Information, Interview with the Prime Minister, Jan. 15, 1970.

33. See National Christian Council of Kenya, Who Controls Industry in Kenya? regarding marketing board operations after independence.

34. Markets, Market Control and Marketing Reform, p. 396.

35. See Green and Seidman, Unity or Poverty? Part III, for discussion of this possibility.

36. For information relating to Kenyan national trading corporation, see, J. Bucknall, "State Trading in Kenya," Ph.D. dissertation, University of Wisconsin, 1971; for Tanzanian corporation, see N. Monck and R. N. Wood, Paper on State Trading Corporation, (Dar es Salaam, Feb. 28, 1967, mimeographed).

37. Republic of Ghana, Economic Survey, 1964, p. 67, and 1965, pp. 53 ff.

38. Gold Coast Cocoa Marketing Board, <u>Annual Report</u>, 1955.

39. For summary of International Monetary Fund Advice, see K. Amoaka-Atta, <u>Budget Speech, 1966</u>, reported in <u>Ghana Daily Gazette</u>, Feb. 23, 1966.

40. Second Five Year Plan, pp. 142-3.

41. E.g., <u>Sunday Nation</u> (Nairobi), April 11, 1971.

11

INTERNAL TRADING INSTITUTIONS

After attaining independence, many African governments have attempted to intervene in internal marketing at various levels for various reasons and with varying degrees of success. The exhaustive research needed to reach definitive conclusions as to the efficacy of these alternatives has not yet been completed, but available evidence permits identification and at least initial evaluation of some of the critical problems that have been confronted. Almost every African government has introduced marketing cooperatives for export crops. A few, especially in East Africa, have utilized marketing boards and developed marketing cooperatives to handle internal domestic foodstuffs. In addition, some states have extended the operations of the state trading corporations to internal wholesale trade.

MARKETING COOPERATIVES

Marketing cooperatives have a relatively long history in Africa. In the former French colonies they were established by the colonial government to facilitate the collection and improvement in quality of export crops produced by African peasants. Membership was made compulsory.[1] The British actively encouraged the peasants to organize cooperatives after World War II in their West Africa colonies,[2] although the trading company buying agents remained the most important collectors of export crops until independence. In Kenya and Northern Rhodesia the European settlers organized their own cooperatives to strengthen their position in the market.[3] African peasants were excluded, since in any event they were prohibited from participating in export crop production until shortly before independence. When Africans were permitted to produce export cash crops, both governments envisaged cooperatives as the means of bringing their crops to market.

Membership in cooperatives was made compulsory in Kenya's "Million Acre Scheme"[4] for all export crops. In Uganda and Tanganyika the peasants themselves took the initiative in the colonial period in organizing cooperatives in an effort to improve their bargaining position vis à vis the Asian middlemen who owned cotton and coffee processing facilities as well as some of the big estates producing coffee.[5] In the postindependence era, the governments of both countries encouraged the rapid spread of cooperatives until membership became essentially compulsory in the case of most export crops.[6] In Tanzania sale through cooperatives was also required in the case of rice and maize for domestic consumption.

Marketing cooperatives have facilitated the rapid expansion of cash crop production and marketing among African peasants since World War II. They provided a means for collecting and selling the produce of tens of thousands of new entrants into the export crop markets. Ghana's cocoa output doubled from 1955 to 1965, and quality was significantly improved.[7] East African countries tripled and even quadrupled the output of cash crops produced by African peasants.[8] Efforts to improve quality to raise the crops' value were often successful there too. One cannot pass this off lightly. It should be emphasized that if increased peasant participation in augmented production is a criterion of success, the marketing cooperatives have achieved a significant degree of success.

This very success contributed much to the greatest problem confronted by most of the young cooperative movements of Africa: the serious decline of the world prices for the export crops with which they had been dealing.[9] Not infrequently peasants, who had only recently begun to participate in the production of cash crops, blamed the cooperatives themselves for the consequent reduction in their cash incomes. When the United Ghana Farmers Cooperative Council (UGFCC was ordered by the marketing board to cut producer prices because of the collapse of world cocoa prices, the UGFCC bore a considerable share of the blame.[10] Yet marketing cooperatives, functioning within the borders of individual African nations, can do little or nothing to solve the problems of world market prices.*

Evidence has also been accumulating to suggest that the rapidly expanding marketing cooperatives have encountered other serious difficulties in the areas both of efficiency and of peasant participation. These two phenomena do not appear to be unrelated.[11] Nor are they unrelated to efforts to restructure the national economy to attain self-reliance.[12] Several major issues appear involved.

1. Inadequate study of pre-existing traditions: One type of problem has been the passage of legislation to establish cooperatives

---

*See pp. 32-43 above.

without a thorough examination of the traditions and realities of the existing working rules in the framework of which that cooperative is supposed to function.

Much has been said about the possibilities and difficulties of building modern cooperatives on the basis of pre-existing communal activities among African peasants. There may, however, be a significant difference between the objectives of traditional cooperative efforts and those of marketing cooperatives as they have been established in Africa. One observer pointed out that the principle of communalism in most traditional African societies involved the sharing of labor in special projects like building a house or a road. There was generally no sharing of material wealth, and when it did take place it was usually confined to kinship units, to secure social cohesion and maintain established loyalties

> By contrast, modern cooperatives have the objective, among others, of creating new loyalties, of securing bonds of cooperation that cut across traditional social units. Moreover, work is performed on a contractual basis and each person is expected to fulfill his duties for the common interest of all members regardless of family ties and kinship obligations.[13]

Efforts to establish working rules for modern marketing cooperatives have on occasion contributed to less than desirable results because they have contradicted local customs. Legislation establishing a pyrethrum cooperative in the Million Acre Scheme in Kenya, for example, provided for payment of earnings to the man in whose name the plot of land was registered; apparently this so reduced incentive for his wife(s), who traditionally grew the pyrethrum crop, that total pyrethrum output actually declined.[14] In another case, an expatriate lawyer formulated rules for range associations for the Masai in Tanzania in which cattle units were to be permanently allocated on the basis of existing numbers of head of cattle owned.[15] Failing to take account of the traditional fluctuations in holdings, for such purposes as the payment of brideprice, this arrangement tended to impose a permanent stratification based on a temporarily existing situation.

It would appear self-evident that the attempt to impose cooperatives within the framework of principles imported from elsewhere without regard to local traditions and needs would be likely to be counterproductive. Research and experience need to be directed to formulation of principles for the expansion of cooperative marketing as appropriate to African circumstances, rather than principles imported from Europe.

2. Lack of trained manpower: Almost every African cooperative movement has suffered the consequences of a lack of trained, dedicated manpower capable of mobilizing peasant participation in decision-making as well as implementing the day-to-day work of bookkeeping and handling produce and other cooperative services. A post-1966 coup investigation of the United Ghana Farmers Cooperative Council[16] revealed that former business agents of the foreign trading companies had been hired by that organization and continued to function after they became secretary receivers of the cooperatives in much the same manner as before. Not a few were accused of short-weighting, underpaying, and in general cheating the peasants. The profit margins of the cooperative buying agents were raised—not lowered—after they had taken over all cocoa sales. The investigation report concluded that the farmers would prefer not to sell through cooperatives at all, and the military government invited the trading companies to return. Significantly enough, the companies refused, indicating that they found it more convenient to permit cooperatives or other country agents to handle the country buying operations and, incidentally, to bear the brunt of the blame for falling world cocoa prices. The government thereupon restored private buying agents, licensed directly by the marketing board. Within a few months time, the press was again reporting complaints of licensing agents utilizing government funds for purposes unrelated to crop purchases as well as of the other practices of which peasants had previously complained.[17]

In Tanzania a thorough investigation of marketing cooperatives, launched in 1966, revealed complaints not unlike those made in Ghana.[18] In this case the government immediately initiated actions in an effort to improve the situation.[19] The two largest cooperatives, those handling cotton and coffee in the Sukumaland and Kilimanjaro areas, respectively, were taken over by the government and reorganized before being restored to their memberships. Education programs were initiated with a view to training personnel for cooperatives. A unified cooperative service, including an inspection prgram, was established for all cooperatives.

The investigations in Ghana and Tanzania were perhaps more comprehensive than others made in the postindependence period, but fragmentary evidence from other areas suggests that the problems they revealed were by no means unique.[20] In an effort to overcome them, training programs for cooperative management personnel are being established in many areas. Usually these emphasize technical skills like bookkeeping. Tanzania has been going further in an effort to orient its cooperative training programs specifically toward fostering the ideas of ujamaa, producer cooperation. That country's political leaders perceive ujamaa as an essential foundation if the personnel thus trained are going to involve peasant participation in cooperative activity without domination by large farmers.[21]

One specific measure that has been suggested, both to improve efficiency and to increase democratic peasant participation in cooperatives, is the devising of internal working rules for cooperatives that link returns to management to efficiency.[22] The peasants themselves could participate in discussion of these working rules to secure their endorsement of the aims and anticipated consequences. The rules should be designed to insure that the managers would receive increased income to the extent that they increased the cooperative's profit margin, over and above costs, within the limits imposed by prices paid to the farmers and those fixed for sale to the consumers.

3. Alleged lack of loyalty: A common complaint among cooperative organizers in Africa relates to the lack of "loyalty" to the cooperatives allegedly evidenced by members. It has been observed— in recent years as well as in the colonial era— that peasants sell their crops outside of cooperatives when they are convinced that they can get higher returns from private traders, even if they have to sell illegally on the black market.[23] This tendency for farmers to sell outside cooperative channels appears to have been fostered by the common practice of imposing local taxes and duties on sales made through cooperatives, because it is much easier to collect them before the cash payments are turned over to the peasant. It has been held to be further aggravated when all members of a given marketing cooperative are held responsible for the failure of individual members to repay debts, so that their earnings are reduced by general deductions until the debts are covered.[24] Complaints to the Commission of Inquiry in Tanzania relating to coffee cooperatives were backed by data showing that the producer actually received only 75 percent of the producer price set by the marketing board because so much was deducted in fees and taxes before he received his final payment. Since the 25-percent reduction came out of the producer's profit margin, it had a significant impact on his real family income.*[25]

The problem of sales outside cooperative marketing channels seems to be far more common in the case of domestically- consumed foodstuffs than export crops. The only significant outlet for export crops available to private farmers and/or traders outside compulsory cooperative marketing channels is, in most cases, smuggling across

---

*In Tanzania the government sought to eliminate this problem by eliminating all local taxes on crops, removing tax powers from local district councils, raising taxes on consumer goods, particularly those consumed in urban areas, and financing local expenditures directly from resulting increases in the central government budget.

the border to a neighboring state where producer prices may be higher. While this illegal trade is of course hard to quantify, it has been estimated in Ghana to run as high as several thousands of tons of cocoa smuggled to neighboring Togo and the Ivory Coast.26 In the case of internally consumed foodstuffs, however, the ease with which private farmers and/or traders can sell produce outside the cooperative is increased by the immediate proximity of the market. Both consumers and farmers can see short-run advantages: a local trader may offer somewhat higher prices to the farmer and sell at somewhat lower prices to local consumers, since he does not need to cover the heavy overheads that a regional or national cooperative must carry. Cooperative supporters argue with the farmers that the private middleman is simply underselling the cooperative now so that later, when the cooperative has gone out of business, he can raise his profit margins to exploit both the farmers and the consumers. There is some fragmentary evidence to justify this claim.27

The alleged lack of farmer loyalty, however, focuses attention on the pricing policies pursued by the marketing cooperatives in relation to efforts to induce greater peasant participation within the framework of a national plan to expand internal specialization and exchange. Many, if not most, African peasants who grow primarily locally consumed foodstuffs produce most of their own requirements. They sell only a little surplus produce to obtain cash for a few items such as cloth, salt, kerosene, and matches. Their participation in marketing cooperatives has not come about primarily as a result of years of struggle with rapacious traders, as was more typically the case in Europe.28 The marketing cooperative in Africa has instead been introduced by the government primarily as a device to bring the peasants into cash crop production while avoiding the emergence of a middleman class. Such a class, in the long run, might speculate not only to the disadvantage of the peasants, but also to the detriment of national development plans requiring the provision of adequate food supplies and eventually raw materials to growing urban-industrialized areas. If cooperative pricing policy discourages farmer participation in cash crop production at the outset, however, it would seem to be defeating the very purpose of establishing marketing cooperatives for dealing with these crops.

Various governments have attempted in various ways to provide markets to expand sales of domestically consumed foodstuffs. Many have simply decided not to attempt to foster marketing cooperatives to handle these crops, concentrating their efforts on expansion of export crops.29 This, however, has tended to leave the would-be domestic foodstuff cash crops at the mercy of existing private marketing interests. On the one hand, farmers have been discouraged from expanding foodstuff production for sale because prices paid by traders have been too low to provide an adequate incentive. On the other hand, shortages of local foodstuffs in urban areas have been a major factor enabling traders to raise foodstuff prices to the urban wage earner.[30] This has contributed to pressures for rising wages, apparently with a distinctly negative effect on efforts to provide more urban employment through expanding industrialization. Holding the line on wages under these circumstances has fostered extensive labor unrest and costly strikes. In Ghana, for example, after the 1966 coup, continued rising prices have contributed to labor strife that has halted production on the docks, the rubber plantations, and the mines more than once. In at least one case, resulting clashes with the police resulted in deaths.[31]

4. Large farmer domination: Evidence from all over the continent suggests that where large farmers exist alongside of small farmers, they tend to dominate cooperative committees and managements, often utilizing their influence to arrogate to themselves a greater share of cooperative services including credit, farm inputs, and marketing facilities. In the Kenya Cooperative Creameries, the role of the large estate farmers (now including some African large estate owners) in dominating the dairy cooperative continues and has been the cause of at least one governmental investigation.[32] In other countries, where the inequalities between large and small farmers have not been so self-evident, the emergence of social stratification with the expansion of cash crop farming has nevertheless created conditions in which larger farmers have not infrequently managed to gain control of cooperative affairs. In some cases they have used the cooperative services to expand their own farm and associated businesses.[33] The former head of the United Ghana Farmers Cooperative admitted, after the 1966 coup, that he had acquired (in the name of various members of his family) several farms employing many laborers, as well as a number of town houses and a transport business.[34]

Hyden summarized the experience with cooperatives in Africa by stating that, while they

> do serve an important function of integrating peasants into the monetary economy, they do not constitute a powerful economic instrument of their ordinary members, the genuine small-holders. Indeed, cooperatives in Africa, including Kenya, have primarily been stepping-stones for ambitious members of the nascent rural "bourgeoisie"—teachers, traders, politicians, and even administrators—

223

and have therefore served to promote rural class formation rather than to prevent it.*35

In the United Arab Republic, where land reform resulted in the
division of the largest landed estates and put a ceiling on the size of
land holdings of the larger farmers, the government has been attempting to prevent the remaining larger farmers from dominating the
marketing cooperatives by excluding farmers with landholdings above
a certain size from participation in governing committees.37

In Tanzania the potentially negative consequences of the emergence of large private farmers were among the considerations leading
party leaders to conclude that it was essential to try to build ujamaa
villages. These are essentially producer cooperatives that seek to
introduce modern productive techniques within a framework of what
is assumed to have been traditional cooperation. It seems probable
that the cooperative movement in each country will need to work out
its own solution to the problem of large farmer domination. What
experience does seem to underscore is the necessity of recognizing
that if this problem is not dealt with, it may lead to serious distortion
of the role of cooperatives.

MARKETING BOARDS FOR DOMESTICALLY
CONSUMED CROPS

The settlers in East and Central Africa had established marketing boards back in the 1930s for major domestically consumed crops,
particularly maize to insure government support for stable prices
when depression conditions threatened the very existence of their
farms. After independence, some efforts were made to restructure
these boards to encourage African peasants to produce foodstuff crops
for sale in urban centers.

In Kenya, for example, the maize marketing board began to
purchase African peasant produce. Its pricing policies apparently

----

*That this was as true in the former French colonies as the
former British colonies is illustrated by the fact that in Senegal the
rapid pace of postindependence expansion of cooperatives has been
reported to have served the unstated aim of absorbing a large pool
of bueaucrats while providing a means for channeling government
services, including marketing, credit, and agricultural inputs, to a
group of well-to-do "notables"—that is, the religious and chiefly
leaders who had already benefitted from cash crop farming and compulsory cooperativization under the French. This model has been
characterized as that of the "cooperative path to capitalism."36

continued to discriminate against the peasants: the large farmers received a fixed price to cover their transport, while the peasants received a lower price calculated by subtracting estimated costs of transport and storage.[38] The board stood ready to purchase all produce at the prices set, but was not a compulsory marketing channel. It handled all large farm maize produce sold, while only handling that portion of the surpluses that peasants desired to sell to it. In the first serious postindependence drought, the policies of the board were investigated in an effort to explain its inability to prevent serious maize shortages and high prices.[39] Since then, however, it still appears to be more concerned with handling the produce of the larger farmers rather than that of the peasants.

The Zambia government[40] at first left the Grain Marketing Board, a lineal descendent of the original settler-created board, to function much as before independence in the settler areas along the line-of-rail. A new board, the Agricultural Rural Marketing Board, established just before independence as a temporary organization, began to formulate policies to encourage African farmers to expand their produce. Gradually, the Grain Marketing Board extended its responsibilities, starting with the operation of a cotton gin in 1965, the taking over of rural marketing in 1967 from the Agricultural Rural Marketing Board, and, in 1969, becoming an importer and distributor of seed, fertilizers, fruits, and vegetables. In 1969 the National Agricultural Marketing Board, NAMBOARD, amalgamated the functions of its two predecessors and expanded still more to further the government's aim to use the marketing board as a major instrument in a broad overall agricultural development program through the provision of marketing facilities for producers of all sorts of commodities all over the country.* At the same time it sought to stabilize the cost of living in urban areas through a wide distribution of local and imported foodstuffs. Line-of-rail farmers were no longer to be favored as they had been in the past.

NAMBOARD encountered many problems in attempting to carry out its mandate. Only some of these were the results of the efforts of the Zambian government to break its ties with Rhodesia after the latter's illegal declaration of independence. Among the problems confronted by NAMBOARD were:

----

*Zambia has three additional boards: the Dairy Produce Board, responsible for marketing milk and milk products; the Cold Storage Board, the residual buyer of all grades of locally produced beef and imported beef when required; and the Tobacco Board, which markets tobacco at the Lusaka auction floor on behalf of the producers.

1. It was unable to provide many of the items it was supposed to sell because of distribution problems. These were aggravated by the Zambian government's efforts to reduce its dependency on Rhodesia.

2. Its retail shops priced their produce comparatively lower than did private shops, but it was apparently unable to prevent the private shops from buying its best produce from its own retail shops for resale at higher prices.

3. The prices that the board was required to pay farmers for various crops, especially maize, after the 1971 drought were set at high levels, presumably to encourage the farmers to expand output so Zambia could achieve self-sufficiency. The result was that NAMBOARD was forced to subsidize these sales. A considerable part of the subsidies went to the larger farmers who continued to produce a major share of the marketed crops.

4. It was difficult to educate the farmers as to the board's role in providing a guaranteed market for some, but not all their produce, and to find a means of estimating the entire amount of produce the farmers would sell to the board, so that it could regularize its operations.

5. The relations between the board and the marketing cooperatives remained unclear, with the cooperatives sometimes complaining that it superceded them unnecessarily; these relationships required more careful definition.

6. NAMBOARD's managerial structure was inadequate for its task. It lacked adequate personnel with sufficient technical knowledge to handle its extended functions.

7. The board failed to keep its accounts up to date and available to the public, rendering it difficult to monitor its activities.

All these problems tended to hinder NAMBOARD from contributing as fully as necessary to enabling small farmers to bring their crops to market in Zambia.

The government of Tanzania sought to require peasants producing rice and maize for the domestic market to sell these through cooperatives to the National Agricultural Products Board in that country. The aim was to involve peasants producing these crops in democratically run cooperatives to facilitate their participation in the expanding internal cash markets, just as in the case of export crops. As the cooperatives become more efficient and peasant participation more effective, it was anticipated that eventually the cooperatives might take over the marketing board's activities.[41]

The Agricultural Products Board and associated cooperatives also encountered serious difficulties in Tanzania. The prices established by the marketing board for the cooperative purchases from the farmers and sales to the consumers were set to cover the total overhead costs of the cooperatives and the board in transporting and storing the crops for sale in the cities, storage of famine relief supplies, and even subsidizing sales of surpluses overseas.* The resulting price structure appeared to discourage farmer sales to the cooperatives. A farmer might sell a bag of maize, for example, immediately after harvest in order to obtain ready cash. Then, as the dry season dragged on, he might be forced to buy back a bag to tide him over until the next harvest. He complained bitterly if the price of the bag he had to buy was ten shillings higher than the price he had received for it, when it had simply remained in the same go-down for the intervening months. He found it difficult to understand why the cooperative should charge him a price high enough to cover its costs not only to store the bag he had sold to it earlier, but for the storage and transport of the rest of the crop to urban areas, a famine reserve, and even the cost of subsidizing surpluses sold overseas.

For the peasant, compulsory participation in a cooperative marketing board complex that appeared to require him to take a reduction in real income appeared unjustifiable. He might even assert that the arrangement by which he received lower prices and the consumer paid higher prices than were available on the private market was a form of exploiting both. The obvious reluctance of the farmers to sell through the cooperatives under these circumstances led to several studies. One proposal was that floor prices might be set at which the government would stand ready to buy through the cooperatives without requiring farmers to sell only through them.[42] This would provide the necessary floor price that would act as an incentive to the farmers to continue to expand their surplus output. At the same time neither the board nor the cooperatives would be required to cover the costs of transport for all surpluses produced in setting prices for resale. One-hundred-percent government ownership of the processing mill, acquired following the Arusha Declaration, would insure control of the final price charged to urban consumers at levels required to cover the storage and transport of only that portion of production sold in the cities. The storage of famine crops, since it was designed to meet a national welfare requirement, might be separately financed by government subsidy. Hopefully, the government would not be burdened with subsidizing sales of surpluses overseas, since it would not need to purchase all surplus crops sold. This path, if adopted, might be viewed as a temporary measure with the longer-range

---

*Both Kenya and Tanzania, when they accumulate surpluses of maize above the national requirements, including that stored for possible future famine, have had to subsidize the sale of the surplus at world prices that are below the domestic price.

perspective that as cooperatives improved in efficiency, and effective peasant participation increased, they might gradually replace all private middlemen, perhaps eventually the board itself.

STATE TRADING CORPORATIONS AND INTERNAL DISTRIBUTION

On the other side of the problem of expanding internal specialization and exchange is the distribution of essential consumer items and farm inputs in the rural areas at prices low enough to enable the poorer peasants to purchase them. Low-cost consumer goods like cloth, kerosene, matches, lanterns, pails, and soap, and eventually maybe consumer durables like bicycles, transistor radios, and construction materials, are necessary, in part, to provide the farmers with an incentive to increase the sales of their crops for cash. At the same time, increased availability of these items should enable the farmers to enjoy improved levels of living. Low-cost farm inputs like cutlasses, hoes, simple standardized plows, fertilizers, and insecticides should enable them to produce more to realize these goals. An adequate system of distribution in rural areas is required to provide for the expansion of the internal markets for these items as they are increasingly produced by the planned industrial sector.

After independence, some African governments also attempted to acquire greater control of internal distribution of imported and locally produced manufactured goods through various forms of state trading corporations. (See pp. 205-208 for the role of these corporations in export-import trade). A brief survey of some of these efforts may help to identify the kinds of problems these corporations have encountered, as well as the extent of their contribution to increasing internal specialization and exchange.

The Kenyan National Trading Corporation,[43] with its primary stated goal of Africanizing internal trade, initially assumed a significant role on the wholesale level in the distribution of a fairly long list of internally consumed items. It provided storage facilities, sometimes transport, and extended credit to would-be African subwholesalers to distribute these items throughout specific regions. It specified the price at which these items could be sold.

Gradually, given constraints on manpower at the management level and the failure of many of the African entrepreneurs to repay loans advanced, the Kenyan corporation relinquished most of its wholesale functions and discontinued the advance of credit. Its primary role became one of identifying African agents, to whom it granted the right to sell specified commodities in specified regions. The fact that African entrepreneurs lacked capital may have created a situation in which some had had, in reality, to resort to the backing of non-African middlemen, in effect simply acting as "fronts" for the latter. It seems dubious whether this approach to trade was likely to contribute significantly to altering the inherited lopsided internal trading patterns.

Ghana's National Trading Corporation[44] had, prior to 1965, gone further than the Kenyan corporation by establishing wholesale and retail stores in regions throughout the country to facilitate the distribution of consumer goods and farm inputs at reasonable prices to the rural as well as the urban areas. A presidential commission[45] was assigned to investigate its evident organizational difficulties in attaining these goals. These difficulties were undoubtedly aggravated by the shortages of imported consumer goods—including essentials like rice, powdered milk, and cutlasses—that resulted from an absolute shortage of foreign exchange because of the collapse of the world cocoa price and the failure to implement a rational set of priorities for utilization of the limited supplies of foreign exchange that did exist. (See p. 204). It also appears to be true that GNTC's own organizational difficulties aggravated the consequences of foreign exchange shortages, especially for the low-income Ghanaian consumer.

The commission's report identified two major problems confronting the Ghana National Trading Corporation. First, on the retail level, it was difficult for the GNTC, with its overheads and salaried employees, to compete with the small African retailer who owned his own little store, perhaps grew some of his own food, and included his salary and that of family members as part of his profit margin. This suggests that in a transitional situation where retailing is sometimes actually a form of disguised underemployment, it may be difficult, if not impossible, for a centrally financed retailing enterprise to replace the many small private retailers scattered throughout rural areas at any saving to the community.

Second, the commission report indicated that the GNTC was plagued by problems of corruption and inefficiency on both the retail and the wholesale level. This was in part a reflection of the shortage of dedicated manpower committed to resolving the problems of expanding internal specialization and trade. It was undoubtedly fostered by the employment of personnel formerly hired—and in some cases fired—by the big private trading firms. It apparently also reflected the fact that well-to-do private African traders utilized privileged connections and occasionally bribes to acquire more than their justifiable allotments of items in short supply, which they could then sell at considerably higher-than-official prices because of the resulting shortage of such items in the GNTC stores.

Whatever efforts might have been made by the Nkrumah government to overcome these problems were cut short by the 1966 coup.

The GNTC continued to function after the 1966 coup, but it was no longer expected to replace private suppliers.

The Tanzanian State Trading Corporation was, in accord with the Arusha Declaration, also expected to assume a major role on the wholesale level in expanding internal trade in Tanzania.[46] It was to replace the domination of wholesale trade by private traders, mostly non-African, and in this sense contribute to Africanization in the trade sector, as in Kenya. But it was also explicitly expected to develop the state's role to insure that wholesale trade contributed to a shift in the inherited pattern of trade in order to facilitate the emergence of a more internally balanced, integrated national economy.

Unlike Ghana's GNTC, the Tanzanian State Trading Corporation actually incorporated the nationalized major foreign trading firms that had previously controlled the major storage, transport, and wholesale facilities for imported manufactured goods. In Tanzania the larger domestic wholesale traders were mainly non-African. Hence they did not hold privileged positions in the political party and government, as had some of the bigger African traders in Ghana, who had apparently exercised their power to continue their businesses and to capture undue shares of scarce supplies. The Tanzanian government also controls the import of manufactured consumer goods more directly through the State Trading Corporation and hence may be able to enforce its priorities for utilization of scarce foreign exchange more rationally in accord with its national plan. That it appears to have done so may reflect the fact that Tanzania's government is perhaps freer of the influence of powerful well-to-do African farmer-cum-trader-cum-businessman influence than was Ghana's.

At the retail level, the fact that the Tanzanian government has control of credit through the nationally owned commercial bank[47] presumably should facilitate insuring that credit-worthy African retailers obtain adequate supplies of commodities for sale at prices set to provide adequate but not unduly high profit margins above the wholesale prices set by the State Trading Corporation. The government is encouraging marketing cooperatives to take over the supply of farm inputs and some consumer necessities. It has experimented with the establishment of consumer cooperatives, but these have not, in Tanzania as elsewhere, been very successful.[48] The party, trade unions, and women's and youth organizations have been encouraged to participate in insuring that price markups at the retail level are reasonable. There has been no public investigation or report on the extent to which this approach is succeeding in attaining the goals set. Nevertheless, the evident distortion of distribution patterns that led to the Ghana government's investigation of the state trading corporation in that country have not been reported in Tanzania as yet.

SUMMARY AND CONCLUSIONS

Upon independence, African nations have faced the necessity of attempting to alter inherited externally dependent trade patterns by focusing on expanding internal specialization and exchange to facilitate attainment of planned goals to increase productivity and raise the levels of living of the broad masses of the population throughout the countryside as well as in urban areas. A review of the efforts of African governments to reshape the institutions governing foreign and internal trade reveals a range of approaches that have had differing consequences. All the governments have been hindered by shortages of high-level manpower. In some corruption has undermined measures formulated with the stated aim of redirecting trade. Measures like licensing and quotas, and even state trading firms designed to provide new incentives and sanctions to facilitate the attainment of new goals within the framework of the inherited set of trading institutions—dominated as they are by foreign firms linked with internal wholesale interests—appear to have been relatively unsuccessful in restructuring trade to support national plan goals. Africanization per se appears to have done little but enable a few politically well-placed Africans to benefit from state assistance, including considerable amounts of credit, and to acquire new positions in the existing trade structure. Marketing cooperatives, designed to replace private middlemen, appear to have been plagued by inefficiency and problems relating to pricing policy. Not infrequently they appear to have been dominated by groups seeking to utilize them for their own gain, while not too much success has been achieved in involving the mass of the peasants in decision-making.

Tanzania's government apparently became convinced, by its own as well as other countries' experiences, that the government itself would have to enter directly into trade, especially at the wholesale level, in order to support national plans directed to reallocating resources more in accord with the needs of the entire population, particularly those in rural areas. A state trading corporation was created by combining existing state trading institutions with wholly nationalized foreign firms, with the stated view of eventual attainment of a monopoly of foreign and internal wholesale trade. It is proposed that the corporation should cooperate with the marketing boards to expand exports, especially of manufactured goods, to new trading partners, both in Africa and overseas. At the same time, the policies of marketing boards and marketing cooperatives appear to be under almost continual review with the aim of finding ways to increase both efficiency and membership participation. It seems to be hoped that the latter will be facilitated by creation of ujamaa villages, which are supposed to stimulate peasant efforts to increase productivity by insuring that

231

all will benefit from the growing output in accordance with the work that they have done.

While the evidence tends to support the hypothesis that state action is required to make essential institutional changes affecting both foreign and internal trade, particularly at the wholesale level, much more research appears to be required relating to implementation of such an approach. It seems apparent that policies relating to pricing, as well as the kinds and amounts of goods made available through expansion of trade, must be closely coordinated with national planning related to the growing productive sectors, industry and agriculture, in order to achieve an integrated, balanced national economy. At the same time, attention needs to be directed to shaping new working rules to enable the broad masses of the population, particularly the small peasants in the countryside and working people in urban areas, to participate effectively in newly created institutions—whether they are marketing cooperatives, marketing boards, or state trading firms— so that policies established do provide the necessary opportunities and incentives to stimulate them to achieve the greater productivity needed to implement nationally planned agricultural and industrial strategies.

NOTES

1. Cf. V. Thompson and R. Adloff, The Emerging States of French Equatorial Africa (Stanford University Press, 1960), p. 168. G. Hyden, in "Can Cooperatives Make it in Africa," Africa Report, December 1970, argues this compulsory nature of cooperatives under colonialism made it more difficult to build cooperatives in these areas after independence.

2. See Registrars of Cooperatives, Reports, in English-Speaking African countries, 1950 on.

3. For summary of preindependence organization of cooperatives among Africans for the first time, see Ministry of Agricultures, African Land Development in Kenya (Nairobi, 1962), p. 292.

4. R. S. Odingo, "Cooperatives in the Kenya Highlands Settlement Schemes," Kampala: University Social Science Council Conference, Dec. 30, 1968–Jan. 3, 1969.

5. For preindependence information regarding history of Ugandan cooperatives, see Uganda Protectorate, Annual Reports of the Registrar of Cooperative Societies, 1947-1960 (Entebbe: Government Printer.)

6. O. Okereke, "The Place of Marketing Cooperatives in the Economy of Uganda," and Paul W. Westergaard, "Cooperatives in Tanzania as Economic and Democratic Institutions," in Cooperatives and Rural Development in East Africa, C. G. Widstrand (ed.) (New York: Africana Publishing Corporation, 1970.)

7. Files of the Planning Commission, 1965.

8. For data regarding crop expansion, cf. Republic of Kenya, 1969 Economic Survey; Republic of Uganda, Background to the Budget, 1968-9; and United Republic of Tanzania, Economic Survey, 1968.

9. Hyden, "Can Cooperatives Make it in Africa?" The prices of the four most important export crops of sub-Saharan Africa (coffee, cocoa, oilseeds, and cotton, which together comprise over a third of the areas exports) have all declined since the mid-1950s peak. (See Food and Agricultural Organization, Annual Statistics of Production, 1969.)

10. This criticism was expressed by critics during the de Graft Johnson Commission hearings (see Report of the Committee of Enquiry on the Local Purchasing of Cocoa [Ghana, 1966]) in comments not unlike those expressed to the Nowell Commission (Report of Commission on the Marketing of West Africa Cocoa, Cond. 5845).

11. Cf. Westergaard, "Cooperatives in Tanzania as Economic and Democratic Institutions."

12. This argument is summarized in G. Hyden, "Cooperatives and Their Socio-Political Environment," in Widstrand (ed.), Cooperatives and Rural Development in East Africa.

13. G. Hyden (ed.), Development Administration—The Kenyan Experience, p. 306.

14. R. Apthorpe, "Some Problems of Evaluation," in Widstrand (ed.), Cooperatives and Rural Development in East Africa, pp. 213-219.

15. J. P. W. B. McAuslan, "Cooperatives and the Law in East Africa," in Widstrand (ed.), Cooperatives and Rural Development in East Africa," esp. pp. 96-99.

16. De Graft Johnson Commission, Report on Local Purchasing of Cocoa in Ghana.

17. For reports and reactions to this allegation, see Ghanaian Times, Oct. 13, 14, and 18, 1969, and The Legon Observer, Jan. 2, 1970.

18. United Republic of Tanzania, Report of the Presidential Special Committee of Enquiry into Cooperative Movement and Marketing Boards (Dar es Salaam: Government Printer, 1966.)

19. G. K. Helleiner, Agricultural Marketing in Tanzania, Policies and Problems, Economic Research Bureau Paper 68. 14 (Dar es Salaam, 1968).

20. O. Okereke, "The Strength and Weaknesses of the Cooperative Movement in Uganda," East African Agricultural Economic Society Conference on Agricultural Marketing in East Africa, June 25-8, 1968; R. S. Odingo, "Cooperatives in the Kenya Highlands Settlement Schemes"; Republic of Kenya, Development Plan, 1966-70, p. 198, and Development Plan, 1970-74, pp. 272-77; G. Rajabu, "Difficulties in Gusii— Troubles Erupt in the Cooperatives," East Africa Journal (June 1966): 7-11; J. Heyer, "Review of Marketing Policies and Problems in Kenya."

21. Cf. B. Harris, "Survey of Agricultural Training Institutes: Implications for Producing Ujamaa Vijimini Extension Workers," Rural Development Research Committee, Rural Development Paper No. 2.

22. McAusland, "Cooperatives and the Law in East Africa," and Westergaard, "Cooperatives in Tanzania as Economic and Democratic Institutions."

23. Cf. H. C. Kriesel, C. K. Laurent, C. Halpern, and H. E. Larzelere, Agricultural Marketing in Tanzania, Background Research and Policy Proposals (Michigan State University, Department of Agricultural Economics, 1970), p. 29; and Report of the Registrar of Cooperative Societies (Accra, Ghana, 1969), p. 13, and 1960, p. 14.

24. For role of cooperatives in advancing credit, see McAusland, "Cooperatives and the Law in East Africa," esp. pp. 111-119.

25. Report of the Presidential Special Committee of Enquiry into Cooperative Movement and Marketing Boards, Appendix B.

26. For discussion of post-coup decline in production and sales of cocoa from Ghana, including an estimate of 25,000 tons of cocoa smuggled to neighboring countries, see Republic of Ghana, Economic Survey, 1967 and 1968, and reports in West Africa, esp. 1/10/70, 3/29/69, 9/27/69, 7/20/68, 7/29/67, and 1/19/70.

27. Cf. Report of Registrar of Cooperative Societies (Accra, 1959, 1960).

28. G. Hyden, "Cooperatives and Their Socio-Political Environment."

29. E.g., in Ghana, where the United Ghana Farmers Cooperative Council was supposed to establish domestic foodstuff cooperatives prior to the coup, it failed to do so; and in fact there is some evidence that they actually dismantled government efforts to assist foodstuff marketing cooperatives to become established (Seidman, Ghana's Development Experience, 1951-1965, Ch. 9). After the coup, however, efforts to build foodstuff cooperatives appear to have been neglected, and the problem of foodstuff marketing remained as a major unresolved problem (ibid., "Postscript: Stagnation").

30. Prices in almost all African urban areas have been rising (see indices in United Nations, Statistical Yearbook, current issues), and in countries like Ghana and Nigeria, domestic foodstuff price increases have persisted, contributing significantly to national unrest both before and after the coups.

31. In Ghana, by 1968, domestic foodstuff prices had increased 80 percent above 1963 levels; for discussion of marketing problems, see R. Lawson, cited in West Africa, 1/31/70. For reports of Lonrho strike, see West Africa, March 8, 15, and 29, 1969.

32. J. Heyer, "Review of Marketing Policies and Problems in Kenya," Makerere, East Africa Agricultural Economics Society, Conference, June 25-28, 1968.

33. As early as the 1950s, the Ugandan Cooperative Registrar noted that larger farmers-cum-traders viewed cooperatives as a means of obtaining funds for entering trade, building businesses, etc. (See Uganda Protectorate, Annual Report of the Registrar of Cooperative Societies, 1947, p. 4.)

34. Jaigge Committee Hearings, reported in Ghana Daily Graphic (Accra), Nov. 22, 24, 26, 29, and 30, 1966.

35. G. Hyden et al., Development Administration, p. 314.

36. D. B. C. O'Brien, "Cooperators and Bureaucrats: Class Formation in a Senegalese Peasant Society," Africa XLI, no. 4 (October 1971); esp. 271.

37. I. F. Harik, "Mobilization Policy and Political Change in Rural Egypt," International Development Research Center, Indiana University, 1970, mimeographed.

38. V. Q. Alvis, "The Marketing of Staple Foodstuffs in Kenya," African Urban Notes (Fall 1970), pp. 9-10.

39. Republic of Kenya, Report of the Maize Commission of Inquiry (Nairobi: Government Printer, June 1966).

40. The following materials relating to Zambia's postindependence marketing boards are analyzed in full in M. T. Ocran, Towards a Jurisprudence of African Economic Development—A Case Study of the Evolution of the Structure and Operations of Zambia's Food Crop and Cotton Marketing Board from 1936 to 1970, Ph.D. thesis, University of Wisconsin, 1971.

41. United Republic of Tanzania, Report of the Presidential Special Committee of Enquiry into Cooperative Movement and Marketing Boards.

42. Helleiner, Agricultural Marketing in Tanzania; for other proposals relating to marketing in Tanzania, see Kriesel et al., Agricultural Marketing in Tanzania, passim.

43. For an analysis of the role of the Kenya National Trading Corporation in internal trade, see Bucknall, State Trading in Kenya.

44. For summary description, see Seidman, Ghana's Development Experience, 1951-1965, Ch. 7.

45. Abrahams Commission Report.

46. Bennett, "Self-Reliance and Foreign Trade."

47. Tanzania nationalized the commercial banks in 1967. (See A. R. Roe and M. J. H. Yaffey, "Money and Banking," Ch. 7; Economic Problems of Tanzania, Svendsen (ed.) (Dar es Salaam, University College, 1968, mimeo.).

48. Cf. United Republic of Tanzania, Report of the Presidential Special Committee of Enquiry into Cooperative Movement and Marketing Boards.

PART

IV

FINANCIAL PLANNING

CHAPTER

12

INTRODUCTION:
THE NECESSITY
OF FINANCIAL PLANNING

Every newly independent African government confronts major problems in financing its development plans. Current government expenditures have doubled and even tripled to cover long-neglected social welfare programs like expanded educational systems, water supplies, and health facilities. Governments' capital expenditures have multiplied to provide essential buildings to house new programs, as well as to build roads, bridges, and ports designed to facilitate the spread of specialization and exchange into areas formerly isolated from the limited modern export enclave sector.

Finance for development in Africa may be broadly conceived as including state revenues and other funds available from internal and external sources, both public and private. The extent of governmental involvement in directly productive sectors, which varies from country to country, will affect its financing program. In some countries government has limited its expenditures primarily to expanding social and economic infrastructure with a view to attracting private enterprise to invest in productive sectors in agriculture and industry. In others government has played a more central role in direct investment in productive sectors. The political-economic philosophy of each government has tended to some extent to shape the measures it has adopted to finance growing development expenditures.

Regardless of whether the form of financing development is public or private, it is generally recognized that for significant increases in per capita income to occur, a considerable financial effort is required. Debate has emerged over the possibility of measuring the extent of the required effort. Some economists hold that[1] the effort to establish a capital-output ratio is a fruitless exercise for several reasons: one cannot assume a causal relationship between growth of capital and output; the statistical problems of estimating the capital-output ratio render the results almost meaningless; noneconomic factors, including the pattern of institutional control, affect the ratio; and the labor-intensity of different projects differs with different national requirements. Others have observed that, given a roughly "guestimated" capital output ratio of 3 or 3.5 to 1, about 25 percent of the total monetary gross domestic product should be devoted to capital investment if the resulting expansion of Gross Domestic Product is to outpace rapidly growing populations.* Whether or not one can identify a valid national capital-output ratio—and admittedly it seems extremely difficult if not impossible in any African country today—it remains true that to finance development will require constraints on consumption and the direction of a major share of the monetary gross domestic product to productive sectors. Twenty-five percent may not be too high.[2]

Initially, most African governments have perforce—given the inherited set of financial institutions—had to adopt a series of essentially ad hoc measures in an effort to finance their increasing development expenditures. As the necessity for more careful physical planning of the productive sectors has become apparent, however, some national planners have simultaneously come to realize the importance of formulating more carefully worked out financial plans to avoid inflation and further distortion of the economy. This is particularly important, given a realistic assessment of the limits of foreign funds (see Chapter 13), to insure that all possible domestic investable surpluses are directed to financing physical plans.

It was suggested in Chapter Four above that financial planning provides, in a sense, the dual of physical planning. It requires careful analysis of all available investible surpluses—existing and potential—and the implementation of appropriate measures to direct them to financing the specific projects incorporated in the physical plans. This implies a study of the way inherited sets of working rules governing existing financial institutions may need to be altered to insure that these surpluses are in fact invested in the critical projects as planned.

A national incomes policy needs to be delineated as an essential foundation for effective financial planning. The incomes policy should identify the way existing and potential investible surpluses could be reallocated for investment to achieve a more balanced, nationally integrated economy. The incomes policy adopted will, in a sense, provide a set of criteria for evaluating proposals for allocation of monetary resources and changes in financial institutions. Each

---

*It is not uncommon for African development plans to include an estimated capital-output ratio of this magnitude.

240

proposal for finance may be scrutinized in terms of its anticipated impact in redistributing investible surpluses away from the export enclave toward creation of productive projects and associated linkages to increase productivity in all sectors of the economy. An appropriate national incomes policy should at the same time insure that each proposal is designed to contribute to advancing the material welfare and social benefits enjoyed by the vast majority of the population; previously neglected by export-oriented "modernization."

Part IV aims to suggest the critical features to be considered in developing financial plans as duals of physical plans. Chapter 13 will indicate the main issues involved in designing an appropriate national incomes policy as a sound foundation for financial planning. The following chapters attempt, on that basis, to consider the evidence as to the consequences of alternative institutional changes that may be introduced to implement the plans made.

Chapter 14 attempts to provide a realistic evaluation of the potential contribution of foreign funds. Chapter 15 considers some of the problems and possibilities of deficit financing. Chapter 16 explores the evidence as to the consequences of various taxation policies. Chapter 17 introduces a preliminary assessment of the possible contribution of public enterprise to public finance. Chapter 18 reviews the role of banking and finance. Chapter 19 considers other financial institutions. And Chapter 20 seeks to summarize the role of financial planning.

NOTES

1. E.g., R. N. Tripathy, Public Finance in Under-Developed Countries, revised (Calcutta: World Press Private Ltd., 1968), pp. 34 ff.

2. E.g., Tanzania has set its capital formation target at 25 percent of total product by the beginning of the Third Plan. See the United Republic of Tanzania, Tanzania Second Five-Year Plan for Economic and Social Development, July 1, 1969 - June 30, 1974, Vol. 1, General Analysis (Dar es Salaam: Government Printer, 1969), p. 209

13

THE INGREDIENTS OF
A NATIONAL
INCOMES POLICY

It would seem that formulation of a national incomes policy ought to be a fairly straightforward proposition: the task is to re-examine the institutions and working rules affecting income distribution to insure that proposed financial measures contribute to attainment of a more balanced, integrated economy capable of achieving increased productivity and higher levels of living for the broad masses of the population.

In reality, African government efforts to arrive at decisions necessary to formulate meaningful national incomes policies have been plagued from the outset by the lack of essential statistical information and the calculated tactics of the more powerful interest groups to obtain verdicts favorable to themselves. These two factors have interacted to obscure the real issues involved at four levels. First, the foreign firms and associated financial institutions have resisted efforts to change the working rules that have, in the past, permitted remittance of a major share of investible surpluses to their home countries in the form of interest, profits, dividends, and salaries of expatriate personnel. Second, members of a small proportion of the domestic populations—including increasing numbers of the so-called African "elites"—have sought since independence to maintain and even increase the high salaries and incomes that have enabled them to capture as much as 50 to 75 percent of the monetary incomes remaining in their countries. Third, participants in the tiny wage-earning sector, a high proportion of whom are employed by the government itself, have demanded higher wages as a visible fruit of independence. And fourth, the vast majority of the populations, who in most African countries still live in the rural areas, are eager to realize the repeatedly promised improvements in their material levels of living.

Almost invariably, inherited sets of working rules favor the economically and politically stronger sets of interests over and against the weaker. The foreign firms and associated domestic elites have tended to try to utilize their wealth and power to exercise overt or covert influence over crucial decisions governing the allocation of financial resources. At the same time, the lack of adequate data has frequently clouded over the real nature of the conflicts of interest involved, rendering it more difficult to determine the actual consequences of specific financial measures adopted.

This chapter seeks to examine in more detail the issues and kinds of data required to resolve these conflicts at these four levels in order to develop a national incomes policy as the foundation for sound financial planning in the context of a perspective of restructuring the national economy.

THE INCOMES OF FOREIGN FIRMS

National planners need to give primary consideration to measures designed to insure that a major share of the investible surpluses, still typically shipped out of the country by foreign interests, are reinvested to achieve the spread of productivity throughout the domestic economy. The amounts involved are not insignificant, as suggested in Chapter 2. In the case of countries with foreign-owned mines, like Zambia, published data reveal direct losses in the form of profits,* interests, and expatriate salaries to have been as much as a third of total export earnings even as recently as 1971. Where African peasants sell their crops to big foreign trading firms, the actual losses are more difficult to calculate, since foreign firm profits are augmented by buying raw materials at low prices and selling back high-priced manufactured goods. Worsening terms of trade, characteristic of the last decade, have involved significant indirect loss of investible surpluses. Between 1962 and 1967, for example, it has been estimated that Tanzania alone lost some £22 million due to the fall in world prices for its major exports, an amount exceeding Tanzania's total government investment in industry after the Arusha Declaration.

Independent African governments have introduced a variety of institutional changes to obtain a greater share of these surpluses. These include higher taxes, acquisition of some or all of the shares of ownership (although here the compensation has typically consumed most if not all the government's share of profits for a number of years),

---

*Including government compensation for its acquisition of shares of ownership in industry, usually paid out of its share of profits.

and the exercise of greater control over the policies of financial institutions. Some of these changes have been discussed in preceding chapters.

It is almost inevitable that foreign firms will oppose enforcement of such measures to reduce their share of profits. One observer remarked that the big United States trading firm Sears, Roebuck, and Co., which rapidly expanded its operations in Latin America in the post war era, does not invest in developing countries "for reasons of philanthropy, but because to be there is good and profitable business."[1] This is no less true of foreign firms investing in Africa. As a Unilever report candidly declared, "We invest money where we hope to make money."[2] It seems self-evident that foreign companies' efforts to pursue these goals will conflict with African government efforts to augment the share of investible surpluses retained in Africa.

It is typically argued that African governments must permit foreign firms to remit profits and interests if they desire foreign investment. But each African government must assess how much each foreign investment is really worth in view of its potential contribution to implementation of explicitly designed physical plans for restructuring the national economy. It is not foreign financial investment per se that is desirable, but rather the acquisition of specific physical capital inputs for establishing a particular physical project for such purposes as setting off a chain of growth or augmenting foreign exchange earnings by processing locally produced raw materials.

African governments must, in effect, bargain with foreign firms to achieve their own goals in conditions in which the latter, with their worldwide marketing and processing operations and gross incomes that exceed many African governments' entire budgets, have a considerable bargaining advantage. The foreign firms may employ well-trained experts who know how to manipulate accounts and price policies to avoid taxes and shift their funds out of African countries undetected. As a Lonrho spokesman has suggested, they may develop personal relations with high government officials to facilitate attainment of their goals.[3] A wealth of evidence indicates that it would be unrealistic to pretend that they do not employ corruption, in Africa as elsewhere, as a means to counteract government efforts to redirect greater shares of investible surpluses to national development.* Various reasons have been advanced for what has been termed "corruption in developing countries," relating it to low levels of economic development, a predominantly agriculturally derived GDP, weak support for formal legal values, and the inability or unwillingness of authorities

---

*For instance, foreign firms admitted to giving bribes to government officials in Ghana to obtain favorable contracts.

to enforce sanctions against departures from stipulated codes of administrative behavior.[4] Riggs[5] asserts that the weakness of functional interest groups renders it difficult for them to hold the bureaucrats accountable for their actions.

Among constraints hindering government efforts to attain a greater share of investible surpluses shipped out of the country by foreign firms are the lack of trained manpower and the difficulty of obtaining adequate data. In the first case, although it is possible to import trained experts from a variety of countries, lack of familiarity with the local situation and short terms of contract reduce their potential effectiveness. This points to the importance of training dedicated Africans to deal with accounting and financial management through introduction of appropriate kinds of educational programs, both on the job and in institutions of higher learning.*

Second, it is vital to obtain accurate data relating to the costs of exports, imports, capital equipment and machinery, and so forth, in order to make wise choices for investments in specific physical projects. Colonial governments, leaving investment decisions entirely to private firms, make little or no effort to gather this essential kind of information. Upon attaining independence, several governments have neglected to alter these colonial working rules. In Kenya, for example, the postindependence government reserved power to grant or withhold permission to private firms to operate industries by licensing. It could grant approved status on certain conditions; influence the availability of credit; restrict imports or levy customs duties; control a company's employment of expatriates; tax company profits; and limit repatriation of dividends in certain cases. A complicated set of boards, committees, and advisory councils was erected to provide channels for discussion and two-way influence between government and private enterprise. Apparently, however, the minimal requirement for making effective use of these techniques was lacking. It was difficult to obtain information about many of the most important companies in Kenya. Subsidiaries of overseas corporations registered as private companies were not required to make public the most elementary facts relating to such issues as turnover, investment, whether they were making profits, and, if so, how much they were used. The

---

*Simply to adopt business school curricula from Western countries (as, for instance, at the School of Business Administration in Lagos University, which was established under a U.S. AID contract with a curriculum basically similar to those at American Universities) which commonly adopt orthodox economic assumptions inappropriate to the African circumstance, hardly seems appropriate for such programs.

laws governing companies were modeled along the lines of British legislation, which tended to favor those who "like to shroud their business in mystery."[6] Yet such information would appear to be a minimum precondition for the formulation of meaningful financial policies.

The necessity of obtaining accurate information and institutionalizing continual checkup procedures is important even in the case of entirely publicly owned enterprises. Firm managers are continually negotiating to purchase machinery and supplies or to sell output to overseas concerns. Individual managers, provided by foreign partners, may take advantage of ignorance of the facts on the part of government personnel. Institutionalized checkups are also essential to provide a means of reducing the danger that foreign firms might bribe government officials.

THE AFRICAN ELITES

Effective financial planning implies the necessity of capturing the major share of the investible surpluses, which have, in the past, accrued to that 7 to 10 percent of the population that has benefitted from narrow export enclave expansion. The members of this group are mostly government officials, managerial personnel in private firms, and a small number of very well-to-do cash crop farmers and wealthy traders. The extent of the gap between the high-income group and the rest of the population is illustrated in Table 11, which shows the salaries of unskilled labor and executive personnel in the government and private sectors in the Western Region of Nigeria.

This pattern is roughly typical of most African countries. The highest-paid executives in the private sector receive salaries about 240 times those of the lowest-paid unskilled workers. This of course does not include possible additions to their incomes deriving from participation in the profits of businesses. Nor does the government executives' salary schedule indicate the extent of fringe benefits— housing and car allowances and the like—as well as private business connections, which may raise their real incomes considerably higher than indicated in Table 11.

The elites, who profit from export enclave business, are unlikely to be eager to make the sacrifices necessary to release investible surpluses for investments designed to attain a more balanced national economy. They not infrequently envisage their welfare as associated with that of the foreign firms that have so long shaped their nations' externally dependent export enclave. Foreign firms have made special efforts to encourage them to do so.[7]

TABLE 11

Some Indicators of Public/Private Sectors Wage and
Salary Differentials, Western Region, Nigeria, 1970
(in Nigeria £)

	Government Sector	Quasi-Government Sector	Private Sector
Entry Point for Daily Paid and Unskilled Labor	90	90	50:8– 174
Initial Salary of Graduate Entrants	648– 720	850–1,200	850– 1,500
(Nonprofessional) Initial Salary of Professional Entrants	840– 950	950–1,200	1,200– 1,600
Chief Executives, that is, Permanent Secretaries, Directors of Companies, and General Managers of Public Corporations	3,000–3,250	3,000–4,500	5,000–12,000

Source: The Nigerian Journal of Economic and Social Studies
13, no. 1: p. 102.

The argument that the members of the African elites must be permitted to retain their high incomes as an incentive for further investment has been refurbished in opposition to measures designed to reduce their incomes—despite the fact that the preponderance of evidence in less developed countries suggests that such incomes are most commonly spent for conspicuous consumption or invested in speculative real estate or trade.[8] A government newspaper in one African country went so far a few years ago as to justify a minister's attempt to line his pocket through his public office. After all, if Africans are to become entrepeneurs, the argument went, how else could they be expected to accumulate the necessary capital? Even where corruption is not publicly condoned, some national legislatures have continued to vote higher salaries and all kinds of fringe benefits to high government officials, despite the fact that this has resulted in furthering the gap between the "haves" and "have nots".

Governments seeking to implement a self-reliant financial policy, on the other hand, have taken measures to attempt to reduce this gap. The Tanzanian government, for example, cut the salaries of higher government officials by 20 percent. The government no longer provides housing and car allowances for senior civil servants. As expatriates are replaced by Africans in the parastatal sector, it is stated public policy to reduce the salaries of the latter as well. Furthermore, the Arusha Declaration forbids party and government officials to hold businesses outside their official posts in an effort to prevent them from lining their pockets while in public office. The government takeover[9] in 1971 of all rental properties valued at about $14,500 or more was in part aimed at reducing the opportunity for such officials to gain additional incomes from them. These measures have been supplemented by the imposition of very high taxes on luxury items as well as a progressive graduated income tax.

It would be surprising if all members of the "elite" welcome such measures. The 1972 military coup in Ghana was reported to have resulted, not from idealism, but Army brass resentment at government measures—forced by persistent economic crises—to reduce their financial rewards.[10] A government desirous of implementing a self-reliant financial program needs to discover ways to educate the broad masses of the population as well as the elites themselves as to the necessity of making such an approach an integral feature of the national incomes policy.

THE CONTROVERSIAL FOCAL POINT: WAGES

The conflict over the appropriate wages to be paid has, perhaps, received more attention than any other aspect of postindependence controversy over national incomes policies, although wage earners constitute only a relatively small portion of the African populations (see p. 242). One reason for this may be the importance that government employment and wages play in the typical monetary sector. In Kenya,[11] for example, public-sector employment accounts for over 36 percent of all employment, and public-sector wages and salaries have been estimated to be about 42 percent of the central government's recurrent expenditure from 1962 to 1967.

Most governments, whatever their stated political persuasion, maintain that workers should exercise restraint in their wage demands to enable the government, the major employer of wage labor, to accumulate investment funds for implementing development plans. This argument has carried over into the private sector as well, where it is likewise argued that high wages will eat up profits that would otherwise be invested for development. Wage restraint has been urged by representatives of the International Labour Organization, government spokesmen, and employers' organizations.

But the issue is a perplexing one. The data relating to it are far from adequate.

Under colonialism, as illustrated by studies made in East Africa, and particularly in Kenya,[12] wages were typically so low that urban workers were forced to leave their families in rural areas; in fact, colonial spokesmen held that the existence of the African "reserves" rendered it unnecessary to pay wages high enough to support the workers together with their families in the cities. The reserves were in fact subsidizing the provision of an urban labor force for industry. But this inevitably had consequences for the stability and productivity of the labor force. Managers could afford to hire many unskilled laborers and paid little attention to training or improving supervision. The high absentee and turnover rates as workers returned to visit their families at home further hindered efforts to increase productivity. In the postwar era, it began to be perceived that higher wages were essential for the creation of a more permanent, productive labor force.

Since independence, the issue of wages has been widely held by public officials, the press, and businessmen to be linked to the urgent problem of mounting urban unemployment. In Kenya, where the unemployed were estimated to total some 500,000 in 1970, even the Secretary General of COTU, also a member of parliament, expressed[13] support for wage restraint as part of a national incomes policy designed "to promote economic growth in order to create more jobs." He apparently accepted at face value the validity of the scanty reported statistics that purported to show that the cause of unemployment lay in the fact that urban unskilled wages had almost doubled since 1960 while peasant incomes had risen by less than half in the same period. He made no more penetrating effort to analyze the extent to which unemployment is in reality inherent in the distorted allocation pattern of the inherited dual economy.

The view that high wages cause unemployment finds theoretical support in orthodox marginal productivity theory, elaborated in the Keynesian framework, that if wages exceed some (assumed) marginal product, unemployment must ensue.[14] But that theory is founded on the assumption of the prevalence of competitive market forces, which can hardly be said to exist in Kenya or any other African country.*

The rural-urban migration characteristic of Africa today, as it has been in Latin America for decades, has tended to be aggravated by postindependence development strategies fostering the expansion

---

*See pp. 109.

of modern productive techniques in relatively capital-intensive projects in the export enclave. Low productivity, underemployment, and growing landlessness prevalent among sectors of the neglected rural populations force increasing numbers to join the pools of unemployed urban slum dwellers competing for jobs in the limited modern sector.

It is conceivable that wages could be raised so high in urban areas that investible surpluses, which might otherwise be invested in rural development, would be consumed. Whether wages of unskilled and semiskilled workers do in fact significantly reduce investible surpluses remains, however, an issue of fact in each country. Unfortunately, few accurate data have been systematically collected and evaluated.

A few facts are available. In the mid-1960s the Tanzanian government, troubled by continuing trade union pressure for wage increases, invited H. A. Turner of the International Labour Organization to study the problems of wages policy. His report[15] reiterated the argument that every increase in workers wages above specified limits would cause unemployment, citing the growth of unemployment after the government had increased minimum wages. But he failed to note that the primary cause of increased unemployment had been the layoff of several tens of thousands of workers in the sisal industry after the drastic fall of world sisal prices. When manufacturing industry alone was considered, the evidence showed a continued increase in employment at the time that wages rose.[16]

A more careful analysis of Tanzanian industry showed that wages constituted only a very small portion of total manufacturing costs, less than 10 percent in all but four industries, less than 5 percent in four industries.[17] The 10 percent of the employees who constituted managers and clerical workers received about 40 percent of the total manufacturing industry wage and salary bill.[18]* This suggested that the sharply skewed income distribution prevalent throughout the economy carried over into manufacturing as well. This survey[19] of the largest manufacturing firms showed that profit and interest, combined, constituted a far higher percent of costs: 38 percent of gross output in paint manufacturing, over 45 percent for beer, 25 percent for matches, 21 percent for tobacco, 27 percent for sugar refining. Profits alone, as a percent of equity capital, were 22 percent for tobacco, 39 percent for matches, 63 percent for beer.

On the other hand, there is evidence[20] to suggest that average wages in Tanzania were barely sufficient to support a worker and his family at the time Turner wrote his report. The average wage earner

---

*In the Kenyan case, about 7 percent of the wage and salary earners received about 44 percent of the total wage and salary bill.

in Dar es Salaam earned barely over 200 shillings a month.* He typically had to borrow money to support his family until the end of the
month when he received his paycheck. Over a fourth of the workers
lived without families, indicating that their wages were still inadequate
to support their families in the cities.

Some wage earners do appear to have used their bargaining
power and political strength to become a sort of "aristocracy of labor."
In Zambia,[21] for example, the wages of the mine workers, who constituted a powerful force in the independence movement, rose much
more rapidly after independence than those of other workers in the
country (see Table 12).

The mines produce about 40 percent of Zambia's Gross Domestic
Product, about 95 percent of its exports, and half to two-thirds of the
government's revenue. They are also the primary available source
of financial surpluses for investment in increased productivity throughout the rest of the economy. The government has sought to discourage
further wage increases for the miners, although in fact wages constitute less than 15 percent of total costs of production of the mines.†

TABLE 12

Monthly Earnings for Mine and Nonmine Labor, Zambia
(in pounds)

Industry	1960	1966
Agriculture	4.5	8.3
Construction	11.0	18.4
Retail	4.0	11.5
Transport	2.0	5.4
Mining	8.8	21.1

Source: R. H. Bates, Unions, Parties and Political Development:
A Study of Mineworkers in Zambia (New Haven: Yale University Press,
1971), Table 2, p. 29.

---

*This is roughly one fourteenth of the wages of the average
United States manufacturing industry employee.

†In 1964 wages had constituted less than 10 percent of total
production costs.[22]

251

Convincing the miners of the validity of the government's position, however, has been rendered more difficult by the persistence of racial differences in salaries and fringe benefits in the mines,* and the continued operation of the mines by the companies. Even after the government assumed 51 percent of shares of ownership in the mines, the two big foreign companies continued to provide the management and received 49 percent of the profits, as well as generous compensation for shares sold to government.

A 1969 report, again produced by International Labour Office official Turner, purported to show that mine labor productivity had declined despite the wage increases. This apparently provided an important argument for the imposition of a wage freeze. Critics of the Turner report emphasized his failure to note causes other than the workers' behavior for the productivity decline, including the impact of Rhodesia's illegal declaration of independence, which created serious fuel and supply problems, as well as the adverse consequences of continued racial frictions in the mines themselves.

Decision as to the appropriate wages to pay the mine workers in Zambia is clearly important to the formulation of an incomes policy directed to restructuring the economy. On the one hand, the growing gap in wages between the mine workers and the majority of the rest of the wage earners and peasants tends to constitute an aspect of the dual economy shaped prior to independence. It will certainly not contribute to and may hinder the necessary reallocation of resources needed to increase productivity in all sectors in order to raise the levels of living of the broad masses of the population. On the other hand, if prices of urban necessities continue to rise, and if the miners remain unconvinced that the government is taking necessary measures to capture and direct mining profits to a broader national development from which they may in the longer run hope to benefit, pressure for rising mine wages seems likely to persist.

Several issues appear to be involved in the wages controversy that has dominated the discussion of national incomes policies in many if not most African countries since independence. First, there are three sets of factual questions.

1. Are the wages of urban workers really so much higher in terms of purchasing power than the real incomes—in cash and kind—of the rural populations? Are they high enough to support and educate the worker and his family—the future source of a skilled, permanent urban labor supply—in the city on a long-term basis? Are

---

*These resulted from differential job classifications for expatriate workers, which continued to exist in large part due to the past failure of management to train and advance African mine workers.

high urban wages really the cause of the rural-urban drift that plagues all African countries? Or is that caused by the dualism of the economy in which social and economic opportunity is concentrated in the cities in the typical narrow, externally dependent modern sector?

2. Should not the issue of wage increases depend primarily on whether such increases contribute to higher productivity by facilitating the growth of a healthier, more stable labor force? Since wages probably constitute less than 15 percent of the costs in all modern African manufacturing industries, and less than 10 percent in most, what is the probable impact on overall costs even if wages are raised significantly, particularly if such increases may be shown to increase productivity? If the line on total wage costs should be held, might it not be preferable to reduce the salaries of the managerial staff while raising the wages of production workers to provide a more highly skilled, stable productive labor force?

3. Is it true, as available evidence appears to suggest, that the greater share of investible surpluses produced in the relatively modern export enclave in most African countries today is still remitted out of the continent by foreign firms or acquired by local elites in the form of high salaries and returns from speculative trade and real estate? If so, to what extent is the widely publicized emphasis on wage increases a smoke screen that clouds the critical issue of how to capture and utilize these investible surpluses to spread productivity and higher levels of living throughout a balanced, nationally integrated economy?

The answers to these sets of questions require, first of all, collection of much more data relating to wages, the relative stability of the labor force and productivity, and overall costs, as well as the comparative levels of living of urban and rural workers. They require, too, a critical analysis of the extent to which government financial policies, backed by essential institutional changes, do in fact direct all investible surpluses to a more balanced, internally integrated national economy capable of providing jobs and higher levels of living for the entire population.

A second issue involved in the wages controversy relates to education. Those workers whose wages really are significantly above the real incomes of the rest of the population—and this may be the case for Zambia's mine workers—need to be convinced that they must show restraint in their own long-term interests as well as those of the rest of the population, including their extended families "back home" in the villages. If the mine workers, for example, consume a major share of the national investible surpluses, these will then not be available for investment in an increasingly productive, integrated national economy; and the remainder of the population, mostly the rural population, will not gain the fruits of independence. Lack of national development may, over time, worsen the future outlook of the miners. If output per worker increases, or if copper prices fall, as they began to do in the early 1970s, copper workers themselves may be laid off. If the remainder of the economy remains undeveloped, workers will have no alternative but to join the growing ranks of urban unemployed or return to the backbreaking labor of subsistence farming.

If education is to help workers to understand their role in planned national development, it needs to permeate down to the rank-and-file trade union members, not merely to top-level union leaders. If trade union officials are seen by their members as participating in decision-making, this may contribute to winning rank-and-file support; but this is not likely to be the case if the workers are not convinced that these leaders continue to represent their best interests. In Zambia the government is reported to have won the cooperation of top union leaders, who were given posts in the government itself; but these leaders were apparently accused by some union members of having been "coopted." If this attitude spreads widely, it is likely to hinder government and top union leaders' efforts to win worker agreement to wage restraint.

Perhaps the most important element in any educational program designed to win worker support for wage restraint is visible evidence that the surpluses thus saved are in fact being invested to attain increased productivity and higher levels of living for the broad masses of the population. Workers will undoubtedly resent efforts to hold the line on wages if prices for food and the other major necessities are permitted to rise as a result of the actions of speculative traders.* Workers may certainly be expected to become cynical if they are convinced that foreign companies and their expatriate personnel are continuing to ship profits out of the country; or if they perceive African businessmen-cum ministers living in high style—as did the colonialists before them—while most of the rest of the population vegetates at bare subsistence levels. In brief, wages policies need to be formulated within the context of national incomes policies that are clearly designed to direct investible surpluses to broad national development. Many more carefully designed factual studies are needed to determine what level of wages is required to insure a stable, increasingly

---

*This certainly appears to have been the case in Ghana,[23] where, after wages were frozen in 1961, prices of local foodstuffs rose some 80 percent, contributing to lack of worker support for the Nkrumah government. After the 1966 coup, as Ghana's currency was devalued and prices rose still further, worker unrest broke out in repeated strikes, leading, just before the 1972 coup, to dissolution of the National Trade Union Congress by the Busia government.

skilled, healthy, productive urban labor force. Education is needed to enable workers to understand their role in the overall development program. But most important of all is clear evidence that investible surpluses produced are, in fact, contributing to the spread of productivity and higher levels of living throughout the economy.

POTENTIAL INVESTIBLE SURPLUSES
IN THE RURAL AREAS

The fourth level of conflicting interest that has emerged in the controversy over national incomes policies involves incomes of the vast majority of the population still living in rural areas. Unfortunately, neither the data nor the analysis of the incomes of the rural populations is as detailed as in the case of the wages—where gross inadequacies of the available information are still all too evident. Yet agriculture remains as the primary productive resource of most African countries and hence is the main available source of existing or potential investible surpluses. The formulation of an appropriate incomes policy and measures implementing it should be directed to capturing these surpluses and insuring that they too are invested to increase the productivity and levels of living of the rural populations in the context of an increasingly integrated and balanced national economy.

The paucity of data relating to the real income of the rural population in cash and kind is one of the greatest hindrances thwarting efforts to formulate an appropriate incomes policy for the rural areas. The lack of concrete data has fostered the somewhat sentimental notion that all African peasants are impoverished. Only fragmentary evidence has been collected to expose the extent to which sharply skewed incomes may already have emerged in cash crop areas long devoted to production of exports, like Ghana's and Nigeria's cocoa belts,[24] Tanzania's cotton areas,[25] or Uganda's coffee farms.[26] Colonial government statisticians explicitly ignored data that might have revealed the dimensions of this problem more fully by excluding from their surveys farmers who lived in towns (absentee landlords) or the top income groups (less than 10 percent of the rural populations) remaining in rural areas, who received incomes several times those of their less fortunate neighbors.[27] The limited information that is available indicates that the higher incomes accumulated by these groups are typically wasted on conspicuous consumption or invested in speculative real estate, trade, and occasionally money-lending.[28] Lack of information, while tending to bolster arguments for measures holding down urban workers' wages, hinders the formulation of policies that might be designed to caputre these surpluses for more productive investment.

255

Data are also scant relating to the extent to which farmers who have commonly been assumed to be subsistence and semisubsistence produce domestically consumed foodstuffs for sale. It is commonly assumed that their production and their "incomes in kind" merely keep pace with the population growth rate. The extent to which they have, or might be induced to, augment productivity for sales when necessary marketing facilities are created is often ignored. Yet historically African peasants have provided surpluses totaling as much as a third to half of their output to support powerful ruling groups, as they still do in Ethiopia.[29] There is a wealth of evidence that once the necessary marketing facilities are created, underemployed labor in semisubsistence areas may be engaged in production of foodstuffs for sale. In this activity too a few farmers may succeed in accumulating significant surpluses that they begin to invest in trade and speculative real estate. More careful studies are required to determine the kinds of policies that might insure that such potential investible surpluses are realized and more productively used.

Incomes policies designed for the rural areas should have a two-fold aim. First, they should provide the necessary incentives to stimulate the rural populations to produce surpluses (by investing both underemployed labor and accumulated funds) in increasingly productive agricultural activities for the sale of foodstuffs and raw materials, as well as export crops, in the context of the national physical plan. Second, they should insure that the increased investible surpluses thus created contribute both to further increases in productivity and to the improved material welfare of the broad masses of the peasants.

The provision of the necessary incentives to stimulate peasants to engage in the increasingly productive activities made possible by the national physical plan may be facilitated by a variety of institutional changes that should be incorporated into the national financial plan. Appropriate prices, which in the last analysis determine the returns to the individual peasant for his increased effort, are crucial, as is emphasized in Part III. Provision of credit for the purchase of necessary available inputs as well as for transport and storage is another essential ingredient. Producer and marketing cooperatives, marketing board funds, and various kinds of local and central government taxes have been suggested as additional institutional devices for directing available and potential surpluses in rural areas to increasingly productive activities.

The second aim, that of insuring that increased productivity leads to increased material levels of living for the peasants themselves, may also be accomplished through a variety of institutional arrangements. Individual peasants make decisions, within the context of constraints imposed by credit, price, and tax policies, as to how much additional labor and what share of their own accumulated funds—if any—they will invest in increased productivity instead of in education, housing, clothing, furniture, and so on. Cooperatives and marketing boards, likewise, if permitted to accumulate surpluses, may decide what share to invest in schools and clinics, what portion in feeder roads, transport, and storage and processing facilities. If the central government takes a major share of these surpluses through taxes, then national planners will have to make this choice.

In formulating national incomes policies relating to the rural sectors, national planners need to keep one important consideration in mind. They need to weigh the relative advantage of having greater centralized control and power to allocate a major share of investible surpluses through reliance on such devices as centralized taxing, financial institutions, and marketing board funds against the necessity of involving peasants themselves in this vital decision-making process in order to provide them with the necessary incentives to continue to increase and sell their output. While the national planners may believe they can make wiser choices, it is possible that the peasants might, given the opportunities to make the decisions themselves, be more willing to invest greater sums of both cash and labor in increasing productivity in order to obtain more of the better things of life. On the other hand, the more decentralized the decision-making, the fewer opportunities national planners will have to redirect surpluses to a more equitable distribution of the benefits of increased productivity among the differing regions of the nation. Given that rural surplus funds exist more as a potential than a reality, and the national planners can more easily exert control over existing surpluses accumulated by institutions dominating the export enclave, it may be hypothesized that they should direct their primary concern to redistributing these latter funds for the attainment of greater national balance. But such hypotheses must be continually re-evaluated in terms of their consequences for national development.

SUMMARY AND CONCLUSIONS: THE SCOPE OF FINANCIAL PLANNING

A national incomes policy is essential to identify and redirect existing and potential investible surpluses to implement physical plans if effective financial planning is to succeed in directing some 25 percent of Gross Domestic Product to proposed physical projects. Efforts of national planners to devise national incomes policies in Africa have confronted conflicting interests at four levels that have tended to render their task more difficult. Formulation of an effective national incomes policy requires (1) altering the institutions and working rules in the export enclave itself to capture a greater share

257

of the profits, dividends, interest, and expatriate salaries siphoned out of the country; (2) devising procedures to reduce the share of the surpluses retained by narrow African elites for conspicuous consumption or investment in speculative trade and real estate; (3) formulation of a wages policy that fosters a stable labor force and increased productivity while insuring that resulting increased investible surpluses are directed to implementing the national plan; and (4) insuring that prices, taxes, credit, and productive policies in the rural areas foster the growth and direction of existing and potential investible surpluses to development projects. The conflicting interests involved in each of these levels have tended to hinder formulation of appropriate national incomes policies.

In part, resolution of these conflicts requires much more information. Fragments of evidence suggest that available and potential investible surpluses are probably not being adequately tapped in most African countries. The controversy that has emerged over wages in the postindependence period, furthermore, has tended to obscure crucial issues relating to other areas.

Beyond the informational problem, the identification of conflicting interests in the process of formulating a national incomes policy reiterates the importance of mobilizing the vast majority of the populations, who will gain from restructuring the economy—the poor peasants, unskilled workers, and the growing numbers of unemployed—to press for essential changes in the inherited sets of working rules to implement effective financial plans. This will require education as to the issues involved, as well as the spread of accounting and statistical techniques to accumulate data to expose the real facts. It necessitates creation of institutions representing the working people and the mass of low-income peasants to insure that they press jointly for measures to capture and direct available and potential investible surpluses to needed physical projects.

An understanding of the basic issues, the inherent conflicts of interest, and the necessity of institutionalizing the joint activities of the broad masses of the population to press for adequate finance for an effective development plan to restructure the national economy—these constitute the parameters of the problem of financial planning to be discussed in the remaining chapters of Part IV.

NOTES

1. J. Z. Kracmar, Marketing Research in the Developing Countries (New York: Praeger Publishers, 1972), p. 23.
2. Unilever Ltd., Capital Investment (London, 1960), p. 6.
3. "Profits from Africa," Newsweek, Jan. 20, 1969, pp. 42-3.

4. H. Bienen, "The Economic Environment," in Development Administration—The Kenyan Experience, G. Hyden, R. Jackson, and J. Okumu (eds.) (Nairobi: Oxford University Press, 1970), p. 60.

5. F. Riggs, Administration in Developing Countries (Boston: Houghton Mifflin Co., 1964).

6. National Christian Council of Kenya, Who Controls Industry in Kenya? (Nairobi: East African Publishing House, 1968), pp. 248-9.

7. "Profits from Africa," Newsweek, Jan. 20, 1969, pp. 42-3. These ties may be reinforced by providing Africans with token directorships and various kinds of "presents."

8. Cf. S. A. Palekar, Problems of Wage Policy for Economic Development with Special References to India (Bombay: Asia Publishing House, 1962), p. 115.

9. Nationalist (Dar es Salaam), April 6, 1971, and Daily Nation (Nairobi), May 6, 1971.

10. West Africa, Jan. 28, 1972.

11. Bienen, "The Economic Environment," pp. 49-51.

12. Summarized in M. W. Forrester, Kenya Today, Social Prerequisites for Economic Development (S. Gravenhage: Mouton and Co., 1962), p. 58; see also Report of the Territorial Minimum Wages Board (Dar es Salaam: Government Printer, 1962).

13. D. Akumu, reported in Daily Nation (Nairobi), May 14, 1972.

14. E.g., M. J. Bailey, National Income and the Price Level— A Study in Macro-Theory (New York: McGraw-Hill Book Company, 1962), pp. 68-70.

15. International Labour Office, United Nations Development Programme, Technical Assistance Sector, Report to the Government of the United Republic of Tanzania on Wages, Incomes and Prices Policy (Dar es Salaam: Government Printer, 1967, Government Paper No. 3; hereinafter cited as "Turner Report.") For critical analysis, see J. Rweyemamu, "Some Aspects of the Turner Report," E. R. B. Paper 69.20; and G. Routh, "Incomes Policy in a Developing Country: A Case Study of the Foreign Expert at Work (Turner in Tanzania)," presented to the 1969 Internship Study Course on Active Labour Policy, Sussex University, England (mimeo).

16. Republic of Tanzania, Central Statistics Bureau, Employment and Earnings, 1966 (Dar es Salaam: Government Printer, 1967).

17. J. Rweyemamu, "The Historical and Institutional Setting of Tanzanian Industry," ERB Paper No. 71.6 (Dar es Salaam: University of Dar es Salaam, 1971), p. 48. This survey produces in more detail results similar to those found in Nigeria, where total wages and salaries constituted less than half the total profits (after depreciation, which alone totaled more than wages and salaries) for larger manufacturing industries reported in the 1965 industrial survey. See Egon Vielrose, "Manufacturing Industries in Nigeria: Notes on Profits,

Growth and Capacity Utilization," (The Nigerian Journal of Economic and Social Studies 12, no. 1 (March 1970): 142.

18. Tanzania, Employment and Earnings, 1966.

19. Rweyemamu, "The Historical and Institutional Setting of Tanzanian Industry," p. 42.

20. Central Statistical Bureau, Household Budget Survey of Wage Earners in Dar es Salaam (May 1967).

21. Unless otherwise cited, the data relating to Zambia are from R. H. Bates, Unions, Parties, and Political Development, A Study of Mineworkers in Zambia (New Haven: Yale University Press, 1971).

22. J. B. Knight, "Wages and Zambia's Economic Development," paper prepared for Institute of Economics and Statistics, Oxford University, 1968, p. 10.

23. See A. Seidman, Ghana's Development Experience, 1951-1966, Ch. VII; and West Africa, Jan. 28, 1972.

24. E.g., Office of the Government Statistician, Survey of Cocoa Producing Families in Ashanti, 1956-57 (Accra, 1958, mimeo); and S. Essang, "Determinants of Income Distribution Among Cocoa Farmers and Buyers in Western Nigeria," unpublished Ph.D. thesis, Michigan State University, 1971.

25. Tanganyika, Central Statistical Bureau, Village Economic Surveys, 1961-62 (Dar es Salaam, 1963).

26. C. C. Wrigley, "African Farming in Buganda," East African Institute of Social Research Conference, 1953.

27. E.g., see Tanganyika Central Statistical Bureau, Village Economic Surveys.

28. This is illustrated by the Ghanaian Survey of Cocoa Producing Families in Ashanti.

29. E.g., M. Taye, "The Impact of Land Ownership Systems on the Development Patterns of Shashamene and Ada Districts," unpublished paper, University of Wisconsin, 1972.

14

EXTERNAL FUNDS:
MYTH VS. REALITY

INTRODUCTION: PURSUIT OF A MYTH?

Initially, almost all African governments tended to plan that a major share of their development budgets would be provided by foreign funds, both public and private.[1] Tanzania, with a per capita income of under $60 a year, projected that foreign funds would cover 78 percent of its government development expenditures in its First Five Year Plan.[2] On the other side of the continent, Nigeria, with a per capita income of barely more than $100, at first planned that half the total projected capital expenditures was to come from foreign aid.[3]

The former British colonies, too, almost without exception, initially assumed they could attract foreign private investment as the main source of funds for expansion of industry. In this they appear to have adopted the argument advanced by Sir Arthur Smith,[4] Chairman of the United Africa Company, who pointed out, "The total national income of most African countries [is] already below the annual sales value of many international companies." He maintained that African enterprises could not hope to free themselves from dependence on foreign capital.

Even the Second Five Year Plan in Tanzania[5]—which since the Arusha Declaration has perhaps made the greatest effort to achieve "self-reliance"—proposes that the government contribute barely more than 20 percent to parastatals in the industrial and tourist sectors.* A share of the remaining 80 percent is undoubtedly expected to come

---

*Unfortunately, these two categories are combined in the plan, and it is difficult to ascertain what percentage is expected to finance each separately.

from reinvestment of surpluses earned by existing parastatals, but since a major portion of the government's earnings is still required to pay compensation for the 51 percent of shares of ownership purchased from foreign firms, it would appear that most of the reinvested funds would have to come from the private foreign partners.*

This approach finds theoretical support in the commonly accepted Harrod-Domar model, which emphasizes capital as the crucial factor in development. But capital is a factor with which few African countries are endowed, given per capita incomes of only $100 or less in most cases. Therefore reliance on the Harrod-Domar model often leads to the conclusion that without foreign funds they cannot hope to achieve "modern" development at all.

It is undoubtedly true that, if sufficient amounts of foreign funds could, without too great a cost, be directed to the right kinds of projects within the framework of an effective development strategy, African nations could increase their productivity and raise the levels of living of the masses of the population far more rapidly than without them. The critical issues then seem to become: how much foreign funds are available at what cost for what kinds of projects?

THE REALITY

Limited Amounts

To date, most African nations have been sorely disappointed as to the amounts of capital they have actually obtained from overseas sources in the form of loans or investment (see Table 13). Only little Sweden, directing half of its assistance to African countries, has come anywhere near contributing 1 percent of its GDP to developing areas as recommended by the first UNCTAD conference in 1964.[7] The biggest Western developed countries, like the United States and Britain, confronted by their own growing balance of payments problems, and in the U.S. case spending heavily for armaments around the world, have in recent years reduced overseas governmental assistance.[8]

It is true that Kenya received some 87 percent of its development revenues in the form of loans and grants from Western countries in 1963/64, but by 1969 this proportion had declined to closer to 55

---

*In almost no African country has enough domestic private capital or know-how been accumulated to contribute significantly to large-scale modern industrial projects; for the most part, private domestic capital tends to flow into trade and speculative real estate.[6]

TABLE 13

Commitments of Bilateral Economic Assistance from
Centrally Planned Economies to Africa,
1954-61 and 1962-65
(in millions of dollars)[a]

Commitments	1954-61 Cumu- lative	1962	1963	1964	1965[b]	1962-65 Cumu- lative
To all developing countries	4,138	316	341	1,246	685	2,588
To Africa	1,247	55	242	874	204	1,375
Algeria	—	—	156	143	—	299
Central African Republic	—	—	—	4	—	4
Congo (Brazzaville)	—	—	—	33	29	62
Ethiopia	114	—	—	—	—	—
Ghana	122	—	—	22	20	42
Guinea	106	13	—	—	—	13
Kenya	—	—	—	55	—	55
Mali	75	10	—	27	—	37
Morocco	5	12	—	—	—	12
Nigeria	—	—	—	—	14	14
Senegal	—	—	—	7	—	7
Somalia	74	—	22	—	—	22
Sudan	22	—	—	—	—	—
Tanzania	—	—	—	51	—	51
Tunisia	48	—	—	—	—	—
Uganda	—	—	—	15	15	30
U.A.R.	681	20	64	517	126	727

[a]National currencies converted into dollars at official rates of exchange.
[b]Provisional estimate.

Source: UN, International Flow of Long-Term Capital and Official Donations, 1961-1965.

percent.[9]* That they have made relatively sizable sums available to Kenya may in part reflect the foreign donors' interest in that country as a "stable" center of the status quo in East Africa. Other African countries have received a far smaller percent of their development requirements than originally anticipated. Tanzania, with a lower per capita income, received barely a third of its development costs from overseas donors in the same period, and was forced to find domestic sources to meet the shortfall.

By early 1971 the Economic Commission for Africa reported that the net real transfer of funds to Africa had probably declined during the Development Decade years. This was because of a decline in official capital, as well as an increase in the outflow of interest and profits on previous loans and investments.[10]

The socialist countries, most of which were themselves "under-developed" at the end of World War II, can only be expected to give limited financial and technical assistance, perhaps at most 10 to 15 percent of the costs of African countries' development programs.[11] (See Table 13, p. 263.) Specific projects may be quite large—as in the case of Soviet-financed Aswan Dam in the U.A.R. or the Tazara Railway being built by the Chinese through Tanzania to Zambia.

Foreign private investment in Africa has expanded even more slowly than foreign government funds, hardly justifying the assertion of the chairman of the United Africa Company[12] that the response of foreign private capital to African needs had been "formidable." His prescription for increased foreign investment was that African governments should treat foreign capital "fairly" in the context of a less nationalistic approach. Business, he held, should press for a new legal, tax, and institutional status for the international company, as well as training staff, Africanizing management, and selling shares to Africans. Most African governments have attempted to comply with such strictures, but Smith himself points out that private capital flow into Africa in 1967 equaled only two-thirds of the official funds obtained from Western countries.

The trend of foreign investment in Africa may be illustrated by the case of investments of private U.S. firms, which have been expanding more rapidly overseas than any others since the end of World War II. U.S. investment[13] in Africa has expanded as fast as new French investments, faster than new British investments. Yet by 1967 less

---

*At least a third of Kenya's external debt at the time of independence consisted of loans by Britain to the new Kenyan government to compensate former British officials for the loss of their jobs and former British settlers for the loss of their estates on that part of the former "white highlands" that was restored to Kenyan farmers.

than 4 percent of all U.S. private investment abroad was in Africa. This is true despite the fact that the overall average rate of profit of U.S. firms in Africa[14] in the 1960s was 21.05 percent, higher than the average U.S. rate of return on all investments in any other area of the world except Asia.

The Costs

African governments have had to pay for the limited amounts of foreign funds they have obtained, usually including interest and profit remittances, in the form of scarce foreign exchange. This has aggravated the growing balance of payments deficits that plague many of them. The extent of this problem may vary from country to country. It depends not only on the amounts of funds obtained, but the share of profits remitted, as well as the rate of interest and the length of the repayment period for loans. These costs may be high. In the case of U.S. investment in Africa,[15] for example, earnings in 1967 ($418 million) exceeded new investments ($220 million). Payout in the form of dividends, interest, and so on, remitted to the United States totaled $367 million (87 percent of all earnings), more than all new U.S. investments made in Africa that year.

The total outflow of investment income—that is, profits and dividends—of selected African countries, as reported by government sources, is suggested by the data in Table 14. It should be noted, however, that such data are subject to considerable question and are undoubtedly underestimated, since it is in the foreign firm's interest to understate its profit remittances in reports available to African governments. As has been noted, import and export prices are manipulated as one means of shifting profits out of a country to avoid taxes, and consequently these profits are not included in official statistics. It has been estimated[16] that about half of the rise in import prices in Tanzania from 1962 to 1967—roughly $4 million—might be attributed to this kind of manipulation.

The cost of repaying both principal and interest on loans to Africa has increased in recent years. An Economic Commission for Africa report[17] projects the 1966-75 growth of debt service repayments from 25 percent to 53 percent of capital inflow, and forecasts that many countries will require rescheduling of repayments to be able to pay at all.

Special problems have emerged as some countries, desperately seeking foreign funds to meet their requirements, have resorted to private suppliers' credits. These tend to have short repayment periods and very high rates of interest. Although they may be easier to obtain than government credit, they may cost more and cause greater balance of payments difficulties in the long run. (See pp. 278-280 for Nigerian and Ghanaian experience.)

TABLE 14

Reported Outflow of Profits and Dividends from Selected
African Countries, 1963-1968

Country	Investment Income (in millions of U.S. dollars; minus sign = outflow)					
	1963	1964	1965	1966	1967	1968
Ghana	-25.2	-17.8	-27.0	-20.1	-24.2	-32.1
Kenya	-25.8	-27.5	-25.1	-34.9	-36.7	-38.3
Nigeria	-47.6	-77.5	-146.7	-208.0	-113.1[a]	-63.5[a]
Tanzania	-15.4	-10.6	-14.4	-19.3	-16.8[b]	- 8.8[b]
Uganda	NA	NA	NA	-17.5	-18.9	NA
Zambia	NA	-82.8	-42.8	-87.0	-70.8	-82.6[d]

NA = Not available in source listed.

[a]Although Nigeria's outflow on investments income appeared to decline in 1967 and 1968, the outflow on "other" account increased significantly in the same years: 1966 = $105.0 million; 1967 = $168.0 million; 1968 = $197.6 million; this suggests that this apparent reported decline may in part reflect changed bookkeeping practices in the face of the tightened foreign exchange controls introduced during the civil war.

[b]This appears to reflect, in part, the consequences of actions taken after the Arusha Declaration.

[c]The figure given in 1968 for Uganda, -$29.0, includes losses on "other" and "travel" accounts, which in 1967 equaled -$0.3 and -$16.4 million, respectively.

[d]Calculated from Central Statistical Office, Monthly Digest of Statistics (Lusaka: April, 1973) p. 59.

Source: International Monetary Fund, International Financial Statistics XXII, no. 12, country data (December 1969).

The Impact on Development

In addition to the insufficiency of foreign funds and the costs of
repayment, the kinds of projects that such funds may finance have not
always coincided with African requirements for restructuring the
inherited economies. Although government-to-government funds may
provide welcome additions to African finance, these need to be scrutinized carefully not only in terms of interest rates, the length of repayment time, and the foreign exchange costs over time, but also in terms
of the kinds of projects financed. Not uncommonly, Western governments, still the source of a major share of official funds, seek to
create conditions in the recipient country conducive to investment or
sales of products by their national private firms. The result has
tended to be that loans have been forthcoming primarily for infrastructure and technical assistance rather than directly productive projects.[18]
The underlying philosophy appears to be that the creation of essential
infrastructure will encourage private firms to invest in productive
sectors. Not infrequently, such loans are tied to purchase of capital
equipment and machinery from the private firms of the lending country.
The advantages to the African countries of building infrastructure and
obtaining technical assistance appear self-evident; yet of themselves
they cannot guarantee the hoped-for increases in productivity. Since
the philosophy behind such funds—backed by advice and sometimes
contractual relations—is that investment in the productive sectors
is best left to the private—typically foreign—investors, the consequences would seem to depend on whether the resulting private investments do contribute to the goal of restructuring the economy. Unless
productivity and national income are in fact increased, the cost of
repayment of the loans may constitute a heavy future burden.

Examination of the postindependence experience of the African
countries suggests that to a significant degree private investments
attracted by such expenditures have not contributed much to increasing
productivity and the real incomes of the national population. First,
foreign private investment, in addition to being limited, has been
directed primarily toward export enclave activities. Mines and oil
wells producing raw materials for developed country factories still
claim by far the greatest share. Investment in plantations and agricultural processing has tended to decline as aid agencies and African
government-sponsored programs have stimulated African peasants
to produce cash crops for export—but falling world prices for these
crops have significantly reduced the resulting real incomes of the
African growers and their governments. Despite the fact that

independent African governments have been competing* with each other and other developing nations to attract foreign investment in industry through provision of essential infrastructure, tax holidays and rebates, and maintenance of low wages, little foreign investment has been attracted into domestic industry. Some has taken place in last-stage assembly and processing of imported parts and materials, primarily to preserve market control behind tariff barriers. A major share of foreign investment in manufacturing in Africa, however, has been concentrated in South Africa.

U.S. investments in Africa, again by way of illustration, while expanding relatively rapidly compared to those of the former colonial powers, are not only limited in scope, but still predominantly directed to export enclave development.[20] Over half (54 percent) of U.S. investment in Africa is in oil, and nearly a fifth (17 percent) more is in mining and smelting. Only 16 percent is in manufacturing, with over half of that in South Africa itself.

Foreign private banks, including Barclays, the Banque de Paris et de Pays Bas, Kreditanstalt für Wiederaufbau, and the Bank of America, have agreed to provide some $350 million or more to finance the Caborra Bassa hydroelectric project in the Portuguese colony of Mozambique. The project will provide power for South Africa, Mozambique, Malawi, Rhodesia, Southwest Africa, Bechuanaland, and Lusotho. The project is one of the largest financed primarily by private funds in Africa—but it is clearly not designed to contribute to the restructuring and development of independent Africa. On the contrary, as one conservative observer has remarked,[21] it is part of a Portuguese program to "stifle left-wing inspired rebel activities" to liberate Mozambique.

It is true that a new trend has emerged in recent years: foreign firms show an increasing willingness to have African governments participate in financing projects in which they are investing. With growing pressure for nationalization throughout the Third World, even foreign mining firms have welcomed 51-percent government ownership (for example, Zambia and Sierra Leone) under conditions in which they continue as managers. They typically receive compensation for shares sold to the government that includes payment of

---

*An advertisement from a Nigerian government corporation, for example, appeared in the New York Times[19] entitled: "People are earning HUGE PROFITS In Nigeria . . . Why don't you?" The ad held forth the following glowing prospect to potential investors: A market of 55 million people; labor at 7¢ an hour; plentiful raw materials; good infrastructure and substantial amenities; and "It is possible to get your investment back in less than three years."

interest—usually 6 or 7 percent—as well as principal estimated at
market value over a period of years. The companies' control of overseas processing and marketing insures them of the opportunity of
continuing to obtain a major share of the profits from the mines'
export. Furthermore, the companies apparently find that government
participation insures political support. Upon buying the Ashanti Gold
Fields in Ghana, for example, Lonrho[22] sold a small share to the
Ghanaian government—and was thus apparently assured of government
support and police action* when the workers went on strike.

   All of this is not to say that African countries should not accept
official funds or private investments from Western developed countries.
What it does argue is that the potential impact of such funds depends
significantly on the extent to which the recipient African government
has formulated a national development strategy in the framework of
which infrastructure and/or productive projects thus financed may
be expected to contribute to the attainment of a balanced, nationally
integrated economy.

   The fact that since independence African nations have been able
to negotiate to some extent among different governments and different
private firms from different countries has tended to give them some
leeway to find foreign-financed projects that they may fit into their
plan strategy—if they already have one carefully formulated and have
sufficiently altered the inherited institutional structure to implement
it. Such a plan and implementation machinery should provide a set
of criteria to enable the planners to evaluate whether the concessions
required to attract foreign funds in any given case render the costs
greater than the benefits. The essential element would appear to be
to retain control of the critical sectors in the economy to insure that
they may continue to exercise self-reliant decision-making so each
project for which finance and/or foreign expertise is accepted will
in fact contribute concretely to implementation of the overall plan.

   A national plan strategy should also provide the criteria needed
to evaluate alternative proposals for assistance from socialist countries. Socialist governments have been willing to lend funds and train
manpower, not only for infrastructural projects but also for industries
within the public sector at low rates of interest (0-2.5 percent)† with
fairly long repayment periods. There is evidence, however, that to
accept a foreign loan for any project without first considering precisely

---

   *Several workers were killed by the police in the violence that
accompanied the strike.
   † The Chinese generally do not charge any interest, although
African governments in this, as in all cases, should compare prices
to insure that the project really is therefore less expensive in the long
run.

what role it will play in overall development can have negative consequences, no matter how "cheap" the loan may appear. Acceptance of
a foreign loan for construction of a giant sports stadium,[23] for example,
hardly seems justifiable since in the long run it involves capital and
foreign exchange expenditures without contributing in any way to increased productivity. Even in the case of industrial projects, to accept
foreign loans without adequate preplanning can be expensive. Machinery
and equipment for a sugar plant was stored in Czechoslovakia at
Ghanaian expense until the Ghanaian planners could decide where to
build it; and when it finally was hastily erected, the failure to plan for
adequate supplies of water or sugar cane led to prolonged heavy
losses.[24] A better use of loans from socialist countries appears to
be the construction of a textiles and a farm tools factory (Chinese
loans to Tanzania),[25] or a textile plant in Northern Uganda linked to
an agreement that the lending country would purchase a significant
share of the output (USSR-Uganda).[26]

International Sources of Funds

Funds from international bodies constitute another potential
source of foreign funds,* but, like all others, these too should be
evaluated in terms of their potential contribution to a carefully formulated development strategy. The World Bank (more formally, the
International Bank for Reconstruction and Development), together with
its affiliates, the International Finance Corporation and the International Development Association, is the largest and best known of
these international agencies.
The World Bank is essentially a financing agency established
by the developed nations of Western Europe and the United States;
its policies are governed by votes in proportion to the financial contribution of participating nations. No African country has as much as
1 percent of the votes. The United Arab Republic, with the biggest
share of all independent African states, has a little over half of 1
percent. South Africa has almost 1 percent.
As recently as 1968, less than 10 percent of all World Bank
commitments had been made to Africa,[28] although in that year bank

---

*The former French and Belgian colonies associated with the
European Common Market have had available to them some additional
multilateral funds through the European Development Fund,[27] but
almost none of these has been available to former British colonies.
Whether this will change now that Britain has entered the Market
remains to be seen.

officials forecast an upward trend in an effort to help achieve "transformation of traditional rural societies and the development of a balancing industrial and commercial economy."

For the most part, prior to 1968, World Bank loans to Africa had been directed to infrastructure (over 75 percent in 1966/67). In contrast, industry and agriculture had been seriously neglected (under 15 percent for industry, including mining, and well under 10 percent for agriculture and forestry). This appears to reflect the World Bank's philosophical outlook—like that of its major sponsoring governments in Europe and the U.S.—that investment in the productive sectors should be left to private firms.

After 1968 the World Bank and its affiliate the International Development Association increased their loans to Africa, particularly to the agricultural sector.[29] By 1970 loans to Africa had increased to almost 20 percent of the total loans of the two organizations. Almost half of the loans were provided by the International Development Association, which provides relatively longer-term loans at lower rates of interest.

World Bank—IDA agricultural loans in the two years from 1968 to 1970 totaled $168.9 million to 16 countries, considerably more than all their loans to agriculture in Africa until 1968 (which had totaled only $151 million to 10 countries). Although World Bank spokesmen admitted the limitations of export agriculture due to world market problems, the Bank continues to help specific African countries produce export crops in "sheer desperation" even when, like coffee, they were in surplus on the world market.

The new World Bank-IDA emphasis in agriculture, in contrast to earlier years, is on small farmers rather than plantations. The latter, it is argued, tend to be "politically vulnerable," and their relatively heavy fixed costs also make them economically vulnerable in a period of softening demand and prices. Hence World Bank-IDA loans have financed package programs to provide seed, fertilizers, and technical assistance for smallholders. These may include programs such as the one for land consolidation and registration in Kenya, resettlement on underutilized land in Ethiopia, and "perhaps" ujamaa villages in Tanzania. It may be significant that D. Gordon, Chief of the Nairobi Office of the World Bank, explicitly welcomed the advice of former British colonial officials and settlers,* for the British had

---

*The Nairobi Office of the World Bank established an Agricultural Development Service including 18 expatriates "with long experience, some in the colonial service, some successful farmers on their own account" to supervise projects. This type of expatriate supervision has been expensive at times; it is estimated, for example,[30] that 43

271

earlier formulated a parallel approach directed to creating a "stable yeomanry" among African farmers in an effort to maintain the status quo in East Africa as independence neared.[31]

Gordon has explained that the World Bank remains unlikely to make many loans to stimulate industry in Africa, aside from mining, processing of agricultural produce, and the manufacture of a few simple consumer goods. It lends money on commercial terms to industry through another affiliate, the International Finance Corporation, which "aims specifically at promoting industrial development through private enterprise and investment." As a practical matter, IFC participation is limited to projects of several hundred thousand dollars at least. These must be in the private sector. In "most African countries there is no great number of industrial projects that fit both criteria." The World Bank is now willing to channel funds through national development banks or finance companies*—it supported four of these in tropical Africa—although it still requires that a major portion of the shares be privately owned. The World Bank has also supported industrial estates and encouraged the development of technical assistance to promote private industry. In most African countries, however, Gordon holds, "there is little possibility of organizing strong private development finance companies—sometimes . . . because of anti-capitalist bias, but also because the short-term investment opportunities are too few or uncertain to make the effort seem worthwhile."

On the other hand, Gordon declares, World Bank officials have "leaped with enthusiasm" to provide support for tourism as "one of the true growth sectors of the world economy."†

Aside from the World Bank and its affiliates, there are few international sources of funds available to African countries. The United Nations offers only a limited amount of funding for technical assistance. Although more than a third of it was going to Africa by

---

expatriates employed on a Malawian smallholder program involving 38,000 peasants consumed one third of an entire $6 million loan from the International Development Association.

*U.S. economist R. F. Mikesell argues that foreign assistance agencies should work through such investment banks to facilitate the development of small private firms to insure the lending agency control of end uses via review or prior approval of projects to be financed through the development bank.[32]

†Not a few social scientists have raised questions as to whether tourism may not hinder efforts to attain development by its demonstration effects on elites as well[33] as its heavy foreign exchange expenditures and speculative character.

the mid-1960s, the absolute amount totaled less than $18 million, considerably less than the British, French, or U.S. programs.[34] About 1,000 UN experts were stationed in Africa in 1965-66, compared to over 9,000 British, 43,000 French (70 percent of these were in education), and 1,376 U.S. experts.

The African Development Bank, established in 1964 as a joint African government-sponsored project to provide essential funds, has been sharply restricted in the amount of funds it could offer.[35] Its main potential appears to lie in helping to promote non-African sources of finance, at least until African governments achieve a sufficient degree of unity in regard to their own plans that they can jointly direct their own funds to essential projects.

In 1969 reports began to circulate[36] that the Development Bank was endeavoring to stimulate creation of a multinational financial corporation, involving worldwide enterprises and looking for "reasonable" profits, to provide managerial and technical expertise to help private investors and contribute to the development of local and regional capital markets. It was to seek participation of African private and public capital, with a minimum of 10-percent local participation, and would sell any "majority interest" to private holders "as soon as possible." It was to give priority to investing in export-oriented enterprises processing local materials, followed by import substitution activities, public utilities, transportation, banking, and financial institutions. The extent of economic integration of a country with its neighbors was to constitute an important criterion in evaluating fund proposals.

It then appeared that a parallel plan, supported by non-African bankers and financiers, including Standard Bank of London, was proposed that, unlike the African Development Bank's proposal, would permit firms dealing with South Africa, like Anglo-American, Shell BP, Lonrho, and Standard Bank itself, to participate. "In a sense, their goal is nothing less than to 'rehabilitate' the image of the private investor in the minds of African leaders."[37]

The upshot of 18 months of these negotiations appears to have been a meeting in Luxembourg, backed by 12 British firms—including Standard Bank and Barclays—as well as 110 to 140 other firms from the U.S., Japan, and Canada, that envisaged an authorized capital of $40 million with a view to mobilizing ten times as much in investment in specific projects. The African governments' safeguard was reported to be their potential shareholding, fiscal weapons, and membership on the board of the consortium.

SUMMARY

In sum, the absolute amount of foreign funds available for African development appears quite limited. The major share of foreign funds obtained must be repaid with foreign exchange earnings, frequently with a fairly high interest and/or profit rate, potentially contributing to future balance of payment burdens. There is an evident bias for major governmental and multilateral fund agencies of the West—still the major potential source of foreign funds—to support rather than replace foreign private investment funds. The latter, limited in amount still more than official funds, are primarily directed to maximizing their investors' profits in existing markets—for the most part the existing export markets and the limited high-income group in associated export enclave activities—with a consequent tendency to reinforce the distorted pattern of Africa's inherited dual economies.

These objective constraints render it imperative for African government planners to work out careful "self-reliant" financial plans to restructure their economies. The Arusha Declaration put the matter plainly:

> We made a mistake in choosing money—something we do not have—to be the big instrument of our development. We are making a mistake to think that we shall get the money from other countries; first, because in fact we shall not be able to get sufficient money for our economic development; and secondly, because even if we could get all that we need, such dependence upon others would endanger our independence and our ability to choose our own political policies.[38]

The necessity for African countries to reduce their dependency on external finance underlines the necessity for reshaping their internal financial institutions to increase their own domestic sources of funds. Once embarked on this path, they may then evaluate specific offers of foreign funds in terms of their anticipated concrete contribution to explicitly formulated physical plans. Any offer of foreign funds, no matter how attractive it may appear in monetary terms, that does not contribute concretely to the implementation of the long-term national physical plan should be rejected. Foreign funds should in any event only be viewed as supplementary, so that if they are not forthcoming on appropriate terms for appropriate projects, it will be possible to forge ahead with the planned program even, if necessary, at a reduced pace.

A footnote might be added here to reiterate that to the extent that African nations can collaborate in the essential political-economic reshaping of their institutions to implement jointly formulated national plans, backed by joint markets, natural resources, and capital, the possibility of attaining more rapid desirable patterns of development— with or without foreign funds—will be considerably enhanced.[39]

NOTES

1. Cf. U. K. Hicks, "Finance and Financial Infrastructure," in M. C. Taylor, ed., Taxation for African Economic Development (New York: Africana Publishing Corporation, 1969), p. 27.

2. Ministry of Economic Affairs and Development Planning, United Republic of Tanzania, Background to the Budget, 1968-1969 (Dar es Salaam: Government Printer, 1968), p. 81.

3. Federal Ministry of Economic Development, National Development Plan, 1962-1968 (Lagos, 1962), pp. 32-33.

4. Sir Arthur Smith, "A Businessman's View of Africa," African Affairs 68 (October 1969): 334-336.

5. United Republic of Tanzania, Second Five-Year Plan (Dar es Salaam: Government Printer, 1969), 1, 212.

6. Cf. O. Aboyade, "A Note on External Trade, Capital Distortion and Planned Development," African Primary Products and International Trade, papers delivered at an international seminar at the University of Edinburgh, I. G. Steward and H. Ord, eds. (Edinburgh University Press, 1965).

7. M. Lowenkopf, "Sweden and Africa," Africa Report 13 (October 1968): 59-62.

8. Organization for Economic Cooperation and Development, Development Assistance, 1970 Review, Report by Edwin M. Martin, Chairman, Development Assistance Committee, December 1970, p. 43.

9. R. Lacey, "Foreign Resources and Development," Development Administration: The Kenyan Experience, G. Hyden, R. H. Jackson, J. J. Okumu, eds. (Nairobi: Oxford University Press, 1970), p. 66. For percent "compensating" former British settlers and colonial officials, see Republic of Kenya, Economic Survey, 1969 (Nairobi: Government Printer, 1969), p. 135.

10. P. Streeton, "Working Capital," reported in West Africa, Feb. 12, 1971.

11. E.g., G. Skorov and V. A. Martynov at University of East African Conference on Foreign Aid, Dar es Salaam, 1964; see also M. Dobb, Economic Growth and Underdeveloped Countries (London: Lawrence and Wishart, 1963), pp. 59-69.

12. Smith, "A Businessman's View of Africa," pp. 335-336.

13. F. T. Ostrander, with assistance of Winifred Armstrong, "U.S. Private Investment in Africa," Africa Report, no. 68 (January 1969): 38-41.

14. Measured as the net returns of U.S. branches and subsidiaries as a percent of investment; U.S. Department of Commerce, Survey of Current Business, September, 1965, cited in J. H. Adler (ed.), Capital Movements and Economic Development (New York: St. Martin's Press, 1967), Statistical Appendix, Table 6h.

275

15. Ostrander, "U.S. Private Investment in Africa."

16. M. J. H. Yaffey, Member of board of directors of State Trading Corporation, Dar es Salaam, interview, July 20, 1968.

17. Streeton, "Aid to Africa."

18. Economic Commission for Africa, Economic Bulletin for Africa 60, 1 June 1969.

19. The New York Times, Jan. 29, 1971.

20. Ostrander, "U.S. Private Investment in Africa."

21. R. W. J. Barnes, "Dawning of a New Era in African Development," Contemporary Review 214 (February 1969): 85.

22. Newsweek, Jan. 20, 1969. For information regarding Lonrho and Ashanti gold fields strike, see West Africa, Jan. 2, 1969, March 8, 15, and 29, 1969, and April 10, 1969.

23. E.g., the Rumanians offered a loan to construct yet another stadium in Ghana in the early 1960s; the Ghanaian planners turned it down as it did not fit their plan.

24. Republic of Ghana, Economic Survey, 1964 (Accra: Government Printer, 1964), p. 85.

25. National Development Corporation, Third Annual Report (Dar es Salaam: National Printing Co., 1968).

26. Sunday News, Tanzania, Aug. 31, 1969, p. 3.

27. For discussion of the role of the European Common Market in relation to Africa, see R. H. Green and A. Seidman, Unity or Poverty? pp. 157-169.

28. The following information and quotations relating to the World Bank and its affiliates, unless otherwise cited, are from D. Gordon, "The World Bank—New Directions in Africa," African Affairs, no. 68 (July 1969): 232-244. Gordon, at the time of writing the article, was Chief of the World Bank's Permanent Mission in East Africa.

29. The data relating to 1968-1970 loans are reported in World Banking International Development Association, Annual Report, 1970.

30. N. McKitterick, "The Role of the World Bank," Africa Report, no. 13 (November 1968): 42.

31. See M. P. K. Sorrenson, Land Reform in the Kikuyu Country (Nairobi: Oxford University Press, 1967).

32. R. F. Mikesell, Public Foreign Capital for Private Enterprise in Developing Countries, International Finance Section, Department of Economics (Princeton: Princeton University Press, 1966), pp. 23-24, 52.

33. E.g., J. A. Paul, "Tourism and Development," Venture 3, no. 23: 21-25.

34. H. E. Caustin, "United Nations Technical Assistance in an African Setting," African Affairs 66 (April 1967): 113-126.

35. For description of African Development Bank, see Green and Seidman, Unity or Poverty? pp. 306-307.

36. E.g., Africa Confidential 7 (March 28, 1969).

37. Africa Confidential 9 (April 25, 1969).

38. J. Nyerere, Freedom and Socialism/Uhuru na Ujamaa (Dar es Salaam: Oxford University Press, 1968), p. 241.

39. For elaboration of this argument, see Green and Seidman, Unity or Poverty? especially Part III.

15

DEFICIT FINANCING

THE RAPID EXPANSION OF PUBLIC DEBT

Since independence, most African governments have increased their public debt to finance their expanded development programs. In so doing, they have typically adopted the Keynesian argument, current in developed Western nations, that deficit financing for capital expenditure is justifiable since the multiplier effect may be expected to stimulate private investment.[1] Furthermore, the government may utilize deficit finance as a means to influence monetary supplies. In the mixed economies of Africa, this argument is buttressed by the recognition that the state is the only domestic agent capable of making major investments in infrastructure required to stimulate growth; and in some cases the argument is extended further to assert that only the state can amass sufficient funds and managerial capacity to finance essential major directly productive investments. In order to carry out this role, given inherent shortages of capital, it is widely held that the state must borrow funds.*

The extent of debt expansion in different African countries has depended on many different factors, including the nature and extent of the proposed development program, alternative available sources of revenue, and the impact of unplanned circumstances like the sharp decline in Ghana's export prices or Nigeria's civil war. Even Zambia,

---

*Governments of developed socialist nations, in contrast, avoid borrowing money if at all possible. Money supplies, socialist theoreticians insist, should be expanded directly in a planned correspondence with increases in production to avoid inflationary price increases that tend to distort the pattern of income distribution.[2]

which was able to appropriate about a fourth of its greatly expanded revenue to development expenditure in 1968, borrowed more than three-fourths again as much to provide for additional development funds.[3] Its net borrowing totaled about $88 million in 1968.[4]

In East Africa,[5] Kenya's external debt rose by about a third, and its internal debt doubled from 1964 to 1968, adding up to a total debt of about $338 million in the latter year. Uganda's external debt remained about constant in the same period, but its internal debt rose from almost nothing to over $13 million, contributing to a total national debt of about $123 million.*[6] From 1965/66 to 1970/71, Tanzania's external public debt almost quadrupled, and its internal debt increased roughly eight times (largely borrowed from the banking system), adding up to a total national debt in the latter year of about $112 million.[7]

Ghana and Nigeria both experienced much greater debt increases than the East and Central African states, in major part due to exceptional circumstances. Ghana's national debt, over half of it from external sources, tripled from 1962 to 1965, to a total of almost $1 billion, as the government sought to maintain an extensive expenditure program in the face of falling world cocoa prices and declining revenues. Over half of its external debt in the latter year consisted of suppliers' credit,[8] and half of its debt was short term. Despite some rescheduling of external debt after the 1966 coup, Ghana's debt servicing in 1969 was almost $40 million.[9] After the 1966 coup, the credit cost of the debt was increased by devaluation. Furthermore, the Busia government, which sought to free imports from all controls, found that it had to borrow further simply to cover the costs of imported goods, so that the estimated short-term commercial debt had risen about $240 million more. The Busia government, with International Monetary Fund advice, therefore proposed another devaluation, this time of 40 percent, the "largest movement by any currency in the world in the recent round of realignments." While foreign firms like Lonrho's Ashanti Goldfields and the International Timber Corporation "generally welcomed devaluation" because it reduced the cost of their exports, the consequent rising cost of living was a major factor generating support for the 1972 coup. The new government rejected the devaluation and repudiated all those foreign debts that could be fairly claimed to have been established through corrupt practices.[10]

The internal debt of Nigeria's central and state governments also nearly tripled from 1962 to 1965, and rose still more rapidly

---

*By 1970 Uganda's internal debt had increased to almost $100 million, over half of it in government stocks, a fourth of them held by commercial banks; nearly a half was held in the form of treasury bills.

during the civil war. By 1970 the internal debt alone stood at $1352 million, about half of it in the form of short-term treasury bills, another fourth in Treasury Certificates. The external debt[11] in 1970 stood at about $750 million, excluding short-term commercial credits* and the foreign indebtedness of the private sector. The Nigerian planners anticipated that the external debt would increase by another $400 million—20 percent of the planned development expenditure—to finance the proposed 1970-74 plan.

THE POTENTIAL IMPACT OF PUBLIC DEBT

One financial authority has observed that the potential impact in Africa of credit, budgetary, and other measures is "frequently discussed in terms of categories of thought of the more 'capitalistic' countries of the West." He emphasizes that

> there is no reason to believe that the transplantation
> of these ideas and weapons of control can be realized.
> On the contrary, they may simply deflect thought and
> energies from dealing with the fundamental obstacles
> which impede the expansion of markets in areas in
> transition from largely subsistence economies. . . .
> For a large part of Africa the problem is less to regu-
> late the column of activity, incomes, and employment
> than to enlarge existing growing points and create more
> productive work for the indigenous people.[12]

While expanding the public debt in an effort to insure increased productivity, African governments need to be concerned with several issues. Most important, they must consider the significant potential influence the public debt may exert on the patterns of growth and distribution of the economy.[13]

Increased borrowing and expenditure by the government contributes to an increasing money supply and potential inflationary pressures that may cause major price increases unless the multiplier functions efficiently to stimulate increased production of real goods and services. The Keynesian prescription has sometimes been held to suggest that a degree of inflation may in itself be a good thing in developing areas, since it may contribute to rising entrepreneurial

---

*These commercial credits—otherwise known as the foreign exchange "backlog"—consisted of unpaid commercial debts accumulated during the war period.

profits that may then be invested to stimulate further production and employment. In the African context, however, built-in institutional constraints tend to inhibit the anticipated multiplier effects, raising prices and windfall profits while reducing the real incomes of the vast majority of peasants and wage earners. Monetary expansion leads also to increased imports of consumer goods, particularly luxury items for higher-income groups gaining from profit increases. This is likely to aggravate balance of payments difficulties. Inflationary pressures appear particularly likely to lead to rising prices and increased imports if the government invests the borrowed funds in social and economic infrastructure (or increased military or "prestige" expenditures) that do not contribute directly to increased domestic production.

These considerations suggest that primary attention should be directed to the purposes for which government borrowing occurs: to what extent does it contribute, for example, to such goals as the establishment of poles-of-growth and essential linkages to insure that productivity is augmented in every sector within the framework of an increasingly integrated, balanced national economy? Only if funds borrowed are directed to insuring increased production of goods and services will it be possible to avoid continuing inflationary pressures and growing balance of payments deficits that are likely to culminate in economic crises. Orthodox efforts to reduce inflationary pressures by reduced government spending, rather than redirecting resources to expand national production in the context of an increasingly integrated, balanced national economy, have, in Africa and elsewhere, tended to result in stagnation.[14]

Within the context of these kinds of general considerations, African countries' experience with rising national debts suggests the importance of considering specific issues, including whether the debt is internal or external and the terms of debt repayment.

Domestic Versus Foreign Borrowing

Funds borrowed internally in developed countries usually come from high-income groups and institutions that have funds to lend. The government taxes the general population to repay the individuals or institutions from which it borrows. This may affect the pattern of income distribution: if taxes are highly progressive the burden of the debt may be carried by high-income groups; but if they are regressive the government may be taxing the poor to repay the rich.

In the African case, governments necessarily borrow primarily from institutions, since few individuals enjoy high enough incomes to lend significant amounts to the government. The few efforts that have been made to borrow directly from the larger low-income groups through compulsory savings programs have contributed little in the way of development funds, and have not infrequently been resisted as an additional form of taxation (for example, Ghana, Uganda, Tanzania).

The consequences of the use of taxes to repay institutional lenders depends in part on whether they are public or private institutions and, in the latter case, whether they are owned domestically or abroad. If the institutions are in the public sector, like a central bank or, frequently in Africa, provident funds,* the impact of the loan repayment depends primarily on the tax structure. (See Chapter 16 for issues involved here.)

If the institutional lenders are privately held, like insurance firms or commercial banks in most African cases, the consequences of repayment depend in part on how the institutions utilize their earnings. If they are domestically privately owned, relatively unlikely in the African circumstance, the consequences of repayment depend on the tax structure, the extent to which the insurance firms contribute directly to investment, and whether those receiving dividends spend them on conspicuous consumption or invest them. The evidence suggests that in Africa both private individuals and the domestic firms are more likely to invest, if at all, where returns are highest—in trade and real estate, including housing and hotels for the wealthy—rather than in directly productive activity. If, on the other hand, the private lending institutions are owned abroad, then repayment is likely to augment the outflow of funds and further aggravate balance of payments problems.

The case of government borrowing directly from abroad has been discussed above. (See Chapter 13.) Here it should only be re-emphasized that repayments, including high interest rates, may constitute a drain of funds that might otherwise have been invested in the country, as well as an added strain on future balance of payments, unless the borrowed funds are used productively and contribute to increased foreign exchange earnings. Kenya's planners estimated[17] that in the course of the 1970-74 plan about $290 million would be

---

*Provident funds, collected regularly under government auspices from all wage-earning individuals, have since independence provided a fairly successful means of mobilizing "savings" from which African governments may borrow. Nigeria's planners estimated the Provident Fund would lend $58 million to the government during the 1970-74 plan.[15] Where pension funds remain foreign-owned, however, the consequences of repayment are similar to repayments made to any foreign firm, insofar as profits and even significant amounts of the principal are remitted to the home country.[16]

required for amortization and interest payments on its current and anticipated external debt, over a third of it owned by the central government. This is equal to about 40 percent of the total current balance of payments deficit anticipated for the period. Nigeria's planners estimated[18] that in the course of their plan for the same period federal and state agencies alone would be required to pay out $190 million to service their accumulated external debts, equal to almost half of their anticipated new foreign loans and investments.

Repayment of such debts constitutes a major burden on these countries' balance of payments. Nigeria's efforts to repay its accumulated short-term commercial wartime debt in 1970 produced a balance of payments deficit, despite expanded foreign exchange earnings for the sale of oil of over $140 million.[19]

Both Ghana and Nigeria have been trying to reschedule their loan repayments with the aid of consultative groups headed by the World Bank.* An Economic Commission for Africa report[21] has noted, however, that such consortiums have not always been helpful. It cites the decline in aid to Tunisia and Sudan subsequent to such "assistance." W. A. Lewis observed that

> if the British or American Governments have political reasons for wanting to prop up the country, one or other may agree to convert the short-term obligations into long-term loans. In other cases, the Government is told to seek help from the International Monetary Fund. This fund will lend money to tide the country over its difficulties, but will normally do this only if the Government undertakes to cut its expenditures, to control credit creation by its banks, and not to repeat the performance which has caused the trouble. Thus the country swings from boom to depression.[22]

The Length of Time Before the Loans Must Be Repaid

The longer the period before repayment is required the better, since the national income will have more time in which to grow

---

*Ghana's post-1966-coup government argued that it should be allowed to refuse to repay foreign loans obtained as the result of proven bribery; but its international advisors rejected this proposal on the grounds that it might undermine the confidence of the foreign business community,[20] considered essential to obtain new loans and investments from abroad. The post-1972-coup government did repudiate these debts in the face of protests from its international advisors.

sufficiently to finance it. The fact that a high proportion of Ghana's and Nigeria's external debts consists of suppliers' credits augments the burden of repayment in the short term. The fact that a high portion of Ghana's, Nigeria's, and Uganda's internal debts consisted of short-term loans, bank overdrafts, and treasury bills has increased inflationary pressures while merely postponing the necessity of cutting expenditures and/or increasing revenues. Short-term debt cannot contribute much to directly increased production, since it must be repaid before any major investments can begin to produce actual goods.

The Rate of Interest

The higher the rate of interest that must be paid, the greater the cost of repayment. One aspect of the high proportion of suppliers' credit obtained by Ghana and Nigeria in the early 1960s was the fact that these usually involve 7-8 percent interest charges, which sharply increase repayment costs. Even a 5- to 6-percent interest rate, the rate typically charged by the World Bank*, may essentially double the cost of the initial investment over a twenty-year period. Domestic commercial bank rates of interest are often relatively high in Africa, at least 8 percent. High interest rates augmented the cost of working capital required by the new state-owned industries established in Ghana in the early 1960s, contributing to serious difficulties in the running-in period.[23] It might have been preferable to provide these essential initial funds through direct government subsidy.

SUMMARY

Most African states have, since independence, expanded their public debt, frequently influenced by the Keynesian argument that the multiplier effects would stimulate development. Given built-in institutional constraints, however, the monetary expansion resulting from internal borrowing, especially short-term loans, has tended instead to stimulate rising prices and the import of consumer goods—aggravating the distortions of the inherited dual economy. Foreign debts have, in addition, worsened balance of payments problems, particularly when they have required short-term repayment or high interest rates, or they have been used for infrastructural projects that have not

---

*The World Bank's affiliate the International Development Agency provides loans for longer periods and lower rates of interest, but has far less resources.

increased national output sufficiently to cover repayment. A government seeking self-reliant financing to foster economic reconstruction must be disciplined in keeping its development expenditures within its ability to pay and must scrutinize proposed loans in the context of its overall financial plan to insure that increased productivity will cover the costs as well as contribute to a more balanced, nationally integrated economy.

NOTES

1. Cf. contra, H. Myint, Economic Theory and the Under-developed Countries, (New York: Oxford University Press, 1971), p. 301.

2. Soviet Financial System, Trans. from the Russian (Moscow: Progress Printers, 1966), Chapter 6.

3. Republic of Zambia, Monthly Digest of Statistics VI, no. L (January 1970): 31.

4. International Monetary Fund, International Financial Statistics 12, no. 22 (December, 1969): 358.

5. Kenya, Economic Survey, 1969; Uganda, Background to the Budget, 1968-69, p. 66; and Tanzania, Economic Survey (Background to the Budget), 1968, pp. 96-97.

6. Bank of Uganda, Quarterly Bulletin 3, no. 1 (December 1970): 870-878

7. United Republic of Tanzania, The Annual Plan for 1971/1972, (Dar es Salaam: Government Printers Office, 1971), p. 5.

8. Ghana, Economic Survey, 1965, p. 28.

9. J. H. Mensah, Budget Statement, 1969-70, pp. 22-24.

10. The Busia government debt figures are estimated in West Africa, Jan. 28, 1972; and the impact of the second devaluation and its relation to the second coup are reported in West Africa, Jan. 7, 14, and 21, 1972.

11. Federal Republic of Nigeria, Second National Development Plan, 1970-74 (Lagos: Federal Ministry of Information, Printing Division, 1970), p. 300.

12. L. H. Samuels, "Monetary and Fiscal Policy in Relation to African Development," in Taylor (ed.), Taxation for African Economic Development, p. 53.

13. See Hicks, "Finance and the Financial Infrastructure," for discussion.

14. Cf. Ghana's experience, described in A. Seidman, Ghana's Development Experience, 1951-1965, "Postscript: Stagnation."

15. Nigeria, Second National Development Plan, 1970-74, p. 300.

16. E.g., for Kenya's experience, see National Christian Council of Kenya, Who Controls Industry in Kenya? p. 179.

17. Republic of Kenya, Development Plan, 1970-74 (Nairobi: Government Printer, 1970), p. 161.

18. Nigeria, Second National Development Plan, 1970-74, p. 300.

19. West Africa, March 25, 1971.

20. For the continuing debate on this ussue in Ghana, see K. Achampon-Manu, "Ghana's Economic Problems and the New Regime," Legon Observer, Jan. 16, 1970.

21. P. Streeton, "Aid to Africa."

22. W. A. Lewis, Development Planning, The Essentials of Economic Policy (New York: Harper and Row, 1966), p. 142.

23. See H. P. Nelson, "Report on the Administration and Operation of State Enterprises under the Work Schedule of the State Enterprises Secretariat for the Period 1955-1965" (Accra, December 1, 1966, mimeo).

16

Given the dangers inherent in increased borrowing, whether at home or abroad, African nations have been forced to search for new ways to increase government revenues. The colonial governments, in keeping with earlier orthodoxies, had sought for the most part to balance their budgets without borrowing; but they had done so at very low levels of government expenditure. Taxes were primarily designed to (1) finance the necessary administration and infrastructure required to facilitate the expansion of private investment in the export enclave, not infrequently through taxes on exports and/or imports, and (2) create the economic necessity, commonly through imposition of some form of hut or poll tax, to "induce subsistence peasants to provide cheap labor supplies for the plantations and mines, or, in some cases, to produce cash crops for export.

Since independence, African governments have mainly attempted to increase their revenues by raising existing taxes and imposing new ones, in an essentially ad hoc manner, primarily based on orthodox taxation principles like equity and incentives for producers.* These efforts have been significantly influenced by pervasive problems of tax collection. Citizens' responses to given tax proposals appear to have depended in large part on their attitude toward the government itself, as well as the taxes' impact on the historical socially determined levels of consumption prevailing in their country.

---

*Kaldor argues[1] that "a great deal of the prevailing concern with incentives is misplaced. . . . It is shortage of resources, and not inadequate incentives, which limits the pace of economic development."

Today far more careful attention needs to be directed to the consequences of specific types of taxes for efforts to implement national plans to finance economic reconstruction. Taxation constitutes the primary source of current government revenue for current expenditures in every African country. Taxation may be used to redistribute income, protect labor, and regulate the flow of capital. It may contribute to industrialization by fostering desired patterns and discouraging unfavorable ones. It may be used as an effective tool for accumulating resources and directing investment. To contribute in these ways, however, taxation policies need to be explicitly framed in the context of the national financial plan based on long-term national development perspectives. Until recently, however, few African governments have directed serious attention to the possibilities of using taxation to reinforce other types of efforts to restructure the economy.

THE EXPANSION OF THE OVERALL TAX EFFORT

The overall tax effort of almost all governments, measured in terms of revenue per capita or revenue as a portion of Gross Domestic Product, has increased since independence, but some governments, however, have made significantly greater tax efforts than others (see Table 15). Examination of individual tax structures (see Table 16) indicates that the extent of each country's effort may be influenced by several factors. Tanzania's stated desire to redistribute domestic incomes as well as to pursue a self-reliant path to development led to major changes in inherited tax patterns, increasing income and sales taxes. Zambia's independent government sharply increased taxes on the export earnings of the two big mining companies that dominated that country's main export, copper, thus tapping the main domestic source of monetary wealth. Kenya's tax effort changed only slightly, apparently reflecting the persistence of the status quo ante in all aspects of government activity. That Nigeria's pre-civil war tax effort actually appears to have declined may be attributable in part to the operation of factors similar to those in Kenya, plus an additional downward pressure fostered by competition among the regions resulting from the regionalization of the tax structure prior to independence. If Nigeria had raised its pre-civil war tax effort to that of, say, Tanzania—which has a considerably lower per capita income—it could have at least doubled its government revenue.

TABLE 15

Relative Tax Efforts: Government Revenue per
Capita and as a Percent of Gross Domestic Product
for Selected Sub-Saharan African Countries,
1962-1967

| | per Capita | | as Percent of Gross Domestic Product | |
	1962	1967	1962	1967
Ghana	$29	$49	14.3	14.2
Kenya[a]	13	16	13.9	17.6
Nigeria[b]	6	7	11.3	10.5
Tanzania[c]	8	11	14.8	23.1
Uganda[d]	15	15	23.2	24.1
Zambia[e]	24	210	7.7	33.2

[a]Only 1963, 1967 data are used here.
[b]Includes both federal and state revenue. The latest date for
the second year is 1966.
[c]The first year employs 1964 data, the second is 1968.
[d]Only 1964, 1967 data are available.
[e]Zambia allocated 13 percent of its current revenue to development finance. The second year is 1968. In accord with the Agreements by which the Zambian government purchased 51 percent of the
shares of the mining companies, however, taxes were to be levied as
a percent of profits. In addition, the Agreements provided for 100
percent tax write-off for investments made by the mines, which reduced the effective 1971-72 tax rate to about 30 percent of profits.
When the copper price and mining firm profits declined, this led to
a sharp fall in government revenue, to about $117 per capita in 1971-72.

Sources: Calculated from data presented in International Monetary Fund, International Financial Statistics 22 (September-December
1969), Economic Surveys (Backgrounds to the Budgets), and Statistical
Abstracts of the respective countries. The difficulties of obtaining
accurate data and different price movements render these calculations
only roughly comparable. Their main purpose is to suggest relative
orders of magnitude.

TABLE 16

Total Government Revenue, Estimated per Head, and
Percentage from Major Sources for Selected Countries, in
Early 1960s and in 1968

Country and Years	Total Revenue		Estimated Revenue per Head ($U.S.)	Percentage of Total Revenue by Major Source								
	Local Currency [a]	$US. (in millions)		Income	Export	Import	Excise, Sales	Licenses	Interest	Other Direct Taxes	Other Indirect Taxes	All State Sources
Kenya												
1964/65	39.7	111.1	14	34.0	1.0	39.0	16.0	4.0		1.0		
1967/68	59.8	167.4	19	38.0	1.0	33.0	17.0	4.0		2.0		
Tanzania												
1964/65	28.7	80.3	8	27.0	5.0	58.0	7.0				3.0	
1968/69 [b]	48.3	135.8	11	31.0	5.0	55.0	6.0				3.0	
Uganda												
1964/65	31.5	88.2	13	13.0	31.0	35.0	15.0	3.0		—	2.0	
1968/69 [b]	44.4	124.3	17	16.0	15.0	39.0	17.0	3.0		3.0	7.0	
Ghana												
1961/62	75.0	210.0	26	14.9[c]	20.3[d]	38.5	20.9		3.3[e]		2.1	
1968	332.0	338.0	37	20.4[c]	29.5[d]	18.1	22.1		2.9[e]		5.0	
Nigeria												
1962	135.0	378.0	6		8.9	41.1	4.7			6.4	21.5	15.2[f]
1968	168.0	472.0	8		8.4	32.3	6.9			13.0	20.5	11.1[f]
Zambia												
1963	63.0	89.0	24	47.3	9.8[g]	6.7[h]					25.9[i]	
1968	306.0	428.0	107	28.2	43.7[g]	15.7[h]					8.6[i]	

NOTES AND SOURCES FOR TABLE 16

a Kenya, Tanzania, Uganda: East African £ (in millions) Ghana: In 1962 Ghana used the Ghanaian £, 1 = $U.S. 2.80; Cedis were introduced in 1965 at 1 = $U.S. 1.70; in 1967 the New Cedi replaced the old Cedi at N¢, 1 = $U.S. 0.98. Nigeria: Nigerian £ (in millions). Zambia: Kwacha (in millions).

b Estimated.

c Includes fines.

d Mainly cocoa.

e Includes profits and rents.

f The states obtain over two thirds of their revenues in the form of Central Government grants (1962 = 68.0 percent; 1968 = 71.6 percent). All percentages from 1968 except export, import, and excise duties are based on 1964 data.

g This was called "Mineral Tax Royalties," but was essentially an export tax. In 1971 and after, as a result of the change in the base of the tax on mining companies, mineral royalties and the export tax dropped to a negligable sum. Taxes on mine company profits were included in income taxes, which became again a more important source of government revenue. The total tax revenue from the mines in 1971-72 averaged about $58 million annually, however, in contrast to $327 million in 1969. This loss was only partially made up by increased taxes on other sectors of the economy.

h Includes excise tax which was still a small percent.

i Includes court fees, earnings of ministries, OJAS reimbursements and loans (compensation), and miscellaneous.

Sources: Kenya: Economic Survey, 1969, Statistical Abstract, 1967; Tanzania: Economic Survey, 1968; Uganda: Background to the Budget, 1969; Ghana: Republic of Ghana, Economic Survey, 1962 (Accra: Central Bureau of Statistics, 1963) and Economic Survey, 1969; Nigeria: Republic of Nigeria, Digest of Statistics, Vol. 17, No. 4, October, 1968 (Lagos: Federal Office of Statistics, 1968); Zambia: Republic of Zambia, Monthly Digest of Statistics, Vol. 6, No. 1, January, 1970 (Lusaka: Central Statistics Office, 1970) pp. 29, 30.

SPECIFIC TAXES

Export Taxes

Prior to independence, export taxes were a major source of governments in countries like Ghana and Uganda, where the producers of exports were mainly small African farmers who had little influence on the colonial government. These taxes, mainly on cocoa in Ghana, and cotton and coffee in Uganda, were relatively easy to collect. Export taxes tend to fall most heavily on the producers (since world market prices are governed by competition among the producing countries confronted with relatively inelastic demand). Export duties in Nigeria, though not as important a source of government revenues as import duties, withheld from 11 to 17 percent of the producers' incomes from 1947 to 1961. Combined with marketing board trading surpluses,* the total share of producers' incomes accruing to the Nigerian state and central governments in that period ranged as high as 39 percent in the case of cocoa and 40 percent in the case of groundnuts.[4]

In East Africa (excluding Uganda), where most of the exports were produced by large settler estates, and in Zambia, where about 90 percent of exports consisted of copper produced by two foreign mining companies, export taxes were a relatively insignificant source of revenue prior to independence.

In the late 1950s and early 1960s, as world prices for most of the crude exports of Africa fell, the governments of countries dependent on export taxes had to search for new tax bases. Only Zambia was able to increase its taxes on exports, raising revenue from copper from less than 10 percent to almost half of its total tax revenue by

---

*Funds accumulated through marketing boards are also essentially taxes on domestic producers whether they are used to stabilize producer incomes or to lend funds for development projects, as became common after independence. They have been expanded by essentially autonomous marketing board authorities with little or no coordinated planning by central governments. The amounts involved have sometimes been high.[2] Nigeria's Western Region Marketing Board accumulated surpluses totaling $54 million from 1962 to 1965. Uganda's Lint Marketing Board accumulated $44 million and its Coffee Board $27 million in the relatively prosperous years 1946-60. Given the importance of these amounts, it has been argued that marketing board surpluses should be incorporated within the national financial plan along with regular government revenues.[3]

1968 (from \$8.7 million to \$187 million).[5] When copper prices fell
in the 1970s, Zambia's tax revenues, too, dropped by about a third.
Most of the other governments found it necessary to increase taxes
on imports, sales, and incomes as export-based revenues stagnated
or declined.

Import Taxes

Taxes on imports, particularly luxuries, were raised in many
African countries after independence. The aim was to capture some
of the surpluses spent for luxury consumption by the limited high-
income group, as well as to reduce imports and save foreign exchange.
In Tanzania, for example, taxes on a number of luxury items were
increased to over 100 percent.[6] In an effort to increase total tax
revenues, some governments have extended import taxes to more
broadly consumed items. This introduced a somewhat regressive
element insofar as lower-income groups must buy such commodities.
Such taxes appear more likely to fall on urban wage and salary earners,
who may not be able to obtain local substitutes.

The establishment of import-substitution industries has both
affected and been affected by import taxation. First, imposition of
high import duties on luxuries may stimulate the establishment of
luxury-type industries domestically,[7] utilizing resources that might
far better be employed for establishing projects directed to stimulating
productivity and/or raising the levels of living of the broad masses
of the population. Secondly, insofar as last-stage assembly and/or
processing industries are established to avoid tariffs, government
revenue has tended to be reduced.[8] Thirdly, since import taxes have
not usually been levied on the import of capital goods and equipment,
there has been a tendency to import these relatively capital-intensive
items for specific investment projects, reducing the potential for
increased industrial employment.[9]

Excise Taxes

Several governments have imposed excise taxes on the manufacture or sale of goods produced domestically, in part to reduce
revenue dependence on import duties.[10] Such taxes are relatively
easy to collect if they are imposed at the manufacturer or wholesale
level.[11]* They may be adjusted to increase the tax burden on luxury

---

*It might be noted that both the Soviet Union and China have
utilized turnover taxes—essentially sales taxes—despite the existence

items while reducing or eliminating it on the more broadly consumed items. As they are extended to items consumed by the lower-income groups, they, like import duties, tend to become increasingly regressive.

In 1970 Tanzania attempted to replace all local taxes by a considerably increased sales tax on almost all items except foodstuffs. This policy appears to have resulted in part from the difficulties of collecting local taxes, in part from an attempt to shift the tax burden to the urban areas since higher cash incomes there were considered to be primarily responsible for the urban-rural drift.* It would seem necessary, however, to avoid reducing real urban wages, on the one hand, and, on the other, to insure that resulting price increases of manufactured consumer items do not constitute a disincentive to predominantly subsistence farmers to increase their output for sales.[14]

Income and Company Taxes

Many African governments have attempted to increase income tax revenues. In capitalist developed nations, taxes on the incomes of individuals and companies have become increasingly important sources of government revenue because of the growth of monetary wealth, as opposed to wealth embodied in land or livestock. In Africa very high monetary incomes are concentrated in the hands of a small minority of individuals and firms associated with export enclave activities. The extent of income taxes imposed depends on both the governments' attitude toward the potential use of private savings for capital formation and on problems of collection. It is frequently observed in Africa that private domestic savings are unlikely to be invested in major productive projects, so that the governments themselves must play an important role to insure that such investments are in fact made. These considerations would seem to justify a high progressive income tax.[15]

---

of state ownership of the major means of production in the industrial sector. Reasons given include (1) the desire to insure direct revenue to the government for reinvestments as well as social services and (2) to provide flexibility in price levels, since the taxes may be adjusted to alter prices for particular items in line with government objectives.[12]

*Whether this assumption is in fact justified would appear to require further study; the Turner Report, which argues that industrial wages are too "high" compared to rural incomes,[13] has been criticized for its inadequate factual underpinning. (See pp. 249-252).

In Tanzania, Kenya, and Zambia,* income taxes already provided an important share of total government revenue prior to independence. Since independence, most countries have made efforts to increase income tax revenue through improved collection and in some cases somewhat higher rates on higher-income groups. Nigeria apparently confronted special problems because the power to tax incomes had been turned over to the regions prior to independence. This rendered it difficult to formulate a unified national income tax policy, which was essential before significant tax increases could be imposed on incomes; otherwise any effort of one region to raise its income tax could be expected to lead to a flight of capital to other regions.[16]

Collection of income taxes is difficult in Africa.† Most African states, given the difficulty of collection, have tended to drop exemptions, since these make collection even more difficult. Pay-As-You-Earn (PAYE) has been introduced in several countries to centralize collection of taxes from wage earners in large establishments. This has tended to increase the tax burden on these groups. In contrast, individual traders, wealthy farmers, real estate speculators, and professionals have been more difficult to tax.[18] Tax evasion by "big fish" while the government is "chasing minnows" has been held to be a major hindrance to the effective administration of income taxes.[19] It is difficult even to assess the incomes of many of those engaged in trade, where incomes of at least a few participants have been shown to be very high. They seldom keep systematic account books. There are seldom enough tax collection agents to check on the individuals' reported incomes. It might be possible to introduce some sort of citizens' assessment committees of the type that have long existed in some communities for rural taxes. (See p. 298.) It would seem probable that it would still be necessary to provide some trained collection agents.[20]

Company taxes tend to constitute a fairly large share of total income taxes in Africa,[21] primarily because a significant share of monetary income accrues to companies. Yet company tax rates have

---

*The apparent decline in the percent of Zambia's revenue produced by income taxes after independence (see Table 16) is attributable to the very large increase in taxes on copper exports, not to an absolute decline in income tax revenues. After the change in the tax base to the profits of the mining companies in 1970, Zambia's income tax again became the most important source of government revenue.

†W. A. Lewis has held that revenue from direct taxes on Nigerian individuals might be doubled by better administration that reduced evasions even without increasing the rates.[17]

remained fairly low, typically between 37 and 45 percent of profits.22
Tax holidays, large depreciation allowances,* and provisions for loss
carry-forward, permitting firms to apply initial losses against subsequent profits, have further reduced the actual taxes paid. In 1969,
for example, Ghana's government, acting with International Monetary
Fund advice, eliminated the tax differential on profits remitted overseas, a differential previously imposed in an effort to reduce the outflow of profits,24 and that year the total balance of payments deficit
increased significantly compared to 1968, due to a "substantial increase in net deficit on invisibles . . ."25 The argument has typically
been advanced that reduced company taxes are necessary to attract
private investors from abroad.26† Kaldor has pointed out, however,
that competitive African government efforts to hold company taxes
down to attract foreign enterprise can be self-defeating.27 Nigeria,
for example, initially granted extensive tax concessions to foreign
oil firms, which sharply reduced the potential tax returns for years.
In 1964/65, six years after commercial production of oil began, the
oil firms still were paying only a little over a million dollars in
taxes.28

Collection of company taxes is difficult in Africa (as noted above).
Taxes on large foreign firms have sometimes been avoided by price
policies designed to shift profits outside of the African country by
overpricing imports or underpricing exports.29 Improved company
tax collection appears to require more and better trained collection
agents. It has been suggested that better pay and status for collection
agents would help to attain this goal.30 It might be, too, that where
the state owns the banking system, as in Tanzania,‡ it might be easier
to check up on tax evasion by both private and public firms.

Land Taxes

In Africa the wealth of many if not most people remains embodied in land and livestock, rather than cash incomes. The increased
necessity of raising funds internally tends to support the proposal,

---

*Insofar as depreciation allowances constitute investment sub-
sidies stimulating the import of capital intensive equipment and machinery, it has been suggested they may actually play a negative role
in the African context.23

†This seems to neglect the fact that today most developed countries permit firms to deduct taxes paid overseas before paying their
own countries' taxes.

‡See pp. 322-28.

long mooted in Africa, of taxing agricultural land.[31] An appropriate land tax might provide an added incentive to predominantly subsistence farmers to increase their production of surpluses for sale, thus contributing to the spread of specialization and exchange in more remote rural areas. This is not to negate the necessity of improving urban property taxes,[32] but rather to emphasize agricultural land taxes because of the importance of wealth embodied in land and livestock in the rural areas in Africa.

Taxes on land are not new in Africa. In the relatively more centralized states of precolonial Africa, like those in Buganda, Northern Nigeria, and Ethiopia, various forms of community taxes were traditionally imposed, based on an assessment of the community wealth and paid through the governing authority of the community.[33] To the extent that local citizens participate in the assessment, collection, and decisions as to the use of the part remaining in the local community, the taxes appear to have received a considerable degree of legitimization in the eyes of the population.

The British Colonial governments imposed poll taxes in most of the areas they ruled. These were usually flat taxes per adult male, primarily designed to force subsistence peasants to join the labor market or, in some cases, to produce export crops in order to earn the required cash. The poll tax obviated the necessity of attempting to assess the actual wealth embodied in the produce or the land allocated by the community to the individual. In Northern Nigeria, in contrast, Lugard empowered native authorities to continue to assess and collect taxes on a communal basis as an integral feature of indirect rule.[34] When the system of indirect rule was extended to the south there were neither traditions of communal assessment nor similar institutions (large emirates with strong native authorities in the north) through which the southern tax could be assessed and collected. Therefore the direct tax imposed in the south was simpler. It was both a poll tax (for adults whose income was not more than a certain assumed minimum) and a slightly graduated income tax (for adults whose incomes were more than the assumed minimum). In operation this tax tended to be regressive and its imposition led to tax riots.*

In Tanzania[36] a similar combination of poll taxes and a somewhat graduated tax was instituted by the British. A study made shortly after independence showed that both the flat rate and the graduated

---

*These historical and practical regional differences in the resulting taxes are said to have "weighed heavily" in regionalizing income tax assessment and collection when Nigeria was carved into regions just prior to independence.[35]

structure varied from district to district, so that local rate payments per assessed tax payer ranged from 23/- in one district to 72/- in another. Difficulties in collecting the tax resulted in collection of only two-thirds to three-fourths of legal local tax obligations. The higher rates of tax were almost invariably collected from wage and salary earners, whose tax was collected at the source; whereas prosperous farmers or shopkeepers, who did not keep books and might not even know their real annual incomes, were generally excluded. Local rates were supplemented by produce cesses collected on a variety of crops and cattle. The relative importance of these cesses, too, varied from district to district. It has been argued that since they were often collected through the marketing cooperatives on the basis of crops sold, they reduced the farmers' incentives to enter cash crop production.[37] As a result of these difficulties of assessing and collecting local taxes and produce cesses, the Tanzanian Government, as noted above, abolished all local taxes.

The principle issues relating to taxing the rural population seem to revolve around the difficulties of assessment and collection as well as the maintenance of equity and provision of incentives to predominantly subsistence farmers to increase their marketed output (or, as a minimum, to avoid disincentives). The approach adopted may depend on several factors, including the changing pattern of land tenure. Where individualized land tenure is an accomplished fact,[38] as in Kenya's Million Acre Scheme and the former "reserves," where land has been consolidated and individual land titles registered, a tax might be assessed at, say, ten-year intervals on the potential average yield of an individual farmer. This might provide an incentive to produce for sale, since the individual would have to pay the tax whether or not he cultivated the land. If he did grow cash crops, he would reap the extra income from any surpluses produced and sold, over and above the average yield, as a result of the introduction of new seed varieties or techniques. Production of specific crops, within the framework of the national plan, might be encouraged by reducing the tax paid. Progressive elements might be incorporated by relating the individual's payments to the size of his family and the total land area. The actual assessment of an individual's land might be carried out, as was traditionally the case in some areas, by committees of local citizens in cooperation with trained government personnel who could help to insure adherence to national standards. Community assessment teams, along the lines reported from Uganda,[39] might submit their findings to community meetings to permit a public evaluation of the results.*

----

*This kind of tax was utilized in China from 1950 to 1957 (after the feudal landholdings were broken up and individual peasants received

On the other hand, in countries like Tanzania that seek to develop modernized agricultural systems on the basis of more cooperative tenure patterns, the ancient community tax system might be adapted to provide a tax paid, not by individuals, but the entire group out of their community production, based on the assessed average potential yield of their entire jointly held land area. This might reduce the tax collection problem, since it would be possible to collect taxes through the community governing authority, rather than from each individual within the community. Where both individualized and group tenures exist, as they do in almost every African sub-Saharan country, both systems might temporarily exist side by side. Presumably Tanzania, which seeks to encourage the emergence of ujamaa villages, could then over time raise the tax on the produce of individual farms to a level above that on the group farms* to provide an added incentive expanding cooperation.

CHANGING TAX POLICIES AND INTER-AFRICAN COOPERATION

One aspect of the shift toward increased sales, income, and company taxes has been a growing differential between the tax structures of different countries. This may have a negative impact on trade and payments between neighboring countries. In Nigeria the consequences of turning important taxing powers over to the regions has been that each has sought to compete for resources by reducing its taxes. As a result, the nation as a whole has remained highly dependent on customs duties with the total national tax effort considerably reduced below that of other countries. The growing competition among the regions for funds and development projects, not infrequently duplicative and wasteful, was an aspect of the conflict that finally culminated in civil war. When the nation was divided into twelve states after the war, the system of revenue collection and allocation was automatically carried over from the previous regional system; this hardly augured well for formulation of a more rational financial plan[42]

---

title to their own land, an objective they had long demanded) and provided almost 20 percent of all tax revenue in 1957. The agricultural taxes were paid in kind and collected in government graneries for distribution as required through the state marketing system; and the returns from their sale were made available to the government through the state-owned banks.[40]

*This procedure was introduced in China as it began to collectivize agriculture in the latter 1950s.[41]

directed toward investing existing or potential surpluses in increased nationwide specialization and exchange.

In a similar way, in East Africa the emergence of differing tax policies, reflecting the differing socio-economic options adopted by the three governments, appears to have contributed to lessening the possibilities of joint efforts to allocate resources. This is not to deny that, as one observer remarked, the preindependence common tax system among the three East African nations acted "as a strait jacket, which restricts the liberty of action of the individual budgets." In particular, it reduced the amount of public revenue obtainable by Uganda and Tanganyika.[43]

Uganda first shifted to a sales tax to offset sagging export tax revenues due to falling world prices for coffee and cotton, and reduced import duties income resulting from import-substitution. In 1970 Tanzania's move to raise sales taxes, especially on luxury items, was a major factor contributing to a significant outflow of foreign exchange as traders sought to avoid the new tax burden. Tanzania therefore found it necessary to establish exchange controls against its East African neighbors—still another barrier to expanded specialization and exchange throughout East Africa. For Tanzania not to have done so, however, would have been to give up the option of increasing its government revenues in pursuit of its policies of self-reliance.

SUMMARY

Despite the overall increase in the tax efforts of most African governments since independence, few have considered the potential for utilizing taxes as instruments for facilitating overall national development in the context of carefully coordinated national financial plans. Ad hoc tax proposals were initially enacted primarily to enable current tax revenues to keep pace with expanding expenditures. These were influenced in part by the difficulties of collection, in part by rough estimates of what the "traffic will bear." Accumulating experience argues, however, that careful attention should be directed to the way specific taxes contribute to or hinder investment of existing surpluses in accord with a carefully considered financial plan. In addition to re-examining the impact of the usual roster of export, import, excise, and income taxes, African governments might do well to consider how agricultural taxes might foster peasant participation in nationally planned specialization and exchange to facilitate increased productivity. Collection of far more data than are now available and continuing on-going evaluation of all tax proposals are essential to insure that they have the desired consequences. It would be preferable if tax policies could be developed in the context of coordinated plans for the joint development of entire regions, but this is unlikely to be accomplished until the attainment of the far higher level of inter-African political unity required to develop joint institutions to control and allocate regional resources in accord with a regional plan.

NOTES

1. N. Kaldor, "Taxation for Economic Development," in Taylor (ed.), Taxation for African Economic Development, p. 158.

2. E.g., A. Adedeji, Nigerian Federal Finance (New York: Africana Publishing Corporation, 1969), p. 168; D. A. Lury, "Cotton and Coffee Growers and Government Development Finance in Uganda, 1945-60," The East African Economic Review 10, no. 1 (June 1963).

3. G. K. Helleiner, Agricultural Marketing in Tanzania, Policies and Problems, Economic Research Bureau Paper 68.14 (Dar es Salaam, 1968); and Adedeji, Nigerian Federal Finance, p. 213.

4. J. F. Due, "Customs, Excise and Export Duties," in Taylor (ed.), Taxation for African Economic Development, Table 1, p. 420.

5. Republic of Zambia, Monthly Digest of Statistics 6, no. 1 (January 1970): 29.

6. For information regarding Tanzania's 1969-70 taxation policies, unless otherwise cited, see United Republic of Tanzania, Speech by Honourable the Minister for Finance introducing the Estimates of Revenue and Expenditure 1969-70 to National Assembly, 19 June, 1969 (Dar es Salaam: Government Printer, 1969), pp. 22-24.

7. Walker, "Fiscal Measures to Promote Foreign Investment," in Taylor (ed.), Taxation for African Development, p. 455.

8. E.g., Republic of Uganda, Background to the Budget, 1967-1968 (Kampala: Government Printer, 1967), section on manufacturing.

9. Ibid.

10. J. F. Due, in "Tax Policy and Economic Development," in Taylor (ed.), Taxation for African Economic Development, p. 196, cites a "universal trend . . . away from customs duties as domestic production rises."

11. Kaldor, "Taxation for economic development," p. 170.

12. G. N. Ecklund, Financing the Chinese Government Budget, Mainland China, 1950-1959 (Chicago: Aldine Publishing Company, 1966), pp. 22 ff.

13. International Labour Office, United Nations Development Programme, Technical Assistance Sector, Report to the Government of the United Republic of Tanzania on Wages, Incomes and Prices Policy (Dar es Salaam: Government Paper No. 3).

14. Cf. Kaldor, "Taxation for Economic Development," p. 180.

15. P. Marlin, Introduction, in P. Marlin (ed.), Financial Aspects of Development in East Africa (Germany: Druckerei G. J. Manz Ag., Dillingen/Donau, 1970), p. 15.

16. A. Adedeji, "The Future of Personal Income Taxation in Nigeria," in Taylor (ed.), Taxation for African Economic Development, p. 274.

17. W. A. Lewis, "Reflections on Nigerian Growth" (mimeo.), cited in M. C. Taylor, "The Relationship Between Income Taxation and Tax Policy in Nigeria," in Taylor (ed.), Taxation for African Economic Development, p. 115.

18. Taylor, "The Relationship Between Income Taxation and Tax Policy in Nigeria," p. 518.

19. Ibid., p. 527.

20. Adedeji, in "The Future of Personal Income Taxation in Nigeria," p. 268, reports that local collection has, in Northern and Western Nigeria, involved a "large number of abuses."

21. N. Jetha, "Company Taxation in East Africa," in Taylor (ed.), Taxation for African Economic Development, p. 281.

22. Due, "Tax Policy and Economic Development," p. 187.

23. Jetha, "Company Taxation in East Africa," p. 287.

24. J. H. Mensah, Budget Statement, 1969-70 (Accra: Government Printer, 1969), pp. 26-7.

25. West Africa, Jan. 23-29, 1971.

26. Due, "Tax Policy and Economic Development," p. 287.

27. Kaldor, "Taxation for Economic Development," p. 164.

28. Adedeji, Nigerian Federal Finance, p. 250; see also p. 181.

29. Kaldor, "Taxation for Economic Development," pp. 174-175.

30. Ibid., p. 177; and Due, "Tax Policy and Economic Development," p. 177.

31. Kaldor, "Taxation for Economic Development," pp. 166-170; and for further discussion, see H. P. Wald, "Basic Design for More Effective Land Taxation," in Taylor (ed.), Taxation for African Economic Development, passim.

32. Cf. Marlin, Financial Aspects of Development in East Africa, pp. 69-70.

33. Cf. Adedeji, Nigerian Federal Finance, pp. 186 ff.; Marlin, in Financial Development in East Africa, p. 51, discusses the modern version of local assessment in Uganda; and P. Schwab, in "Ethiopia: Paying for Economic Progress," African Development, pp. 25-27, describes the problems that ensued when the central government sought to assess individuals' produce from individually farmed land, an effort reportedly perceived by local farmers as an attempt to destroy the semicommunal landholding system.

34. Adedeji, Nigerian Federal Finance, p. 186.

35. Ibid., p. 188.

36. R. G. Penner, "Local Government Revenues in Tanzania," Agricultural Economics, University College of Dar es Salaam, 1968-69.

37. Report of Presidential Special Commission of Enquiry into Cooperative Movement and Marketing Boards (Dar es Salaam: Government Printer, 1966), pp. 74-75.

38. Due, in "Tax Policy and Economic Development," p. 200, argues that land taxation requires registered land titles.

39. Marlin, in Financial Development in East Africa.

40. Eckland, in Financing the Chinese Government Budget.

41. Ibid.

42. Adedeji, in Nigerian Federal Finance.

43. Marlin, in Financial Development in East Africa.

17
**PUBLIC ENTERPRISE
AND PUBLIC FINANCE**

PUBLIC ENTERPRISE'S FINANCIAL ROLE

Potential Contribution to Finance

Regardless of their political leanings, all African states envisage some degree of government participation in investment in productive sectors. In particular, the state is commonly expected to invest in projects that are expected to contribute to development but in which private enterprise is unlikely to invest. Few public enterprises in sub-Saharan Africa have as yet contributed significantly to increased government revenues except, in some cases, through company taxes. Profits from industrial projects owned by government are seldom included in the budget, and interest payments seldom total over a few percent of government revenues. In most cases, the state enterprises in the productive sectors are owned by "autonomous" state corporations that keep separate books—in accord with British tradition that they should function like private commercial enterprises—and the books are not even always available to the public.

While a government may subsidize some projects, for example to initiate a chain of growth throughout an entire region, overall its participation in production should contribute to increased funds for further investment. This certainly must be true if the state anticipates assuming more and more control of the means of production in a process of transition to socialism.* The inherited set of working rules

---

*In China, for example, the combined profits and depreciation funds of state enterprises increased from less than 15 percent of government's budgetary revenue in 1952 to 60 percent in 1959.[1]

that holds that development corporations should turn profitable public
enterprises over to the private sector might well be questioned in
this context; it certainly appears contradictory to any effort to insure
that, over time, public enterprises should contribute significantly to
the government budget.*

The way public enterprise profits are obtained and invested
should be planned in the context of the overall government financial
plan along with taxes and the national debt. Taxes on enterprises may
reduce the profits of publicly owned firms as well as private ones.
Rising prices stimulated through the expansion of the public debt may
augment profits of public as well as private enterprise. At the same
time, they may reduce the incomes of the lower-income groups, and
hence limit the potential mass purchasing power required to consume
a major share of the planned output of expanding productive public-
sector enterprises.

It is, of course, equally true that the pricing and output policies
of public enterprises also affect the distribution of incomes and taxes,
as well as their own profits.† If they provide necessary services to
the public sector at low prices—for example, low-cost electric power
for water supplies, or low interest rates for funds loaned by private
firms while reducing the share of investible surpluses retained by the
public sector. Even where such low-cost services are sold to public
sector firms, if these are joint private-state firms, part of the resulting profits will still end up in the private sector. If the private partner is foreign-owned, they are likely to be shipped out of the country.
All of these, and other possibilities need to be carefully considered in
incorporating financing for public enterprise into the overall national
plan.

Bailing Out Private Enterprise

The failure of public-sector enterprises to contribute significantly
to governments' overall revenues in Africa, despite their increased

----

*The persistence of this notion is illustrated by the fact that in
Tanzania, Mr. Paul Bomani, while Chairman of both the National
Development Corporation and Devplan, described the development
corporation subsidiary, TAFCO, as the instrument through which the
government intends "to sell off part investments of our equity to the
people of Tanzania and to use the proceeds for investment in new
projects."

†These possibilities may be systematically analyzed in the
framework of a useful scheme designed by I. Sachs that suggests how

role, may in some cases be explained by the fact that they have been saddled with projects taken over by the government in a process of bailing out private firms on the verge of going out of business. Uganda's Development Corporation, for example, purchased a textile plant (Nytil) from the private sector before independence when it appeared to be failing.[3] The Nkrumah government of Ghana purchased several gold mines in 1961 when their foreign owners complained that as a result of new minimum wages and increased company taxes, they would have to go out of business. The government operated the mines at a considerable financial loss—accumulated losses totaled £6 million by 1964—in order to insure continued employment for the 14,000 miners and to earn the much-needed foreign exchange brought in by the sales of their gold.[4] The government left the largest and most profitable gold mining firm, the Ashanti Goldfields Corp., in the hands of its British owners, who reported a profit of £904,203 after taxes in the one year of 1965 alone.[5]

In accord with the Arusha Declaration, the Tanzanian government purchased about two-thirds of the nation's sisal estates after many of them had run down their assets and threatened to go out of business when world sisal prices collapsed. The more profitable sisal firms, on the other hand, appear to have been left in the hands of their private owners.

The Tanzanian government, after considerable pressure by the foreign private owners, also purchased the Kilombero sugar project for $8.6 million (present value of $6.4 million plus 7 percent interest over 16 years) because the consortium that originally built it was losing money.[6]

One cannot draw up hard and fast rules as to when governments should acquire shares of projects in the productive sector. But it would appear necessary to consider how the industry might be expected to contribute to the overall national plans from a financial point of view as well as in terms of employment, foreign exchange earnings, and the more general perspective of restructuring the overall economy.

The actions of the Tanzanian and Ghanaian governments were undoubtedly influenced by consideration of the unemployment problem that plagues all African countries. Some 30,000 sisal workers had already been laid off from the Tanzanian sisal estates, and another 100,000 jobs might have been at stake. The Ghana government's concern with unemployment apparently also led it to hire redundant workers in state enterprises outside the mining sector. It was reported that the post-1966-coup military government laid off some 50,000 allegedly

_____

alternative public sector pricing policies may affect the availability of investible surpluses to the public sector.[2]

306

redundant workers—about a fifth of the wage-earning labor force—from state enterprises in industry and agriculture. Several state plants allegedly began to show profits after that time.[7]

The concern with unemployment is widespread in Africa. The Kenyan government sought immediately after independence to require not only the state, but also private firms, to augment their payrolls to provide more jobs.[8] But it would appear unwise to saddle public-sector projects with welfare programs. One cannot build the industries and other projects required to restructure the economy without investing a major share of the surpluses produced by all sectors of the economy in additional productive projects. If these surpluses are absorbed in social welfare schemes instead, industrial growth is likely to be choked off, thwarting the basic restructuring of the economy, the only way to eliminate the causes of unemployment permanently.

MAXIMIZING PUBLIC-SECTOR SURPLUSES

Price and Output Policies

Even if the government has included only potentially viable projects in the public sector, the price and output policies will inevitably affect their profitability. They will also affect the tax incomes of the government.*

A higher rate of profit in a state-owned basic industry providing, say, iron and steel materials and parts for privately owned consumer goods industries, may reduce the share of profit accruing to the owners of the latter, whereas a low rate may permit them to increase their own profits without passing along the benefit to the consumers. Or a subsidized state transport industry may reduce the costs of production

---

*When all productive enterprises are in the public sector, so that prices and output are planned in relation to national goals, the question of whether budgetary revenue is to be obtained directly as enterprise income or indirectly as tax revenue essentially becomes a matter of government decision. The Soviet Union tended to set relatively low prices on heavy industrial products and acquired only a small part of its investment funds from the profits of heavy industry. The Chinese, on the other hand, price basic industrial products relatively high, compared with industrial costs and the prices of consumer goods. In some years, the Chinese obtained more than half the funds used for economic construction from industrial profits alone.[9]

of private industries, but the private firms may raise their profit rather than reduce final prices. On the other hand, subsidization of transport might permit many small private or cooperative producers to sell their goods in remote markets, thus expanding their sales. These, and a host of similar issues relating taxes, prices, credit, profits, and investment to planned national economic development perspectives need to be weighed carefully in formulating a national financial plan.

In the case of government-owned public utilities in Africa, prices have sometimes been set at low levels to the advantage of private firms utilizing their outputs, while reducing the returns to government. For example, the government-owned Uganda hydroelectric project contracted in 1955 to sell almost half its power to the Kenya Power Company (to meet the needs of Kenya's settler-dominated export enclave) at such a low price (three East African cents) that the project had not yet become profitable by the time of independence.[10] The Nkrumah government in Ghana agreed to sell about two-thirds of the Volta Dam project's power to a U.S.-owned aluminum smelter in Tema (which used imported bauxite instead of buying Ghana's and received a range of additional tax incentives) at a price about one-third that paid by Ghanaian consumers.[11]

The price-output policies, even of those firms in which the African government owns over 50 percent of the shares, tend to be determined by commercial considerations, much as if the firms were still privately owned. In most cases, because of the lack of adequately trained African personnel, the foreign partners continue to manage the projects for a fee; this creates the possibility that prices for imported items may be artificially raised, while those for exports may be artificially lowered as a means of shifting profits out of the country.

One might expect that Zambia's shares of the industrial sector, with total assets of $200 million, would contribute significantly to the national government's financial program. Indeco's group profits, however, equaled about 13.5 percent of shareholders' equity and 7.7 percent of the net group assets.[12] This rate of profit appears fairly low, given that the average rate of return of U.S. firms in Africa in manufacturing has been reported at almost 20 percent of investment, and for all investments somewhat higher. Whether Indeco's profits might be expected to contribute a greater share, however, could only be determined by examination of its price and output policies through a careful auditing of the books of each of its subsidiaries.

Careful study may also be required of the profits accruing to the Zambian government after it purchased 51 percent of the shares of the big mining companies. These were expected to equal the taxes the companies had been paying since independence. The companies were reported to be content with the arrangements, since the profits,

unlike the taxes they had been paying since independence, could be
expected to fluctuate with world prices and sales of copper.[13] The
companies' continued ownership of the overseas marketing apparatus
gave them considerable control over these variables. As world prices
for crude copper fell after the 1970s, Zambia's government share of
profits as well as foreign exchange fell, introducing serious problems
for the entire government financial program. How the government
and its foreign-managed affiliates handled their price and output policies
clearly could be expected to exert a major influence on that country's
overall development plans.

The Case of Tanzania's National
Development Corporation

Some of the possibilities and problems of augmenting government
funds from public enterprise profits may be illustrated by examining
the sources of income and investment available to the Tanzanian National Development Corporation.

Tanzania's Second Five Year Plan anticipated that the National
Development Corporation as well as the other parastatals would be
able to generate sources of funds outside of those contributed by the
central government.[14] The NDC alone was expected to invest a total
of about $110 million over the five-year period. Together with the
National Agricultural and Food Corporation, the Tanzanian Tourist
Corporation (whose assets were included under the NDC umbrella
until 1969), and the Small Industries Corporation, the National Development Corporation was expected to invest a total of about $150 mil-
lion, about half of all parastatal investments anticipated in the five-
year period. Of this, the government was to provide only $35 million.
Unfortunately, the plan does not indicate how much of the government
funds are to be invested in the Industrial sector, which is to make
roughly a fifth of the investments by this group, and how much in the
agricultural sector, which is to make a tenth of the investments by
this group.

It seems clear that the National Development Corporation was
expected to obtain its future financing mainly from its own surpluses,
its existing or new foreign partners and/or loans, and whatever funds
it could obtain in the form of loans or investments from such local
institutions as marketing boards, cooperatives, the Workers Development Corporation, and the Provident Fund. The sources of funds
available to the National Development Corporation and its subsidiaries
for this purpose will be affected by overall policies of pricing, taxing,
and investment formulated by the government. One way in which the
National Development Corporation could augment its surpluses, for

example, would be to raise the prices on its subsidiaries' products, especially since in many areas it essentially exercises monopolistic or at least oligopolistic control. This would simultaneously raise the profits of its foreign partners and probably increase the drain of surpluses from the country. At the same time, high prices on such items as cement would raise the costs of construction activities throughout the economy, thus perhaps hindering further development.

On the other hand, increased taxes on corporate profits would increase surpluses available to the government, reduce the drain of profits to foreign partners, and make funds available for new projects in the country. Given these interrelationships, it would seem essential to make decisions as to profits, taxes, prices, and investments within the framework of an overall national finance policy, rather than leaving them to be made on an ad hoc basis by individual parastatal. This would appear to be the preferable way to insure that the surpluses collected and the investments made contribute most effectively to restructuring the economy.

These considerations argue that an African government seeking to become self-reliant financially must plan the price-output policies of projects in the state or joint state-private sector in terms of the nation's overall development requirements. These need to be analyzed not only in terms of the role of each specific project in restructuring the economy—that is, how its output will be used and the kinds of linkages it may establish—but also its potential contribution to government revenues for further investment.

The Need for Audit and Control

In many African states, even today, however, the assumption that development corporations should function autonomously, as much like private firms as possible, has tended to create an environment in which the state lacks even the most minimal information to exercise essential control over the financial decisions of the development corporations' subsidiaries. This may be illustrated by the Ghanaian case. The Ghanaian Seven Year Plan (1962/3 to 1969/70) anticipated that a significant share of the nation's cocoa earnings—estimated at £240 a ton—would be available for financing a rapid expansion of industry. These hopes were shattered when the world cocoa price plummeted to £90 a ton. As has been noted, a number of the public enterprises sought to complete their plans by using foreign suppliers' credit, which saddled them with heavy short-term repayment burdens as well as aggravating the national balance of payments problem. (See pp. 279-280.) It was admitted, however, after the 1966 coup, that large foreign firms, eager to sell machinery and equipment for these projects, had given managers and directors bribes. In some cases the prices paid were considerably higher than the actual costs of the equipment purchased. But the government lacked the basic information needed to detect these situations. In 1966 the Finance Minister called[15] for further measures to improve the management of state enterprises, including what would appear to be a bare minimum—the requirement that they report their accounts for the year.

If African planners are to incorporate the price-output policies of public enterprises into effective national financial plans for restructuring their economies, then the inherited sets of working rules— exemplified in the Ghana case—must be drastically altered. It is vital that procedures for continual accumulation of essential information and checkup on the financial plans and policies of public enterprises be institutionalized at every level. This kind of institutionalized data collection and checkup is required as the foundation of rational decision-making about the role of public enterprises in public finance. The developed socialist countries still emphasize the further improvement of cost-accounting as crucial to effective financial planning.[16]

SUMMARY

As African governments have begun to seek to influence the economy through more direct intervention, they have begun to expand the public sector. As yet, however, public enterprises contribute relatively little to the typical government budget, over and above the taxes that they might have been expected to pay even had they remained in the private sector. In some cases, if the public enterprise sector is to continue to expand, it is essential that public firms begin to contribute significantly to the government budget. Furthermore, careful analysis should be initiated as to the working rules under which they operate in order to insure that their overall price and output policies conform to the requirements of the national financial plan. Not only is it important that each project contribute to the implementation of the physical plan for restructuring the economy, but also that it play an appropriate role in respect to overall financing.

NOTES

1. G. N. Ecklund, Financing the Chinese Government Budget, Mainland China, 1950-1959 (Chicago: Aldine Publishing Co., 1966).
2. I. Sachs, Patterns of Public Sector in Underdeveloped Economies (Bombay: Asia Publishing House, 1964), pp. 73-8.

3. A. Baryaruha, "Case Study of Nyanza Textiles Inds., Ltd.," EDRP No. 69 (Makerere), March 25, 1966.

4. Ghana, Mines Department, Annual Report, 1960-61 (Accra, 1961), p. 3; see also W. Birmingham, I. Neustadt, and E. N. Omaboe, A Study of Contemporary Ghana, Vol. One: The Economy of Ghana (London: George Allen & Unwin, 1966), Ch. 11, passim, esp. pp. 262-266. Prior to the takeover, the government had subsidized these mines since 1956.

5. Ashanti Goldfields Corporation, Ltd., Annual Report, 1965, p. 2. EGI,281,393 were deducted to pay Ghana taxes and £46,416 more to pay the United Kingdom tax on investment income.

6. Tanzania, Annual Economic Survey, 1968, p. 76.

7. Daily Graphic (Accra), Nov. 7, 1966.

8. See African Digest, June 1965, regarding Tripartite Agreement by which employers were to hire 10 percent more workers and the government to hire 15 percent more in hopes of increasing employment by 30,000.

9. Ecklund, Financing the Chinese Government Budget, p. 78.

10. E.g., the prices of electricity of the Jinja hydroelectric plant in Uganda, about half of it shipped to Kenya's settler economy, were originally set at rates so low that the project had not become profitable prior to independence; see National Christian Council of Kenya, Who Controls Industry in Kenya? p. 83.

11. A. Seidman, Ghana's Development Experience, 1951-1965, Ch. 8.

12. T. Holmes, "Zimco—Still More in the Pipeline," in Zambia Six Years After—African Development Economic Survey, 1970.

13. Africa Confidential, no. 25 (Dec. 19, 1969).

14. United Republic of Tanzania, Second Five Year Plan for Economic and Social Development, 1st July, 1969-30th June 1974, Vol 1: General Analysis (Dar es Salaam: Government Printer, 1969), p. 212.

15. Amoako-Atta, "Budget Statement, 1966," reported in Daily Gazette (Accra), Feb. 23, 1966.

16. E.g., Soviet Financial System, trans. from the Russian (Moscow: Progress Publishers 1966), esp. Ch. 7.

18

THE BANKING SYSTEM

THE NEED FOR BANK CREDIT

The complex of financial institutions existing in any country may play a vital role in influencing the extent and direction of development through determining the amount and distribution pattern of short- and long-term credit for the productive sectors. Upon attainment of independence, the African countries all confronted the problems of redirecting the activities of existing financial institutions or creating new ones to finance projects required to restructure and develop the economy. Among the most essential kinds of finance needed are:

1. Funds for industry: (a) long-term loans for the initial heavy investments in plant and basic capital equipment (these might also be financed by the sale of shares of ownership or outright grants by government); (b) medium-term credit for financing the purchase of some kinds of machinery; and (c) short-term credit to finance the day-to-day operation of the industry, that is, the working capital.

2. Funds for small farmers: (a) land finance, to acquire and clear land, irrigation or drainage, or other basic preparation of land; (b) cultivation finance, to assist in the purchase of farm inputs—seed, fertilizers, insecticides—during planting and growing but before they are processed and sold; (c) development finance for the introduction and extension of farming and processing operations; and (d) consumer credit to enable the farmer and his family to provide shelter, clothing, and food until he can sell his crops.

3. Funds for expansion of internal commerce: transport, storage, and handling of goods between urban and rural centers.

The Colonial Banking System

In the colonial era in Africa, such institutions as were established functioned primarily to finance the expansion of the export enclave. Currency boards, rather than central banks, provided currencies backed by the colonies' foreign exchange earnings, which were held in London. Thus the money supply tended to fluctuate directly with the quantity and price of exports, reinforcing the boom-bust effects of international price fluctuations on the monetized sector dependent on export enclave activities.[1] The commercial banks were, with few exceptions, British.* For the most part, they only advanced the short-term commercial credit to finance export-import production and trade. Little bank credit was available for domestic industry or African farmers. Insofar as Africans acquired credit at all, they obtained it from the big trading companies or their agents or, commonly, at exorbitant rates, from local money lenders. Other financial institutions were practically nonexistent, or functioned primarily to meet the needs of settler communities; they were most developed in East and Central Africa, where the settler communities were largest.[2]

Initial Postindependence Policies

One finance authority, R. S. Sayers, has objected to "the not very happy tendency for the less developed countries to follow too closely the patterns of financial structure seen to exist in the more highly developed centers." He maintains,

If progress in the development of financial institutions is really to contribute to economic growth, it must be based on a thorough understanding of the problems rather than on a slavish imitation of what now exists in the countries whose financial institutions developed first.[3]

At the outset, however, most of the former British colonies did try to create the same pattern of monetary institutions as had emerged over the centuries in England.

---

*Barclays DCO and the Bank of West Africa, in West Africa, and Barclays, National Grindlays, and the Standard Bank (in which the Chase Manhattan Bank of New York acquired shares in the 1960s), in East, Central, and South Africa, carried on almost all the banking business. With the exception of two small banks in Nigeria, no African-owned private banks existed.

TABLE 17

Distribution of Branches of British Commercial Banks in Africa
Immediately After World War II

Bank	(1) Total Branches	(2) Gold Coast	(3) Nigeria	(4) Kenya	(5) Tanganyika	(6) Uganda	(7) Southern Rhodesia	(8) Northern Rhodesia	(9) Nyasaland	(10) Total: Columns (2)-(9)	(11) Column (10) as percent of Column (1)
British Bank of West Africa, Ltd.a	41	14	18	–	–	–	–	–	–	32	78
Barclays Bank, D.C.O.	691	11	10	12	11	5	21	12	2	84	12
National Bank of India, Ltd.b	46	–	–	9	4	8	–	–	–	21	46
Standard Bank of South Africac	540	–	–	10	10	5	26	12	6	69	13
Total	1,318	25	28	31	25	18	47	24	8	206	16

aThe British Bank of West Africa was partly owned by Lloyds, Westminister, and National Provincial banks and the Standard Bank of South Africa and interlocked, by common directors, with the Midland Bank, Coutts and Co., and the Yorkshire Penny Bank.
bThe National Bank of India, though independent of the "Big Five" banks in the United Kingdom, owned the share capital of Grindlays Bank, which had total assets equal to half its own.
cThe Standard Bank of South Africa had common directors with Lloyds, Midland, and Westminister Banks. It later became partially separated from the South African office and in the 1960s merged with the British Bank of West Africa and the U.S.-owned Chase Manhattan Bank to operate a "chain of branches stretching across Africa."

Source: Bankers Almanac and Yearbook, 1951.

1. Central banks and monetary policies: The first step was to establish a central bank along the lines of the British model.* The enabling legislation typically empowered them to issue currency in their respective countries, to establish maximum interest rates and the liquidity ratio of commercial banks, and to direct commercial bank policies relating to credit as long as they did not "discriminate" between potential borrowers.

Initially, most African governments linked their currencies to the British pound sterling, but the differing circumstances surrounding their separate monetary and fiscal experiences led to significant divergences within a few short years.[4] Ghana devalued its currency after the collapse of world cocoa prices and the emergence of serious balance of payments deficits, but it still found it necessary to maintain exchange controls. The main consequence of its devaluation was to raise internal consumer prices. When Britain devalued in an effort to surmount its own balance of payments difficulties, Nigeria, the East African countries, and Zambia maintained the value of their currencies as before.† The war in Nigeria led that country to impose severe exchange control regulations. Tanzania, after introducing a new tax program related to its own development strategy in 1970, found it necessary to extend exchange control to its East African neighbors to reduce the outflow of funds the following year.

2. Commercial banks: Initially, all the African governments permitted the foreign banks to conduct business much as before independence. Gradually, however, each began to formulate its own policies in terms of its particular requirements and perspectives.

A study of branch bank expansion in 1964[6] shows that from 1950 to 1964 branch banking expanded more rapidly in the former British colonies than the French, but, nevertheless, tended to remain concentrated in expatriate urban communities and linked predominantly to financing foreign trade.‡ Furthermore, the authors attributed a decline in the growth trend from 1957 to 1964 to the transition from colonial to independent status, "which inevitably influenced the banks' outlook and their propensity to open new offices." The exodus of Europeans reduced bank lending and deposit growth and cut the

---

*The former sub-Saharan French colonies, with a few exceptions, participated in joint central monetary systems that remained centered on Paris.

†In contrast, when France devalued the franc, all the African member countries of the franc zone devalued simultaneously.[5]

‡"Indeed," the authors asserted, "it was largely the prospective profit opportunities in trade financing which brought the banks in the first place; this is also reflected in their loan portfolios."

profitability of the banks. Government emphasis on Africanization of bank personnel was also alleged to have contributed to this trend.

By the end of the 1960s, the private commercial banks still tended to direct their credit primarily to the commercial sector. Even in Kenya,[7] with the largest industrial sector relative to its Gross Domestic Product of all the former British colonies, 45 percent of all credit was directed to trade, compared to 12 percent for agriculture, 22 percent to manufacturing, and barely 2 percent to building and construction. Little credit was advanced to Africans. Evidence indicates that where credit was directed to agriculture, it tended to go primarily to larger farms.[8] This policy was explicitly adopted for government agricultural credit institutions in the Kenyan 1970-74 Development Plan.[9]

The commercial banks made little medium-term credit available in Africa. Prior to independence, Barclays had established an Overseas Development Corporation that advanced small amounts: in the first 20 years of its existence, it made about $84 million available in medium-term loans to about 1,300 projects, two-thirds of them in Africa. Of the total, 28 percent were to industry, 15 percent to agriculture and forestry, 18 percent to commerce, 20 percent to building, and 19 percent to public works. Barclays' Chairman indicated the bank's reluctance to reveal the details of its business:

> Exactly how much "development finance" the banks as a
> whole are today carrying cannot be stated—so far the
> banks have been able to resist the nosiness of govern-
> ment statisticians and preserve some secrets.[10]

He concluded, however, that the greatest lack was not money but men—managers and entrepreneurs.

The British commercial banks have initiated a limited degree of Africanization of their personnel, and even have accepted the necessity of permitting African government participation in their local business. In 1968 Barclays complied with Nigerian legislation to transfer its business to a locally incorporated company and made plans to sell shares to the Nigerian public. It announced[11] similar plans for its branches in Ghana, Sierra Leone, and Kenya, with the proviso that the Barclays' management retain a "significant shareholding and . . . the day-to-day management." Barclays' management pointed out that local participation reduces local demands on its overseas resources.

The banks have attempted to cement their ties with local elites by inviting prominent individuals to participate on the local boards of directors. In 1971, for example, Alhaji Sanusi Dantata, head of the largest groundnut purchasing organization in the northern states of Nigeria, was appointed the first African director of the Standard Bank of Nigeria.

The evidence suggests that whatever the consequences may have been for development of the African countries involved, the bankers' policies have been profitable. Barclays, for example, with two-thirds of its business in Africa, reported[12] a 1971 profit of $73 million ($38 million after taxes), a 22 percent increase over the previous year.*

Postindependence Government Loan Schemes

The experiences of African countries with foreign commercial banks prompted most of their governments to sponsor various schemes to extend credit to agriculture and industry.

1. State commercial banks: Several countries, including Ghana, Nigeria, Kenya, Uganda, Tanzania, and Zambia, established state commercial banks with the aim of stimulating extension of banking to African citizens and into previously neglected rural areas. This aim was to be achieved primarily by opening state bank branches in new areas, and hopefully, through resulting competition, forcing the private banks to do likewise.

The Ghana state bank reportedly had opened some 85 branches throughout the country and one in London, and claimed to have been a factor in stimulating the opening of new branches by the British banks as well: 9 in 1962, 19 in 1963, and 16 in 1964.[13]

Expansion of state banks appeared somewhat slower elsewhere. The Kenyan government established the first entirely state-owned commercial bank in 1968, which planned to open two or three more branches in other major urban centers in the following year.[14] Uganda's government transformed the state-owned Uganda Credit and Savings Bank into a state-owned commercial bank in 1965, and by 1969 it had opened 12 branches in various parts of the country. It owned about a fifth of the total number of branches of all banks and provided about 14 percent of the bank credit available in the country.[15]

2. Rural credit schemes: The marketing cooperative movement, which spread rapidly throughout the former British colonies,† was frequently assisted by governments in establishing some form of

---

*This includes its profit from its share of business in the Standard and Chartered Banking Group, one of the other two big British banks with important African Business.

†In some countries participation in marketing cooperatives became compulsory, particularly for farmers producing export crops.

cooperative bank or credit scheme to advance loans to the farmers through the cooperatives. The World Bank affiliate the International Development Agency provided long-term loan funds at low interest rates to facilitate the operation of some of these schemes.

Most loan schemes for small farmers have encountered serious problems, particularly in respect to securing repayment. An early Ghanaian scheme for lending funds to cocoa farmers through the Cocoa Purchasing Company foundered in part due to the rapid accumulation of unpaid debts,[16] and thereafter no new form of providing government rural credit was established for several years, despite evidence of high interest rates charged by local money lenders.[17] In 1970 the members of 780 out of a total of 900 registered cooperatives in Kenya were reported to be ineligible for loans until their repayment position improved.[18] In Uganda a so-called Progressive Farmers Loan Scheme, under which the Uganda Credit and Savings Bank made loans available to "progressive farmers," was suspended in 1964, at which time about half of the farmers were in default.[19]

The persistence of repayment problems may reflect in part the attitudes as well as the economic status of subsistence peasants who have only recently entered the cash market. Studies of the reasons why farmers borrow indicate that loans are often desired for schooling, housing, or emergencies, as well as for productive purposes. A loan may be perceived as a kind of windfall to be used for such items— even if they are not productive. Insofar as productivity is not thereby increased, the farmer, operating at little more than subsistence level, may be unable to repay. Even if the loan is used for productive purposes, the peasant may see no valid reason why he should not be allowed to use the surpluses thus obtained to raise the level of living of his own family, rather than repay it with interest.* There is some evidence, too, that local political leaders have sometimes viewed the opportunity to obtain credit as one of the plums of office, and used their position to avoid repayment.[21]

Various approaches have been tried to resolve repayment problems. One has been to collect the debts through marketing cooperatives by deduction from payments made after sale. This, unfortunately, may tend to reduce the farmers' incentive to sell through the cooperative. Another method has been the provision of credit in the form of

---

*In the case of the Kenyan Million Acre Scheme, the participants have been reported to be reluctant to repay that portion of their debts that is attributable to payment for the recovery of their land from the British settlers, since they argue that the land was unjustly taken from them in the first place.[20] It is conceivable that this argument is then extended as a rationale for refusal to pay all debts.

actual tools and equipment, with the implements themselves constituting security. This may reduce the use of credit for other than
productive purposes, so that the farmers' output will in fact be in-¬
creased, contributing to his ability to repay.

Arguments relating to the security of credit have been introduced
to support proposals for altered land tenure patterns. A major argument for land consolidation and registration of title in Kenya was that
it would enable the individual farmer to provide security for loans.*
In Tanzania, where the emphasis on producer cooperation has been
held to be contrary to the type of individualization of land ownership
envisaged in Kenya's land registration program, the state banking
system has been directed to make loans to ujamaa villages.[23] The
experience is fairly recent, however, so that no definitive conclusions
may be reached as to consequences.

Insofar as there is any truth to the hypothesis that peasants'
attitudes are partially responsible for their failure to repay loans,
it would seem necessary not only to develop institutions directed to
providing credit at low rates of interest† in order to reduce the future
burden on the farmer, but also to accompany loans by some form of
education. The use of extension agents to collect repayments has
tended to foster negative attitudes among the peasants toward the
agents themselves. But extension agents might be used more effectively to educate farmers as to the use of loans to acquire more effective inputs, simultaneously explaining the necessity of repaying
the loans obtained.‡

3. Proposals for financing private industry: Since most African
countries seek to develop industry, attention has been directed to

---

*Evidence from Tanzania[22] suggests, however, that even this
might not insure repayment under some circumstances, since the
banks may find it difficult to sell the land reclaimed.

†Further studies directed to this issue would be useful.

‡It has been argued[24] that rates of interest charged to small
farmers may have been too low, actually subsidizing borrowing. The
major reasons appear to be (1) that inflation may result in turning
low rates into negative rates of interest and (2) low interest rates
subsidize larger farmers' purchases of capital-intensive machinery
with negative consequences in terms of employment as well as losses
of foreign exchange. It would appear that these contingencies might
best be dealt with through effective financial planning to control inflation and physical planning to produce appropriate farm inputs domestically. Rates of interest, like other prices, cannot be left to "free
market" forces—since these can hardly be said to exist in Africa—
and therefore should be established in the context of careful evaluation of consequences.

developing institutions with the aim of helping to provide long-term investment funds as well as shorter-term credit for industrial projects. In line with the philosophy that private enterprise should be expected to provide most of the long-term investments in industry, both Nigeria and Kenya established stock exchanges.[25] The assumption appears to be that the greater facility with which shares of ownership may be purchased and sold in locally established stock exchanges will stimulate greater local investment. In reality, only a limited number of the largest firms, usually foreign-owned, list their stock, apparently hoping to obtain some local participation. The resulting acquisition of a few shares by a handful of wealthy Africans does not appear to have significantly altered the patterns of the firms' investment decisions. It appears more likely to serve primarily to link the interests of the African elites more closely to those of the foreign firms.

Provision for longer-term loans to industries has in some cases been provided through a government-sponsored national investment bank, since private commercial banks have shown a considerable reluctance to enter this field. For the most part working capital has been obtained through the regular commercial banks.

Governments have sponsored various loans schemes to assist small-scale African entrepreneurs to promote African business. Schatz, who made perhaps the most extensive study of the consequences of schemes to lend funds to Nigerian would-be entrepreneurs, concluded[26] that programs providing credit to small-scale African entrepreneurs are of doubtful value, as well as being very costly to the government. The Nigerian governments spent on the average over $2,000—about two-thirds of the value of the average loan—for each one that actually resulted in productive activity. Political status apparently influenced the granting of loans and the treatment of borrowers. Deficiencies of staff led to inadequate appraisals. But the more fundamental problem appeared to be the absence of viable projects. A "false demand for capital" apparently emerged as persons, tempted by the availability of loan funds, proposed projects regardless of their lack of economic feasibility. Although thousands of projects were rejected, there was an abysmally poor record of repayment on the part of the few hundreds that were accepted. Schatz concludes that there had been too many overexpectations of the potential of such programs: the economic problems facing the government agencies seeking to assist small-scale private enterprise are "insuperable" even if the administrative difficulties can be solved.

In Kenya Industrial and Commercial Development Corporation was established to lend funds to African entrepreneurs. After five years of a not very successful loans program it began to establish industrial estates with an extension service to provide guidance for participants. After nearly a decade of efforts along these lines, the Kenyan Economic Survey of 1969 observed,

321

Early hopes that African entrepreneurs would come forward in response to the opportunities have not been borne out due to both lack of capital and experience.[27]

The attempt to foster Africanization of trade through loans to African distributors culminated in similar failures in Kenya. Eventually, as the government loan funds dried up because of borrowers' defaults, the program itself was terminated.[28]

NEW TRENDS

Several African governments have sought to exert greater control over and direction of the commercial banks and financial institutions of their countries as these early initiatives proved relatively unsuccessful in contributing to broad development goals. The approaches adopted and their probable consequences have varied significantly. The Kenyan government, for example, apparently viewed the merger of government and foreign-owned private commercial banks as the answer. It announced an agreement[29] with National and Grindlays Bank to exchange shares: the Kenyan government would retain 60 percent of the shares in the state commercial bank and 40 percent in the Kenya branch of National and Grindlays, while National Grindlays would hold the remaining shares in both. Whether this would serve to increase government ability to redirect credit more successfully to productive sectors or merely ally government personnel and policies more closely to those of the foreign bankers remained to be seen. Tanzania went furthest of all the former British colonies by the outright nationalization of all the banks and other financial institutions as part of the Arusha Declaration policy of attaining government control of the "commanding heights."*

The Tanzanian government viewed nationalization as essential to insure efficient direct control of banking policies so that credit

---

*The Uganda government initiated efforts in 1970 to take over 61 percent of the shares of banks and financial institutions. The evidence suggests the post-1971 coup government is unlikely to pursue this path further but that the government will retain 49-percent ownership of the banks.[30] At the end of 1970, the Zambian government announced it would assume 51-percent ownership of the four foreign commercial banks operating inside its borders,[31] but as of this writing the only action taken has been to establish a small state owned commercial bank and buy 60 percent of the shares of the smallest foreign owned bank. The bulk of the commercial banking business is still conducted by the three remaining wholly foreign owned private banks.

expansion would contribute in the most effective way possible to development. The Chairman and Managing Director of the Tanzanian National Bank of Commerce, Mr. A. J. Nsekela, explained:

> In developing countries investment resources are so
> pitifully small and the demands upon them so excessively
> large that their prudent allocation becomes a matter of
> paramount importance if development is to proceed at any
> politically acceptable rate. Efficient resource allocation
> and avoidance of waste should in theory become matters
> of the highest priority. . . . As a consequence of this
> change in ownership [of productive enterprises] we have
> not only increased the volume of resources available to
> Tanzania by reducing outflows of scarce foreign exchange
> and by retaining profits in Tanzania for use in the devel-
> opment budget, but we have also gained complete control
> of the policies of those enterprises. . . .[32]

The National Bank of Commerce was created by combining the operations of seven expatriate banks, one locally incorporated bank, and the State Commercial Bank. It was heir to a full range of banking services and assets totaling about $1,400 million. Following initial consolidation of its operations under new management, it began mobi- lization of the personnel and branch systems of its predecessors. In the first year, the branch location patterns were redesigned to meet the need for banking facilities rather than interbank competition. As a result, eleven duplicative branches in major urban centers were closed, two more opened in new areas, and mobile rural services were expanded. Rural and small-town branch managers were urged to follow a more active lending policy to stimulate development out- side the main urban centers.

Despite problems created by the precipitate withdrawal of key expatriate staff and the blocking of external balances, the new state bank successfully built up the central office operations and overseas correspondent relationships. These had formerly been operated from Nairobi or the overseas head offices of the foreign banks. In 1967 operations would have shown a net profit before tax comparing favor- ably with previous years, except for nonrecurring losses resulting from the fact that part of the foreign exchange reserves were held in British sterling, which was devalued.* In 1968 the National Bank

---

*The National Bank of Commerce holds relatively few reserves, only those needed for working balances. Surpluses are sold immedi- ately to the Bank of Tanzania. After nationalization, the Bank of Tanzania began to diversify its overseas holdings. As a result, the

of Commerce showed a net profit of about $4 million.[34] Total credit
advanced by June 1969 had increased by 20 percent over the previous
year to over $130 million. A major share of this was directed to
seasonal financing of crop payments. Of the remainder, over half
was an increase in loans to manufacturing. The relative share of
credit to the commercial sector had declined.[35]

The extent to which the Bank should enter into provision of
medium-term credit was examined. It was discovered, after nationalization, that the private banks had been terminating medium-term
credit in Tanzania. In 1969 the Bank established a general loan scheme
to provide facilities for loans for up to ten years with a maximum
moratorium period of three years to facilitate plant erection and
running-in time. Interest rates were to be 7 to 9 percent with pre-
ferential rates charged for projects in the nine towns designated as
priority areas in the Second Five Year Plan.[36] By 1971 this loan
scheme had been separated from the NBC to establish the nucleus of
a new Tanzania Investment Bank, designed to act as the principal local
source of long-term loans for industrial and other large projects.[37]

After the first year of operation, the new management of the
National Bank of Commerce began to have time to begin to consider
a host of questions.[38] The first was the appropriate criteria to use
in evaluating loan proposals. Profits alone were no longer to be the
deciding factor, while public ownership was not expected to excuse
inefficiency or uneconomical administration; considerations other
than profitability might take priority in certain cases. Additions to
local employment, savings of foreign exchange, complementarity with
and linkages to existing plants, exploitation of local raw materials,
production of capital rather than consumer goods, production of basic
consumer as opposed to luxury consumer items, creation of poles-of-
growth in less developed areas—all these could be considered as additional criteria in selection of some projects in preference to others
even though the latter might promise better returns in purely financial
terms. Traditional financing techniques remained important for
assessing the viability of large projects, but they might need to be
qualified to the extent that government policy placed a different price
upon certain inputs or outputs than that prevailing in the market, or

---

losses due to British devaluation were somewhat less than they might
have been otherwise, probably considerably less than those sustained
by Ugandan and Kenyan banks, which held most of their reserves in
sterling.[33] To the extent that its reserves were held in U.S. dollars,
the Tanzanian banking system, like those of all other developing
countries with their reserves in dollars, must have suffered negative
consequences from the U.S. devaluation.

to the extent that relatively poor financial aspects might be offset by other redeeming features of a project. At the same time, any subsidy element must be clearly identified to avoid a false picture of a project's overall contribution to the economy and should be met by the government directly, not by the Bank.

A second, related question was the appropriate interest rate structure to be set by the state banking system. It was decided that—even though savings in Tanzania appeared to be relatively insensitive to interest rate changes—interest rates should be raised to 3.5 percent for savings deposits.

The selection of appropriate interest rates to charge to borrowers also involved consideration of other issues. If interest rates charged by the bank were lower than commercial rates elsewhere, the Bank would in effect be subsidizing private profit as well as state projects. In this respect specifically it would seem to be sound principle to insure that any subsidy to state industry should be granted in well-defined terms directly from government funds, rather than concealed in the form of low interest rates provided by the state banks. On the other hand, if interest rates were set too high they might discourage both public and private investments that might benefit the economy.

Third, the formulation of new criteria for loans implied the necessity of increased coordination and centralization of decision-making within the government to insure that investment funds would be directed as needed within the framework of overall government development strategy. This raised the question of the relationship of the Ministry of Economic Development and Planning, the parastatals, the National Bank of Commerce, the National Cooperative Bank, and other financial agencies.

Problems that emerged as to the relation of the credit policies of various government agencies to the national development strategies may be illustrated in the case of agriculture and industry. In the agricultural sector, since the entire commercial banking sector was in the public sector, should a separate bank, the pre-existing National Cooperative Bank, continue to finance crop movements, or would a unified system provide greater flexibility in the use of surplus funds in the off-crop moving season for short-term loans in other sectors of the economy? By 1971 the Tanzanian Rural Development Bank was established on the foundation of the former National Credit Development Agency to play an "innovative role in rural development." The largest source of funds for this bank in the immediate future was expected to be foreign loans to the treasury.[39] Another problem emerged as provision of credit primarily to "progressive farmers," the larger, more well-to-do farmers—as effected by some East African credit schemes—appeared to foster consequences contrary to ujamaa perspectives. Provision of credit to tobacco farmers to hire laborers, for example, appeared to have been a factor contributing to the break-up in the mid-1960s of government-sponsored cooperative tobacco farms, since it enabled farmers to obtain labor supplies without co-operating.[40] By the 1970s the banks were directed to provide more credit to ujamaa projects.

Additional problems of credit-policy coordination arose in the industrial sector. The National Development Corporation continued to provide credit at lower rates of interest for its subsidiaries than did the National Bank of Commerce.[41] The legislation establishing the National Development Credit Agency permitted it to provide commercial finance to encourage small industries and trade, another potential source for conflicting policies. Commercial loans to small rural business require a great deal of supervision, including assistance in procuring inputs, marketing, bookkeeping, and banking. A sufficient staff of commercial officers is required to do these jobs. This work might be coordinated with that of the national Small Industries Corporation established in 1967,[42] as well as with activities of branch banks of the National Bank of Commerce.

A strong case was made[43] for concentrating financial analysts in the Ministry of Economic Affairs and Development Planning and the Industrial Studies and Development Center for appraisal of large projects to assess their financial viability, their place in the nation's industrial strategy, and any special nonfinancial virtues they might have that warrant government support. At least, if this degree of centralization could not be attained, Devplan could assist the many boards and bodies taking decisions independently by stipulating minimum and maximum rates of return to be earned by various categories of investment projects over a certain size. A project earning more or less could be referred to Devplan to consider whether circumstances warranted its going ahead unaltered. In 1971 a new Programming and Reporting Division was set up in Devplan to monitor the progress of the plan and to operate more systematic project selection procedures.[44]

Fourth, there was the question of the extent to which the Bank should be encouraged to exercise its role as a main provider of credit to check up on the fulfillment of plan targets.[45] At least once a year, bank staff scrutinizes the balance sheet and profit and loss accounts of its borrowers. Large enterprises are usually requested to furnish cash flow projections to permit formulation of forward calculations of probable bank involvement. Each of the assumptions on which figures are based is carefully checked. The Bank is, therefore, in a unique position of having extensive information, built up over a number of years, on almost every business in Tanzania; and because almost all day-to-day transactions of these businesses pass through the Bank's books, it is possible to watch their progress carefully.

In socialist countries, this intimacy between banks and business enterprises has evolved into financial control over the enterprises' fulfillment of planned targets.[46] In Tanzania, where private firms still constitute a significant sector of the economy, the Bank's role has been limited to providing financial expertise and assistance, of course keeping information confidential and observing normal banking secrecy. This should not, in principle, hinder the Bank from advising on the financial structure of new public and state-private investment projects within the framework of the overall plan. This again raises the issue of the extent of autonomy in financial matters to be retained by other fund-providing agencies, including the National Development Corporation and such of its subsidiaries as the Rural Development Bank and the National Insurance Corporation.

Critical objective constraints hindered Tanzanian efforts to arrive at decisive conclusions concerning some of these issues. The lack of highly trained Tanzanian personnel was probably the most serious. There was a reduction in the number of expatriate personnel from over 50, located in branch offices as well as the head office in 1967, to no more than 10 in 1969, all of them in the head office.* Nevertheless, the choice appeared to be to continue to hire high-quality expatriate personnel for some of the key posts or to employ less well-trained, less experienced local personnel, which might result in less efficient use of existing scarce resources. Tanzania chose to continue to hire expatriates and at the same time to institute extensive training of Tanzanians within the Bank. As President Nyerere put it, "To employ an inefficient person just because he is a Tanzanian, when the job he has to do is crucial for our development, is not self-reliance, it is stupidity."[47]

The importance of maintaining an efficient, well-trained staff was considered crucial for assisting business with financial management to translate short- and long-run production plans into financial terms and to advise on how various alternatives would affect the enterprise's cash flow position, profit and loss account, and balance sheet over a number of years. The problem of training adequate financial personnel was recognized as particularly important in Tanzania because much of the country's industrial investment is undertaken hand in hand with foreign investors whose equity participation is less than the government's, but who contribute long-term contractor finance or debenture loan finance and who usually participate on a managing agency basis. It was held to be of utmost importance that

_____

*Most of these expatriates were provided by technical assistance arrangements with foreign governments, so that their cost to Tanzania was limited primarily to housing, and so on.

the real returns to the overseas partner be calculated clearly in advance and that forward projections be made of the implications of alternative capital-debt structures.

The government also needed to train middle-level personnel—accountants and bookkeepers, auditors and cashiers—who could contribute to accumulation of accurate data and control of expenditures. The government directed greater attention to strengthening government training institutions and colleges to produce large quantities of well-qualified financial administrators at all levels.

SUMMARY

The banking system plays a crucial role in development by determining the amounts, kinds, and costs of the long- and short-term credit available for productive projects. The colonial banking system was established in Africa primarily to finance the private foreign firms and settlers expanding the export enclave. After independence, the African governments initially tried to redirect the banking system through establishment of central banks along lines typical in Western countries. In addition, limited state banks, rural credit schemes, and industrial loans were introduced in an effort to spread credit more broadly.

By the latter 1960s, it was becoming increasingly evident that these schemes were not contributing much to stated broader development goals. A number of governments began to intervene more directly in the banking system. Among the former British colonies, Tanzania went the furthest, nationalizing the entire banking and financial system with the express aim of husbanding its limited investible surpluses more effectively. The new banking system functioned increasingly rationally in the context of overall national planning. Gradually longer-term credit facilities and extended rural banking institutions were established. The nationalized banking system began to cope systematically with such questions as evaluation of loan proposals, interest rates, coordination and centralization of credit decisions, and checkup on credit use in the context of increasingly explicit national financial plans designed to allocate investible surpluses more effectively to restructuring the national economy. These kinds of measures appeared to be essential to the attainment of the more self-reliant financial program envisaged in the Arusha Declaration.

NOTES

1. N. T. Newlyn and D. C. Rowan, Money and Banking in British Colonial Africa (Oxford: Clarendon Press, 1954).

2. For description see National Christian Council of Kenya, Who Controls Industry in Kenya? Ch. 15.

3. R. S. Sayers, Modern Banking, 6th ed., Oxford, 1964, pp. 299-300.

4. See International Monetary Fund, International Financial Statistics, country data.

5. Africa Confidential, no. 17 (Aug. 22, 1969).

6. H. L. Engberg and W. A. Hance, "Growth and Dispersion of Branch Banking in Tropical Africa, 1950-1964," Economic Geography 45: 195-208.

7. Kenya, Economic Survey, 1969, Table 2.5, p. 29; and National Christian Council of Kenya, Who Controls Industry in Kenya? p. 167.

8. E.g., for Uganda, despite long-standing participation by small African farmers in export cash crop production, see J. H. Gervers, "Preliminary Results of a Survey on the Financing of Large-Scale Enterprise in Uganda," Economic Development and Research Project (EDRP) Paper no. 122, Mar. 17, 1967; and G. R. Rose, "Results of a Survey of Financial Demand by Small-Scale Enterprise in Uganda," EDRP No. 111, Oct. 28, 1966.

9. When projected Agricultural Finance Corporation credit is combined with direct Central Government credit, the total available to large farmers is about twice as much as that for small farmers (see Kenya, Development Plan, 1970-74, pp. 214 and 216.)

10. B. Macdona, "Financing Development in Africa—The Role of the Commercial Banks and their Overseas Investment Corporations," African Affairs, 66 (Oct. 1967): 328.

11. Advertisement, West Africa, Jan. 2-8, 1971, p. 16.

12. West Africa, Jan. 7, 1972.

13. Ghana, Economic Survey, 1964, p. 59.

14. Kenya, Economic Survey, 1969, p. 29.

15. Bank of Uganda, Annual Report, 1967-8, pp. 23-4.

16. Report of the Commission of Enquiry into the Affairs of the Cocoa Purchasing Company, Ltd. (Accra: Government Printer, 1956).

17. E.g., See Cocoa Research Studies (reports of economic surveys carried out by P. Hill and C. McGlade, Economic Research Division, University College of Ghana, Legon), esp. No. 2, pp. 8-9, and No. 4, p. 13.

18. Kenya, Development Plan, 1970-1974, pp. 276-8.

19. D. Hunt, "Some Aspects of Agricultural Credit in Uganda," EDRP No. 106, Aug. 26, 1966.

20. R. S. Odinga, "Resettlement Schemes in Kenya," lecture to Geography Department, University College, Dar es Salaam, Jan. 23, 1969, based on Ph.D. thesis, "The Kenya Highlands, Land Use and Agricultural Change."

21. E.g., Report of the Commission of Enquiry into the Affairs of the Cocoa Purchasing Company, Ltd. (Accra: Government Printer, 1956), passim; and G. K. Helleiner, "The Fiscal Role of the Marketing Boards in Nigerian Economic Development," in Taylor, ed., Taxation for African Economic Development, esp. pp. 434-7.

22. M. P. Collinson, "Agricultural Credit in Tanzania," in Helleiner, ed., Agricultural Planning in East Africa, pp. 139-140.

23. Tanzania, Second Five-Year Plan, p. 37.

24. Agricultural Development Council Workshop on Small Farmer Credit, Washington, D.C., April 6-7, 1972.

25. E.g., see National Christian Council of Kenya, Who Controls Industry in Kenya? pp. 130-131.

26. S. P. Schatz, Economics, Politics and Administration in Government Lending; The Regional Loans Boards of Nigeria, 1970; see also Helleiner, "The Fiscal Role of Marketing Boards in Nigerian Economic Development," pp. 434-7.

27. Kenya Economic Survey, 1969, p. 91.

28. J. Bucknell, "State Trading in Kenya," unpublished Ph.D. thesis, University of Wisconsin, Agricultural Economics Department, 1971.

29. "Banks—Partnership in Kenya," African Development, Jan. 1971, p. 35.

30. Gen. Amin's May Day Message, Uganda Argus, May 3, 1971.

31. "Banks and Zambia," African Development, Jan. 1971.

32. A. J. Nsekela, "The Place of Financial Management in Industrial Development," lecture in UNIDO Seminar, Dar es Salaam, 27 January 1969.

33. Hoarnmann, "Bank of Tanzania," lecture to Economic Research Bureau Seminar, University College, Dar es Salaam, 1969.

34. United Republic of Tanzania, National Bank of Commerce, Annual Report and Accounts for Year ended 30th June, 1969, p. 4.

35. Bank of Tanzania, Economic and Operations Report, June, 1969, p. 17.

36. National Bank of Commerce, Annual Report, 1969 (Dar es Salaam, 1970), pp. 9-10.

37. United Republic of Tanzania, The Annual Plan for 1971/1972 (Dar es Salaam: Government Printer, 1971), p. 8.

38. Discussed by Nsekela, "The Place of Financial Management in Industrial Development."

39. Tanzania, The Annual Plan for 1971/1972, pp. 8, 59.

40. D. Feldman, "The Economics of Ideology—Some Problems in Achieving Rural Socialism in Tanzania," paper presented to Economic Research Bureau Seminar, Oct. 25, 1968.

41. See Seidman, Comparative Development Strategies in East Africa (Nairobi: East African Publishing House, 1972), p. 118.

42. For progress as of 1969, see National Bank of Commerce, Annual Report, p. 12.

43. Nsekela, "The Place of Financial Management in Industrial Development," p. 8.

44. Tanzania, The Annual Plan for 1971/1972, p. 9.

45. National Bank of Commerce, Annual Report, 1969, p. 10.

46. Soviet Financial System, passim.

47. Cited by Nsekela, "The Place of Financial Management in Industrial Development," p. 5.

19

**OTHER FINANCIAL
INSTITUTIONS**

Medium- and longer-term loans are essential for the longer-range investments required for development in Africa. British banking traditions inherited in Africa had generally restricted commercial banks to making relatively short-term loans; in England medium- and longer-term loans were for the most part provided by a complex of other financial institutions. In Africa additional institutions that constituted potential means of channeling savings into productive sectors of the economy included marketing boards, insurance and pension funds, post office savings banks, building and hire purchase funds, and credit and savings societies. The African governments were confronted with the possibilities and problems of trying to reshape these institutions and perhaps develop new ones to insure that they too contributed more effectively to investment in proposed development projects.

It has become increasingly apparent that the policies of these institutions should be incorporated into the overall financial plan to maximize their contribution to attainment of overall development goals and to minimize the danger that their separate activities might interfere with other governmental plans.

MARKETING BOARDS

The marketing boards were probably the most significant of these other financial institutions at the time of independence, particularly in Uganda and West Africa, primarily because of the importance to the entire economy of the export crops they handled.

Reserve Funds

The marketing boards accumulated significant surpluses in periods of relatively high world prices—especially the 1950s—by saving in their reserve funds the difference between the prices paid to the farmers for their crops and the world market prices. In reality, these funds constituted an additional form of export tax on the producers themselves. The British viewed them[1] as giving the colonial governments a firmer grip on the territories, enabling them to control purchasing power and reduce inflation. Producer prices were perceived, too, as an instrument for encouraging or discouraging particular lines of production. For the independent governments, marketing boards potentially constituted, in addition, a major channel for directing savings from agriculture into investment.

The amounts of money accumulated by various marketing boards were on occasion quite large. In Ghana high world cocoa prices in the 1950s permitted the board to accumulate some £87 million from 1947 to 1961 by holding payments to farmers to only 54 percent of the total cocoa proceeds.[2] Ghana's Second Development Plan assumed that the Cocoa Marketing Board reserves would provide about a fifth of its proposed development finance. These were "forced savings," it has been argued, that would not have been made voluntarily; the wealthier cocoa farmers tended to invest their own funds, if at all, aside from expanding their farms, in middle- and upper-class urban housing. If the board's policy of setting low producer prices discouraged further cocoa expansion, it may have been all to the good. Ghana produces 30 to 40 percent of world output. The world expansion of cocoa production—to which Ghana contributed by doubling its own output from 1955 to 1965—led to price declines that all but wiped out Ghana's benefits from the increased production that occurred.

All the marketing boards in Nigeria, by the time the 1953 Constitutional Conference placed them under regional control, had accumulated a sum of £75.5 million.[3] These reserves were distributed among the regions, enhancing their financial autonomy. The regional governments thus attained an important fiscal weapon. The regional boards became so closely integrated as to be veritable departments of the regional governments that made the critical decisions relating to producer prices and allocation of the boards' surpluses among loans, grants, and direct board expenditures.

The 1953 division of the marketing boards widened the disparities in financial resources among the regions of Nigeria. Initially the West received almost half, the North a third, and the East less than 20 percent of the amounts accumulated by that date. The boards' contributions to the separate regions after that date reflected and aggravated the consequences of the fluctuating world market prices for

the individual crops on which each depended. Marketing board loans
and grants contributed about a fourth of the total revenues of the Western Region between 1955 and 1959, dropping to about 12 percent in
1959-66 when world cocoa prices fell. The Eastern Region Marketing
Board's contribution to government, on the other hand, increased from
0.9 percent in the first period to 6.3 percent in the second. The Northern Region Marketing Board increased its contribution to current
revenue from 0.4 percent in the earlier period to 9.8 percent in the
latter period.

In East Africa, where the European settlers had successfully
opposed the imposition of export taxes that would reduce their incomes,
marketing board surpluses, too, were far less significant than in West
Africa. Only in Uganda, where African peasants produced the major
export crops, were large sums retained by the boards. From 1945 to
1960 the Ugandan Lint Marketing Board accumulated £15.9 million
in its Price Assistance Fund and the Coffee Board accumulated £9.9
million.[4] In Tanzania only those boards that were engaged in the sale
of peasant-produced crops accumulated significant sums. The Lint
and Seed Marketing Board had accumulated £5.3 million by 1959, although this had been reduced to £2 million by 1967 due to the fall in
world cotton prices; the Tanganyika Tobacco Board was estimated to
have about £150,000 by 1967, although it had not published any figures
on its financial position since its inception; and the National Agricultural Products Board reportedly deducted about £250,000 a year from
the value of its turnover.[5]

Investment Policies

The boards were empowered to use their accumulated funds for
financing crop movements, supplementing them by bank overdrafts
if necessary. They could also either lend funds to the government or
invest in processing plants, storage and transportation facilities to
handle crops under their jurisdiction. The Coffee and Lint boards of
Uganda provided major sources of funds for storage, processing, and
transport of the crops with which they dealt in the 1950s. The Tanzanian Lint and Seed Marketing Board invested in its own warehouses
and provided grants for research, maintenance, and improvement of
roads, tracks, and piers in cotton areas, and seed stores for cooperatives as well as bale stores for the railways. It loaned funds to cooperatives for construction and acquisition of ginneries, as well as
working capital to construct buying stores. It also loaned funds through
the cooperatives to members for purchase of fertilizers and agricultural equipment at interest rates of 7.5 percent. The Second Tanzanian
Five Year Plan projected further investments to be made by the marketing boards.[6]

The much larger amounts accumulated by the Nigerian boards were used for a variety of purposes as directed by the state governments.[7] The Northern and Western regional governments borrowed heavily from their boards in the early 1960s for development projects. The Eastern Board was required to contribute to the Consolidated Revenue Fund of the government. To a large extent, the funds of all three were used for social services like education. When cocoa prices collapsed in the 1960s, the Western Region government, in particular, faced a serious financial crisis in its efforts to maintain the flow of funds to education while attempting to pay off these loans and maintain the incomes of the cocoa producers.

Two sets of problems emerged as marketing boards became important sources of funds for development. First, to the extent that they invested outright in processing facilities and sought to provide management for facilities provided, some question began to be raised as to their competence in this area. In Tanzania it has been argued that it might be preferable for all management of such facilities to be handled by the government's major instrument for industrialization, the National Development Corporation, since the best national managerial capacity for industrial projects is centered in that agency.

The second set of problems related to coordinating the use of funds within the framework of the overall national development strategy. There is a need for a conscious analysis of the extent to which such savings—essentially "forced" savings from producers—should be used for investment in development and what types of investments should be made. Political problems have arisen when producers have seen their funds used for investments and were convinced those investments were not related to projects in which they have an interest.[8]

In Nigeria[9] additional difficulties were encountered when domestic firms desiring to use traditional export crops as raw materials sought to gain competitive advantage by buying them at producer prices rather than the considerably higher world prices. As a result, the purchases of cocoa by a chocolate factory in the Western Region, for example, might reduce the revenues of that government. On the other hand, a textile mill in the West, built on the assumption that it would purchase cotton grown in the North, was denied the potential competitive advantage because the Northern Region Marketing Board refused to sell cotton to it at less than the world price.

A third set of problems concerns the impact of marketing board policies on overall monetary supplies. In Ghana, for example, Cocoa Marketing Board payments to the cocoa farmers represented 8.6 percent of Gross Domestic Product at current prices from 1954 to 1962.[10] The government dipped into the marketing board funds to maintain producer prices and to finance the balance of payments deficits that emerged when world cocoa prices began to fall; in a sense it attempted to use the funds to finance a form of pump priming. By the early 1960s, new cocoa crops were being financed through the Ghana Commercial Bank by means of loans and advances against special government deposits. This contributed further to inflationary pressures by significantly increasing the money supply. As one observer remarked, the major impact of Cocoa Marketing Board prices argued strongly for the formulation of a comprehensive policy relating to cocoa prices, incomes, and national development and monetary supplies—"The difficulties of formulating a confident and well-informed policy should not be an excuse for not formulating one at all."[11]

In Nigeria regional control over marketing boards further aggravated the difficulties of formulating an effective monetary policy.[12] When the Western Region Marketing Board reduced producer prices for cocoa from £141 10s to £92 10s per ton in 1961-62, it reduced the money incomes of the producers by some £9.11 million, about a twelfth of the total regional money supply that year. Revenue needs and political considerations played important, even decisive roles in the board's decisions—and these could easily counter nationally oriented attempts to relate money supplies to real production.

Special problems have arisen in connection with the operations of the marketing boards handling domestically consumed crops. The National Agricultural Products Board in Tanzania has been required to hold maize as a famine reserve at a cost of about £517,000. It has been argued that to the extent that these are held in the national interest, the government, rather than the producers should finance the reserve.[13] This would, of course, only shift the incidence of the burden; it would not eliminate it.

Zambia's National Agricultural Marketing Board encountered problems in attempting to develop pricing policies that could (1) encourage the farmers to increase output in the face of food shortages aggravated by efforts to reduce dependence on Rhodesia and South Africa and (2) hold down consumer prices in urban areas. The board subsidized the farmers to the extent of millions of dollars in an effort to attain these goals.[14] This could only be a temporary expedient, however; over time the board's pricing and financial policies should be considered in the context of an overall national financial plan.

In brief, to the extent that marketing board funds are to be invested in development, all such investments should be planned to conform to the overall pattern of development. As the Ross Report asserted in Tanzania in 1965:

In general, arbitrary capital transfers from one public or semi-public body which happens to have funds to another quite different body which happens to need them can only result in a loss of central government control over the general pattern of financing.[15]

INSURANCE FUNDS

Colonial Insurance Policies

In colonial Africa almost all insurance firms were foreign-owned, their activities designed to facilitate the activities of the narrow high-income group associated with export enclave activities. Whereas in developed countries insurance premiums paid by those seeking insurance in case of accident or death commonly provide large sums for investment, in Africa a major share of these investible funds were shipped out of the country. Here the task confronting African governments upon independence was to design new working rules to shift the insurance funds accumulated to investment in projects in Africa itself.

The problem may be illustrated by the experience of the three East African countries. There the foreign-owned insurance companies, some with headquarters in Kenya, either shipped their funds home or invested them in the Nairobi-Mombasa area. At independence, all but four of the insurance companies in Kenya were foreign-controlled, and the distributed profits were therefore largely repatriated, subject to normal exchange control regulations. Available information about insurance companies was limited. Nevertheless, it was estimated that about 8 million pounds was shipped out of East Africa in the five years 1960-1964.[16] Of the remainder, most was invested in Kenya. The holdings of Kenya-based insurance companies, accumulated over the preceding half century from insurance business in Tanganyika and Uganda as well as Kenya itself, totaled slightly over £25 million in 1965. Of these holdings, K£6.4 million were invested in mortgages and loans, K£9.1 million in government securities, K£2.3 in stocks and shares, K£3.1 in real estate, with the remainder in cash, the banks, and miscellaneous categories.

Government controls over the insurance industry in Kenya were those set out in the Insurance Act of 1960. This provided that each company must have a paid-up capital of not less than K£50,000 before it began to operate, a safety provision that excluded would-be African insurers since few could accumulate so much capital. Otherwise government requirements were related to "sound" insurance principles supervised by an advisory board on which sat representatives of the Attorney General and the Treasury. The government intervened very little with the existing firms' investment policies. It did take steps to withdraw income-tax relief from payments on policies that mature outside East Africa to offer an incentive to insurers to take out policies payable in the country. In 1969 a Parliamentary Committee of Inquiry led to the limitation of increases in insurance premiums to 20 percent instead of the proposed 25-30 percent.

A new "local" company, the Kenya National Assurance Company, Ltd., was established in 1964 through the Development and Finance Company of Kenya, with financial backing from a consortium of British, Kenyan, and other Commonwealth and international European insurance companies, together with the Kenya government. In 1967, in accord with a new arrangement and in full agreement with the existing shareholders, the Kenya government was issued 51 percent of the capital, thus obtaining a controlling interest without reducing the holdings of the other partners. The company began by undertaking general insurance. In 1967 it was announced that all insurance business from government bodies, statutory boards, local authorities, and cooperative societies would be placed with the company.

The 1970-74 Development Plan announced[17] that the government planned to establish the State Reinsurance Corporation to end a outflow of funds that occurred because all insurance firms reinsured overseas. No mention was made of possible coordination of all East African reinsurance.*

The insurance companies in Uganda functioned much as in the colonial era for several years after independence. In 1967 the Insurance Companies Act was amended to require the companies to hold the greater part of their assets in approved securities in the country itself.[18] The decisions as to the kinds of securities purchased, within the general limitations on insurance companies, however, appear to have been left with the private company directors.

In 1970 the Obote government announced it would take over 60 percent of the shares of the banks and financial institutions, but the post-coup policies of the Amin government appear to have left the insurance companies much as before.

The Tanzanian government established a government-owned National Insurance Company in 1963 to provide competition with existing insurers, which were mostly based in Kenya. The company had acquired about a sixth of the nation's insurance business by 1966, but was not yet in a position to make significant investments except in the form of bank deposits.

Nationalization of Insurance in Tanzania

Tanzania nationalized the local branches of all insurance companies at the same time that it took over the banks following the Arusha Declaration. The National Insurance Company was enlarged to handle their business. The 1967 Act expanding the company provided

*See footnote, p. 339.

that it should create all types of insurance with adequate service and facilities throughout Tanzania without discrimination. The government recognized the potentially expanded insurance business as an important source of investible funds as well as a provider of increased security for the population.[19]

The National Insurance Company found it possible to reduce costs to some extent after nationalization by reducing the fees of insurance agents. It continued the agency system in an effort to continue to expand insurance not only in the urban areas, but also in the rural areas. At the same time, the company increased its employment from 60 to 260 persons in the first year of operation to handle the larger volume of work it undertook in Tanzania itself. Here, as in the case of banks, the main problem continued to be one of training local personnel as rapidly as possible, reducing the expatriate staff to only a few experienced individuals at the top levels.

With nationalization, the National Insurance Company's nonlife insurance premium income increased from £0.2 million to £1.35 million. Life insurance premium income did not increase as spectacularly, since the previously existing companies were permitted to continue to collect premiums on existing policies. Life insurance premium income in 1967 was only £100,000 and was expected to increase to about £300,000 in 1968.

The Tanzanian National Insurance Company confronted the task of formulating an investment policy that would provide adequate security for its insurers and at the same time contribute to economic development in the country. Initially, it invested its income from short-term nonlife insurance and longer-term life insurance in government paper. It began to invest in mortgages in 1968. The preservation of these investment funds in the country was expected to save foreign exchange.* By 1971 it was estimated that the National Insurance Company had invested about $2 million in government stock.[22]

The interest rate structure of the National Insurance Company was initially linked to long-term borrowing rates of the government.

---

*The National Insurance Company continued to reinsure major risks—for example, the Tiper Oil Refinery—abroad. In 1969 Mr. Nsekela, Chairman of the National Bank of Commerce, urged the East African Legislative Assembly to establish a reinsurance firm in East Africa.[20] Unless Uganda and Kenya also nationalize their insurance businesses (which are held by private firms that continued to reinsure more of their risks abroad) or at least require them to reinsure most of their risks with the East African firm, its establishment would do little to help solve the problems of reinsurance confronted by Tanzania.[21]

For example, if the government long-term interest rate was 8 percent, the National Insurance Company might charge a half percent more. The theory appeared to be that lower rates should not be charged, since this would constitute a hidden subsidy of projects. Furthermore, lack of information as to actual insurance business profits—which would only be known after years of operation provided actual experience—made lowering of interest rates risky for the policy holders. It was held, too, that if company income was adequate to give bonuses to policy holders, these would constitute an added incentive to purchase insurance.

Provident Funds

Pension plans and provident funds potentially constitute another insurance-type channel for savings that might contribute to investment. Collected regularly from workers and employers at their places of work, these funds are usually accumulated over long periods of time to be paid out to the workers in case of accident, illness, or old age. Private funds collected in Africa in the past were frequently invested by stockbrokers in England. Even as late as 1967[23] Noble Lowndes Finance (E.A.) Ltd., which continued to handle pensions in Kenya, was the local subsidiary of Noble Lowndes Holdings Ltd.: The latter, a British firm specializing in investing pension funds, obtained a third of its group profits from overseas operations, including those in Kenya.

Most African governments began to move toward increased state establishment of and participation in provident funds to insure that minimum standards of security were provided for the workers, while at the same time attempting more effectively to direct the accumulated funds to local investment needs. The Kenyan government,[24] for example, established a National Social Security Fund, which by 1967 covered virtually all classes of workers. In 1968 it proposed to introduce a Workers' Investment Trust to hold funds transferred from private pensions and provident fund schemes. This was held to give trade unions some influence on investment decisions, but the total trust investment in any one project would be so small that the unions could be expected to have little say in industrial policy.

The Tanzanian government also established a National Provident Fund, initially covering employers of 10 or more workers. By 1968-69 employers of 4 to 9 workers were covered, increasing the members to more than 400,000 by January 1969. Contributions reached almost $10 million in 1971. The National Provident Fund, with cumulative investments in government stocks in 1969 of over $24 million, was the largest single source of finance for domestic borrowing to carry out plan implementation.[25]

Hire-purchase funds, building societies, post office and other
types of savings schemes are among the other kinds of financial institutions inherited by African countries. At the time of independence
these too were predominantly linked to the interests of the narrow
high-income group in the export enclave. The amounts of money
involved tended to be small. The problems and possibilities of these
institutions for channeling surpluses to investment may again be illustrated by the East African experience.

Hire Purchase

Finance houses in Africa mostly functioned to provide loans to
consumer durables like cars, radios, and refrigerators. The amounts
of funds were never very large, running into several hundreds of
thousands of pounds at most.

In Kenya the biggest finance houses are still foreign-owned,
although in some cases local citizens—typically European "Kenyans"—
sat on their local boards of directors.[26] For the most part, they
engaged in financing purchases of private automobiles. The United
Dominions Corporation's principle business, for example, immediately
after independence, was with the Kenya Government Car Loan Scheme.
In 1966 the company had advanced K£981,639 in loans; reported profits
for the year were K£36,679 before tax of K£11,285. Another of the
"big three," Credit Finance Company, Ltd., held outstanding loans in
the three East African countries amounting to K£1.3 million, though
it reported, after making a profit of K£57,000, that it still carried
forward a net accumulated loss from past operations of K£164,705.*
Its chairman was Harold Travis, also a director of 42 other Kenyan
companies. Smaller finance companies included Traction Finance
Corporation, Ltd., a subsidiary of Cooper Motor Corporation, and
others that specialized in financing the purchase of vehicles such as
buses or lorries on a deferred payment basis. The bigger hire-
purchase firms usually charged 10-14 percent flat interest on their
loans on the initial amount borrowed. No allowance was made for
repayment of the loan, so the effective rate was over 20 percent.[27]
In 1968 the Kenyan government passed a Hire-Purchase Act seeking
to "strike a balance between the conflicting interests of hirers and

---

*Careful examination of the company books would be required
to determine whether this bookkeeping loss concealed profits shipped
out of the country.

owners."28 The act prescribed conditions under which a hirer could terminate a hire-purchase agreement. It also provided for licensing hire-purchase companies and registration of all hire-purchase agreements with a Registry of Hire-Purchase Agreements.

Efforts to impose more stringent controls over the foreign firms' hire-purchase practices tended to encounter company resistence. Tanzania passed a Hire-Purchase Act in 196629 in an effort to increase protection for those seeking to purchase commodities by installment. Essentially the act aimed to reduce the danger that once the hirer had made a major portion of the payments for an item with a view to ultimate purchase, he would not lose the entire sum invested in the event that the company repossessed it. The foreign hire-purchase companies objected to the act and actually withdrew their business from the country following its passage, apparently at least in part to influence the Kenyan and Ugandan governments not to pass similar statutes. Some companies that had been financing their own hire-purchase arrangements with their clients—for example, Singer Sewing Machine—apparently continued to do so, however, despite the act.

After nationalization, the National Bank of Commerce in Tanzania made arrangements in 1969 for a wholly owned subsidiary, Karadha Company, Ltd., to finance the purchase of commercial vehicles, plant, and machinery. A public debate emerged over whether the company should make hire-purchase facilities available to civil servants for purchase of automobiles, refrigerators, and other durable luxury consumer items. The government newspaper, The Nationalist, argued editorially that government credit should be directed to expanding public transport and other facilities rather than private consumption by a limited high-income group.

Building Societies

Building societies may constitute a significant potential source of funds for investment in housing. Generally, they accept savings in deposit and savings accounts, much as do banks, and relend these savings to people who wish to take out a mortgage (a long-term loan, secured by the property) for the purpose of buying a house. The repayment of the mortgage represents an additional form of saving, making funds available for the provision of more mortgages. The total saving channeled through a building society is thus equal to initial funds put in the deposit and savings accounts plus the total repayment on the mortgage.

Building societies operated on an East African-wide basis until 1966, when efforts were made to establish separate companies in each country. The funds of the Kenyan and Tanzanian societies declined sharply when settlers withdrew their deposits in the 1960s: Tanzania's companies temporarily went out of business. Those in Kenya could not have continued without special assistance from government and a variety of other financial agents. Four companies, three of them privately owned, continued to operate in Kenya. The Savings and Loan Society, Ltd., is a wholly owned subsidiary of the British Pearl Assurance Co., Ltd., with public deposits of $7 million and loans in the form of mortgages on houses amounting to $8.6 million in 1968. The East African Building Society, established in 1959, is an entirely local firm, the smallest of the three, with some 9,000 members and $1.4 million in loans in 1968.

The First Permanent (East Africa), Ltd., a subsidiary of the British Commonwealth Development Corporation, had public deposits in 1967 of $12 million, but the CDC began to run its assets down. In 1968 it transferred $6.1 million in public deposits to the Housing Finance Company of Kenya, a Kenyan government company, on the board of which sit representatives of CDC and the Kenya government, and which is managed by First Permanent. The Housing Finance Company offers mortgage facilities up to $14,000 for up to 15 years to Kenya citizens to build housing costing from $4,000 to $21,000, that is, for the higher-income group. A Sessional Paper on Housing Policy[30] noted that many would-be houseowners find it hard to raise the initial deposit; but this was apparently anticipated. In 1967 the company reported a net loss.

KBS, Ltd., formerly the Kenya Building Society, was also a subsidiary of the Commonwealth Development Corporation, but it went out of business altogether in 1965.

In sum, by March 1968[31] 65,861 investors had loaned funds to the building societies in Kenya and 2,735 people had borrowed. The total assets of all companies were $29 million. The only action taken by the Kenyan government as late as 1970[32] to direct the policies of these societies was to announce that "it may be necessary to bring them into the scope of monetary policy" through central bank regulatory powers.

Building societies were never as firmly established in Tanzania as in Kenya.[33] Until 1960 the First Permanent (E.A.), Ltd., had been operating with reasonable success, but the large-scale withdrawal of the accumulated deposits of the society as independence neared forced it to the point where it could only operate by means of extensive borrowing from the Commonwealth Development Corporation, which took it over in 1961.* The CDC subsequently announced its intention to phase the society out of existence.

----

*This led to severance of the company's Rhodesian connections, which had existed since its formation in 1950.

In 1962 the Tanganyikan government established the National Housing Corporation to provide some incentive for saving for house ownership.[34] One hundred houses had been built for tenant purchase. The main activities of the National Housing Corporation during the First Five Year Plan period were construction of houses under the slum clearance scheme for rent and tenant purchase, site development, and loans to urban local authorities for roof loans to individuals. By the end of the period, the central government expenditures through the corporation totaled $9.5 million to build 6,327 houses. Some 5,705 of these were in a relatively low-cost range, almost four-fifths of them in Dar es Salaam as part of the slum clearance program. The net addition to housing stock was under 400 houses a year.

Under the Second Plan,[35] the Housing Corporation was to build about 2,000 houses a year, limiting their size to the $800 to $1,400 range. It was also to prepare some 5,000 sites with water, drainage, and foundations for people to build their own homes. The National Housing Corporation aimed to encourage people to build their own houses on these sites by promoting building cooperative societies through TANU, NUTA, and cooperatives; encouraging employers to form credit unions of their employees; deducting agreed savings regularly from their pay; and providing technical assistance for building cooperatives. In the rural areas, research and locally available construction materials were provided to improve traditional houses, assisted by 15 building teams under Maendeleo.

In 1964 the British Commonwealth Development Corporation indicated its willingness to assist Tanzania to develop a new institution designed to provide housing finance facilities. In 1967 the Permanent Finance Housing Corporation was created to provide a source of finance for owner-occupied house construction for middle-income groups.[36] It took over the assets of the Tanzania section of the First Permanent and received new injections of capital from the government and the Commonwealth Development Corporation. It had an issued capital of $16,000 and could borrow up to $320,000 from the government and $1.4 million from the CDC.

The Tanzanian government stopped providing housing for its employees except in special cases.[37] Under the Second Five Year Plan, the Permanent Housing Corporation was to finance construction of about 400 houses a year in the medium-cost range, lending up to 76 percent of the cost of the house for a maximum cost of $14,000. Repayment was to be made in 20 years with an 8.5-percent interest charge on outstanding debt (9.5 percent if the property is rented). The corporation began operations in Dar es Salaam, Tanga, Moshi, and Arusha and planned to extend its operations to Mwanza.

Additional Institutions for Mobilizing Small Savings

Post office savings banks were established throughout East
Africa by the British in the colonial era, primarily to encourage thrift.
Theoretically, post office savings banks have the advantage of providing
savings facilities in rural areas. Since independence, however, the
post office savings banks have made relatively little contribution as
a channel for directing small savings into productive industry in any
of the three countries.

In Kenya the Post Office Savings Bank deposits totaled $6.4
million in 1966, while annual withdrawals totaled about $6.3 million,
and the total balance of the bank had declined from about $14.4 million
in 1961 to $12.7 million. The Economic Survey of 1967 suggested
that the Bank was "providing a rate of interest on accounts which are
more in the nature of demand rather than savings deposits and, in
consequence, is unable to operate profitably without Government support."[38]

In Uganda withdrawals exceeded deposits in every year from
1962 to 1966. The total balance in 1966 was $2.64 million. The Uganda
government appointed a committee of inquiry to review the policy and
law governing the Bank.

In Tanzania,[39] although the numbers of depositors increased
from 1966 to 1968, the average deposits declined in size, so that total
deposits tended to fluctuate around $5.6 million. The low average
value of individual deposits and the high average deposit turnover
resulted in a high-cost structure for the system.

Savings and credit societies may provide another means for
voluntary collection of small savings. They were introduced in Tanzania, for example, in the early 1960s, with assistance from credit
unions from the United States and Canada, as a means of encouraging
rural savings by individuals. The amounts actually saved appeared
small. By 1967 some 1,969 societies had been formed, 23 percent
consisting of members working in the same occupations, 65 percent
in the same communities, 12 percent by various associations and
organizations. Only 21 were sponsored by cooperatives. These societies collected regular deposits from their members and provided
them with loans as required for bicycles, furniture, tools, roofing
for houses, payment of school fees, medical bills, purchase of land,
and even to pay a bride price. Many societies provided that each
shilling saved by a member, up to $2,000, before age 55 was to be
matched by a shilling of life insurance arranged through the National
Insurance Corporation. By the end of 1967, some $350,000 had been
saved by members of the society, of which $330,000 were outstanding
as loans to members. These societies were managed separately from
marketing cooperatives, an arrangement that had the advantage that

it avoided submerging the thrift interests of the members in the far larger business of marketing coops. The new National Bank of Commerce in Tanzania began to develop mobile savings units to operate in rural areas in a manner complementary to the Post Office Savings Bank and, presumably, other small savings institutions.

SUMMARY

The other financial institutions inherited by the African countries, outside the banking institutions, varied from country to country, depending on the circumstances and particularly the relative importance of European settlers. In West Africa and Uganda the marketing boards played an important monetary role through their imposition of policies of "forced savings" on the African peasants that involved tens of millions of pounds. These accumulated funds influenced pricing, incomes, and purchasing power but were seldom integrated into overall national monetary policies, far less into any kind of nationally oriented financial plan designed to implement physical plans for restructuring the economy. In Nigeria the regionalization of the marketing boards rendered the possibility of attaining any kind of nationally unified monetary and investment policy even more difficult.

The other institutions—insurance companies, hire-purchase firms, building societies, and small-savings schemes—involved less funds. Nevertheless, postindependence experience underlined the necessity of evaluating potential sources of funds and integrating them into the national financial plan.

NOTES

1. C. Leubusher, Bulk Buying from the Colonies (London: Oxford Press, 1956), p. 11.

2. The following material relating to Ghana's marketing board is in T. Killick, "The Economics of Cocoa," in W. Birmingham, I. Neustadt, and E. N. Omaboe (eds.), A Study of Contemporary Ghana, Vol. 1: The Economy of Ghana (London: George Allen and Unwin, Ltd., 1966), Ch. 15.

3. A. Adedeji, Nigerian Federal Finance (New York: Africana Publishing Corp., 1969), pp. 111-12, 142-3.

4. See D. A. Lury, "Cotton and Coffee Growers and Government Development Finance in Uganda, 1945-1960," The East African Economic Review 10, no. 1 (June, 1963).

5. H. H. Binhammer, "Financial Infrastructure and the Availability of Credit and Finance to the Rural Sector of the Tanzanian

Economy," University Social Science Council Conference, Makarere, Dec. 30, 1968-Jan. 3, 1969.

6. Tanzania Second Five Year Plan for Economic and Social Development, 1st July, 1969-30th June, 1974, Vol. II: The Programmes (Dar es Salaam: Government Printer, 1969), pp. 54-58.

7. P. N. C. Okigbo, Nigerian Public Finance (Evanston: Northwestern University Press, 1965), pp. 166-9.

8. Cf. D. Austin, Politics in Ghana, 1946-1960 (London: Oxford University Press, 1964), pp. 275 ff.

9. Adedeji, Nigerian Federal Finance, pp. 168-9.

10. T. Killick, "Cocoa" and "The Monetary and Financial System," in Birmingham, Neustadt, and Omaboe (eds.), The Economy of Ghana, pp. 236-318.

11. Killick, "The Possibilities of Economic Control," in Birmingham, Neustadt, and Omaboe (eds.), The Economy of Ghana, p. 390; see also pp. 412, 418, 430.

12. Adedeji, Nigerian Federal Finance, p. 256.

13. A. Seidman, Comparative Development Strategies in East Africa (Nairobi: East African Publishing House, 1972), pp. 208 ff.

14. M. T. Ocran, "Towards a Jurisprudence of African Economic Development," unpublished Ph.D. thesis, University of Wisconsin, 1971, pp. 209 ff.

15. Report of the British Economic Mission on the Tanganyika Five Year Development Plan, C. R. Ross, Chairman, Dec. 1965 (hereinafter cited as "Ross Report"), paragraph 48.

16. J. Loxley, "Financial Intermediaries and Their Role in East Africa," University of East Africa Social Science Conference, December 1966.

17. Republic of Kenya, Development Plan, 1970-74, p. 570.

18. Republic of Uganda, Background to the Budget, 1968-1969, p. 46.

19. S. N. Vaidya, General Manager of Tanzania's National Insurance Company, Economic Research Bureau Seminar, Oct. 25, 1968, University College, Dar es Salaam.

20. The Standard (Dar es Salaam), Nov. 19, 1969.

21. J. Loxley, interview, Nov. 19, 1969, University College, Economics Department, Dar es Salaam.

22. Tanzania, The Annual Plan for 1971/72 (Dar es Salaam: Government Printer, 1972), p. 15.

23. National Christian Council of Kenya, Who Controls Industry in Kenya? p. 179.

24. Ibid.

25. United Republic of Tanzania, Economic Survey, 1968 (Background to the Budget for 1969-70), p. 39.

26. National Christian Council of Kenya, Who Controls Industry in Kenya? pp. 172-73.

27. Ibid., p. 174; and interview, J. Loxley, Sept. 25, 1969.

28. Republic of Kenya, Development Plan, 1970-1974, pp. 546-565.

29. P. Picciotto and C. Whiteford, "The Impact of Tanzanian Hire-Purchase Act, 1966," Law Faculty Staff Seminar Paper, (Dar es Salaam, University College, Nov. 13, 1968).

30. Republic of Kenya, Development Plan, 1970-74, p. 164.

31. National Christian Council of Kenya, Who Controls Industry in Kenya? p. 178.

32. Republic of Kenya, Development Plan, 1970-74, p. 563.

33. A. R. Roe and M. J. H. Yaffey, "Money and Banking," in Svendsen (ed.), Economic Problems of Tanzania (Dar es Salaam: University College, 1968, mimeo), p. 18.

34. Ross Report.

35. United Republic of Tanzania, Second Five Year Plan, I, 187-192.

36. Tanzania, Background to the Budget, 1967-8, p. 78.

37. Tanzania, Second Five Year Plan, I, 189.

38. Kenya, Economic Survey, 1967, p. 16.

39. Tanzania, Background to the Budget, 1968-69, p. 40.

The model of underdevelopment outlined in Chapter 1 suggests that current efforts to plan in Africa, typically based on assumptions underpinning orthodox Western economic theories, are likely to fail to attain declared development goals. Effective planning, designed to spread increasingly productive employment opportunities to all sectors of the economy as the essential foundation for raising the levels of living of the broad masses of the population, requires fundamental alteration of the institutional structures inherited from the colonial past. Despite attainment of political independence, these institutional structures continue to perpetuate African economies' dependence on uncertain foreign markets dominated by powerful multinational corporations that drain away a major share of the investible surpluses produced on the continent. Most of the surpluses remaining in Africa accrue to wealthy farmers-cum traders-cum politicians who largely perceive their advantage as bound up with externally dependent export enclave growth.

Evidence drawn from the postindependence experience of the larger former British colonies in sub-Saharan Africa argues that only state action can adequately reshape the institutions that dominate what President Nyerere has called the "commanding heights"—basic industries, external and internal wholesale trade, and finance—to reallocate physical resources and investible surpluses to build a more balanced, nationally integrated economy. For such state action to achieve development as defined, new political channels are needed to insure that the interests of the peasants and wage earners—the vast majority of the population, who would most benefit—are represented in critical areas of state decision-making machinery; but lack of space here prevents exploration of this issue.

Parts II through IV of this book have attempted only to assess the consequences for planned development of institutional changes

351

made in the key areas of the economies of several African countries. Evaluation of this cumulative experience underlines the importance of planning the detailed physical backward and forward linkages of major projects to attain balanced, mutually reinforcing expansion of industrial and agricultural production. The inherited set of trading institutions needs to be reshaped to insure that they facilitate, rather than hinder, the spread of specialization and exchange leading to increased productivity in all sectors of the economy. The marshaling of available and potential investible surpluses through all channels— taxes and public debt, banking and finance, price and profit policies— must be worked out in a comprehensive financial plan to insure realization of essential physical projects and their linkages.

These conclusions are best conceived as a series of hypotheses formulated after weighing the available evidence drawn from the brief postindependence experience of the larger former British colonies of sub-Saharan Africa. They seek to direct attention to the essential ingredients of more effective physical and financial planning designed to enable the masses of the African populations to achieve levels of living commensurate with the technological possibilities of the twentieth century. It is hoped that further critical research and analyses along these lines will help to build the essential foundations of more effective national planning throughout Africa.

Africanization: of banks, 317-318;
Blundell on, 65-66; loans for,
197-198, 321; of trade, 205-206,
322 (see also credit, entrepre-
neurship, trade)
agriculture: land tenure and rural
institutions, 159-181; in relation
to industry, 103-127, 175-176,
351-352 (see also cooperatives,
credit, exports, rural development, taxes)

balance of payments problems, 265-
266 (see also exports, imports,
investable surpluses)
banks: African Development Bank,
273; Africanization, 317; central
banks, 316; colonial, 49-50, 61-
62, 63-64, 314-315; commercial
bank growth, 316-318; and credit
for development, 313-314; and financial planning, 313-328, 352;
medium and long term loan institutions, 332-346; national investment banks, 320-321; post-independence money and banking policies, 314-322; post office savings
banks, 345-346; relations to African governments, 317-319, 322-
327; World Bank (International
Bank for Reconstruction and Development) and associated activities, 270-272
Blundell, M., 65-66, 172
Building Societies, 342-344

classes in Africa, 54-75; colonial
impact, 58-69; definition of, 55-56;
Nyerere on, 272; and political-
economic reconstruction, 69-75;

pre-colonial, 57-58; and the
state, 54-55
capital-intensive (see technology)
capital-output ratio, 239-240
capital (see finance, investible
surplus, savings)
cash crop farmers, 161-165 (see
also export crops and food crops)
cattle complexes, 161
cocoa: cooperatives in marketing of,
209, 218; credit to Ghana cocoa
farmers, 319; efforts to obtain
international price agreement, 43;
Ghana agreement to sell to USSR,
212; and marketing boards, 332-
333, 335-336; oligopolistic buyers,
38-39; smuggling, 221-222; stratification of farmers, 63-64; world
cocoa market, 32-33 (see also
Ghana and Nigeria)
coffee: International Coffee Agreement, 42; main exporters, 32-33;
oligopolistic buyers, 38 (see also
Kenya, Tanzania, Uganda)
Common Market, East Africa, 203-
204, 300 (see also integration)
"commanding heights," efforts to
control, 86, 90, 92, 351
competition: colonial efforts to
avoid African competition, 59;
inability of African entrepreneurs
to compete, 202; unreality of
theoretical assumption, 29-30,
83-84, 198-199
cooperatives: (see also participation, rural development) colonial cooperatives of settlers, 17-
18); (of peasants, 217-218); corruption, 72-73, 220; credit, 318-
319; domination by large farmers,

72-72, 223-224; inadequacy of legislation and working rules, 218; investigations of (in Ghana, 73); (in Tanzania, 220-222); marketing, 217-224; post-independence growth, 72-73, 218; price problems, 218, 222; problems of 218-224; producer cooperatives, 172-176; reasons for establishment, 322; sales outside of, 221-223, 227-228; shortages of skilled leadership, 220-221; women, and, 219; ujamaa approach, 220, 224 (see also Tanzania)

copper: main exporters, 43-51; oligopolistic copper buyers, 45-49, 211; Zaireis policies re copper, 48-49; Zambian policies re copper, 48-50, 211, 292-293, 308-309 (see also Zambia and Zaire)

cotton: buying interests and textiles industry, 38-39; Egypt, 32; main exporters, 36-38 (see especially Uganda, Tanzania)

corruption, 18, 204-205, 244-245, 246, 310-311

credit: for African entrepreneurs, 197, 321-322; rural, 178-179, 318-322; suppliers', 83, 279-280, 283-284, 310

currency: colonial policies, 314; effect of devaluation of sterling, 316; exchange control, 316; notes re French franc, 316n, 317n; post-independence, 314-322 (see also monetary crisis and money supplies)

data, inadequacy: for incomes policies, 242-243; re insurance companies, 337; re investable surpluses and foreign firms, 245-246; for planning, 82; re rural foodstuff output, 256; re rural incomes, 255; re wages,

248-249, 250-253

decentralized planning, 90-92 (see also participation)

deficit financing (see public debt)

development corporations: colonial, 137, 140-142; and financing, 305-310; foreign managements, 145-146, and ministerial system, 144-145; role of development corporations in implementing industrial strategy, 140-144; structure and policies, 138-141, 144-146

dualism, 12, 16-17, 107, 164, 196, 198, 351 (see also export enclave, rural underdevelopment)

Dumont, R., 121-123

Education, 7-8, 62-63, 74, 125, 178, 245n, 253-255

elites: composition, 15, 64-66; and education, 62-63; incomes, 246-248; influence in independent governments, 18, 70-71, 87; relations to foreign firms, 242-243

employment: (see unemployment, wages, labor reserves)

entrepreneurs: colonial policies towards African entrepreneurs, 63-65; dispersed investments, 153; limited investments, 17-18, 88, 321-322 (see also trade)

exports: inadequacy as "engine growth," 5-7, 12-20, 32-51; major exports, 32-38; possibilities and problems of increasing export value, 41-43, 191-195, 208-212; taxes on, 289-292; worsened terms of trade, 40, 69, 83 (see also export enclave, marketing boards)

export enclave, 12-14; perpetuated by dominant institutions, 8-9, 15,

31-32, 107-108, 163-164, 191-196,
267-268; relation to underdeveloped rural areas, 16-17, 66-67
(see also labor reserves, rural
underdevelopment, urban drift)

financial planning: need for, 89-
90, 239-241, 336-337, 351-352;
relation to incomes policy,
240-241, 257-258
food supplies and prices, 18-19,
164, 198-199, 222-223, 256
foreign firms: in common markets, 203-204; competition to
attract, 267-268; corruption,
244-246; in finance, 268, 317-
318, 337, 340; government efforts to regulate, 29, 30, 112,
135-136, 244-246; and government participation in, 268-269,
308-309; oligopolistic control
of foreign trade, 31-32, 38-40,
44-51, 210; profits, 49, 243-246,
265-266, 296; restrictive policies,
8-9, 17 -18, 111, 197-198, 203,
267-268; role in export enclave
(see export enclave)
foreign funds for development,
261-274; African Development
Bank, 273; arguments for, 261-
262, 264; costs of, 50, 243-246,
265-268; debt repayment problems, 281-284; expectations of,
261-262, 264; limited amounts
available, 262-264; relation to
development strategy, 267-270;
from socialist countries, 264,
269-270; World Bank and affiliates, 270-272, 319

Georgescu-Roegen, re institutional
content of economic theory, 5, 9
Gezira scheme, Sudan, 168
Ghana: classes in, 58, 64, 66-67,
255; cooperatives, 72-73, 209-

210, 218-220; external debt, 83,
279-280, 283-284, 310; international Monetary Fund advice,
279, 296; Lonrho in, 269; marketing boards, 210, 332, 335-336;
National Trading Corporation,
204-206, 229; state commercial
banks, 310-311, 318; state enterprises in, 137-138, 141-144, 153,
169, 306, 310; taxes, 290-291,
292; unemployment, 108; Volta
Dam, 308; worker participation,
151-152
Gordon, D., re World Bank policies, 271-272
goals of development, 3-4, 62, 82,
87-89
government (see state, nature and
role of)

Harrod-Domar model, 6, 262
hire-purchase institutions, 341-342
Hyden, G., on cooperatives, 223-
224

imported goods: auto imports,
113, 196, 206; efforts to change
pattern of, 196, 202-208; high
prices and profits tax evasion,
265, 296; import substitution on
industries, 6-7, 17, 111; import
taxes (tariffs), 202-203, 293;
kinds, 19, 113, 196, 205-206;
lack of tax on capital goods and
equipment imports, 203, 293;
socialist imports, 195 (see also
industries)
income: of elites, 246-248; of
foreign firms, 243-246; lack of
data on, 242-243; national incomes policies, 242-258; of
rural areas, 256-257; skewed
distribution, 69; taxes on, 281-
282, 288, 294-297; of wage
earners, 248-254

indirect rule, 61
industry: consumer goods, 124-125; [sugar, 119, 122-123; cement, 108, 146; fertilizer, 124; textiles, 124-125, 195; meat-packing, 145; iron and steel, 122, 124; breweries and cigarettes, 139]; distorted growth, 63, 107-113, 267-268; and economic integration, 117-118, 194; finance of, 73-74 (see also banks, finance, foreign funds); foreign investment in, 19, 110-111, 112, 139, 146, 195-196, 267-268; governments and foreign partners, 139, 146; inadequacy of import substitution policy, 6-7, 17, 111; location and rural underdevelopment, 105-108, 112, 114-125, 135-136, 153-155; need for balance with agriculture, 103-127; oligopoly and, 109 (see also oligopoly, competition); poles of growth, 118-119; technology (labor vs capital intensity of), 108-109, 120-125; unemployment and, 108-109, 124-125; workers and, 67-69, 147-153
industrial strategy, 107-156; institutional changes to implement, 135-156; kinds of industry, 114-118; stimulation of rural areas, 118-120, 135-136, 154-155 (see also industry)
inflation, 19, 280-281
infrastructure, 121-122, 267-269 (see also trade)
insurance, 337-340
integration, economic, 29-30, 88-89, 194, 203-204, 299-300 (see also unity)
interest rates (see credit, banking, foreign funds)
international agreements re export prices, 41-43 (see also exports)
International Bank for Reconstruc-

tion and Development [IBRD] (also known as World Bank) and affiliated agencies, 270-273, 319
International Development Association [IDA] (see International Bank)
International Finance Corporation [IFC] (see International Bank)
International Monetary Fund, 279, 283, 296 (see also monetary policies, currency)
investible surpluses: and income distribution, 246-248; investment in productive sectors, 240-241; lack of information, 245-246; loss of, 15, 243, 351; potential in rural areas, 255-257; in public sector, 307-310 (see also financial planning, incomes, profits, elites)

Johnston, B. F., re industrial development, 110, 115, 123-124
Johnstone, H., re colonial division of labor, 60

Kaldor, N., re taxes, 296
Kenya: Africanization policies, 64-65, 171-172, 205-206, 322; cooperatives, 217-219, 222-223; decentralization of planning, 90-92; development corporations, 138, 322; finance, 245-246, 262, 264, 316-317, 321-322, 337-338, 340-341, 343, 345; industrial development, 108-109, 138, 146, 195; land policies, 163-164, 170-171 (see discussions of tenure); marketing boards, 209, 224-225; taxes, 288, 292, 298; trade unions, unions, wages, and influence on government policy, 148-152, 249, 340; unemployment, 108-109, 249, 307-307 (see Common Market)
Kilby, P. re industrial development,

110, 115, 123-124

labor, "aristocracy of," 73, 251-
252
labor-intensive (see technology)
labor reserves, 7, 15-16, 60-61,
66-67, 161-162, 249, 287, 297
(see also urban drift, rural
areas, wages)
W..A. Lewis: on technology, 120-
121; on international debt repayment and IMF, 283; on tax
collection, 295
Lonrho, 244, 269
Lugard, Lord: on colonies' importance to England—on taxes,
297

manpower (see education, labor
reserves, technology, unemployment)
marketing, in rural areas, 176-177
(see also exports and imports,
marketing boards, trade, state
trading agencies)
marketing boards: in colonial period, 208-209, 224; and finance,
209-210, 332-337; post-independence, 192-193, 209-210, 224-
228; problems, 225-226, 336
(see also exports)
mining (see Zaire, Zambia, copper,
exports)
model of underdevelopment and
economic theory, 5-6, 8-9, 10,
20-21 (see also dualism,
problem-solving)
money and monetary policies, 314,
316-322, 343 (see also currency,
International Monetary Fund,
monetary crisis)
monetary crisis, 103-104, 193-194
(see also currency, money)
Mozambique, Caborra Bassa hydroelectric project, 268

multinational corporations (see
foreign firms, oligopoly, exports)
Myint, H.: re theoretical model, 9;
re competition in exports, 29-30
Myrdal, G., re theoretical models,
9

Nigeria: classes, 58, 63, 67; efforts to assist African entrepreneurs, 321; federation, 71,
297, 333-335; incomes data, 246,
255; indirect rule, 61; marketing
boards, 332-333, 335-336; suppliers' credit, 83, 279-280, 283-
284; taxes, 288, 290-291, 292,
296-297, 299-300; unemployment,
108-109
Nyrere, J.: re ujamaa, 171-172;
re 51% industrial takeovers, 139;
re commanding heights, 351

oilseeds, 33-36 (see also exports)
oligopoly: in foreign trade, 8-9,
17, 31-32, 38-41, 44-51, 203;
in internal trade, 109-110, 196-
198 (see also foreign firms, exports, profits, competition, trade)

Parsons, K., re requirements of
tenure system, 165
participation, 55, 71-72, 74, 87,
89-92, 231, 245, 352 (see also
planning); and rural development,
71-73, 90, 153-155, 256-257 (see
also rural development); trade
unions and, 73-74, 150-153 (see
also trade unions)
planning, 81-97; in colonial period,
82; decentralization and, 90-92;
evaluation and, 93-96, 352; exports and, 50-51; first post-independence plan failures, 4-5, 20,
71-72, 82-83; inadequacy of
orahodox theories and, 4-5, 20,
84-85, 351; institutional changes

and, 69-70, 74, 86-89, 93-96,
351; long and short term, 88-89
population growth, 7-8
Prebisch, R., re import substitution industry, 6
problem-solving orientation, 10-12
profits, 40-41, 49, 196, 243-246,
251-252, 264-266, 295-296, 308-
309 (see also foreign firms,
balance of payments, incomes)
proletariat, 66 (see also classes)
provident funds, 340
public debt, 83, 278-284, 310, 352
public enterprise (see state enterprise, development corporations,
state trading corporations)

rural underdevelopment and development: and decentralized planning, 90-92; and industrial location, 104-105, 107-108, 112, 114,
118-120, 126, 135-136, 153-155;
and labor reserves, 4, 7, 14-16,
66, 67, 108, 161-162, 249-250;
land tenure, 159-181; and marketing institutions, 176-177 (see
also cooperatives, marketing,
trade); and mobilizing rural
incomes, 161, 176-179, 254-257
(see also credit)

Sayers, R., re banking institutions,
314
Schatz, S , on credit to African
entrepreneurs, 321
Schumpeter, J., on theory as a
rationalization for political policies, 54
South Africa, 60-61, 66-67, 268
state, nature and role of: "commanding heights," 86, 90, 92,
136-140, 239, 351; foreign firms,
145-146, 242-245, 268-269, 308,
317-318, 321-322; postindependence, 18, 69-71, 74-75, 87 (see

also state enterprises, development corporations, marketing
boards, state trading agencies)
state enterprises, 137, 141-144,
169, 261-262, 297-311 (see also
state trading corporations,
foreign firms, industrial strategy,
banking, marketing boards)
State trading corporations, 205-
208, 211-212, 228-230
stock exchanges, 321
strikes, 68-69, 147-148, 269 (see
also trade unions)
Sudan, Gezira scheme, 168-169

Tanzania: commanding heights,
control of, 86, 139, 231, 351;
cooperatives, 218-221, 227-228,
257; decentralized planning, 74,
92, 231; Development Corporation, background and functioning
of National, 137-39, 144-147,
306-307, 309-310; foreign exchange reserves, 9, 323-324
(see also imports, exports,
foreign funds); foreign finance,
261, 274; industrial development,
122-124, 139-140, 144-146, 261-
262 (see also development corporation); local taxes, 297-299
(see also taxes); marketing
boards, 209-210, 226-227, 272-
273, 336; mobilizing savings,
338-340, 342-346; National Commercial Bank, possibilities and
problems, 296, 322-328, 342;
State Trading Corporation, 207-
208, 212, 230; TANU, 74; ujamaa,
72, 92, 154, 171, 173, 220, 224;
wages and incomes, 248-251;
World Bank and U.S. Agency for
International Development, advice, 144 (see also Nyerere,
Common market)
taxes, 287-301; difficulties of col-

ABOUT THE AUTHOR

ANN SEIDMAN is Professor of Economics, University of Zambia, Lusaka, Zambia. Previously, she was Lecturer, Land Tenure Center, University of Wisconsin, and Chairperson, Subcommittee on Africa. She has also taught at the Universities of Dar es Salaam, Ghana, and Bridgeport.

She is the author of Comparative Development Strategies in East Africa, Ghana's Development Experience, An Economics Textbook for Africa, and Unity of Poverty: The Economics of Pan-Africanism.

Professor Seidman received her Ph. D. in Economics from the University of Wisconsin.

AFRICA IN THE SEVENTIES AND EIGHTIES:
Issues in Development

edited by
Frederick S. Ackhurst

ARMS AND AFRICAN DEVELOPMENT: Proceedings
of the First Pan-African Citizens' Conference

edited by
Frederick S. Ackhurst

MILITARY RULE IN AFRICA: DAHOMEY, GHANA,
SIERRA LEONE, AND MALI

edited by
Anton Bebler

SOCIAL CHANGE AND ECONOMIC DEVELOPMENT
IN NIGERIA

edited by
Ukandi G. Damachi
and Hans Dieter Seibel

TOWARD MULTINATIONAL ECONOMIC COOPERATION
IN AFRICA

B. W. T. Mutharika

URBANIZATION THEORIES AND REGIONAL PLANNING
IN AFRICA

edited by
Salah El-Shakhs
and Robert Obudho